Serial Publications

Serial

Second edition,
revised

Andrew D. Osborn

Publications

Their Place
and Treatment
in Libraries

American Library Association
Chicago 1973

Library of Congress Cataloging in Publication Data

Osborn, Andrew Delbridge, 1902–
    Serial publications; their place and treatment in
libraries.

    Bibliography: p.
    1. Periodicals. I. Title.
Z692.S508 1973   025.17′3   72-4519
    ISBN 0-8389-0118-2

International Standard Book Number 0–8389–0118–2 (1973)

Copyright © 1973 by the American Library Association

Library of Congress catalog card number 72–4519

Printed in the United States of America

To the memory of my old chief,
colleague, and friend

KENNETH BINNS

formerly Librarian of the National Library
of Australia, Canberra

with affection
and esteem

Contents

Illustrations

Preface

There has been impressive progress in library technology for the handling of serial publications since information was gathered for the first edition of *Serial Publications* in 1954. As a consequence of these advances, the text has had to be completely rewritten.

Two developments stand out above all others; they give promise of transforming control methods. The first is the advent of the book catalog of serial holdings, reissued annually. Already in the eyes of readers and staff this type of catalog has proved to be superior to card cataloging, which it is bound to supersede sooner or later. The second is the availability of systematic coding for serial titles. Coding has far-reaching consequences for manual and automated checking systems, as well as for the production of book catalogs and union lists. Not only that, but coding now provides the distinct possibility of making computer checking methods sufficiently economical so that they can compete with the visible index in terms of both cost and effectiveness. One major reason for this is that coding can dispense with the process of opening and sorting second-class mail before checking can begin.

These are timely events because, although the greatest amount of experimentation has taken place in smaller institutions, a number of large libraries have been casting around for an automated system that will serve for tens of thousands of titles at a modest cost. Among these libraries are the Harvard College Library, the Library of Congress, and the National Agricultural Library.

The enthusiasm of serial librarians was fully in evidence in the contributions which they made to the preparation of this second edition. The rewriting could not have been achieved, especially at a distance of ten thousand miles, without the help of so many of them.

I am tremendously grateful for all the willing assistance that I have received.

Above all I want to thank the staff of the Library of Congress for very extensive help. Robert D. Desmond, assistant chief of the Serial Record Division, has been a tower of strength, going out of his way continually and efficiently to supply up-to-the-minute information about the work of the Division in carrying out its key role in serial affairs. I want to express my appreciation to C. Sumner Spalding, assistant director for cataloging, who contributed extensively to the first edition and who has again helped in the areas of descriptive and subject cataloging. Mrs. Elaine W. Woods saved me a vast amount of time by making her large files of serial documentation available. Among others on the staff of the Library of Congress I am especially grateful to William J. Welsh, chief of the Processing Department, and Samuel Lazerow, chief of the Serial Record Division, for contributing the services of their staff so generously on my behalf. The book could not have been reworked so successfully without the whole-hearted support of so many members of the staff of the Library, colleagues who are keeping that institution in the very forefront of serial activities and policy making.

Several librarians gave me an unusually large amount of help and documentation. K. P. Barr, deputy librarian of the National Lending Library for Science and Technology, not only supplied data on the operations of that outstanding library, but also discussed his estimates of the number of scientific periodicals which are being published contemporaneously. Miss Elizabeth F. Beder, acting chief for preparation services in the Research Libraries of the New York Public Library, was extremely helpful in reporting the numerous changes and developments which have taken place in her library since 1954. Miss Susan M. Haskins, associate librarian, and Miss Mary Hanley, who is in charge of serial cataloging at Harvard, have completely updated the record of Harvard College Library practices. Miss Natalie N. Nicholson, associate director of the Massachusetts Institute of Technology Libraries, generously gave me much data and supplied a number of documents, all of which I value very much. Foster M. Palmer, associate librarian in the Harvard College Library, gave excellent aid with the chapter on reference work. Mrs. Lucille J. Strauss, of the Pennsylvania State Library, went to much trouble to supply me with advance information from the 1972 edition of *Scientific and Technical Libraries*. Mrs. Marie Toerien, deputy director of the United Nations Library, went out of her way to review all references to the work of her institution. To each of these colleagues I am genuinely and warmly grateful.

Other friends and associates who assisted in a wide variety of ways included: Jean Adelman, librarian of the University Museum Library, University of Pennsylvania; Judith A. Baskin, chief acquisition librarian in the National Library of Australia; Albert L. Batik, director of publications operations, American Society for Testing and Materials, whose aid with *Coden for Periodical Titles* was very fine; William S. Budington, executive director and librarian of the John Crerar Library; Forrest F. Carhart, Jr., director, Library Technology Project; Martha A. Connor, associate librarian, Swarthmore College Library; William H. Crane, documents librarian, Public Library of Fort Wayne and Allen County, Indiana; Arthur Curley, director, Montclair (N.J.) Public Library; Margaret Currier, librarian, Peabody Museum of Archaeology and Ethnology, Harvard University; R. R. Dickison, chief librarian, Oak Ridge National Laboratory Library; Glyn T. Evans, acting deputy librarian/research associate in machine methods, School of Medicine Library, Washington University; F. Bernice Field, associate librarian for technical services, Yale University Library; Fred Folmer, librarian, University of Texas Library; John E. Galejs, assistant director for resources and technical services, Iowa State University Library; Herbert Goldhor, dean of the Graduate School of Library Science, University of Illinois; Mrs. V. K. Greenbie, director, Hampshire Inter-Library Center, Amherst, Mass.; Warren J. Haas, director of libraries, Columbia University Library; Arthur T. Hamlin, director of libraries, Temple University Library; Donald P. Hammer, head of library systems development, Purdue University Libraries; Harvey Hammond, assistant biomedical librarian, Biomedical Library, University of California at Los Angeles; Carl W. Hintz, librarian, University of Oregon Library; Robert R. Kepple, librarian, Applied Physics Laboratory Library, Johns Hopkins University; Dorothy M. Kesseli, head of Serials Department, University of California Library; Carma Russell Leigh, librarian, California State Library; T. N. McMullan, director, Louisiana State University Library; Monica J. Maier, librarian, Detroit Edison Company; Robert F. Munn, director, West Virginia University Library; Wyman W. Parker, librarian, Wesleyan University Library; Beatrice M. Quartz, associate librarian, technical services, Wellesley College Library; Mrs. Frankie G. Runzo, director of technical services, Los Angeles Public Library; Marion Sanner, chief of processing, Enoch Pratt Free Library; Robert Severance, director, Air University Library; Joseph C. Shipman, director, Linda Hall Library; George A. Strait, acting librarian, Harvard Law School Library; Robert L. Talmadge, director of technical departments, University of Illinois Library; Wilbur K. Turk, head of data processing, Baker Library, Harvard University; Melvin J. Voigt, librarian, University of California at San Diego Library; I. A. Warheit, Information Systems Marketing, International Business Machines Corporation; Dudley A. Weiss, executive director, Library Binding Institute; Mrs. Anne M. Wickersham, library manager, Standard and Poor's Corporation; and Mrs. Edith C. Wise, head of reference, New York University Libraries.

I also wish to express my deep sense of appreciation to the following librarians who were formerly members of my staff at the University of Sydney and who did much to supply information and resources at this distance from the great libraries of the United States: Jennifer M. E. Alison, Margaret Lundie, Barbara J. Palmer, Gwen Tucker, and Jean P. Whyte.

Finally I wish to express my gratitude to Miss Pauline A. Cianciolo, executive editor, Richard A. Gray, senior editor, and Helen Cline, production editor, American Library Association. Their patience and understanding have been truly remarkable.

In addition to the collaboration of all these and other colleagues, I would like to thank the following authors and publishers who have given me permission to quote from their publications: American Library Association (*Anglo-American Cataloging Rules: North American Text*); Aslib (David Grenfell, *Periodicals and Serials* and *Handbook of Special Librarianship and Information Work*); Association of College and Reference Libraries (Charles H. Brown, *Scientific Serials*, and Mary R. Kinney, *The Abbreviated Citation—A Bibliographical Problem*); Robert L. Collison, *Indexes and Indexing* (Benn); E. J. Crane, A. M. Patterson, and Eleanor B. Marr, *A Guide to the Literature of Chemistry* (Wiley); D. E. Davinson, *The Periodicals Collection* (Deutsch); P. M. Handover, *Printing in London from 1476 to Modern Times* (Allen & Unwin); Ingeborg Heintze, *Shelving for Periodicals* (Bibliotekstjänst); University of Illinois Graduate School of Library Science, *Library Trends* and *Serial Publications in Large Libraries*; International Business Machines Corporation, *Library Automation—Computerized Serials Control*; Antony Kamm and Boswell Taylor, *Books and the Teacher* (University of London Press); Frank L. Mott, *American Journalism, a History, 1690–1960* (Macmillan); Theodore Peterson, *Magazines in the Twentieth Century* (University of Illinois Press); Scarecrow Press (David A. Kronick, *A History of Scientific and Technical Periodicals*); Special Libraries

Association, San Francisco Bay Chapter, *Acquisition of Special Materials*; Erwin C. Surrency, Benjamin Feld, and Joseph Crea, *A Guide to Legal Research*; and John Wiley & Sons, Inc. (Lucille J. Strauss, Irene M. Shreve, and Alberta L. Brown, *Scientific and Technical Libraries*).

ANDREW D. OSBORN

St. Ives, N.S.W.
Australia
25 August 1972

Preface
to First Edition

This book has been designed as a theoretical and practical introduction to the library aspects of serial publications. These publications are now so profuse and at the same time so significant for library purposes that librarians generally should have a good grasp of their nature and of the modes of controlling them. Like rare books, serials give rise to frequent and sometimes intricate technicalities with which not only specialists but also head librarians, department heads, and others should be acquainted, since serials are part and parcel of the workaday library. At all times throughout the text I have tried to present these technicalities in such a way that both the specialist and the non-specialist can comprehend and benefit by the discussion.

Theory has been emphasized because libraries ought to base their practice on sound principles. When they do, local practice can be individualistic in many respects, for which reason the book does not attempt to codify practices, but instead refers to representative libraries from time to time.

The working hypotheses I have followed in developing and organizing the book may be summarized as follows:

> Serials are an indispensable feature of most library programs by virtue of their informational and research value.
>
> Serials of all types should be accorded equal status. No main type should be discriminated against. This principle applies most particularly to government documents, which all too often have been set apart from the classified collection and given substandard treatment in their cataloging, classification, current housing, and binding.
>
> Specialized serial records should as a rule be developed for control purposes and economy of effort. Primarily these

include the visible index, the shelflist, the *Union List of Serials*, and *New Serial Titles* (or other appropriate union lists).

For all parts of a library the specialized records should to the fullest extent be regarded as a joint concern, no matter in which department they may be located.

The specialized records should serve clearly defined ends, and the serial entries in the general card catalog should be complementary to them. Recognition of this principle is essential if duplication of effort is to be avoided.

The rules for serial cataloging require revision to allow fully for the contributions made by the visible index, the *Union List of Serials*, and *New Serial Titles*.

Serial functions, notably those connected with processing and current servicing, should when practicable be in the hands of specialists, partly because of the unpredictable nature of serials and partly because of the technicalities which must endlessly be faced in larger collections.

On both the local and the national level, extensive cooperation between libraries is a prerequisite for the sound development of serial resources.

Indexing and abstracting mediums, as well as union lists, must be promoted on a larger scale than heretofore. They should be more comprehensive and less duplicative in their coverage.

Microreproduction and other copying devices must play an ever-increasing role in the rounding out and preserving of serial files, as well as in making them widely available; but the microreproduction program should be carefully planned, because some forms of serial micropublication give rise to major service problems.

In terms of library economy, serial publications will really come into their own in the comparatively near future when libraries of all kinds are linked up in national networks of television facsimile reproduction machines.

Special libraries have been taken into account equally with general libraries. Though these two types are in some ways distinctive, each has much of value for the other to study. Perhaps because of their intense preoccupation with serials, special libraries have somewhat more to offer general libraries than the other way around. It is certainly true that general libraries can often benefit by investigating the ways in which special libraries learn of new titles of worth and by examining the businesslike methods of control which they adopt. This text is in keeping with special library traditions when it argues for enterprising, economical, and efficient procedures.

I owe an immense debt of gratitude to those colleagues who have supplied information or illustrative material and to those who have read through part or all of the manuscript. The contribution of the Library of Congress has been truly notable; there I am especially grateful to C. Sumner Spalding, Chief of the Serial Record Division, for all the help and advice he has given. For assistance in various ways I want to express my deep appreciation to Eleanor S. Cavanaugh, Librarian of Standard and Poor's Corporation Library; F. Bernice Field, Assistant Head of the Catalogue Department, Yale University Library; Elizabeth Kientzle, Gifts and Exchange Librarian, John Crerar Library, and Editor of *Serial Slants;* Robert E. Kingery, Chief of the Preparation Division, New York Public Library; A. Ethelyn Markley, Associate Professor, University of California School of Librarianship; Bella E. Shachtman, Chief of the Catalog and Records Section, Department of Agriculture Library; Beatrice V. Simon, Assistant University Librarian, McGill University; and Vernon D. Tate, Director of Libraries, Massachusetts Institute of Technology. Also I want particularly to thank my colleagues at Harvard, above all Susan M. Haskins, who helped especially with the bibliography, William A. Jackson, who contributed much to the chapter on rarities, and the staff of the Serial Division.

Special thanks are due those who have given permission to quote from their publications, including a number of those mentioned in the previous paragraph. Grateful acknowledgment is also made to the following: Dr. William Warner Bishop (*The Backs of Books, and Other Essays in Librarianship*) ; Catholic University of America Press (Bernard M. Fry, *Library Organization and Management of Technical Reports Literature*) ; Columbia University Press (Alice I. Bryan, *The Public Librarian*, and James L. McCamy, *Government Publications for the Citizen*) ; Cresap, McCormick and Paget (*Survey of Preparation Procedures, Reference Department, New York Public Library*) ; Dr. John F. Fulton (Dr. Harvey Cushing, *Consecratio Medici, and Other Papers*) ; Harcourt, Brace and Company (William S. Learned, *The American Public Library and the Diffusion of Knowledge*) ; Margery C. Quigley (*Portrait of a Library*) ; The Special Libraries Association (*Technical Libraries, Their Organization and Management*) ; and the University of Minnesota Press (John L. Lawler, *The H. W. Wilson Company*) .

Finally I wish to express my thanks to the Publishing Department of the American Library Association. Upon completion of the manuscript, it is a pleasure to look back upon the friendly advice and help of so many people.

ANDREW D. OSBORN

Widener Library
Cambridge, Massachusetts
January 8, 1955

1

Libraries
and Their Approach to
Serial
Publications

1

Definition of a Serial

The elements which, by and large, constitute a serial publication are: (1) a name and (2) either periodical or serial numbering of the successive parts of the work which are issued under that name or under the name which eventually comes to replace the earlier one. The qualification "by and large" is significant because once in a while the name of the serial is lacking,[1] as are more frequently the elements of periodical or serial numbering, yet a work which is defective in any or all of these ways can still be regarded in libraries as a serial. On the other hand, all elements can be present, but the publication may be considered by librarians to be a book.

Quite often the name of a serial is a brief, striking word designed simply for publicity purposes, e.g., *Choice, Life, Nature, Time*. Sometimes it indicates the subject coverage in a very broad way, e.g., *American Libraries, Philosophy of Science, School and Society*. At times an expression is incorporated in the name to emphasize the serial character of the work, such as "annual report," "bulletin," "journal," or "review": e.g., *Annual Report on the Progress of Chemistry, Bulletin of Bibliography, The Journal of Philosophy*, and *American Historical Review*. In cataloging circles there is an established practice which says that generic terms such as "annual report" and "journal" may not be used as a title main entry or a title added entry when for the

[1]Two examples of serials without titles are given by K. I. Porter, "Standards for the Presentation of Information, with Particular Reference to Serial Publications," in Bernard Houghton, ed., *Standardization for Documentation* (London: Bingley, 1969) , p.35. He says that "List and Index Society" implies but does not state a word such as *Publications* as the title, and that "Air Force Cambridge Research Laboratories" is in effect the annual report of that body and requires those words in its title.

sake of meaning they must be eked out by the addition of the name of a corporate body. The practice holds in most libraries, even when usage in the field is clearly otherwise; this can be seen from an acronym such as JAMA, which indicates that medical people, unlike librarians in general, think of *Journal of the American Medical Association* as a name in its own right.[2] Names, too, are subject to constant change; *American Libraries* was formerly the *ALA Bulletin*, and the *Saturday Review of Literature* shortened its name to *Saturday Review* for the sake of terseness and because its scope was somewhat wider than the world of books.

Periodicity is expressed in serials by means of dates, principally day, month, quarter, or year. There are many variations, however. For example, a quarterly published in the Northern Hemisphere may call the four issues "Winter," "Spring," "Summer," and "Fall," while one in the Southern Hemisphere may say "Summer," "Autumn," "Winter," and "Spring"; or the quarters may be designated by the month in which the issue normally appears, giving a sequence such as January, April, July, October; or they may be numbered: first, second, third, and fourth quarter. Especially on annual, biennial, and triennial reports and budget statements, the date as given on a publication may or may not represent the calendar year, with the notational consequence that in libraries the form 1970–71 is used to cover two full calendar years whereas 1970/71–1971/72 serves to cover twenty-four months of divided years. In any event, from the idea of periodicity, of parts issued periodically, whether regularly or irregularly, there arises the concept of a periodical. Essentially, then, a periodical is a work whose parts are issued periodically, that is, whose parts bear dates of one kind or another. From the point of view of the Anglo-American cataloging code, though, there is a limitation: for an item to be considered a periodical, it must be issued more frequently than once a year. So, on technical grounds, an annual, biennial, or triennial is regarded by catalogers as a serial publication, not a periodical. On the other hand, the North American text of the

---

[2]Some medical libraries constitute an exception to the general library practice. The Harvard Medical Library lists and shelves the JAMA under its title, not under the name of the association (see Ann T. Curran, "The Mechanization of the Serial Records for the Moving and Merging of the Boston Medical and Harvard Medical Serials," *Library Resources & Technical Services* 10:362 [1966]). Lela Spanier says, "Medical librarians generally seem to consider title listing superior to the use of corporate entries for serials with non-distinctive titles" (Lela M. Spanier, comp., *Biomedical Serials, 1950–1960, a Selective List of Serials in the National Library of Medicine* [Washington, 1962], p.v).

cataloging code excludes newspapers from its definition of periodicals, whereas the British text includes them.

Seriality is most commonly expressed on publications by means of cardinal numbers in the form of arabic numerals. Present-day practice in libraries is to convert roman numerals into arabic for record purposes and on bindings. Ordinal numbers tend to be found on annual reports, the sessional papers of international and other recurring conferences, and in other cases when the numeral in the edition statement is pressed into service as the numbering device for the serial publication. As with dates, there can be complications with numbers, and this quite apart from mistakes in numbering, which are fairly frequent on the issues of newspapers. It is not uncommon for a serial publication to have more than one set of numbers. An issue can be called volume 10, part 6, or it can carry one number because it is part of a main series and another number because it is at the same time part of a subseries. When only one term is on the issue itself, it is customary to omit the word "volume" or its equivalent from library records and bindings, but in compound situations each of the terms may be given along with the numbers. Occasionally letters are substituted for numerals, especially in the subdivisions of learned society and other scientific publications. So the *Journal of Polymer Science* is subarranged by letters: part A–1, polymer chemistry; A–2, polymer physics; B, polymer letters; and C, polymer symposia.

Often both periodical and serial numbers occur on one and the same item. The numbers then duplicate each other, at least as far as concerns either the arrangement of the parts of a volume or the posting on library checking records. The dual system is followed extensively in the United States because it is required by the regulations which govern second-class mailing privileges.

In themselves the characteristics of periodicity and seriality are not always sufficient to distinguish between a serial publication and a nonserial work which (1) looks as though it may be the first volume of a new serial or (2) is issued in parts, sometimes as unbound numbers, sometimes as a bound volume in what will eventually be completed as a monographic set. Schneider put his finger on two factors which in doubtful cases could possibly aid in distinguishing serials from nonserials. He found the first difference between the two types of material in the publication program for serials:

> By nature they are unlimited. They may be suspended, but they do not conclude. External circumstances, but scarcely exhaustion of the subject, bring about their end. A second difference lies in the num-

ber of their authors. Apart from collections and composite works, books possess more than one author only by way of exception. With periodicals it is the reverse.[3]

Handover expresses the bibliographer's point of view when she says:

> It is obvious that a periodical publication differs in format from a book, and that it does so because it must be printed and distributed at regular intervals; the shorter the intervals the greater the distinction in format. Because these publications must be produced regularly, the price must be kept low; the more frequent the intervals, the lower the price. It is periodicity that distinguishes newspapers, journals, magazines, reviews and even some annuals from books and from jobbing (posters, cards, tickets, etc.) , and it is periodicity that dictates format and price.
>
> Moreover, a periodical publication is distinguished from a book or a piece of jobbing because it is dated and numbered. By giving this information the publisher indicates that at a certain interval the next number will appear. The method of dating often reveals this interval: daily, weekly, monthly or quarterly. The number identifies the place in the series and also serves as a promise by the publisher to produce further numbers.[4]

Schneider and Handover, working toward the definition of a serial, reflect the needs of the bibliographer and historian, both of whom require guidance as they face problems of inclusion and exclusion in their bibliographical and historical studies. But these scholars tend to represent a world in which there are inherent difficulties in sorting out the forerunners of serial publications from conventional serials, difficulties which pervade research into ancient, medieval, and more particularly early modern works. For such a reason it was possible for Mott, in his *History of American Magazines,* to avoid a definition. Instead he could say that in the United States the terms journal, magazine, newspaper, periodical, etc., "are all more or less indistinct and confused in common usage, and the more so when one looks back over the last two hundred years. It would be pedantry to insist upon erecting . . . arbitrary distinctions which do not actually exist in usage, and it would be bad philology and bad history as well."[5] He is talking

---

[3]Georg Schneider, *Handbuch der Bibliographie* (4th ed.; Leipzig: (Hiersemann, 1930) , p.369.

[4]P. M. Handover, *Printing in London from 1476 to Modern Times* (London: Allen & Unwin, 1960) , p.98–99.

[5]Frank L. Mott, *A History of American Magazines* (Cambridge: Harvard Univ. Pr., 1939) , v.1, p.8–9.

of American conditions when he says that format is the decisive characteristic of a newspaper, because in Great Britain, for example, book format was standard practice for all publications until the 1640s, when a distinctive format began to emerge for newspapers.[6]

A sound definition of a serial and, for that matter, of a newspaper or periodical has long been sought, especially in book-trade, legal, and library circles, as well as by bibliographers and literary historians. The futility of the quest can be seen from the attempts made by Du Prel,[7] Kienningers,[8] and Lehmann.[9] The last named, for instance, is at pains to list nine characteristics of periodicals: association with an editorial office, collectiveness, continuity, mechanical reproduction, periodicity, popularization, publication program, timeliness, and universality. After thirty-six pages of elaboration, in the course of which he points out that libraries adopt a very wide interpretation of what a serial is, Lehmann arrives at the following definition:

> A periodical is a printed work appearing regularly, founded with the expectation of unlimited duration, which is not predominantly concerned with events of the day, or else it pays attention only to the latest developments in a special field. Its issues are manifold both in their contents and in their layout, yet they present—the whole continuing series of them—an internal and external unity which is brought about by established editorial policy. For the most part periodicals serve limited fields; the extent of their audience is therefore varied. In their form they correspond to the needs of a circle of readers who are often widely scattered and who are accordingly only loosely connected with the place of publication.[10]

A number of writers have pointed out that the connotation of the various terms applied to serial publications has changed from century to century. Kirchner, for instance, has defined a seventeenth- or eighteenth-century periodical,[11] but his definition will not suffice for later

---

[6]Handover, *Printing in London*, p.116.

[7]Maximilian Du Prel, *Der Zeitungsbeitrag im Urheberrecht unter besonderer Berücksichtigung der Unterscheidung zwischen Zeitung und Zeitschrift und die Autorrechte* (Zeitung und Leben, no.5 [Munich, 1931]) .

[8]Werner Kienningers, *Die Einteilung der periodischen Pressschriften* (Straubing: Attenkofer, 1932) .

[9]Ernst H. Lehmann, *Einführung in die Zeitschriftenkunde* (Leipzig: Hiersemann, 1936) .

[10]Lehmann, *Einführung*, p.81.

[11]Joachim Kirchner, *Die Grundlagen des deutschen Zeitschriftenwesens* (Leipzig: Hiersemann, 1928) , v.1, p.32–33. Kirchner's definition, as well as his seven charac-

times. Likewise, the close connection that exists between periodicals and the postal service has been brought out.[12] That connection developed in the nineteenth and twentieth centuries; before that, periodicals tended to be sold issue by issue as though they were books, so much so that in 1716 it was suggested that the name "bookstore" be supplanted by "periodical store."[13]

Contemporaneously in the United States a periodical must satisfy the following requirements if it is to qualify for second-class mailing privileges:

1. The newspaper or periodical must be regularly issued at stated intervals, as frequently as four times a year, bear a date of issue, and be numbered consecutively.
2. It must be issued from a known publication office.
3. It must be formed of printed sheets.
4. It must be originated and published for the dissemination of information of a public character, or it must be devoted to literature, the sciences, arts, or some special industry.
5. It must have a legitimate list of subscribers.[14]

Legal definitions of a periodical or a serial stem from statutory law relating to second-class mail, which consists of newspapers and periodicals, or else from cases in court. The following, while it is not a good definition, is still good law, coming as it does from the leading case:

A periodical, as ordinarily understood, is a publication appearing at stated intervals, each number of which contains a variety of original articles by different authors, devoted either to general literature or some branch of learning or to a special class of subjects. Ordinarily each number is incomplete in itself, and indicates a relation with prior or subsequent numbers of the same series. It implies a continuity of literary character, a connection between the different num-

---

teristics for periodicals as they were at the end of the eighteenth century, can be found in David A. Kronick, *A History of Scientific and Technical Periodicals; the Origins and Development of the Scientific and Technological Press, 1665–1790* (Metuchen, N.J.: Scarecrow, 1962), p.29–32.

[12]Gerhard Menz, *Die Zeitschrift, ihre Entwicklung und ihre Lebensbedingungen; eine wirtschaftsgeschichtliche Studie* (Stuttgart: Poeschel, 1928), p.121ff. At the time of the manuscript newsletters there was a different kind of connection between periodicals and the postmaster.

[13]Lehmann, *Einführung*, p.4.

[14]*United States Code*, Title 39, Section 4354.

bers of the series in the nature of the articles appearing in them, whether they be successive chapters of the same story or novel or essays upon subjects pertaining to general literature.[15]

A 1967 case, *Fifield* v. *American Automobile Association,*[16] hinged on whether the AAA *Northwestern Tour Book,* published annually, could be classed as a periodical. The court held that the publication was a book, not a periodical. Two cases were cited in which a work was ruled to be a periodical: in 1892 a weekly magazine of serial stories and in 1945 a monthly magazine of cartoons. In two other cases the work was ruled to be a book: the 1904 Houghton case, which involved a series of paper-covered items, consecutively numbered, each one of which contained a novel, short stories, or poems; and, in 1912, a weekly each issue of which contained a complete story. In the 1967 AAA case the test of "common understanding" was reaffirmed; in the Houghton case the Supreme Court had ruled that, in addition to having periodicity, a work must be a periodical in the ordinary meaning of the term. In the AAA case the court said it was advised that in library science six months is the upper limit for a periodical: that is, a publication issued twice a year or less is classed as a periodical or serial, whereas one issued annually or in single volumes is classed as a book. Actually the library ruling is that a periodical must generally be issued more frequently than annually.

In both the British and North American texts of the Anglo-American cataloging code a serial is defined as "a publication issued in successive parts bearing numerical or chronological designations and intended to be continued indefinitely." This statement, identical in the two texts, is followed by a sentence which is punctuated differently in the two editions, and the punctuation implies variant practices. The British text reads: "Serials include periodicals (e.g., newspapers, journals, and the memoirs, proceedings, transactions, etc., of societies), annuals (reports, yearbooks, etc.) , and numbered monographic series."[17] The North American text reads: "Serials include periodicals, newspapers, annuals (reports, yearbooks, etc.) , the journals, memoirs, proceedings, transactions, etc., of societies, and numbered monographic series."[18] Similarly, the definition of a periodical is identical: "a serial

[15]*Houghton* v. *Payne* (1904) 194 U.S. 88, 24 S. Ct. 590, 48 L. Ed. 888, affirming (1903) 22 App. D.C. 234.

[16]262 F. Supp. 253 (1967) .

[17]*Anglo-American Cataloguing Rules: British Text* (London: The Library Assn., 1967), p.268.

[18]*Anglo-American Cataloging Rules: North American Text* (Chicago: American Library Assn., 1967) , p.346.

appearing or intended to appear indefinitely at regular or stated intervals, generally more frequently than annually, each issue of which normally contains separate articles, stories, or other writings." The British text stops at that point, but the North American text goes on to say: "Newspapers disseminating general news, and the proceedings, papers, or other publications of corporate bodies primarily related to their meetings are not included in this term."[19]

These definitions reflect much more the periodicals of the early 1900s than the extremely varied product of today, and their intension carries on the unsatisfactory separation of society publications from periodicals, more particularly in their subject cataloging. There are extremely important periodicals, notably national bibliographies and statistical publications, as well as others, which do not fit the Anglo-American cataloging-code definition.

Ulrich's International Periodicals Directory has adopted another American Library Association definition which is more satisfactory: "A periodical is a serial publication which constitutes one issue in a continuous series under the same title, usually published at regular intervals over an indefinite period, individual issues in the series being numbered consecutively or each issue being dated."[20] The directory also includes United States government periodicals, which are usually listed in the February issue of *United States Government Publications: Monthly Catalog*. It also lists newspapers which do not appear more often than five days a week.

The inclusive term "serial" has established itself in American library usage. The word is in the title of major tools such as *New Serial Titles* and the *Union List of Serials*, and since 1942, when the Central Serial Record (now the Serial Record Division) of the Library of Congress was first mentioned, the *Annual Report of the Librarian of Congress* has made frequent and important reference to serial publications, whereas it paid scant attention to them earlier. European practice has generally inclined to "periodical" as the inclusive term. As evidence there is the *British Union Catalogue of Periodicals* (not "of Serials"), as well as the *World List of Scientific Periodicals*. Both Davinson[21] and Grenfell[22] elect to continue the British preference for "periodical" as against "serial." Grenfell says:

[19]*Ibid.*, p.345.

[20]This definition is taken from *Library Statistics, a Handbook of Concepts, Definitions, and Terminology* (Chicago: American Library Assn., 1966), p.139.

[21]D. E. Davinson, *The Periodicals Collection; Its Purpose and Uses in Libraries* (London: Deutsch, 1969), p.33–38.

[22]David Grenfell, *Periodicals and Serials; Their Treatment in Special Libraries* (2d ed.; London: Aslib, 1965), p.1, 183–88.

The term "serial" is becoming unpopular and a more comprehensive interpretation is being given to the term "periodical." The latter term finds almost universal favour in other European countries, added to which it is one which is more easily interpreted by the layman. Whether a distinction is necessary is a highly debatable point and warrants the closest examination by those responsible for the various aspects of international standardization in library work.[23]

Grenfell was writing before the adoption in 1967 of the word "serial" in the British text of the Anglo-American cataloging code. Added to that development is the position taken by the editor of the *British Union Catalogue of Periodicals*, who says:

As for the class of document I am mainly concerned with, it will have been noticed that I have referred principally to "serial publications," when "periodical" is the word used in the name of the publication of which I am editor, as well as in BS 2509 (1959). "Serial" is to become the preferred term with "periodical" representing a sub-class of the term "serial." Although I do not propose to advance any definitions myself, I would point out that any definition for "serial" will have to include publications appearing in a continuous, indefinite or "open-ended" sequence under a common title and with some sort of sequence designation. "Serial" will have to be distinguished from "periodical" and "series"; it will also need to specify a relationship to the term "monograph," since a "monograph series" is a "serial." The term "monograph" is often taken as being the opposite of the word "serial," and can be applied to single works whose nature can be described as "polygraphic" in that they consist of papers, or sections, by different hands, such as a symposium or a manual. The word "symposium" opens the way to other classes of document, serial or non-serial, monographic or polygraphic, which need precise definition, such as research and development reports, administrative reports, conference proceedings, etc.[24]

The great advantage which the inclusive term "serial" enjoys is that it is not ambiguous, even though in some respects it may of necessity be vague. "Periodical," on the other hand, is decidedly ambiguous, in addition to being somewhat vague; it may mean "serial" in general, as it tends to in Europe, or it may, in Europe and elsewhere, mean "journal" or "magazine" in particular. Beyond this, in subject cataloging a periodical issued by a society was formerly distinguished from one issued by a nonsociety, particularly when it

[23]*Ibid.*, p.188.
[24]Porter, "Standards," p.30–31.

contained the transactions and other official notices of the organization. So there arose mutually exclusive subject headings such as Mathematics—Periodicals and Mathematics—Societies, a practice that persisted at the Library of Congress until 1971 (see chapter 13).

It is clear that a truly precise series of definitions, if indeed they can ever be contrived, will entail a large amount of elaboration, in part because the essential characteristic of a serial—namely, its formation by periodical or serial numbering—is by no means always present. On the one hand, there is a whole category of publications known to librarians as unnumbered series; there are numbered series whose first or later volumes lack numbering; there is an increasing number of serials which are republished in simple monographic form; and there are serial publications, many of them pseudoserials, whose numerical or chronological arrangement is derived from the edition statement or from the date of publication as given in the imprint— even from the sales number, as in the case of some League of Nations and United Nations documents. On the other hand, there are the so-called author series (that is, successions of works by a single author but held together by a serial name and numbering), which most libraries do not regard as serials, and there are nonserials (for example, the Pauly-Wissowa *Real-encyclopädie der classischen Altertumswissenschaft*) which have all the earmarks of serials: their volumes are numbered, they never seem to exhaust their subjects, they have a plurality of authors, and so on.

One other significant factor must be borne in mind. The most experienced serial librarians cannot always tell whether an item is a serial or a nonserial when it first appears. On occasion they counsel treatment as a monograph until such time as it may be necessary to reopen the case, i.e., on receipt of other issues; or a work, originally thought to be a serial publication, may have to be recataloged as a monograph because no further issues ever appeared. It is all very well to say that periodicity and seriality are the infallible signs of a serial; difficulties arise because the intent of the publisher is not always known or ascertainable. It is not at all an uncommon experience for a library to decide on the evidence of the first issue, or what may be taken possibly as the first issue, that a work is or is not a serial, only to reverse the decision when the publication's true character has at length been discerned. The editors of the *Union List of Serials* and *New Serial Titles* have frequently been confronted by titles which some libraries have treated as serials while others have taken them to be monographs, further evidence of the uncertainties which prevail through lack of an exhaustive, authoritative definition.

On all counts, therefore, it seems wiser to adopt a working definition than to confuse both theory and practice with endless exceptions and borderline cases. In these respects librarians are like the bibliographers and historians who look for a definition of terms such as "newspaper" and "periodical" so they can tell whether a title should be included in their studies or not. The librarian needs definitions to enable him to channel publications as surely as he can along the special lines which have been laid down for monographs, newspapers, periodicals, and society publications.

It was customary once to try to make hard and fast distinctions, particularly among government publications, newspapers, periodicals, and society publications. Nowadays there is a tendency to operate with as much latitude as is possible. Bella E. Shachtman represented this trend when, in the National Agricultural Library, she interpreted the term "serial" broadly "to include any title issued in parts which is incomplete in the library collection, thus periodicals, annuals, biennials, and even incomplete works-in-parts are considered serials."[25] The Enoch Pratt Free Library, which formerly drew a rather interesting distinction between periodicals and serials,[26] has now eliminated the distinction and employs just the term "serials." Within its Processing Division it has a Serials Unit which is charged with the responsibility for checking in all serials, placing subscriptions and claiming missing issues, preparing serials for binding, and maintaining a shelf-list for bound volumes.

In keeping with the times, then, a serial can be defined for library purposes as any item which lends itself to serial treatment in a library; that is, to listing in its checking records, whether they are manual or computerized; to cataloging and classifying as a serial; and to shelving in the current-periodical room or among the bound volumes of serials in the bookstacks. It is not necessary for a publication to go through all these serial stages; the current checking records will suffice for most works in parts, or the current checking records and cataloging. In doubtful cases one's judgment, based on the insights gained through years of handling serial publications, is all that is needed to decide on serial or nonserial treatment of an item, pending the possible receipt of any future issues. That is, just like the law courts, libraries

[25]"Current Serial Records—An Experiment," *College and Research Libraries* 14:240 (1953). In an earlier article, "Simplification of Serial Records Work," *Serial Slants* 3:6 (1952), Miss Shachtman says simply: "Our definition of a serial is: Any title issued in parts, which is incomplete in the library collection."
[26]For the former practice see footnote 25, p.16–17 of the first edition of *Serial Publications*.

can operate successfully on the basis of the "common understanding" of what a serial is.

In accepting as a serial any item to which a library chooses to apply serial techniques of one kind or another, three borderline types must be distinguished. They are continuations, provisional serials, and pseudoserials.

Continuations

When a library acquires part of a nonserial set for which it places a continuation order, it commonly lists the title in a special acquisition record for follow-up purposes. This kind of set is generally referred to in library parlance as a "continuation." Many libraries do not class continuations as serials in any way, especially when there are only one or two volumes still to come; when the set will be completed in the very near future; or when the volume numbering is by no means complicated, for example, when volumes and parts are not involved.

At the Library of Congress in 1953, when the Serial Record Section was detached from the Order Division to become the Serial Record Division, the pendulum swung the other way, and an effort was made to eliminate entries which could not be considered true serials. The Order Division then placed orders for the monograph continuations on an "until-completion" rather than a "continuation" basis.

However, the advantages lie with incorporating continuations in the current serial records. A single follow-up system becomes possible, and there are considerable economies in having the successive issues marked with their call number and sent directly to the shelves instead of having them go through the more elaborate and costly open-entry procedures in the catalog department.

Provisional Serials

Allied to the continuation is a mixed type, with the base quite definitely a nonserial and the continuation equally definitely a serial. The Library of Congress author catalog in book form is a good example. The work began in 1942–46 as a 167-volume set. There have been several cumulative supplements to the main work, and one publisher has cumulated the main work and the supplements in a single alphabet. At the same time, since 1948 there has been an annual supplement based on monthly and quarterly cumulations. This part of the catalog is clearly serial in character, just as surely as the foundation set is nonserial. Without doubt, too, the entire publication should be cataloged as a unit under the latest title, *The National Union Catalog*. It should be cataloged as a single entity, and by skillful manipulation of the book numbers the whole should be arranged on the shelves as a continuous set. Issues and volumes which are duplicated in any of the cumulations should be discarded or transferred to a storage warehouse.

Provisional serials are increasing in number, especially in the case of library catalogs and of encyclopedias which issue annual supplements. Whenever a complex work of this kind is held together as a unit on the shelves, good service to staff and readers inevitably follows. When the work is held together, the argument is in favor of treating it by serial methods, which will naturally keep the set intact and make automatic provision for the disposition of superseded parts and volumes.

Pseudoserials

A pseudoserial is a frequently reissued and revised publication which quite properly may be, and on first publication generally is, considered to be a monograph. After the work has been revised and issued several times, however, it may conveniently be regarded as a serial, whether the library keeps merely the latest issue or whether it keeps a back file as well. Commonly the serial numbering for pseudoserials must be taken from the edition statement or the date of publication.

The *Guide to Reference Books* (see figure 1) and *Ulrich's International Periodicals Directory* (see figure 2) are examples of potential pseudoserials which became actual serials in two different libraries. In terms of library economy it costs much less to make a single serial entry than to catalog the work afresh each time a new edition comes out or, in addition to that, to cancel the previous set of cards when the latest edition is the only one a library retains.

In volume 22 of the *Catalog of Books Represented by Library of Congress Printed Cards* there were no fewer than sixty-four separate catalog entries under Sir John Bernard Burke for editions of *Burke's Peerage,* a file that was difficult to consult because of constant variations in the wording of the title. In volume 6 of the 1942–47 supplement, however, a serial entry under *Burke's Genealogical and Heraldic History of the Peerage* replaced the monographic entries. The ratio of sixty-four to one gives some idea of the savings in descriptive and

Latest   = $\begin{cases} \text{RR } 1.6 \\ \text{Ref } 600.4 \\ \text{Doc R } 1.10 \\ \text{also Lamont Lib.} \end{cases}$

Earlier = KSF 544

Guide to reference books. Chicago, etc.
   1902 [1st] and later editions
   Published by the American Library Association
   Title varies: 1st-3d ed, Guide to the study and use of reference books; 4th ed., New guide to reference books
   Many other Harvard libraries also have sets

                        (See next card)

Guide to reference books. (Card 2)

   First-second editions by Alice B. Kroeger, third-sixth editions by Isadore G. Mudge, seventh, etc. editions by Constance M. Winchell

Figure 1. Catalog entry for a pseudoserial in the Harvard College Library

subject cataloging which are possible when a potential pseudoserial is actually treated by serial methods. Readers and staff are helped, too; in the case of *Burke's Peerage* it is no longer necessary to thumb through many cards to find the latest edition, regardless of the wording of the titles on the successive editions.

In volume 153 of the same catalog there are many examples under "U.S. Laws, statutes, etc." of laws on a particular subject which were issued and reissued constantly. Between 1919 and 1941, for instance, the pension laws were published and cataloged individually by the

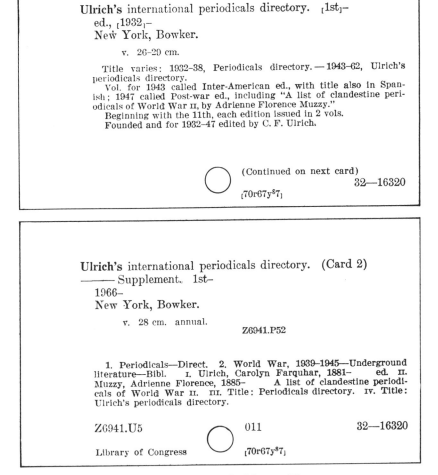

Figure 2. Catalog entry for a pseudoserial in the Library of Congress

Library of Congress no fewer than thirteen times. In recent years, however, the Library has converted the records for many of these publications to serial form (see figure 3).

Note the gains to a library which follow from the serial handling of pseudoserials:

1. Serial follow-up methods are applicable once the title of a pseudo-serial is included in the current serial checking record.

U. S. *Laws, statutes, etc.*
    Laws relating to social security and unemployment compensation. 1958–
Washington, U. S. Govt. Print. Off.

     v. 24 cm.

    Compiler: 1958–   G. G. Udell.

    1. Old age pensions—U. S. 2. Insurance, Unemployment—U. S.
    I. Udell, Gilman G., comp. II. Title.

                                 60–64640 rev

    Library of Congress   [r65f1]

Figure 3. Library of Congress catalog entry for laws frequently issued and reissued

2. When desired, particularly in special libraries, a simple program for the discarding of superseded issues can be established. For United States government publications the regulations of the Superintendent of Documents permit the discarding of any publication after a revised edition of it has been received by a depository library.

3. The number of titles which must be cataloged each year is reduced desirably. At the same time the latest edition should be on the shelves sooner than when it must await individual cataloging.

4. Processing costs of various kinds are decreased, e.g., because there are fewer cards to make and file and because the shelf-listing function is simplified.

5. Readers and staff can more readily locate entries in the catalog, both because the mass of cards under a heading such as Burke or "U.S. Laws, statutes, etc." is somewhat reduced and because the filing of the entries is not affected by the vagaries of wording in the titles of the successive editions.

6. In libraries which have closed stacks the latest edition, which is the one most commonly sought, can be called for in a simple way, just by writing the word "latest" in the space for volume or year. When the latest edition is shelved in the reference collection, the serial entry can bring this fact to the attention of the reader or staff member in a

simpler and clearer way than can be achieved with a series of cards.

In 1969 the Library of Congress had 4,621 pseudoserials listed in its Serial Record Division. There were 1,310 on its visible index and 3,917 in its Old Serial Record, some items being listed in both catalogs. While the Library of Congress is still converting frequently issued publications into serials, it is not including law materials because the K classification arranges these items by date, not by a common serial-type number; and less is being done with pseudo-serials in the era of shared cataloging because of the feeling that other libraries prefer separate cards for all editions. Actually the Library has little in the way of established policy on pseudoserials; a decision is made on each title as it occurs.

Local custom and a readiness to take advantage of favorable circumstances are more important than theoretical considerations in the determination of what shall be treated by serial methods in any given library. Hence serial practice may and does vary in some quite important respects from one institution to another. Obviously the desideratum in the treatment of serials, as in other library operations, is a large measure of agreement in principle together with great latitude in practice. Reflections such as these are what make a liberal, working definition of a serial of greater value than a series of definitions each of which has loopholes.

Bibliography

Davinson, D. E. *The Periodicals Collection; Its Purpose and Uses in Libraries.* London: Deutsch, 1969, p.33–37.

Grenfell, David. "What Is a Periodical?—or Serial?" in his *Periodicals and Serials; Their Treatment in Special Libraries,* p.183–88. 2d ed. London: Aslib, 1965.

Kronick, David A. "Definitions of the Periodical," in his *A History of Scientific and Technical Periodicals; the Origins and Development of the Scientific and Technological Press, 1665–1790,* p.28–38. Metuchen, N.J.: Scarecrow, 1962.

2

Historical and Statistical Background

Serials, which are indispensable for information and research, two important objectives of present-day libraries, are a relatively recent type of publication. Overwhelmingly they are the product of the past three centuries of the printing press and of a single century of near-print. Serial forerunners of one kind or another, including spoken newspapers, existed for better than three thousand years before Gutenberg's invention, while in the first two hundred years of European printing there were publications such as almanacs, courants, newsbooks, news pamphlets, newssheets, and eventually early forms of the newspaper.

On a decidedly conservative estimate, well over 900,000 serial publications have appeared by means of print or near-print since the first printed newspaper was issued in 1609. In 1957 the Library of Congress estimated that eleven major lists had 434,000 serial titles under bibliographical control and that 630,000 was the total number that could be safely assumed. *New Serial Titles* has averaged 13,125 new serial publications a year, so for 1950–70 an annual increase of 15,000 is a conservative estimate for world production. For the last three decades of the twentieth century an average increase of 20,000 titles a year can be anticipated (figure 4). In the twentieth century the figures for periodicals are probably in the vicinity of a fourth of the totals for serials of all kinds.

Possibly the earliest serial was represented, some 4,700 years ago, by the annals transcribed on the tombs of the fifth-dynasty kings of Egypt who reigned from 2750 to 2625 B.C.[1] According to Suetonius, in 60 B.C., "Caesar's very first enactment after becoming consul was,

[1] James H. Breasted, *A History of Egypt* (2d ed.; London: Hodder & Stoughton, 1924), p.109.

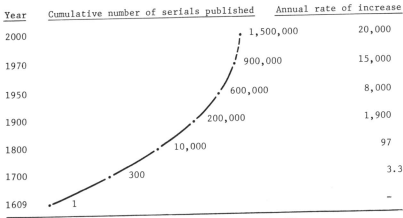

Year	Cumulative number of serials published	Annual rate of increase
2000	1,500,000	20,000
1970	900,000	15,000
1950	600,000	8,000
1900	200,000	1,900
1800	10,000	97
1700	300	3.3
1609	1	—

Figure 4. World production of serial publications, 1609–2000

that the proceedings both of the senate and of the people should day by day be compiled and published."[2] This manuscript newspaper, which was posted in a public place before being copied by scribes, was referred to by a variety of names, among them *acta diurna, acta populi,* and *acta publica.* It covered political affairs, news of the emperor and his family, and daily happenings of all kinds. It ceased only when Constantine made Constantinople the capital of the Roman Empire in 330 A.D.[3]

Bücher says:

> Long before Caesar's consulate it had become customary for Romans in the provinces to keep one or more correspondents at the capital to send them written reports on the course of political movement, and on other events of the day. Such a correspondent was generally an intelligent slave or freedman intimately acquainted with affairs at the capital, who, moreover, often made a business of reporting for

[2]Suetonius; tr. J. C. Rolfe (London: Heinemann, 1928), v.1, p.25.

[3]For the Roman newspaper see Pauly-Wissowa, *Real-encyclopädie der classischen Altertumswissenschaft; neue Bearbeitung* (Stuttgart: Metzler, 1894), v.1, p.290–95, under the caption *acta urbis.* For the linguistic expressions see *Thesaurus linguae latinae* (Leipzig: Teubner, 1903), v.4, p.1409–10, under the heading *acta diurna.* Emphasis shifted during the Middle Ages from *acta,* "acts" or "proceedings," to the adjectival form *diurnalis,* "daily." The shift led to forms such as "diurnal," a term that was used in the title of many English seventeenth-century forerunners of the newspaper, and "journal," with its variant spellings in languages such as Italian, Russian, and Spanish. The word "news" did not become common in English until after 1500. Prior to that date "tiding" was the prevalent term, and it had as its cognate in German the word "Zeitung," which has persisted as the German expression for "newspaper."

several. He was thus a species of primitive reporter, differing from those of to-day only in writing not for a newspaper, but directly for readers. . . .

The innovation made by Caesar consisted in instituting the publication of a brief record of the transactions and resolutions of the senate, and in his causing to be published the transactions of the assemblies of the Plebs, as well as other important matters of public concern.

The first were the *Acta senatus*, the latter the *Acta diurna populi Romani*. The publication was made by painting the text on a white tablet smeared with gypsum. The tablet was displayed publicly, and for the inhabitants of the capital was thus what we call a placard. For those abroad copies were made by numerous writers and forwarded to their employers. After a certain interval the original was placed in the archives of the state.

This Roman Public Bulletin was thus not in itself a newspaper, though it attained the importance of such by what we would consider the cumbersome device of private correspondence to the provinces.

The *Acta senatus* were published for but a short time, being suppressed by Augustus. On the other hand, the *Acta diurna populi Romani* obtained such favour in the eyes of the people that their contents could be made much more comprehensive, while their publication was long continued under the Empire.[4]

The earliest newspaper in China was *Ti-pao*. It began as a handwritten paper in the Han dynasty, which extended from 206 B.C. to A.D. 220. It continued through the era of block printing and into the age of movable type. The paper terminated in 1736 and was succeeded by *Ching-pao*.[5]

In Europe, from the thirteenth century on, it was not uncommon for long series of handwritten letters to be sent to great mercantile houses. The newsletters would originate with correspondents who were principally in major ports (e.g., Antwerp, Cologne, and Venice) or in cities where fairs were held (e.g., Frankfurt). In addition to commercial information the correspondents would convey word of notable military, political, and other events or personalities. The most extensive of these series was undoubtedly the Fugger newsletters, some 17,600 numbers written on 35,230 pages between 1568 and 1605 which are preserved in twenty-seven volumes in the National Library in Vienna.

[4]Carl Bücher, *Industrial Evolution* (New York: Holt, 1912), p.218–20.
[5]Paul T. H. Huang, "Tipao, the Earliest Chinese Newspaper," *Canadian Library Journal* 27:96 (1970). See also Roswell S. Britton, *The Chinese Periodical Press, 1800–1912* (Shanghai: Kelly & Walsh, 1933), p.1–15.

Following the manuscript newsletters came printed ones, as well as a number of other antecedents of serial publications. The first printed newspaper was the *Avisa, Relation oder Zeitung*, which was issued in Augsburg and bears the date 15 January 1609 on the first number. Fifty weekly parts were published in 1609, fifty-two in 1610. The only known copy of the paper is in the State Library in Hanover.[6] The name of the newspaper was composed of three of the terms which were often applied to the forerunners of newspapers in the early days of printing.

The first newspaper in French was printed in Amsterdam in 1620; not until eleven years later was one printed in France. The first newspaper in English was likewise printed in Amsterdam from 2 December 1620 to 18 September 1621; it usually bore the title *Corrant out of Italy, Germany, &c.* What has been called the "first truly English newspaper"[7] did not appear until the end of November 1641; it was a weekly entitled *The Heads of Severall Proceedings in This Present Parliament.* Nearly twenty years more had to elapse before the first daily paper was published in England, *A Perfect Diurnal of Every Dayes Proceedings in Parliament,* which ran for twenty-one issues in 1660.

The first American newspaper appeared in Boston on 25 September 1690. It was called *Publick Occurrences* and was suppressed after a single issue. Fourteen years later the *Boston News-Letter* began and lasted for seventy-two years.

Handwritten letters were the immediate antecedents of periodicals, as well as of newspapers. Porter says:

> At the beginning of the 17th century, written scientific communication was primarily through books and gazettes. Soon there arose in science, however, this important formula: one experiment equals one communication or publication. This formula was of significance because it meant that current methods of publication were inade-

---

[6]Walther Heide, *Die älteste gedruckte Zeitung* (Mainz: Gutenberg-Gesellschaft, 1931) .

[7]Joseph Frank, *The Beginnings of the English Newspaper, 1620–1660* (Cambridge: Harvard Univ. Pr., 1961) , p.21. Two other papers were issued that December. "At least eight different newspapers, most of them running to only two or three consecutive issues, rose and fell during the first three months of 1642" (*ibid.,* p.22) , affording evidence of the competition which has generally existed among serial publications and of the high mortality rate which has also been characteristic. Another matter of interest in Frank's book can be found in the index under the heading "Firsts," where forty-one items are listed, among them the first advertisement, article on flying, editor, and foreign-language weekly.

quate. The characteristic book was inappropriate for presenting the results of one new experiment or observation, because an author had to wait until he accumulated several results before he could justify publication. . . . The early gazettes or newspapers consisted mainly of reports from so-called intelligence offices, and they were not suitable for transmitting scientific information.

By 1660 the men of science recognized that they were dependent on private correspondence to keep abreast of the new knowledge being discovered throughout the world. . . .

Communication by letter writing simplified the spelling and form of many words and phrases in use at the time, and the letters provided records of scientific experiments. But just as the book was inadequate for publishing the results of one scientific experiment, so it was soon realized that correspondence among small groups was not ideal for the rapid and widespread dissemination of new ideas and knowledge. Many letters were personal, and they were not sent usually to people who would criticize or debate their contents. As a result, unsound theories were frequently not disputed or rejected for some time. Because questions of priority often arose between two men, or among groups of scientists, ciphers or systems of shorthand were devised by some to maintain secrecy. The answer to the defects in handwritten correspondence became clear to several people. The printing press had rendered the making of books in quantity a simple matter. Now these same presses could save time and labor by printing multiple copies of letters for wide distribution.[8]

The first weekly number of a periodical[9] entitled *Journal des sçavans* (from 1816 on *Journal des savants*) appeared in France on 5 January 1665. The aims were stated in the preface. They were: (1) to provide a list of the principal books published in Europe, together with a statement of their scope and findings; (2) to present obituaries of notable people and note their achievements; (3) to record contributions in chemistry and physics, as well as discoveries and inventions in the field of the arts and sciences; (4) to cite decisions handed down in civil and ecclesiastical courts, in addition to censure of the Sorbonne and other universities; and (5) to inform

[8]J. R. Porter, "The Scientific Journal—300th Anniversary," *Bacteriological Reviews* 28:211, 216 (1964).

[9]David A. Kronick, *A History of Scientific and Technical Periodicals; the Origins and Development of the Scientific and Technological Press, 1665–1790* (Metuchen, N.J.: Scarecrow, 1962), p.235, says: "The periodical falls between the book and the newspaper; it is usually addressed to a more limited audience than is the newspaper, and is not as firmly bound to the events of the day. The periodical resembles the book more than the newspaper in the range of ideas in which it deals."

readers on current events. For many years the first of the objectives was the dominant one, so the periodical grew principally as a book-reviewing medium. Except for the period from December 1792 to August 1816, the *Journal des savants* has been published continuously for over three hundred years. Naturally, there are not many complete sets in existence, but the rarest volumes are those for 1790–92, the numbers for January through November 1792 being excessively scarce.[10] In 1683 a cumulative index, covering the years 1665–81, was published in Holland; it too was the first work of its kind.[11]

Three months after the inception of the French work there appeared in Great Britain a journal which demonstrated quite clearly the historical connection between scholarly correspondence and the periodical press. The editor, Henry Oldenburg, was secretary of the Royal Society and in that capacity had the responsibility for corresponding with European scientists. Kronick says:

> The editors of the early learned journals had their prototypes in those men who constituted themselves communications centers for the scholarly world and through whose hands a great deal of the early correspondence passed. These were men like Mersenne, Peiresc, Haak, Collins and finally the two journal editors Oldenbourg and Mencke. The nature of the correspondence in the period preceding the introduction of the learned periodical anticipated the contents of the learned journal; it was impersonal in tone, and contained scientific news and notices of new books. Early periodicals might in a sense be considered printed letters addressed to a wider audience than could be reached by the written letter.[12]

The British journal began publication on 6 March 1665 as *Philosophical Transactions: Giving Some Accompt of the Present Undertakings, Studies, and Labours of the Ingenious in Many Considerable Parts of the World*. The subtitle, which was not to last, indicated the reliance which the editor placed on information that came in letters.

---

[10]Eugène Hatin, *Bibliographie historique et critique de la presse périodique française* (Paris: Didot, 1866), p.31. Hatin gives the history and bibliography of the *Journal des savants* on p.28–32. A full-length study of its formative years will be found in Betty T. Morgan, *Histoire du Journal des Sçavans depuis 1665 jusqu'en 1701* (Paris: Presses Universitaires, 1929). Kronick, *History of Scientific and Technical Periodicals*, has numerous passages on the history of this journal, which, although it was general in character, published a number of early scientific contributions.

[11]For the early history of periodical indexes see Kronick, *History of Scientific and Technical Periodicals*, p.220–32.

[12]*Ibid.*, p.235.

Since the aim of the periodical was to be more truly scientific than the *Journal des savants*, it naturally avoided the historical, legal, and theological matters found in its rival. The Royal Society adopted the journal as its official organ in 1753. The *Philosophical Transactions* are still being published,[13] though there was a period of suspension from 1676 to 1683.

In a field which for three centuries has been more noted for early mortality than for long life, it is very much of a coincidence to find that a third serial which started in 1665 is still in existence. When it appeared on 16 November 1665 its title was *Oxford Gazette*, but in the following February the name became *London Gazette*.[14]

The earliest American periodicals, although both were dated January, were actually issued in February 1741, with no more than three days at the most intervening between their appearance. Priority is generally accorded to Andrew Bradford's *American Magazine, or a Monthly View of the Political State of the British Colonies*. There were three numbers, dated January through March. The close rival was Benjamin Franklin's *The General Magazine and Historical Chronicle for All the British Plantations in America*. It ran for six issues, dated January through June.

Without doubt the seventeenth and eighteenth centuries represent a late start for serial publications. But the nineteenth century made up for that, while their growth in the twentieth century has been nothing short of phenomenal. The history of serials falls into four main periods,[15] that is, apart from the manuscript beginnings in ancient and medieval times.

1. To 1700. This was the so-called incunabula period. In the sixteenth and seventeenth centuries there were numerous forerunners of serial publications. They included almanacs and calendars, annual

13*Ibid.*, p.111–12. Kronick points out that society publications have a longer life than do those serials which are not connected with an organization. See Kronick, *passim*, for the early history of the *Philosophical Transactions*. Porter, "Scientific Journal," also gives the story of its foundation. There is an account of Oldenburg and his journal in Sir Harold Hartley, *The Royal Society, Its Origins and Founders* (London: Royal Society, 1960).

14For the story of this publication see P. M. Handover, *A History of the London Gazette, 1665–1965* (London: H.M. Stationery Office, 1965).

15C. T. Hagbert Wright, in the *Encyclopaedia Britannica* (Chicago, [1951]), v.17, p.512, divides the history of serials from a literary point of view into five periods, as follows: "It may be said, generally, that there have been five definite epochs in periodical literature: its birth in the 17th century; its jubilee in the 18th century, when Addison and Steele did their brilliant work; its rapid expansion in the first half of the 19th century; the revolt of the specialists in the latter half; and the vast output of the present, with popular approbation as its objective."

book catalogs, courants, newsbooks, manuscript and printed news-letters, news pamphlets, and newssheets. In the seventeenth century came weekly newspapers, followed by periodicals in the last third of the century.

2. 1700–1825. Although it persisted, the weekly newspaper began to give way slowly to dailies. Newspapers increased in numbers and spread from the big cities to the country. The literary periodical and the gentleman's magazine flourished. With the founding of several hundred learned societies there came the proceedings of these organizations, since three-fourths of them published their own journals. As a counterpart to the learned society publications came numerous scientific periodicals. Porter says: "Today's characteristic form of the scientific paper appeared about 1780–1790, with the publication of specialized journals in physics, chemistry, biology, agriculture and medicine."[16] There were law reports, parliamentary debates, and statutes. National bibliographies were started in France and Germany.

3. 1825–1890. This was a period of great expansion, in terms of the number of periodicals published as well as their circulation figures. Technical advances led to high-speed printing, and after 1870 wood pulp led to an adequate supply of printing paper. Along with the technological developments went a large-scale movement for the popularization of knowledge, simultaneously with enormous growth in the fields of science and technology, which in turn led to a spectacular rise in the number of scientific, technical, and industrial periodicals. As Kirchner exclaimed: "From now on, the specialized research journal!"[17] Many agricultural periodicals were published. Of the period 1833–60 Mott says: "There were also many journals in the fields of medicine, law, and education. And there were periodicals for the bankers, insurance men, druggists, hardware dealers, railroad men, telegraphers, and coach-makers. The children had their papers, too, of which the *Youth's Companion* (1827-1936) lived to become the most famous."[18] And from 1860–72, as he goes on to say:

> Expansion and specialization were leading trends in periodical publication in the years immediately following the [Civil] war. The number of periodicals (exclusive of newspapers) in 1865 was about 700; by the end of the period under consideration the number had approximately doubled. One observant weekly was fearful lest what

[16]Porter, "Scientific Journal," p.225.

[17]Joachim Kirchner, in the *Lexikon des gesamten Buchwesens* (Leipzig: Hiersemann, 1937) , v.3, p.613.

[18]Frank L. Mott, *American Journalism, a History, 1690–1960* (3d ed.; New York: Macmillan, 1962), p.322.

it called "a mania of magazine starting" should "spend itself by every successful writer becoming possessed of a magazine of his own." Religious papers showed a marked tendency to desert the general news field and become either denominational reporters or journals of opinion. Medical, legal, agricultural, educational, industrial, and trade journals flourished; and there were periodicals begun in the single year 1868 for such diverse groups as the stamp collectors, the brewers, the spiritualists, the booksellers, the dentists, the railway men, the insurance men, the Odd Fellows, the Masons, communists, artists, and sportsmen.[19]

The illustrated magazine had its inception. Women's periodicals began, *Godey's Lady's Book*, for instance, founded in 1830, with its hand-colored engravings. There were innumerable serial publications other than periodicals, such as annual reports, college and university catalogs, and directories, as well as government publications at the local, state, and federal level. This was also the golden age of the newspaper.

4. From 1890. Through the last decade of the nineteenth century and throughout the twentieth century serial publications passed into the era of mass communications, an era made possible by cheap paper[20] and the progression from the linotype to faster and faster equipment, culminating with the photocomposing machine operated by the computer. Near-print gave rise to myriads of processed publications whose elusiveness quite commonly makes them difficult to track down, to record, to count. Tabloid newspapers thrived at a time when newspapers, alone among serial publications, began to decline in numbers. Pulp magazines multiplied; as Mott says:

> Large numbers of ten- and fifteen-cent magazines—referred to as pulps because their rough-finish paper makes its origin in woodpulp particularly apparent—were issued in the twenties and thirties. This type of cheap periodical began with Munsey's *All-Story Magazine*

[19]*Ibid.*, p.395.

[20]Gerhard Menz, *Die Zeitschrift, ihre Entwicklung und ihre Lebensbedingungen; eine wirtschaftsgeschichtliche Studie* (Stuttgart: Poeschel, 1928), p.114–20, links paper production and costs to the rise of the twentieth-century serial. To give a graphic idea of the amount of paper consumed by a modern periodical in a single year, he analyzed the requirements of *Jugend*, which in 1913 had a circulation of 85,000. Six thousand trees, each about fifty feet high, had to be pulped in a factory where fifty men labored day and night for two months to produce the paper. A freight train would require fifty-seven cars to transport the 8,700,000 sheets. Thereupon eighteen presses and sixty-three men would be occupied throughout the year printing the magazine.

in 1905, and it was characterized in general by its almost exclusive devotion to action fiction as well as by its paper-stock. Most pulps were specialists in their content, one group dealing wholly with western adventure, another with love stories, another with mysteries, and so on.[21]

Sports periodicals and other journals for men multiplied, as did publications for youth. This was the period of little magazines and later on of the underground press and the politically radical publication. Color printing reached considerable heights. Technical reports came into being. The great flood of serial literature in one form or another had to be supported by several thousand abstracting and indexing services. To government publications now were added the serial publications issued by more than two thousand international organizations, both governmental and nongovernmental.

So vast was the proliferation of periodicals in the twentieth century that Peterson could say:

> The American of 1900 could probably have found at least one magazine devoted to his special interests no matter what they were. Magazines had begun to appear in profusion after the Civil War, and never before had they so completely represented the diverse tastes of the public. Politics, religion, science, fashions, society, music, drama, art, literature, sports, and recreation—by 1900 there were periodicals covering all of those fields and dozens of others. . . .
>
> The American of the early sixties had an even more diversified field to choose from, and the magazines he chose were likely to be superior in technical execution if not necessarily in content. Magazines of politics ranged from the extreme left to the extreme right. Religious magazines of many faiths abounded, and several denominations maintained sizable publishing companies; but freethinkers also had their organs. There were magazines for lovers of classical music, for lovers of jazz, for amateur magicians and amateur astronomers, for believers in astrology and students of the occult, for collectors of coins, stamps, and antique automobiles, for ex-servicemen, yachtsmen, women bowlers, campers, ham radio operators, folklorists, teen-agers, retired persons, and square dancers.[22]

Awareness of the turn of events in the twentieth century led Esdaile to protest that "the periodical has added a new terror to research." He went on to say:

[21]Mott, *American Journalism*, p.733.
[22]Theodore Peterson, *Magazines in the Twentieth Century* (2d ed.; Urbana: Univ. of Illinois Pr., 1964), p.362–63.

A century ago there were few and all but a handful of those that existed were insignificant. But the most worthless literature, if it be popular, is in time of value as an index to social habits and ideas. Now the periodical contains a very large proportion of the first appearances of important literature of the imagination, criticism, essays and the like, and practically the whole of the original work done in science. A bibliography which ignores articles in periodicals is a one-eyed leader of the blind.[23]

Statistics of Serial Production

As the twentieth century progresses, insight into the mounting problem brought about by serial publications is of fundamental importance to librarians who must adjust their collections, services, and thinking to the new state of affairs. It would be unwise in the extreme to think that world reliance on serials will abate. The decline in the number of newspapers published cannot be taken as a straw in the wind, and adequate supplies of paper for printing are certain to be maintained in spite of the concern expressed in the FAO and Unesco surveys. Porter's counsel about scientific periodicals can be applied to serial publications in general. He says:

> We have reached a period in science somewhat similar to that encountered by our colleagues of 300 years ago. Creative and inventive minds must now discover new methods for coping with the scientific literature. If this is not done, science will face a real crisis within a generation and may suffocate from its own immense production. I challenge each of you to ponder the formidable and perplexing difficulties associated with communicating and comprehending the scientific literature.[24]

In former times people were exercised about the number of periodicals which were being produced; yet, despite expressed concern, the number of titles has increased generation after generation, and to a high degree ways have been contrived to manage the outpouring. In 1716 apprehension was felt about the overproduction of periodicals, whose remainders would have to be bundled up and sold like rotten old cheese. In 1739 the cry was: "Journals! Journals! They are the

[23]Arundell Esdaile, *Manual of Bibliography;* rev. ed. by Roy Stokes (The Library Association Series of Library Manuals, no.1 [4th ed.; London: Allen & Unwin, 1967]), p.321.

[24]Porter, "Scientific Journal," p.229.

means whereby our present century distinguishes itself from all others."[25] In 1831 it was declared:

> This is the golden age of periodicals. Nothing can be done without them. Sects and parties, benevolent societies, and ingenious individuals, all have their periodicals. Science and literature, religion and law, agriculture and the arts, resort alike to this mode of enlightening the public mind. Every man, and every party, that seeks to establish a new theory, or to break down an old one, commences operations, like a board of war, by founding a *magazine*. We have annuals, monthlys, and weeklys—reviews, orthodox and heterodox—journals of education and humanity, of law, divinity and physic—magazines for ladies and for gentlemen—publications commercial, mechanical, metaphysical, sentimental, musical, anti-fogmatical, and nonsensical. . . .
>
> Whether we travel, or stay at home, we are feasted with periodicals to a surfeit—they pervade the atmosphere of the country like an epidemic. Go to a tea-party, and you find souvenirs served up with the confectionary; dine with a friend, and you get reviews with your wine; walk in the street, and a fellow assails you with a prospectus; take refuge in a book-store, and your retreat is cut off by huge piles of periodicals.[26]

In 1845 the theme was still the same:

> Whatever may be the merits or demerits, generally, of the Magazine literature of America, there can be no question as to its extent or its influence. The topic—Magazine literature—is therefore an important one. In a few years its importance will be found to have increased in geometrical ratio. The whole tendency of the age is Magazine-ward.[27]

Thus each of the last three centuries has been impressed with the number of serial titles it has produced. With this reading of history, the only wise conclusion to draw is that the serial production of the hundred years that lie ahead will dwarf the accomplishments of the past ten decades, stupendous though they have been.

[25]Ernst H. Lehmann, *Einführung in die Zeitschriftenkunde* (Leipzig: Hiersemann, 1936), p.6.

[26]"Periodicals," *Illinois Monthly Magazine* 1:302–303 (1831).

[27]"Graham's Magazine," *The Broadway Journal* 1:139 (1845). Cf. Frank L. Mott, "A Period of Expansion in Periodicals," in his *A History of American Magazines* (Cambridge: Harvard Univ. Pr., 1939), v.1, p.340–42. Mott points out that "in most of the estimates and tables given throughout this period the newspapers form about nine-tenths of the total periodicals."

Anyone who attempts a census of today's output of periodicals in the narrow sense of journals, or of serials in the broad sense, is plagued by problems of inclusiveness and exclusiveness. No figures should be quoted or compared without reference to the types of publication which they include or exclude. Davinson says:

> The problem in attempting any count of the number of periodicals is to know what it is one is trying to count. As already indicated there is difficulty in attempting to define "periodical." The use of qualifiers such as "major," "significant," "frequently cited," etc. in the counts already attempted indicates a difficulty—what do such terms themselves imply? Gottschalk and Desmond ignored House Journals, International Organization periodicals and Technical Report series in their reckoning but estimated that there were a further 17,000–19,000 in these and other such categories. The other estimators . . . do not make clear what they have included.
>
> Whatever the truth of the numbers game, which is energetically pursued in the librarianship press, it is easy to agree with Huff when he says, "How many periodicals are there? The elementary nature of this question is not matched by the complexity of the answer." Without wishing to enter into debate as to whether there will be one hundred thousand or one million current periodical titles by the year 2000, as various advocates of an exponential growth theory have argued, it is quite clear that however many there are today there will be many more tomorrow. The problem of their bibliographical control will increase before there is any chance of electronic salvation via computers.[28]

The first edition of the *Union List of Serials* omitted almanacs, annual denominational church reports, annuals, gift books, government publications, law reports, monograph series, state and local trade-union publications, and many titles which seemed to the editor to have limited or ephemeral value. The scope of the second and third editions was considerably enlarged by the addition of annual publications which record or summarize the progress of research in specific fields, children's magazines, numbered monograph series and, when the run of volumes justified inclusion, those usually discarded magazines known as pulps. The exclusions were specified as administrative reports of corporations, societies, universities, etc.; publications of agricultural and other experiment stations; almanacs; alumni, undergraduate, and intercollegiate-fraternity publications;

[28]D. E. Davinson, *The Periodicals Collection; Its Purpose and Uses in Libraries* (London: Deutsch, 1969), p.21–22.

American newspapers; publications of boards of trade and chambers of commerce; English and other foreign newspapers after 1820; gift books; government publications, except for the periodicals and monograph series issued by governments; house organs, unless they had scientific or technical value; law reports and digests; publications of local fraternal, labor, and religious organizations; national and international conferences; trench papers; and in general all titles which had a highly limited or ephemeral value. *New Serial Titles* is much more comprehensive; its exclusions are administrative reports, books in parts, filmstrips, loose-leaf publications, motion pictures, municipal government serial documents, newspapers, phonorecords, and publishers' series.

In the circumstances it is difficult to compare figures for these union lists, yet in 1969 the Library of Congress said:

> The number of new titles listed by *New Serial Titles* in its 16 years of operation now totals 210,000, which exceeds the number listed in the *Union List of Serials* (1665–1949) and its two companion volumes, *International Congresses and Conferences* (1840–1937), and the *List of Serial Publications of Foreign Governments* (1815–1931).[29]

The one sure statistic in this statement is that the libraries of Canada and the United States have recorded the publication of an average of 13,125 new serials for each of the sixteen years of *New Serial Titles* up to 1969. Kuhlman breaks this figure down into 3,000 new periodicals and 10,000 new serials a year.[30] Another way of interpreting the figure is that on the average at least 36 new serials are born for every day in the year or 53 for every working day.

For long it has been difficult to tell how many newspapers are published because of the question of editions. Do the morning and evening editions count as one paper or two? Now the problem has spread to periodicals, several hundred of which are issued in a variety of national and international editions. Peterson says of this development:

> Since publishers began to exploit regional editions in 1959, the geographic regions have become smaller and smaller. Now several magazines sell space in copies going into such cities as Chicago, Los

[29]*Library of Congress Information Bulletin* 28:489 (1969).

[30]A. F. Kuhlman, *A Report on the Consumer Survey of New Serial Titles* ([Washington, D.C.: Library of Congress], 1967), **p.66.**

Angeles and New York. *Farm Journal*, which has published more than 125 different editions of a single issue, will sell circulation in any one of 3,070 counties in the United States. . . .

About a year ago *Fortune* began publishing a special edition going to 120,000 computer-selected subscribers who are associated with manufacturing concerns. *Time* has had editions for physicians, educators, and students, and the *Reader's Digest* has had one for pupils in grades seven through twelve and their teachers.[31]

In the United States alone the number of magazines with regional editions has increased from 126 in 1959 to 186 in 1965 and 235 in 1969. Is the count for 1969 to be taken as 235 or 470 or still more periodicals? Sometimes it is only the advertising which varies from one regional edition to another, but sometimes it is the text, too, as in the case of a Canadian edition of an American periodical in which part of the American text is regularly replaced by Canadian.

Distinctions which are made between types of serials give rise to other problems of counting. The Serial Record Division at the Library of Congress has separated out no fewer than fifty-six types, the largest of them being "unknowns."[32] However, if trade journals were removed from the category of "unknowns" and were considered as periodicals under a broader definition of that term, then periodicals would constitute 21 percent of all serials and not 12.3 percent, as now given in the Serial Record Division tables. The figure of 21 percent could rise if a number of other categories were counted as periodicals, e.g., abstracting journals, book reviews, house organs, and little magazines.

In 1969 the Library of Congress had 180,180 current titles on its checking records together with another unduplicated 247,044 titles, live and dead, on its old serial records, making a total of 427,224 serial publications listed in the Serial Record Division's files.[33] In 1950 it was estimated that the Library of Congress held at least half of the serial titles possessed by American research libraries.[34] On that basis it can be assumed that those libraries are receiving some 360,360 current titles and that they have something like 854,448 serial publications in their collections.

No less than three-fourths of the volumes that find their way into

[31]Theodore Peterson, "The Bright, Bleak Future of American Magazines," in Walter C. Allen, ed., *Serial Publications in Large Libraries* (Allerton Park Institute, no.16 [Urbana, Ill.: Graduate School of Library Science, 1970]), p.6.

[32]Library of Congress, *Serial Record Sample* (Washington, 1969), p.69–80.

[33]*Ibid.*, p. 62–63.

[34]*Annual Report of the Librarian of Congress* 1950 (Washington, 1951), p.113.

the nation's largest library are serial in character. One reason for this is that two-fifths of all monographs are nowadays published in series; another is that 80 percent of all United States government publications are serials.

The number of scientific serials currently being published has been the subject of a series of investigations. The most dependable is that of Gottschalk and Desmond, which shows that in 1961 there were 35,300 current scientific and technical periodicals, plus or minus 10 percent.[35] The figure could have been increased by 50 percent by including house organs, the proceedings of international organizations, publishers' series, technical-report series, and cover-to-cover translations.

The National Lending Library for Science and Technology in Great Britain took exception to the Gottschalk and Desmond figures, the reason being that to a certain extent they tended to be based on lists which cannot altogether be trusted because of the mortality rates for serials. At the end of 1965 the National Lending Library had 22,600 current titles, with another 3,600 on order, and these figures did not exclude proceedings of international organizations, technical-report series, or cover-to-cover translations. Since no more than 26,200 titles could be obtained or traced, the library considered that this must be the number of current scientific and technical periodicals in existence.[36] However, in 1970 it reported that it was receiving 36,000 current titles, with another 2,000 on order, but included in the total were many serials in the area of the social sciences.

It seems reasonable to say that from now on the annual figure for scientific and technical journals produced throughout the world can be taken, for working purposes, as the number of current periodicals in the National Lending Library, the social science journals compensating for the margin of error. If so, this will be a remarkable state of affairs, because for many years it has been recognized that no major library can be complete in itself,[37] and in particular that the

[35]Charles M. Gottschalk and Winifred F. Desmond, "Worldwide Census of Scientific and Technical Serials," *American Documentation* 14:188 (1963). In their careful study they decided that the sections of a journal would not be counted individually; so the forty sections of the Russian abstracting service, *Referativnyi Zhurnal*, which existed in 1962 would be counted as one, although quite properly they could have been tallied as forty different titles.

[36]K. P. Barr, "Estimates of the Number of Currently Available Scientific and Technical Periodicals," *Journal of Documentation* 23:110 (1967).

[37]Gertrude L. Annan and Jacqueline W. Felter, eds., *The Handbook of Medical Library Practice* (3d ed.; Chicago: Medical Library Assn., 1970), p.76, say, e.g.: "Not even the National Library of Medicine regularly acquires every issue of all the estimated 18,000 journals of medical and related interest."

smaller special libraries with their tremendous range of subject specialization add extraordinarily to the holdings of the larger research libraries.

Bonn, who accepts the Gottschalk and Desmond figure, adds that the number of serials is growing at the rate of 5–10 percent every year. He goes on to say that 93 percent of all the literature cited in chemistry is published in serials, 90 percent in physiology, 88 percent in physics, 80 percent in zoology, and 76 percent in mathematics.[38]

Estimates for the number of scientific journal articles written each year vary even more widely. Schur and Saunders say:

> To take but one field, chemistry, it took well over two centuries for the first million papers to be published, and over 30 years, from 1907 to 1938, for the first million to be abstracted in Chemical Abstracts. We are now at the stage where one million papers have been abstracted in a five-year period—1962–1967—and before 1975 the point will have been reached where one million papers, equal to the output of the whole pre-war generation of chemists, will be published and abstracted in a single year.[39]

Vickery estimates that in 1965 there were 850,000 articles in the 26,000 periodicals held by the National Lending Library for Science and Technology.[40] In 1963 Price set a lower figure. He said: "Since science began, about 10 million scientific papers have been published, and we are adding to them, with a doubling in 10 years, or about 6 percent a year, about 600,000 new papers every year."[41] Bourne gives estimates which range from 790,000 articles in 1957 to a Russian figure of 3.5 million in 1961.[42] Adams and Baker say:

> NSF estimated the annual number of scientific and technical articles to be 1,700,000 in 1964. Other estimates range from one to two million articles per year while a Russian estimate suggested that there

[38]George S. Bonn, *Literature of Science and Technology* (New York: McGraw-Hill, 1966), p.3. This item is reprinted from the *McGraw-Hill Encyclopedia of Science and Technology,* revised edition.

[39]H. Schur and W. L. Saunders, *Education and Training for Scientific and Technological Library and Information Work* (London: H.M. Stationery Office, 1968), p.1.

[40]B. C. Vickery, "Statistics of Scientific and Technical Articles," *Journal of Documentation* 24:193 (1968).

[41]Derek J. De Solla Price, *Little Science, Big Science* (New York: Columbia Univ. Pr., 1963), p.73.

[42]C. P. Bourne, "The World's Technical Journal Literature," *American Documentation* 13:159 (1962).

may be 4.5 million articles per year. A later study by the System Development Corporation (SDC) estimated conservatively that 2,-573,000 individual items were abstracted or cited by 220 abstracting and indexing publications in 1966.[43]

In addition to the problems created by sheer numbers, library handling of serials is complicated because on the average they have a brief life-span. Kuhlman found that the defunct titles in the first edition of the *Union List of Serials*, which was published in 1927, had existed for an average of 9.9 years, while the continuing titles averaged 25.1 years.[44] The Library of Congress compiled comparable data for the second edition, which was published in 1943. By then the average life-span of defunct titles had increased to 11.4 years and of continuing titles to 27.2 years.[45] Since items in the *Union List of Serials* constitute a select group, it is extremely improbable that statistics as high as these would stand for serials of all types. In 1943, and certainly in 1927, the life-span of the average serial would have been closer to five than to ten years. However that may be, it can be seen from evidence presented by Brigham and Mott that the life expectancy of a serial has steadily increased as the years have progressed. Brigham said: "The mortality in newspapers before 1821 was notable. Over half of the total of 2120 papers in this period, to be exact, 1118 papers, expired before they had reached two years of existence."[46] Wroth comments: "This high mortality among the newspapers can be best accounted for by the lack of capital of their promoters, an ever-present factor in lost causes, and by the difficulty experienced at various times and places of securing a steady supply of reasonably cheap paper."[47] In another place he adds: "This was indeed a high mortality rate, but a more interesting reflection upon the figures is that the rate was not higher, even, than here shown in

[43]Scott Adams and Dale B. Baker, "Mission and Discipline Orientation in Scientific Abstracting and Indexing Services," *Library Trends* 16:311 (1968).

[44]A. F. Kuhlman, "Administration of Serial and Document Acquisition and Preparation," in William M. Randall, ed., *The Acquisition and Cataloging of Books* (Chicago: Univ. of Chicago Pr., 1940), p.96–97.

[45]C. Sumner Spalding, *Certain Proposals of Numerical Systems for the Control of Serials Evaluated for Their Application at the Library of Congress* ([Washington], 1954), p.21.

[46]Clarence S. Brigham, *History and Bibliography of American Newspapers, 1690–1820* (Worcester, Mass.: American Antiquarian Society, 1947), v.1, p.xii.

[47]Lawrence C. Wroth, *The Colonial Printer* (Portland, Maine: Southworth-Anthoesen Pr., 1938), p.233.

view of the difficulties under which periodicals must be published in an undeveloped country."[48]

Mott, whose figures do not include newspapers, says: "Sixty per cent of the magazines of 1741–94 did not outlast the first year, and only four reached the ripe age of three and a half years. Four died a-borning at one month."[49] In these circumstances it is not surprising to find Noah Webster saying pessimistically in connection with his *American Magazine:* "The expectation of *failure* is connected with the very name of a Magazine."[50] As late as 1828 a journal in its sixth year stated that "the average age of new periodicals in this country is found to be six months—some have reached nine—and a few dragged on a lingering existence to the mature age of twelve."[51] But Mott is inclined to set the average age of periodicals from 1825 to 1850 at nearer two years. From 1850 to 1885 he calculates the average age generously at four years.

Gottschalk and Desmond find quite high mortality rates continuing into the twentieth century. They say:

> The burgeoning of a science and the springing up of new technologies built around discoveries increases the number of periodicals as increasing numbers of articles are produced and demand fresh outlets. A number of these new journals pass out of existence or merge with others and gradually generate a factor—the mortality rate—which is not accounted for in many estimates of the number of journals published during a given period. By examining a given application in the field of physics—radioactivity—and by analyzing the growth and death of the serial literature in that field from the discovery of X-rays and radium in the late 19th century through the mid-20th century, the authors drew several interesting conclusions. . . . Of the journals examined, two-thirds of the total had come into existence between 1900 and 1930, and one-third of these had ceased publication during that time. By the mid-50's over one-third of the new total had ceased publication. One might conclude from this that at least in one field over the period of half a century there is a 33% death rate for journals. . . .
>
> Mortality can also be studied in subject bibliographies. *Aeronautical and Space Serial Publications: a World List* published in November

[48]Lawrence C. Wroth, in Hellmut Lehmann-Haupt, *The Book in America, a History of the Making and Selling of Books in the United States* (2d ed.; New York: Bowker, 1951) , p.38.

[49]Mott, *History of American Magazines*, v.1, p.21.

[50]*American Magazine* 1:130 (1788).

[51]"American Periodicals," *The New-York Mirror and Ladies' Literary Gazette* 6:151 (1828) .

1962 by the Library of Congress, demonstrates the high death rate in that field from the early 20th century to the present. Of the 4,551 titles listed, only 1,553 are known to be current, a mortality of approximately 66% for the 60 years and 10% for the decade 1950–1960. The National Library of Medicine, in its *Biomedical Serials,* cites approximately 9,000 titles, of which over 3,000 are presumed dead. A sampling of the Library of Congress Serial Record indicates an approximate 40% mortality rate over an undefined period. A sampling of 100 pages from the *World List* indicates a mortality rate of 33%, or some 15,000 titles.[52]

Barr adds that a similar sample check of the fourth edition of the *World List of Scientific Periodicals* shows that only 40 percent of the entries, that is, 24,000 titles, represent actual current titles.[53]

Peterson rounds out the story by saying:

> Certainly the death of the *Saturday Evening Post* should remind us of the essential mortality of all magazines. Many of the magazines that led in circulation, advertising and prestige preceded the *Post* in death. And in the same month that the *Post* died, *American Builder* slipped quietly into the grave. Eight years earlier, *American Builder* had been its publisher's number one magazine, and only the previous November it had observed its hundredth anniversary. In April, 1969, *Western Farm Life* died at age seventy-one. In April, too, the Hearst Corporation gave up its attempts to sustain *Eye,* a two-year-old monthly for young swingers. Over the years, death has come with democratic impartiality to the young and old, to the poor and to the once wealthy.[54]

The present situation is that over one-half million serial publications are being issued every year. Since the publications have a relatively short life on the average, continual alertness is necessary if libraries are to maintain complete files and to acquire new titles as they appear. The names of the publications change frequently, and it is estimated that the corporate bodies with which many of the serials are connected change their names on an average of once every fifteen to twenty years. Harriet Pierson mentioned a work which experienced forty-one changes in corporate name or title in fourteen years. Strange things happen to the collation and numbering of the

52Gottschalk and Desmond, "Worldwide Census," p.192–93. They used the third edition of the *World List of Scientific Periodicals.*
53Barr, "Estimates," p.111.
54Peterson, "Bright, Bleak Future," p.1.

publications. They have been known to come to life again after being thought dead for a century: witness the *Memorias* of the Academía de Buenas Letras de Barcelona, volume 1 of which was published in 1756 and volume 2 in 1868; also the *Memoirs* of the Connecticut Academy of Arts and Sciences, volume 1 of which appeared from 1810 to 1816 and volume 2 in 1910. Moreover, new types of serials keep rising to the fore. The most recent type to assume major proportions is the technical report. The demand for greater speed than even the periodical could afford has led to this development, as Lieutenant General Kuter indicates:

> The era in which we live is one of incredible speed. Many, many years ago, it was already apparent to writers and teachers that the production of books as a means of recording current knowledge was far too slow. That was the time when journals were established and came to take the place in our lives that they now have. It was and still is possible for new and valuable facts to be publicized rather swiftly through journals. However, more recently the journal has proved to be too slow, and a new form of literature, the near-print document or ephemeral paper, has come to take its place in our working lives. Recorded information can be made available in this special form much more simply and rapidly.[55]

Forewarned is forearmed. Realizing the complexities of the situation as well as the ever-increasing trend toward publication in serial form, libraries should be ready to make considerable adjustments in principle and practice in the last part of the century. As Miss Ditmas says: "The literary, scientific or technical periodical has come to stay—more, it has won such an honoured place amongst the tools of research that it has attained the right to be treated *sui generis*, and not as a poor relation of the book."[56] This is perhaps the sternest lesson to be learned by the general library, a lesson which, as Miss Ditmas observes, the special library learned at its inception. Implied here is the all-or-nothing theory of serial treatment which is all too prevalent in serial cataloging, classification, and binding. It is wise to aim at a compromise between overelaborate methods and comparative neglect, two treatments which seem to go hand in hand in so many libraries, where a minor periodical or an annual report is cataloged in detail but a major government publication is neither

[55]Laurence S. Kuter, "What Makes a Special Library Special in an Academic Institution," *Special Libraries* 45:159 (1954).

[56]E. M. R. Ditmas, in David Grenfell, *Periodicals and Serials; Their Treatment in Special Libraries* (2d ed.; London: Aslib, 1965), p.v.

catalogued nor classified, or upwards of a dollar is spent for lettering on the spine of an approved serial but nothing for the spines of other serials.

Bibliography

History

Frank, Joseph. *The Beginnings of the English Newspaper, 1620–1660.* Cambridge: Harvard Univ. Pr., 1961.

Kirchner, Joachim. *Die Grundlagen des deutschen Zeitschriftenwesens.* Leipzig: Hiersemann, 1928–31. 2v.

Kronick, David A. *A History of Scientific and Technical Periodicals; the Origins and Development of the Scientific and Technological Press, 1665–1790.* Metuchen, N.J.: Scarecrow, 1962.

Mott, Frank L. *American Journalism, a History, 1690–1960.* New York: Macmillan, 1962.

———. *A History of American Magazines.* Cambridge: Harvard Univ. Pr., 1939–68. 5v.

Peterson, Theodore. "The Bright, Bleak Future of American Magazines," in Walter C. Allen, ed., *Serial Publications in Large Libraries,* p.1–10. (Allerton Park Institute, no.16) Urbana, Ill.: Graduate School of Library Science, 1970.

———. *Magazines in the Twentieth Century.* 2d ed. Urbana: Univ. of Illinois Pr., 1964.

Porter, J. R. "The Scientific Journal—300th Anniversary," *Bacteriological Reviews* 28:211–30 (1964).

Statistics

Barr, K. P. "Estimates of the Number of Currently Available Scientific and Technical Periodicals," *Journal of Documentation* 23:110–16 (1967).

Gottschalk, Charles M., and Desmond, Winifred F. "Worldwide Census of Scientific and Technical Serials," *American Documentation* 14:188–94 (1963).

Price, Derek J. De Solla. *Little Science, Big Science.* New York: Columbia Univ. Pr., 1963.

Vickery, B. C. "Statistics of Scientific and Technical Articles," *Journal of Documentation* 24:192–96 (1968).

3

Librarians as Serial Specialists

The figure of speech which librarians in general and special libraries in particular have repeatedly applied to serial publications is that they constitute the backbone of the research collection. Serials are basic to organized reference work in the broad and the narrow sense in almost any kind of library. They comprise much of the librarian's stock in trade—many of them are his daily working tools—just as they are essential to the scholar, the research worker and, in fact, to people generally who are carrying out investigations of one kind or another. As Margaret Hutchins remarks:

> It is no longer necessary to argue for the importance of periodicals and newspapers in reference work. From childhood up the present generation has read them and used them for information more than books. In view of the innumerable enthusiastic testimonials of reference librarians as to the supremacy of periodicals as reference materials it may become necessary to write an apologetic for books, lest the periodicals elbow them entirely out of libraries, and serials departments monopolize reference work.[1]

Some testimonials of the kind she refers to follow.

Brown says: "Studies have shown that over 95% of the references cited by scientists are to scientific periodicals and society publications."[2] The first edition of the *Handbook of Medical Library Practice* states:

[1] Margaret Hutchins, *Introduction to Reference Work* (Chicago: American Library Assn., 1944), p.103.

[2] Charles H. Brown, *Library Resources in Selected Scientific Subjects at Louisiana State University* (Baton Rouge: Louisiana State Univ. Library, 1950), p.2.

A well-rounded medical library must consist in major part of periodical material, including journals and serials of many types. . . . They contain the first recorded reports of scientific discoveries and additional ever mounting comments, criticisms and supplements on these reports. After periodical literature, monographs and textbooks on special subjects are a necessary part of the library.[3]

The third edition expresses the primacy of the periodical over medical books as follows:

Science, and especially medicine and its allied fields, produces primarily a periodical literature. The medical journal, and its cousins, the serial and the periodical, has a long and crowded history. One of the major differences between a medical and a public or school library is that the collection of the "average" medical library will be roughly two-thirds periodicals and one-third books.[4]

Strauss, Shreve, and Brown, from the point of view of special libraries in the field of science and technology, say:

Periodicals constitute a most important part of a science-technology library's resources because they publish the immediate results of experimental research and technological developments. A continuous record of scientific advance is presented in these journals, although it is not an account easily read since related information is usually scattered among many papers. The more volumes of periodicals in any one collection, particularly of long runs of basic titles, the more of this record there will be at hand to be put together, and it is for this reason that these publications, in contrast to most monographic works, appreciate in value with time. Papers accepted for publication by prestigious journals have had to be approved by authorities in the subject fields, a requirement that has kept standards high, thereby creating a body of literature of inestimable significance.[5]

The Public Business Librarians Group of the Special Libraries Association states that "rapid changes in the business and economic world

---

[3]Janet Doe, ed., *A Handbook of Medical Library Practice* (Chicago: American Library Assn., 1943) , p.65.

[4]Gertrude L. Annan and Jacqueline W. Felter, eds., *A Handbook of Medical Library Practice* (3d ed.; Chicago: Medical Library Assn., 1970), p.76.

[5]Lucille J. Strauss, Irene M. Shreve, and Alberta L. Brown, *Scientific and Technical Libraries; Their Organization and Administration* (2d ed.; New York: Becker & Hayes, 1972) , p.138.

today have caused emphasis to be placed on periodicals rather than books."[6]

In the past law libraries have lagged in collecting periodicals, although they leaned heavily on other types of serials, notably law reports and statute laws. In 1953 Roalfe reported that 40 of the 184 law libraries he surveyed did not receive any legal periodicals currently, while another 60 received only from one to ten titles. Moreover, he found that 76 of the 184 did not subscribe to the *Index to Legal Periodicals.*[7] But Surrency, Feld, and Crea say:

> Within recent years, legal periodicals have become an important source of persuasive authority. It is in the periodicals that the results of legal research and articles discussing developments in the law first appear. Many of these articles are generally scholarly and thorough. The subjects covered in these articles range through all fields of the law, from "how to do" type to a more scholarly exploration of legal problems. Anyone engaged in legal research overlooks the periodicals at his peril.[8]

They also say: "One of the best sources for a critical analysis of any decision is the case-notes found in the various law reviews. To determine if the case has been the subject of a law note, one should turn to the index of the decisions in the *Index to Legal Periodicals.*"[9]

In the latter part of the twentieth century there are few, if any, libraries which can adequately fulfill their functions without recourse to serials of one kind or another. An obvious reason for the high priority which libraries in general and research and special libraries in particular accord serial publications, the reason for the never-ending accumulation and consultation of serial files, is that the volumes contain facts and figures which are necessary for both general information and research work: bibliographical references, contributions by authorities, news, popular presentations of knowledge, statistics, up-to-the-minute data, and so on. The closest analog to a serial is a pamphlet; each of them is noted for its timeliness. Out of the

[6]Special Libraries Association, Public Business Librarians Group, *Business and the Public Library; Steps in Successful Cooperation;* ed. by Marian C. Manley (New York: Special Libraries Assn., 1940), p.41.

[7]William R. Roalfe, *The Libraries of the Legal Profession* (St. Paul, Minn.: West Pub. Co., 1953), p.51–52.

[8]Erwin C. Surrency, Benjamin Feld, and Joseph Crea, *A Guide to Legal Research* (2d ed.; New York: Oceana, 1959), p.62.

[9]*Ibid.*, p.53.

pamphlets and serials of the day will come many of the books of the future.

The historian Sir Charles Oman, writing in 1921, gives an illustration of the way in which contributions in periodicals so often precede, outrun, and make possible the writing of books. He says:

> No general manual or authoritative work on Early British coins, before the Roman Conquest, has appeared since Sir John Evans published his monograph on them more than a generation ago. But in the last forty years an immense amount of information concerning these primitive but interesting coins has cropped up. The discoveries of numerous hoards of issues unknown in 1860 have enlarged the facts at the disposal of the archaeologist, and have even enabled the historian to add some undoubted deductions to the annals of Early Britain. But all these new facts and deductions are preserved only in the numbers of the *Numismatic Chronicle,* and certain other journals of learned societies. If these journals did not exist, the knowledge would never have got into print, but would have remained in the brains of the researcher, and have perished with his death—to be discovered perhaps again by another researcher in another generation, with much waste of duplicated labour.[10]

This to Sir Charles is an evidence of the way in which a great part of historical, literary, and scientific research "first takes shape in papers or monographs, which appear in periodicals of the more specialised sort." It leads him to conclude: "I regard therefore the Proceedings and Journals of learned societies as one of the most important sections of every library."

But the full impact of the ascendancy of serial publications does not begin to dawn on us until the realization sinks in that a good three-fourths of the 16 million and more volumes in the Library of Congress are serial in character in one way or another. In an epoch-making statement the Library of Congress says:

> Serial publications (including newspapers, periodicals, bulletins, reports, most Government documents, and books in series) constitute perhaps 75 percent of all publications, an indispensable part from the viewpoint of research. It is in serial publications that advance information and discussion are found; in them are found also the detailed records which support most scientific, legal, and historical

[10]Sir Charles Oman, "Note on the Present Hindrance to Research Caused by the Enhanced Price of Printing," *Library Association Record* 23:326 (1921).

> study. Attention to the acquisition and recording of serial publications is, therefore, of first importance to every large research library. Because the separate issues of serials cannot be treated individually as are books, but must be considered in conjunction with other issues, they represent the form of publication which is most difficult to control at all stages—acquisition, accessioning, processing, and service.[11]

Note that this statement refers to books in series in addition to the vast mass of government serials, newspapers, periodicals, and other conventional serial publications. In themselves the component parts of monograph series are so numerous that in Schneider's estimation "more than a third of all books nowadays appear in this form."[12] Another indication of the extent of books in series is the Card Division's statement that "about one-tenth of the cards in stock in the Library of Congress are for publications in series."[13] In 1971 the Card Division estimated that since the beginning of the Title II program the number of cards printed with series notes has increased to 40 percent.

Probably the most picturesque account of the librarian's approach to serials was made by Dr. Bishop in an address to library-school students in 1922:

> Periodical publication is now truly *the* fashion of the day in all lines the world over. This form came into vogue in the seventeenth century with the *Journal des Savants* and other similar learned publications. For seventy-five years now it has been increasingly *the* mode for the publication of the results of study in any and all fields. Thousands of journals keep hundreds of thousands of specialists abreast of the growth of knowledge in their several lines of investigation. Yea, more, thousands of other journals inform the banker, the merchant, the artisan, the tradesman, the professor, the teacher, even the librarian, what is going on in his field. The journals are usually about five years ahead of the books in every subject. They form the record of progress in the sciences and the arts, in the crafts and trades and occupations. They wax more numerous with every month and in every clime, despite rising costs of paper and presswork, and in the face of a severe mortality in journalistic circles.

---

[11]*Annual Report of the Librarian of Congress* 1946 (Washington, 1947), p.400.

[12]Georg Schneider, *Handbuch der Bibliographie* (4th ed.; Leipzig: Hiersemann, 1930), p.370.

[13]Library of Congress, Card Division, *List of Series of Publications for Which Cards Are in Stock* (4th ed.; Washington, 1932), p.1. See also the Library's *Handbook of Card Distribution* (8th ed.; Washington, 1954), p.50.

Well may the perplexed and devout librarian say with the Psalmist —*"Lord, how are they increased that trouble me!"* How to get, how to keep, how to index this mass of periodical and serial printed matter! We must have it—we never have enough journals—we never have enough indexes to the mass of original materials concealed beneath their multitudinous and multiform varieties of publication. Woe to the librarian who fails to get and to bind and to use these journals. They are the present-day mode of retailing (and frequently rehashing) thought and discovery. "Fractions drive me mad" was a favorite tag in my boyhood. How true of these days! It is not the sound and single volumes which come from the publisher which trouble us and bring our grey hairs in sorrow to the grave. Rather it is these *lieferungen, heften, livraisons,* parts, fascicles, special numbers and supplements which do drive the poor librarian frantic. And how solid the satisfaction, how firm the reward which attends the completion and binding of any fractious and long-broken set! Journals—and still more journals—all printed on wood-pulp paper destined doubtless to disintegrate in the lifetime of these students of library economy—here you have the chief problem of the careful librarian of any research library. Will the fashion change? How long *can* it last? Will the whole literary output of the world soon be in periodicals? Shall we always be paying subscriptions, writing postcards for title pages and indexes, preparing for binding, paying for binding, buying older sets, renewing our worn-out *Poole's Index* and *Index Medicus?* These questions I leave with you to ponder. I and my generation shall never get away from journals; perhaps the journals will get away from you younger folk—by the simple process of chemical decomposition.[14]

That was the story in 1922. While the problem areas have grown in extent and complexity, the story was very much the same in 1970 when Allen said:

If ever there was a perplexing area in librarianship, it is the handling of serial publications. It is inconceivable that any library could operate without them. It is equally inconceivable that any library can cope with them without experiencing some sort of trauma. The enormous numbers of them, their endless variety, their lasting qualities (as to both physical properties and content), their arrangement and handling present daily and frequently difficult problems. And, the larger the library, the more these problems emerge to plague the many librarians who have to deal with them.

14William W. Bishop, *The Backs of Books, and Other Essays in Librarianship* (Baltimore: Williams & Wilkins, 1926), p.324–26.

> Users face difficulties too, and it is, of course, the aim of the librarians to minimize these.[15]

Most disconcerting of all, at the Allerton Park Institute Professor Peterson, dean of the College of Communications at the University of Illinois and keynote speaker, felt called upon to say, "Librarians are not specialists in magazines."[16] The statement was made with reference to the selection of serials, and more particularly the selection of types of periodicals which the historian of magazine publishing desires to study for historical and cultural reasons, yet which are seldom found in library collections. So he went on to say:

> Librarians are eminently respectable; many of the magazines that tell us a great deal about our century do not seem to be respectable. *Night and Day, Dude, Clyde, Eros, Sir, Modern Romances, Dime Western, Doc Savage*—they seem shabby companions to share library shelves with such upright citizens of the magazine world as the *National Geographic* and *Reader's Digest.*
>
> Moreover, people, librarians included, form mental images of some magazines without bothering to read them. Those images, whether or not they have a basis in reality, linger on in perpetuity. I still encounter people who think of *Esquire*—which is surely one of the best magazines in the U.S.—as something to be read furtively in barbershops. I still encounter people who think of *Playboy* as the greatest threat to the moral fiber of the nation since the abolition of the 72-hour week.
>
> Serial librarians have the beneficent task of selecting the magazines that best disseminate current knowledge and of preserving some of the most representative aspects of our subcultures. Their task is already a big one, and I am afraid it will not get easier.[17]

There is too much truth for comfort in the pronouncement that "librarians are not specialists in magazines." And yet, of course, in general as in special libraries, from the days of Childs, MacNair, and Pierson on, there have been and there always will be librarians who dedicate themselves to the difficult field of serial publications, who will continue to make notable contributions in this area. But admittedly there are shortcomings, and it could be that the most damaging one is the fact that of the serial titles which "have been collected

---

[15]Walter C. Allen, ed., *Serial Publications in Large Libraries* (Allerton Park Institute, no.16 [Urbana, Ill.: Graduate School of Library Science, 1970]) , p.v.
 [16]*Ibid.*, p.9.
 [17]*Ibid.*

in the United States and Canada, only 35 percent are represented by complete runs."[18]

Possibly it is the small public library which has most to learn about exploiting periodicals and other serials such as government publications. In his home the average reader may be less familiar with books than he is with newspapers and magazines, so a public library might succeed in broadening tastes through devoting more attention to the accumulation, display, and servicing of serials. The idea is not new. In 1920 Dana said:

> Many a small library could do more to stimulate its community, broaden its views and sympathies, encourage it to study, if it diverted a larger part of its income than it now does from inferior books, and especially inferior novels, to weekly journals and popular and standard magazines. What a community needs is not a "library"—it may have a street lined with "libraries" and still dwell in outer darkness—but contact with the printed page. Get this contact, then, by means of attractive rooms and clean, wholesome, interesting books and periodicals.[19]

Clearly serials have their part to play in the smallest public library, in its capacity as a community information center, just as they do in the greatest research library.

[18]Joint Committee on the Union List of Serials, *A Permanent Program for the Union List of Serials* (Washington, 1957), p.ii
[19]John Cotton Dana, *A Library Primer* (Boston: Library Bureau [1920]) , p.68–69.

4

General Organization of Serial Work

There are three main areas of serial activity in libraries which are large enough to require specialization of functions. Each of the three may have one or more staff members who work exclusively with serials. The areas are: the acquisition department, which procures serials and commonly has the current checking records under its supervision; the catalog department, where there is usually a serial cataloging section or division; and the current periodical room, which is sometimes supplemented by a document or a newspaper room. Naturally other parts of a library have much to do with serials, notably the circulation and reference desks; but their concern is as a rule incidental to their general duties, as can be seen from the fact that only rarely is one of their assistants a serial specialist.

The upper limits for specialized serial staff have long been set by the Library of Congress. In 1953 it had 129 full-time serial specialists; in 1971 the figure was 208. On both occasions there were numerous people who spent part of their time working with serials. The distribution for full-time staff is as follows:

	1953	1971
Administrative Department		
Binding Office	2	5
Congressional Research Service	1	2
Law Library	2	1
Processing Department		
Descriptive Cataloging Division	9	7
MARC Development Office	–	1
Order Division	3	6
Serial Record Division	53	104
Subject Cataloging Division	4	5

	1953	1971
Reference Department		
Music Division	1	1
Orientalia Division	7	10
Serial Division	43	62
Slavic and Central European Division	4	4
Total	129	208

It is possible for any one of the three departments—acquisitions, cataloging, or the periodical room—to assume the major responsibility for serials and to be called the serial section, serial division, etc. From 1939 on there has been a slight tendency to centralize serial activities to the extent that a full-fledged serials department is created, coordinate with acquisition, cataloging, and other departments. In point of theory it is difficult to lay down hard and fast rules for the location of the primary serial functions. A good case can be made for each of the three departments already named—and for none of them.

The orthodox arrangement is to divide the work among the three. The Library of Congress followed that plan until 1953, when it established the Serial Record Division as a separate recording unit. The change was brought about because of the highly specialized nature of the function of recording incoming serials, the considerable size of the operation and of the staff necessary to perform the daily work, the development of *New Serial Titles,* and the prospective idea of a comprehensive union list of serials. In 1968 the scope of the division was expanded by the transfer of serial cataloging from the Descriptive Cataloging Division. The outstanding example of the highly successful operation of checking functions in the serial division of a cataloging department, under the direct supervision of the serial catalogers, was in the Harvard College Library, but the function has now been transferred to the acquisition department. The University of California Library at Berkeley is the notable example of the concentration of serial functions in the periodical room. As such the Serials Department comprises Binding Preparation and Mending; the Newspaper and Microcopy Room, where the checking records for newspapers are maintained; and the Periodical Room with its checking records. In the Washington Square Library of New York University a separate Serials Division was established to care for virtually all phases of work with serials. Realignments which culminate in the formation of a processing department commonly have as an objective the correlation of what could otherwise be overlapping serial functions in the traditional acquisition and catalog departments.

The Acquisition Department

The concern of an acquisition department with books and pamphlets exists for the most part only until they have been absorbed in the library's collections. With serial titles, however, the department tends to have a continuing interest because year after year renewals must be arranged, bills paid, and so on.

There is actually an affiliation between books and serials at the acquisition stage. Dealers frequently combine books and serials in a bundle or on a single invoice, especially when the serials are works such as annuals, directories, items in monograph series which are received on a standing order, and who's whos. On occasion items which are ordered as simple monographs may, on report from the dealer or on receipt, prove to be parts of a monograph series. Hence there is something to be said in favor of receiving and checking both books and serials in the acquisition department, where mixed bundles can readily be processed and cleared for payment (but see chapter 6) and where it is customary to acquire or claim items and to check them off after they have been received.

The unwrapping of periodicals, as of books, is an untidy operation that should be performed in as inconspicuous a spot as possible. Even the bins into which the wrappings go are difficult to keep looking neat and attractive, all the more so in a large serial section. These are arguments in favor of receiving and checking serials in the acquisitions department, which is essentially a work area. In some library buildings it is possible to plan for a workroom adjoining the periodical room where behind-the-scenes work can be undertaken, though this is principally the preparation and accumulation of material to be sent to the bindery. When current periodicals are received and checked in a periodical room, there is the risk that the overall serial acquisition program may be weakened because current periodicals may receive special attention while other serials may be relatively neglected. There is much to gain from having one strong unit care for all incoming serials impartially, especially when there is informed and capable supervision of the serial activities. Finally, the fact that the current checking records are quite generally located in acquisition departments suggests that there are good practical reasons for that disposition.

The Catalog Department

Most, if not all, of the serial staff in an acquisition department are clerical assistants. The claim of a catalog department to be the principal center of serial activity is based primarily on the presence there of serial librarians who are professional in grade. These are the people who become fully conversant with serials and their intricacies. Their work has been basic to serial operations throughout the library—for instance, up until now the checking records in most libraries have used entries supplied by the serial catalogers. Their enthusiasm, knowledge, and skill are essential to the building of sound serial collections.

When all serial processing is concentrated in a single section of the catalog department, there is opportunity for superior direction of the operations by experienced serial catalogers. There is, however, one danger in this type of organization. It stems from the fact that the processing of current issues is the most demanding phase of serial activities; the staff at the checking records must be maintained at full strength at all times so that the work will not fall behind. Catalogers may therefore on occasion have to interrupt their regular duties to serve as interim checkers, but even greater claims on their time come regularly: resolving problems for the checkers, answering reference questions in person or on the telephone, and otherwise performing a variety of activities connected with the checking records. Accordingly, if the serial catalogers are to give their undivided attention to their primary job of cataloging, there is something to be said for keeping the checking function out of the catalog department. A similar comment can be made about the combined operations in a processing department: care must be taken to see that the catalogers are left free to do their own work without constant interruptions.

The Periodical Room

The desire to give prompt and efficient service to readers justifies the checking in of magazines in a periodical room. Otherwise a reader may have to wait while a telephone call to the acquisition department discloses whether the latest issue of a given title has arrived or whether an issue not on the shelves was ever received. The reader may have to wait much longer than that for his information, especially when he goes to the periodical room in the evening, on a holiday, or over the weekend when the acquisition department is closed and its records can be consulted only as an emergency measure.

In the general library of the University of California the serials file is restricted to nongovernment serials and is a record of receipt, holdings, claims, and binding. After posting in the Serials Department (i.e., the Periodical Room), the periodicals are shelved in the Periodical Room or the stacks, while some go to branches and other services. The serials file is not directly accessible to readers, but is consulted extensively by assistants in the Acquisition Department and elsewhere.

Administratively it may be expedient, especially in a college or university library, to combine the checking and public-service duties in order to justify the manpower necessary to staff a periodical room at all times when the library is open. As in a catalog department, the disadvantage can then be that the clerical function of checking may at times devolve on professional personnel; or, if the staff of the periodical room is clerical or subprofessional, the checking process, follow-up work, and preparation of volumes for binding may lack proper supervision. In a research library the partial conversion of a periodical room into a processing unit can result in an unfortunate division of serial functions, the opportunity to develop a strong serial processing section may be lost, and many serials may have to be handled in the acquisition department without benefit of expert serial supervision.

The Self-Contained Serial Department

In a few libraries the idea of specialized serial services has been carried so far that a separate department has been set up with responsibility for all phases of work with serials: acquisition, cataloging, housing, servicing, etc. The Washington Square Library of New York University moved in this direction in 1939. It expressed its philosophy as follows:

> The major place of serial publications in the modern university collection is ... given recognition by the organization of a separate serials department within the Washington Square library. Virtually all phases of collecting, binding, shelving, and servicing are handled here, ensuring proper attention to the whole field. The Commerce library has taken a similar step by establishing a serials division, which includes among its other functions the acquisition and administration of Government publications.[1]

A year later it added:

[1] New York University Library, *Report of the Director of the Libraries* 1938–39 (New York, 1939), p.6–7.

Work with serials was organized and carried on under a separate department for the first time in 1939–1940. This type of organization is in line with a general trend in the library field, a recognition of the importance of serials and the special problems connected with their administration. . . . Under the new setup, all serials, except in law, were shifted to the serials stacks in order to coördinate all work with serial publications.[2]

It was the considered opinion of Rothman (who established the unit) and Ditzion that the self-contained serial department is the best type of organization. Their conclusion, based on a survey of methods in 126 public, college, and university libraries, was that "complete centralization of functions relating to serials offers the best solution of vexing problems."[3] Beatrice Simon has likewise stated her preference for a consolidated serial department. She says:

The amount of time wasted on cross consultation; the number of costly mistakes made because each assistant knows only part of the tale at any one time, is fantastic. Time costs money and money buys more periodicals, or hires more staff, so I am very jealous of time. That is the reason why I believe so wholeheartedly in the separate serials division. If you can delegate all operations concerning serials to one person, or one group of persons, and you have the courage to set up a separate serials division, where periodicals are received, processed and serviced as a continuous operation, you will find that great economies will ensue and you will have, in addition, an unusually competent group of people ready to give reference service of a very high quality.[4]

Complete centralization is, of course, out of the question. Because a great many library tools, reference books in particular, are serial publications, they will naturally be located where they are of most use. Rothman and Ditzion themselves made an exception to the centralization of serial collections in favor of subject departments:

In virtually every instance where there is a serials division in a library, there are also subject departments. The only difference is

2New York University Library, *Report of the Director of the Libraries,* 1939–40 (New York, 1940) , p.16.

3Fred B. Rothman and Sidney Ditzion, "Prevailing Practices in Handling Serials," *College and Research Libraries* 1:169 (1940) . See also Rothman's "Pooh-bah of the Serials Division," *Library Journal* 62:457 (1937) .

4Beatrice V. Simon, "Cataloguing of Periodicals," *Ontario Library Review* 33:239 (1949) .

that the serials division handles these serial publications up to the point where they go to the shelves; only at that time are they sent to the subject department. In other words, serials falling within the scope of a departmental collection are separated from serials in the main collection for purposes of shelving and circulation.[5]

Certainly a self-contained serial department solves many problems, just as it gives due recognition to the importance of the publications it services. At the same time, though, it gives rise to problems of another kind, and in the area of cataloging it can easily lead to serious trouble. Serials and nonserials overlap in significant respects in cataloging, just as they do on the classified shelves in the bookstacks. Many of both kinds are intimately connected through the corporate entry; others are connected through the series entry. In general it must be realized that classification, subject heading, the shelflist, and above all the card catalog itself, are in themselves only parts of a unitary organizational pattern that should come under a single jurisdiction. It is true that the responsibility for cataloging serials and nonserials has been divided in some libraries, but unless extremely favorable circumstances exist, difficulties and problems are bound to arise. One difficulty is that the catalogers in a self-contained serial department will be forced to work at a distance from their principal tool, the card catalog, or that, to avoid this, the catalog may have to be divided at the risk of splitting corporate entries and duplicating references—history cards, too, if they are made.

Organization of the Document Collection

Ethelyn Markley divides document collections into three types: the nondepository, the selected, and the complete depository.[6] In the nondepository type all documents which are acquired are specially wanted; they are therefore incorporated in the general bookstock, though some items may be treated by self-cataloging methods, in vertical files, for example. In the selected-depository type, Miss Markley favors segregation of most of the documents in a self-cataloging collection exploited through printed indexes. She advocates generous use of references in the card catalog, particularly from subjects and from the names of government agencies, so that readers will learn

[5]Rothman and Ditzion, "Practices in Handling Serials," p.168.

[6]A. Ethelyn Markley, *Library Records for Government Publications* (Berkeley: Univ. of California Pr., 1951), p.7–16.

about the document collection and its indexes. In the complete depository she again favors segregating most documents in a self-cataloging collection. She would catalog items which are not covered by the printed indexes as use demands or as the budget permits.

The critical element in this schematization is the amount of material to be detached from the document collection for integration in the regular bookstock. On this point Miss Markley says:

> Certain titles or series may be more useful in the ready reference collection or in the general collection or with the periodicals, than in the documents collection. There should be no hesitation in placing such titles in the collection best suited to their use, but these cases should be regarded as exceptions made for cause and they should be kept at a minimum. Some libraries select such titles by artificial means, choosing all documents not members of a series or all entered by L.C. under personal name rather than corporate name, but this seems to be evading the issue. There is general agreement that the Congressional set should be arranged separately by serial number, but in all other cases permanence and convenience in use should determine the policy. The advantages of placing a document with the book collection should be so obvious that there can be no question of keeping it with the separate collection. Repeated and frequent evidence that patrons look for it in the book stacks or expect to find it entered in the card catalog are useful criteria.[7]

This statement can be interpreted in two ways. It can easily be taken as a defense of past practice in libraries which have been content to write off documents as frugally as may be, or it can be taken as a statement of enlightened policy not too far removed from Library of Congress practice. The former would be unfortunate. Many librarians have skimped on the processing of their document collections, which contain extremely valuable informational and research materials that should be in place on the classified shelves and should be represented in the card catalog by a serial entry. There is no doubt, e.g., that the political-science shelves are robbed when the publications of the Department of State are not in their normal place in the bookstacks together with works about that agency. It is true, of course, that there is a core of general documents that ought to be held together, as the Library of Congress recognizes in its J classification, but there is also much that should be scattered by subject.

[7]*Ibid.*, p.9–10.

Unlike Miss Markley, Ellen Jackson is completely in favor of separate and frugal treatment for documents as a distinct species of serials. She says:

> The library must give its government documents separate and special consideration, for the origin, the method of publication, the format, and the methods of indexing of publications of government agencies set them apart from publications of the commercial press and even from those of non-governmental research agencies, learned societies, and other privately sponsored organizations. . . .
>
> Unity of intent and effort is basic to the efficiently operating research library, but as must be clear from the nature of government publications, their origin, their form, their indexing, their methods of distribution, they can be handled most efficiently as a separate and cohesive unit by a specially trained and experienced staff.[8]

The distinction Miss Jackson draws might have been truer in earlier times, but today it is difficult to distinguish many items and types. For example, one has to look very carefully to discover who issued a Latin American tourist magazine which is so like an ordinary periodical that it comes as something of a surprise to learn that it is a government publication, and a technical report series may originate in either a government or a nongovernment source and yet have identical format. But apart from such considerations, the distinction between government and nongovernment serials is false and unwise when it results in uneven treatment. An all-or-nothing policy for serials is bad. Serials are serials, no matter what the issuing body may be. This is fundamental in the general library, just as it always has been in special libraries. There can be no doubt about it: Serials in an uncataloged or self-cataloging collection have been given substandard treatment.

There is an interesting comparative study in Pittsburgh, where the Carnegie and university libraries are within a few hundred yards of each other. The public library has cataloged and classified its government publications so that its downtown business branch and its science and technology division, as well as the main collection, are well served at all hours the library is open. The university library, on the other hand, has a self-cataloging collection, open 9–5 Monday through Friday. University staff and students commonly prefer to go to the public library, where they can readily find what they are look-

---

[8]Ellen P. Jackson, *Administration of the Government Documents Collection* (ACRL Monograph, no.5 [Chicago: Assn. of College and Reference Libraries, 1953]) , p.1, 9.

ing for, but the interesting point is that it apparently costs the public library no more to operate its program than it costs the university to run its restrictive scheme.

The uncataloged documents collection certainly hampers union-catalog work. The National Library of Canada, which is highly successful in locating copies of nongovernment publications, can help with only about a tenth of the requests sent to its union catalog for government documents.

Government serials must be posted on current checking records, whether they are in a self-cataloging collection or not. It costs approximately the same to check them in in one place or the other, and the consolidated checking record certainly makes it easier for staff and readers to know where to turn for help.

Whatever the overall organization of serial work may be, then, no library should rest content until document serials are acquired, checked in, cataloged, and made available to readers in the same way as other serials. Self-cataloging methods are just not good enough for the Department of State *Bulletin*, the *Farmers' Bulletin*, the *Monthly Labor Review*, the *Report* of the Atomic Energy Commission, *School Life*, the *Statistical Abstract of the United States*, the *Yearbook of Agriculture*, and a host of other government serials. If a research library wants to economize on its documents collection, it can put the less used ones in a storage library, and the Center for Research Libraries has had many government serials transferred to it. But it is false economy to conceal the serials from readers, just as it is a mistake to exclude them from the general checking records. The substitute, which may be a combination shelflist and checking record,[9] is at best a makeshift. On all counts it is desirable to treat documents like other serials; substandard treatment is nothing less than a counsel of expediency.

Organization of the Newspaper Collection

There is considerable justification for according collections of bound volumes of newspapers special treatment because of the bulk of the volumes and because checklisting is better for them than cataloging. Nevertheless, some libraries post the current issues of newspapers in their regular checking records and house the papers in the periodical room. Checking is frequently dispensed with when the newspapers

[9]Cf. Markley, *Records for Government Publications*, p.22–27, 59–62.

are expendable. In public libraries a separate newspaper room was more often provided in the past than is the case now.

In many libraries the microfilm reading room has taken over as the center for back files of newspapers. Readers in the New York Public Library, for instance, work with microfilm copies of newspapers, though they may go to the library's storage collection if they wish to work with the bound volumes themselves. Newspapers published before 1800 are commonly housed in the rare book room.

Organization of a Technical Reports Collection

World War II turned the production of technical reports into a large-scale enterprise. Special organization is required for the housing and servicing of reports because so many of them are security classified by governments or by companies. In 1968 it was estimated that perhaps half a million reports are produced each year.[10] Bedsole says:

> At one time distribution of a technical report was considered only an interim step preceding publication in the open literature, but in many fields today, the technical report is the final step. Any scientist or engineer who ignores the report literature does so at his own peril, since in large segments of research and development the technical report is the primary means for written communication, with books and journals being of secondary importance.[11]

Technical reports collections cannot fit into the ordinary organization of a general library or of most special libraries because they comprise both classified and unclassified documents; the latter are accessible to uncleared as well as to security-cleared personnel, whereas the former require security clearance for handling or consultation. Fry says of the university security-classified library: "Although such projects are under university contract, they tend to become separate organizations for operational purposes, with separate library service distinct from the university library system."[12]

[10]Federal Council for Science and Technology, Committee on Scientific and Technical Information, *The Role of the Technical Report in Scientific and Technological Communication* (Washington, 1968), column 26.

[11]Danny T. Bedsole, "Technical Reports," in Isabel H. Jackson, ed., *Acquisition of Special Materials* (San Francisco: San Francisco Bay Region Chapter, Special Libraries Assn., 1966), p.73.

[12]Bernard M. Fry, *Library Organization and Management of Technical Reports Literature* (Catholic Univ. Studies in Library Science, no.1 [Washington: Catholic Univ. Pr., 1953]), p.35.

Collections are of two types: one in which all documents are integrated under security conditions, the other in which security-classified documents are housed separately and recorded separately from the unclassified or declassified ones, which therefore are free from security restrictions. The latter practice, Fry says,

> permits access of uncleared personnel to the unclassified collection, and also is more economical of filing equipment in that open shelves or unlocked cabinets can be used to house unclassified documents, as contrasted to expensive combination-lock safes required for classified storage. The principal disadvantage of this method is that it frequently breaks up the group of reports issued by an organization and separates them without regard to program or project unity.

He goes on to point out that some libraries which segregate the two types of report file their unclassified documents with the general bookstock:

> This appears to reflect a recent tendency among technical libraries holding collections of both types of literature to integrate as far as possible the unclassified reports with the large body of traditional scientific literature. This practice makes good sense because many, perhaps one-third, of the unclassified reports eventually will be published as journal articles. Thus, it is possible to have a Secret report moving successively to the declassified (unclassified) collection and later to the periodical shelves.[13]

Here then is a rapidly expanding area of serial activity which is closer to documentation in some respects than it is to regular library techniques. Because of the security aspect, however, technical reports will continue to call for special types of organization.

Centralization of Serial Checking

In every library system it must be determined whether economy and efficiency result from centralizing or scattering the checking records or, in some cases, from duplicating them. In public libraries there is room for much latitude because branch subscriptions are usually expendable duplicates. It may be better for multiple subscriptions to come to the main library from which the order originates;

---

[13]*Ibid.*, p.29.

there the copies can be checked off and prepared for use as simply and economically as multiple copies of books. On the other hand, time and routine can be saved when newspapers and other expendable items go directly to the branches. As a rule branch libraries do not require checking records, certainly not when the branches are small: in simple circumstances checking instructions are not needed, complete files are not wanted for binding, and titles are quite standard and virtually check themselves in automatically. Whenever warranted the checking records may be decentralized or duplicated, and some public libraries prefer to have the checking done in the branch which receives the publications. Note that decentralization of serial receipts will call for certain processing routines in the branch library: checking, stamping, covering, and adding book pockets, etc.

At Enoch Pratt Free Library serials for branches are received at the central library, where they are stamped for Pratt ownership, marked with the branch number,[14] and sent to the Extension Circulation Department for delivery to branches. A majority of the periodicals are circulated from most of the branches; the more popular titles are reinforced before they leave the Central Library. A card checklist is kept in each branch to register the issues as they are received. When an imperfect copy is noted, it is returned to the Serials Unit at Central, which arranges for a replacement.

Since 1958 the Research Libraries of the New York Public Library have used a system whereby most current periodicals are sent by the publisher directly to post office boxes for the particular divisions which take care of them: the Periodicals Division, the Science and Technology Division, and so on. In this way the divisions receive their publications directly, and each division has its own visible index. At the same time there has been a great reduction in the tremendous quantity of material which formerly was recorded in the Central Serial Record located in the Acquisition Division. When bindable volumes have accumulated in the divisions, they are routed to the Central Serial Record to be added to the tabulated records there.

Some university libraries centralize all their processing functions, but there is a much better argument for the decentralization of checking activities in a university library system than there is in a public library system. Multiple copies are infrequent, almost invariably files are intended for preservation, and normally much gift and exchange

[14]It is generally more accurate and convenient to use numbers as branch symbols when there are more than a few branches in a public library system. A number is not as meaningful as an abbreviation based on the branch name, but it is more convenient as a checking and routing symbol when there are several branches whose names begin with the same initial or letters.

material comes directly to a departmental library from the publisher or others. Moreover, the processing of current numbers tends to be simpler: few university libraries reinforce them or make book cards for them, since current periodicals do not circulate enough to require such public library apparatus. The most compelling reason for decentralization in a university library system, though, is that the departmental libraries are thereby left free to adopt progressive special library methods.

A Separate Serial Catalog

Whenever there is talk of a self-contained serials department, separation of the official catalog into serials and nonserials should be considered so that the serials department can have on hand the basic records it needs. A few libraries have divided their catalogs in some such way. In the Research Libraries of the New York Public Library, for instance, the official catalog has been divided by putting personal-name entries and books entered under their titles in one file, non-government serials and corporate-entry nonserials in a second, and government serials in a third. This arrangement is of interest because it demonstrates the strong affinity that exists between serials and corporate entries.

In the Serial Record Division at the Library of Congress there is a notable serial catalog which in 1969 contained 481,478 titles and 707,294 cards. When the unduplicated entries in the visible index were added, the Serial Record Division had bibliographical control over 640,991 serials. The functions of the serial catalog are to serve as: (1) a record of the receipt and internal distribution of unbound serials; (2) the shelflist for bound serials; (3) the center for information on the assignment, processing, retention, and routing of serials; and (4) a key element in the library's system of bibliographical controls. Some features of the catalog are:

1. Corporate entries constitute 53 percent of the total file.
2. Government publications amount to a fifth of the total file.
3. There are 73,676 entries for monograph series, or 11.2 percent of the total file.
4. Only 97,427 titles, or 15 percent of the file, are represented by printed Library of Congress cards, which, however, were not incorporated in the file after the early 1950s.

5. Eight titles have between 250 and 1,135 cards. They are:
   Canada. Department of Agriculture. Publications.
   Gt. Brit. Aeronautical Research Council. Report and memoranda.
   Unesco. Documents (English).
   United Nations. Documents (English).
   United Nations. Documents (French).
   United Nations. Documents (Spanish).
   U.S. Congress. Congressional record.
   U.S. War Dept. Training publications. Field manual.
6. All entries beginning with "Akademiia Nauk..." are broken out of the normal sequence, as are entries beginning with "U.S."

A Problem in Organization

The preceding sections have indicated some of the pros and cons of the complex problems which ought to be considered in the organization of growing serial collections. If outright centralization is not the answer, and generally it is not, at least much can and should be done in many a library to coordinate serial functions better, to eliminate areas of overlap, to provide more adequate staff and quarters for all phases of serial work, and to conserve for the future all the files of serials which should be available to the historian and the bibliographer as well as to the research worker.

2

Selection
and
Acquisition

5

Principles of
Serial Selection

Until the middle of this century two major difficulties confronted those who were engaged in building up serial resources. The first of them was the lack of reasonably complete and prompt tools for serial selection. Now there are a number of such works, the most important and extensive of them by far being *New Serial Titles—Classed Subject Arrangement*. It is compiled and issued by the Library of Congress from copy supplied by large numbers of American and Canadian research libraries as well as by itself. It is a monthly noncumulated publication which began in 1955 and essentially is a subject rearrangement of entries from *New Serial Titles*. Its express purposes are to make known to acquisition librarians the existence of upwards of 15,000 new serials which are published throughout the world annually and to supply the information required to place an order, information which *New Serial Titles* does not provide.

The subject coverage is by short Dewey numbers. Thus 020 stands for new library periodicals, 022 for serials on library buildings, and 026 for special library publications. Three-digit numbers generally suffice, but the decimal point is called into play when necessary. Accordingly 331.88 represents trade union material and 510.78 computer items. Bibliographies are listed under both 016 and the pertinent subject, e.g., 016 960 for a bibliography on Africa, in addition to 960 016.

New Serial Titles—Classed Subject Arrangement is a must for all libraries which are enterprisingly building up their serial collections. Since it is arranged by subject, it is possible to photocopy segments to submit to specialists, for instance, in university departments, for their advice on titles which should be considered for acquisition. The work is not a complete world listing; it must be complemented in a wide variety of ways; but it has been unquestionably, since its inception in 1955, the number one selection tool for every library that is diligently accumulating serial resources.

Although *New Serial Titles—Classed Subject Arrangement* possesses such high potential, a survey carried out in 1966–67 disclosed that in March 1967 there were only 235 subscriptions to it, and that no more than 180 libraries were using it for acquisition purposes.[1] Perhaps the title has mitigated against its widespread adoption and exploitation; perhaps it should be something like *New Serial Titles—Acquisition Edition*, because that is precisely what the publication is: a serial selection tool of the highest possible order, designed specifically to facilitate acquisition operations.

The suggestion has been made that the lack of cumulations has greatly limited the usefulness of *New Serial Titles—Classed Subject Arrangement*. Kuhlman says:

> One of its major purposes should be to enable university faculty members and subject-specialist librarians to discover which new serials are appearing in their subject specialty. Few of them, including serial and special librarians, have time to scan through twelve monthly issues per year to make their recommendations for new subscriptions in their respective subject fields. Quarterly and annual issues and/or cumulations would save much time.[2]

On the other hand, one of the complaints made about *New Serial Titles*, and hence about the acquisition edition, was that the listings were not sufficiently prompt—that delays of six or nine months often occurred for foreign serials, and that there have been delays of even a year and more. Kuhlman's comment on this is:

> The importance of prompt listing in NST is self-evident, but how to achieve it requires further study. A part of the delay in listing new entries grows out of the fact that some librarians do not catalog a serial until the first volume is completed. Cataloging information is taken from the title page of the volume, not from the cover or masthead of issues. Hence, the delay in reporting. One solution to this problem would be for libraries to send in a preliminary or temporary entry containing such information as called for in Instructions and forms for reporting serials to NST.[3]

[1]A. F. Kuhlman, *A Report on the Consumer Survey of New Serial Titles* ([Washington, D.C.: Library of Congress], 1967), p.48.

[2]*Ibid.*, p.49–50.

[3]*Ibid.*, p.31.

First-issue cataloging is the real solution to the problem of prompt reporting, especially now that the Library of Congress has decided to adopt the practice.

A question asked in the consumer survey was: "Would your library be interested in proof slip service at possibly $65 annually assuming a minimum of 100 subscribers?" A mere 74 libraries said yes; 322 said no. Such a service is highly desirable; it would simplify selection routines appreciably. It would no longer be necessary to photocopy segments of *New Serial Titles—Classed Subject Arrangement;* instead, the slips could quickly be sorted by subject for submission to specialists who make recommendations for acquisition. Quarterly or annual cumulations are not the answer; selection from them would result in fewer files that begin with volume 1, number 1, the reason being that the early issues of periodicals go out of print soon after publication. This much is sure: any acquisition librarian who does not have time to go through carefully—not scan—twelve monthly issues of *New Serial Titles—Classed Subject Arrangement* lends support to the charge laid by Peterson and reported in chapter 3 that "librarians are not specialists in magazines."

Book Selection versus Serial Selection

The second major difficulty has its roots in publications on the theory and practice of book selection and, consequently, in library school courses on the building up of library resources. Examination of works on book selection shows how far serial selection has been neglected, how far the topic has been subordinated to the selection of nonserials. The neglect and subordination might be condoned in books published in the first half of the century, but it is extraordinary that no postwar writing on book selection has devoted a major section to serial publications. Brown expresses similar concern when he says: "Much attention has been given in professional library circles to the selection and acquisition of books, but comparatively few articles can be found on the selection of scientific journals for purchase by research libraries."[4]

It is not sufficient to say in extenuation of the situation that serial selection follows the same pattern as book selection does; that would be a serious oversimplification. Actually pamphlets are closer to serials

4Charles H. Brown, *Scientific Serials; Characteristics and Lists of Most Cited Publications in Mathematics, Physics, Chemistry, Geology, Physiology, Botany, Zoology, and Entomology* (ACRL Monograph, no.16 [Chicago: Assn. of College and Reference Libraries, 1956]), p.57.

than books are, and the thought that goes into determining the number of copies of a book to be acquired for a library system is roughly the equivalent of the deliberation that should go into every single serial selection. The following points should be noted:

1. At least four-fifths of all serials are not trade publications, the exact opposite of books. They are therefore more elusive; existence of new titles must be watched for in many special channels.

2. Bookstock is held by dealers, jobbers, and publishers; commercial publishers of periodicals hold no stock. The out-of-print problem is a serious one with books, but periodicals issued by the book trade tend to be out of print on the day of publication.

3. All too often libraries consider acquisition of a serial when the first or second volumes have already been published. It is then a case of deciding to go along with an incomplete file or of attempting to acquire the earlier issues by one means or another. No serial that is under way should be acquired until a decision has been made about acquisition of back numbers.

4. Every decision to acquire a new serial title should be accompanied by a further decision on whether it is to be procured by exchange, gift, or purchase. Libraries buy most of their books, but at least half of their serials should come by exchange or gift.

5. The interdependence of libraries comes to the fore with their serial holdings, as can be seen from the fact that union lists of serials outnumber union catalogs of books by a wide margin. So a decision to acquire a new serial title takes into account the holdings of other libraries in the vicinity, with regard to enriching the resources of the area. Books are considered in this way mostly when expensive sets or items are concerned.

6. The cost of books is generally known, but with serials there are many hidden costs, so that a $5 subscription can easily turn into $20 a year when all the record work, handling charges, and binding are taken into account. Serial subscriptions represent fixed charges which are a first lien on the annual book budget, and every year since the end of World War II the total amount has risen substantially because of increases in subscription and postal rates. In some libraries more money is spent on serials than on books. For example, in the 1970–71 budget for the Harvard Law Library, twice as much money was allocated to serials as to books: $93,334 as against $46,666. In times of financial stringency it is difficult to cut the serial budget without the risk of serious if not irreparable harm. More than one library looks back with regret to an across-the-board decision to curtail serial subscriptions so that the level of book purchases might be

maintained. The Harvard College Library has regretted on many occasions the termination in 1920 of subscriptions to French local history periodicals, an area in which the library has notable strength. In general it is possible to acquire most nonserials at a later date, whereas it is difficult if not impossible to fill serial files later.

7. Serial selection requires more time per title than book selection does; a number of officers may have to partake in the making of a decision. It is a time-consuming operation; it involves an exacting routine when carried out promptly, as it should be.

8. It is more difficult to select serials than it is to select books. A mistake can be more serious. The skills take beginners much longer to learn; it takes a good deal of poise, for example, to admit that the original decision was made in error and to reverse it, a course of action that must be taken from time to time. Much sound judgment must be exercised to strike a proper balance: on the one hand, to grasp at opportunities to obtain serials so that some day effort and expense will not have to be spent to repair omissions which never should have been allowed to occur and, on the other hand, to see that the sorcerer's apprentice does not unloose a perfect torrent of serials in his enthusiasm.

Guiding Principles

Serial selection, like book selection, is an art, not a science. Its skilled performance depends primarily on the exercise of trained, informed judgment. There are certain principles and procedures that are relied upon by the experienced librarian in determining whether or not to add a serial title to the bookstock. Among them the following should be emphasized:

1. Checking the monthly issues of *New Serial Titles—Classed Subject Arrangement* promptly and systematically.
2. Acquiring and putting to good use the tools that open up the literature of a country or subject.
3. Acquiring titles that are analyzed in abstracting and indexing services.
4. Giving special attention to the acquisition of the basic journal or journals in all fields of interest.
5. Whenever desirable and possible, obtaining a sample copy of a periodical in order to make the selection process as judicious as can be.

6. Enriching the resources of a locality, region, or group of libraries by carrying out as far as possible a program of cooperative acquisition.

7. In each area developing a coordinated program for the preservation of local publications.

8. Building up serial files on the basis of long runs, not broken files. In the case of annuals and other low-frequency serials, however, rather than doing without a worthwhile title altogether, the librarian should consider subscribing to every second or third issue.

9. Acquiring microreproductions in moderation. Except for newspapers, originals should be preferred to microcopies. If a microcopy is to be obtained, favor the form which facilitates the making of photocopies whenever the serial is available in two or more forms.

10. Being ready to take advantage of opportunities as they occur by budgeting for the purchase of sets and back files to enrich the bookstock.

11. Being ready to accept the responsibility for going beyond immediate needs and acquiring all the items in a monograph series when by so doing a valued contribution will be made to the resources of an area.

12. Controlling duplicate subscriptions on the basis of relative values: will extra copies or additional titles further the library's program better?

13. Always remembering the possibilities of acquiring a title by exchange or gift, because these methods of acquisition help immeasurably in enriching the bookstock.

14. Reviewing each entry on the checking records at least once every three years to see whether the title or the extra copies are still worth while.

Using *New Serial Titles—Classed Subject Arrangement*

Every month on receipt of *New Serial Titles—Classed Subject Arrangement* all entries should be examined as a matter of priority to see which items should be considered for possible procurement. If a library does not subscribe to the acquisition edition of *New Serial Titles*, then a trip should be made to a neighboring library to go through its copy. Between a fourth and a fifth of the new titles are periodicals; the rest are serials of various kinds. In a departmentalized system where there is, e.g., a business or a science and technology library, the relevant sections of *New Serial Titles—Classed Subject Arrangement* should be photocopied so that simultaneous action can be taken on the listings with a minimum of delay.

Professional Tools

Libraries that contribute entries to *New Serial Titles* have already worked with a wide variety of selection aids and tools; the compilation could not exist if they had not operated in that way. Acquisition librarians must be alert to all sources of information about serials that have just appeared and those that are forthcoming. Among their many ways of learning about titles that have just been published or are about to be published, serial selection officers: (1) are on mailing lists to receive prospectuses from publishers of new serials; (2) examine accession lists from other libraries; (3) go through trade and national bibliographies systematically; (4) keep their ears to the ground, locally and among colleagues and specialists, for hints of new titles; (5) look for new items that are covered in abstracting and indexing services; (6) scan notices and reviews in journals; and (7) take counsel with other selection officers for any information which they can supply.

The librarian, just as much as the craftsman, engineer, or surgeon, should have all the tools he needs to discharge his daily activities effectively and skillfully. First in line are the current publications which open up the literature of a country or subject. It is astonishing how few libraries acquire all the national bibliographies, and yet they should be checked regularly and systematically for the new titles which they can disclose. Current checklists of government publications should likewise be on hand for the development of the document collection. The quarterly *Bucop Journal*, the British counterpart of *New Serial Titles*, should be checked thoroughly even though it is not in a classed arrangement.

With inadequate tools an inferior job can be anticipated. With fine tools an excellent result is possible whenever the staff will make the fullest possible use of them.

Abstracted and Indexed Periodicals

The periodicals which are of greatest potential value in a library are those that are covered in abstracting and indexing services. *Ulrich's International Periodicals Directory* makes a feature of recording the services which include a given title; it should be checked to see whether or where a journal is abstracted or indexed when an item is being considered for acquisition. Catalogs put out by periodical dealers also make a point of saying where a periodical is indexed; e.g., the annual catalogs which for long the F. W. Faxon Company has issued. University Microfilms also indicates those items that are covered in thirty-two abstracting and indexing services, just as it has special lists of the microfilms it has made for the titles in four of the H. W. Wilson indexes. Because of the importance that libraries attach to indexed journals, they sometimes note on their checking records the services in which a periodical is represented. The original binding policy at the Linda Hall Library was that only indexed serials would be bound for preservation.[5]

The principle of paying special attention to the acquisition of abstracted and indexed items applies equally to back files. For example, libraries consider that a title which is indexed in *Poole's Index to Periodical Literature* is especially worth getting because the reference staff and readers have at hand a detailed listing of its contents.

Basic Journals

When a library does not aim at inclusive collecting in a field that it wishes to cover, its primary endeavor should be to secure the basic journal or journals. It then knows that it is well served, that it has up-to-date information, even though its holdings are thin. There are several ways of determining whether a journal is basic: (1) see if the title is included in abridged indexing services, e.g., the *Abridged Index Medicus* or the *Abridged Readers' Guide to Periodical Literature;* (2) note whether it occurs in one of the selected indexing services, e.g., those published by the H. W. Wilson Company or the Library Association; (3) seek the advice of a specialist, for instance, a department head or a faculty member; (4) at least for smaller subject areas, list the titles in *Ulrich's International Periodicals Directory*, obtain sample numbers, and determine which of the journals will serve the library best; (5) consult standard lists to see whether the title is recorded in them. Winchell's *Guide to Reference Books* has a section called "Selection of periodicals" which names standard lists for libraries of different sizes and types; it also has a section "Selection of books," which should be consulted because standard lists of books often cover periodicals as well.

[5]Edgar G. Simpkins, "A Study of Serials Processing," *Serial Slants* 2:8 (Jan. 1952).

A sixth technique for determining basic journals in scholarly fields is to check footnotes in periodicals on a given subject to see which titles are referred to most frequently. Duly weighted, e.g., to allow for new but highly significant titles, the most cited journals can be considered as the basic publications other than abstracting services, which, as Brown says, "a scientist uses . . . more frequently than any other journal."[6] In 1927 Gross and Gross applied the method to chemical journals.[7] In 1942–44 tabulations were made by Brown in the fields of agronomy, animal pathology, astronomy, botany, chemistry, mathematics, physics, physiology, and soil science.[8] For a brief time they were used by the Association of Research Libraries as a criterion for membership. In 1950 they were employed by Brown in his listing of lacunae in the Louisiana State University Library. The feeling of that library is that such compilations may be used only as a starting point in building up resources. Few libraries would purchase everything on the lists even if the budget permitted. In university libraries serials, other than a few basic ones, are purchased to support research, teaching, and undergraduate needs peculiar to each institution. After they reach a certain point in growth, university libraries need journals to sustain research and teaching in areas in which serials may not fall into the heavily cited category.

In 1956 in *Scientific Serials* Brown published lists in the fields of entomology, geology, and zoology as well as revised lists for botany, chemistry, mathematics, physics, and physiology. Among the findings which have a bearing on serial selection are:

1. For the latest decade the percentage of citations to volumes of serials ranges from 75.6 to 33.9. Accordingly, recent literature is more essential to scientists in physics, physiology, and chemistry than in botany, mathematics, geology, entomology, and zoology, in that order.
2. The percentage of citations to volumes of serials published before 1904 ranges from 0.5 for physics to 10.2 for zoology. These figures can be used as guides in retiring older volumes to storage collections, transferring them to other libraries, or even discarding them outright.
3. The decades which must be considered if a library is to make available 90 percent of cited literature are: two for

---

[6]Brown, *Scientific Serials*, p.72.

[7]P. L. K. Gross and E. M. Gross, "College Libraries and Chemical Education," *Science* n.s. 66:385 (1927).

[8]The lists are reproduced in appendix B in Brown, *Scientific Serials*, p.170–89.

physics; three for botany, mathematics, and physiology; four for chemistry and geology; and five for entomology and zoology.

4. The percentage of citation to books is very low in relation to the total number of citations to books and serials; it ranges from 6.4 for chemistry to 23.2 for mathematics. The percentage for all the eight disciplines studied is 14.8; therefore, chemists, geologists, physicists, and physiologists are below the average, while those above are botanists, entomologists, mathematicians, and zoologists.

5. The number of journals which cover 90 percent of the citations is 37 for chemistry and physics, 53 for mathematics, 57 for physiology, 62 for geology, 67 for zoology, 68 for botany, and 83 for entomology.

6. The journals which appear on four to eight of the lists are:

All eight lists

Académie des Sciences, Paris, *Comptes-rendus*
Royal Society of London, *Proceedings*

Seven lists

Nature
Science

Six lists

Akademiia Nauk S.S.S.R., *Doklady*
American Chemical Society, *Journal*
National Academy of Sciences, Washington, *Proceedings*
Naturwissenschaften

Five lists

Biochemical Journal
Journal of Biological Chemistry
Société de Biologie, *Comptes rendus*
Society for Experimental Biology, *Proceedings*

Four lists

Analytical Chemistry
Canadian Journal of Research
Industrial and Engineering Chemistry
Journal of General Physiology
Physical Review
Royal Society of London, *Philosophical Transactions*

Brown cautions against the indiscriminate application of lists of most cited periodicals. He says:

Complaint has been made that some libraries ordered periodicals on such lists without any consideration of the needs of their communities. Any list, whether of books or periodicals, must be considered from the viewpoint of the community to be served. In most universities some periodicals not on the list may be of more value than those listed. For example, in Louisiana, some periodicals covering the chemistry of sugar could be much more valuable than other periodicals high on the "Most Cited Lists."[9]

Miss Brodman applied the Gross and Gross technique to physiology and came to the conclusion that the underlying assumptions were not altogether valid. She says:

> The Gross and Gross method has been extremely valuable in helping administrators to build up periodical collections in many diverse fields about which they would not themselves have expert subject knowledge. For this reason it has probably been accepted more or less uncritically, with the feeling that any method was better than no method. Yet it appears to be a somewhat unscientific and unscholarly method as well as one which gives untrustworthy results. In spite of these extremely grave drawbacks, the method will probably continue to be employed by librarians until the library profession is presented with a better one. Individuals using the method, however, should be aware of the small dependence which can scientifically be placed on the results.[10]

Postell has presented additional evidence "to bolster the conclusions of Miss Brodman that the Gross and Gross method for evaluating journals cannot always be relied upon as a valid criterion of the selection of the outstanding journals in any particular field."[11] In a systematic review, Stevens concluded that, despite Miss Brodman's basic criticisms, the reference-counting method has proved its usefulness in a number of ways.[12]

[9]Charles H. Brown, quoted in *Serial Slants* 1:25 (Jan. 1951).

[10]Estelle Brodman, "Choosing Physiology Journals," *Medical Library Association Bulletin* 32:482 (1944). On p.483 there is a list of twenty-two items which were compiled by the Gross and Gross method; they cover fields such as agriculture, chemistry, child guidance, dentistry, education, electrical engineering, geology, and mathematics. Miss Brodman's findings are given in full in her Columbia Library School thesis, "Methods of Choosing Physiology Journals" (1943).

[11]William D. Postell, "Further Comments on the Mathematical Analysis of Evaluating Scientific Journals," *Medical Library Association Bulletin* 34:109 (1946).

[12]Rolland Stevens, *Characteristics of Subject Literature* (ACRL Monograph, no.6 [Chicago: Assn. of College and Reference Libraries, 1953]).

Brown responded to Miss Brodman by saying:

> When specialists are working in different subfields of a discipline
> any agreement on the most important serials on a general list is
> almost impossible. . . . A biochemist interested in plant physiology
> would probably place at the top of any list in botany certain bio-
> chemical journals, while a phytopathologist would want a different
> ranking and an ecologist would want still a third.
>
> This point was well emphasized when a list of the most cited
> serials in the field of physiology was referred to physiologists in a
> medical school. Naturally, too much correlation cannot be expected
> between lists suitable for specialists in human physiology in medical
> schools, for specialists in comparative physiology in veterinary
> schools, and for plant physiologists. . . . The argument was made
> that if a list of most cited serials in physiology does not agree with
> the subjective opinion of the physiologists in a school of medicine,
> then the most cited list is of little value.[13]

Raisig has reported on what he considers to be a more objective
method of reference counting that makes allowance for periodicals
that consist of shorter articles, reduce their scope, or suspend publication temporarily.[14] Vickery presents four approaches to the determination of basic journals: (1) reference counting in both articles and
bibliographies, an examination of borrowing records, the appraisal of
reference questions, analysis of abstracts, and lists of periodicals; (2)
diaries and questionnaires to be written up by scientists as they do
their reading; (3) questionnaires which record the opinions and
estimates of scientists on their reading; and (4) observation of the
way in which scientists actually spend their time.[15]

An interesting and significant application of the reference-counting
method is found in "Is American Attention to Foreign Research Results Declining?" by Karl W. Deutsch, George E. Klein, James J.
Baker, and associates.[16] The study arrived at the conclusion, supported
by twenty-three graphs, that American scientists are becoming far
more nationally self-preoccupied in absolute terms but are becoming

[13]Brown, *Scientific Serials*, p.9–10.

[14]L. Miles Raisig, "Mathematical Evaluation of the Scientific Serial," *Science*
2d ser. 131:1417 (1960).

[15]B. C. Vickery, "The Use of Scientific Literature," *Library Association Record*
63:263 (1961).

[16]"Is American Attention to Foreign Research Results Declining? A Tentative
Attempt at Measurement for Selected Data from Seven Fields of Pure and Applied
Science, 1889–1954" (submitted for the Committee on International Relations of
the American Academy of Arts and Sciences, 9 June 1954).

slightly more international in their reading, if the shift in their sources of relevant information is taken into account. For librarians there is much food for thought in this study. To what extent have selection policies influenced the domestic/foreign ratio of what scientists are reading?

There is a useful variation on the reference-counting technique. Bishop and Osborn have introduced the concept of translation frequency as a guide in serial selection.[17]

Sample Numbers

Just as the book-selection process is facilitated whenever books can be obtained on approval, so too the procurement of specimen copies of periodicals and some other serials can be a distinct aid in selection. Sample numbers are generally available on request to the dealer or publisher and should be obtained unless there is a clear case for subscribing or not subscribing. Farmington Plan dealers have been instructed to supply sample copies whenever possible.

Cooperative Acquisition

The total number of serial titles published each year, both domestic and foreign, is so great that libraries have become increasingly aware of the need for dividing the fields of collecting activity among themselves. On a national scale Public Law 480 has brought much material to the participating libraries, but most cooperation has been at the local level. Two or more libraries in a locality develop a plan whereby they confer and decide which institution will subscribe to a new title or a back set when a single file will suffice. There have been quite notable achievements along these lines in several small groups of colleges, e.g., those comprising the Hampshire Inter-Library Center in Massachusetts. Its first annual report showed the benefits that derive from cooperative serial acquisition:

> The branch of activity first begun ... concerned periodical subscriptions, 119 of which have now been placed by the Center in the interest of its members. During the year the faculties of the three

---

[17]D. Bishop and L. K. Osborn, "Translation Frequency as a Guide to the Selection of Soviet Biomedical Serials," *Medical Library Association Bulletin* 52:557 (1964).

member colleges [Amherst, Mount Holyoke, and Smith] examined their own current subscription lists and recommended journals which might be foregone on the local campus if the Center would take responsibility for them. . . . Agreement in these 119 instances represents a remarkable accomplishment when viewed against the background of local self sufficiency and autonomy which had previously prevailed. They fall into two broad categories: (a) journals previously maintained by one, two, or three of the members (a total of 98), (b) journals new to the area (a total of 21). The former represent economies effected by reducing what had been 180 subscriptions to 98 journals nearly by half. The latter exemplify the Center's constructive potentialities.

A third purpose has also been served in at least two instances where substantial journals threatened by cancellation for reasons of economy have been taken over by the Center. Thus, in this area of current subscriptions alone, three types of service have been rendered: reduction of expenditures, increase of resources, conservation of resources.[18]

Fifteen years later it was possible to say:

An analysis of the current subscription list shows 313 titles replacing subscriptions formerly carried in the area by one or more member institutions, 398 newly brought to the area by HILC, and a score of revivals of subscriptions which had formerly been carried in the area by member institutions but which had been dropped, usually for reasons of economy. . . .

The substantial collection of back files—so necessary to support the many new programs particularly in graduate and faculty research which have been announced—was further enriched this year with the addition of *Allgemeine musikalische Zeitung*, v.1–50; *Revista nacional; literatura-arte-ciencia*, no.1–218; *Ethnohistory*, v.1–10; *Egypte contemporaine*, v.2–55; *Vizantiiskii vremennik* [*Byzantina chronica*], v.1–10; and the *Daily Herald, London*, 1919–1926, 1930–1938—the last on microfilm. . . .

But current subscriptions and other purchases account for only a portion of HILC's holdings. After depositing back files of titles currently received at the Center, then closed files of periodicals which had been terminated, member libraries also curbed duplication and needless binding costs by establishing a class of materials known as "Current issues in member libraries, back files in HILC"; furthermore, a number of journals received under Public Law 480 from newly developing areas of the world by arrangements through

[18]Hampshire Inter-Library Center, *First Annual Report 1951–52* (South Hadley, Mass., 1952), p.1–2.

the Library of Congress, have been deposited at HILC, assuring that one file of each journal already selected by another member will be available in the area. HILC now maintains the area files of over 100 titles in this class.[19]

In retrospect the achievement at the Hampshire Inter-Library Center can be described as follows:

> HILC's holdings concentrate on important but infrequently used publications and on serials and sets rather than on monographs. These fall into two classes: those it acquires by purchase or gift, and those which are transferred to it by member libraries. Current subscriptions to periodicals and other serials—by intention titles not elsewhere in the area—receive major emphasis in the Center's acquisition program. HILC now receives more than 750 serials and their number is regularly increasing. . . .
>
> Incoming issues of most journals are routed on receipt to the libraries of the three colleges. They are displayed for a fortnight by each library in turn, returning thereafter to HILC where they become available for loan or consultation. . . .
>
> The collection exceeds 30,000 volumes and grows at a rate of approximately 2,500 volumes a year. This count does not reckon materials in all the four varieties of microform.[20]

While agreements of this kind are all too few and should be multiplied a thousandfold, it has been a fairly common practice, when the purchase of a serial set is being considered, to check the *Union List of Serials* to see whether there is already a copy in a neighboring institution or in the region. A library on the West Coast may well buy an item if the only recorded holdings are in the East or Middle West. But the same library might put its money into another title if it saw that the file was in another West Coast institution. The objective of all acquisition librarians should be to reduce duplication of foreign-language material, highly specialized titles, and little-used publications generally, at the same time that they conserve the means of enriching the resources of an area. Beatrice Simon, in speaking of "the utter impossibility of any of us being able to acquire and house every serial we might like to have, even if we had the money," says:

---

[19]Hampshire Inter-Library Center, *Sixteenth Annual Report*, 1966–67 (Amherst, Mass., 1967), p.1–2.

[20]"A Guide to the Hampshire Inter-Library Center" (Amherst, Mass., 1968).

It doesn't really matter much if six libraries in the same city buy the same book, but is it sensible, even sane, for six neighboring libraries to buy, bind and store complete sets of the *Commercial and Financial Chronicle....* Yet that is exactly what is happening all over the country to a greater or lesser degree and, at the same time, other valuable contemporary records are not being bought, bound or stored at all....

Whether we like it or not, this is the age of co-operation, and only through co-operation are we going to survive and have libraries. Co-operation extends all the way from nations to such seemingly small matters as whether two libraries in the same city will preserve the same periodical. Certain titles will be duplicated currently in nearly all libraries of the same type; others need not be. But complete sets, dealing with all phases of our own culture, and foreign titles should be preserved somewhere on this continent. Those universally useful should be dotted about . . . at strategic spots. Nor should this be considered impossible in this day of microfilm. Some kind of co-operative, regional planning for the acquisition, preservation and use of serials should be substituted for the haphazard and "isolationist" policies now in operation in so many of our libraries.

Furthermore, it is perfectly feasible and possible to carry out such a program with all types of libraries participating: public, university and even the private libraries of societies, research institutions, industry and business, to say nothing of the government libraries. On a modest scale, and in select groups of libraries, co-operative buying and storing has already been put into successful operation.[21]

This statement goes to the heart of the matter. Some titles are so significant that complete sets must be acquired, bound, and stored in neighboring libraries. Some should be acquired currently but do not need to be bound or preserved permanently except in the institution that undertakes the responsibility on behalf of others. For other titles one library can accept full responsibility so that nearby institutions do not have to acquire even the current issues.

Cooperation should apply most definitely to less used and marginal materials. Classes that deserve special attention are: annual reports; directories; foreign-language publications, particularly those in less known languages; government documents, notably at the state and local level; learned society journals and proceedings other than those of major organizations; local imprints; and press releases and other mimeographed matter. In applying this principle the Center for

[21]Beatrice V. Simon, "Let's Consider Serials Realistically," *Library Journal* 71:1297 (1946).

Research Libraries listed among the initial classes of material it collected: American newspapers, especially the foreign-language press; college catalogs; foreign newspapers; foreign parliamentary proceedings; house organs and trade journals; processed federal documents; and state government publications.

Local Publications

No one has any conception of the number of serials which are issued in local communities of all sizes throughout the world. There is a tremendous profusion of them: annual reports in manuscript as well as printed form; directories of various kinds; house organs; near-print and printed magazines; newspapers intended primarily for advertising purposes as well as regular newspapers; plus many additional types of serial. Among other groups, they originate with churches, firms, local government bodies, local societies, newspapers, and schools and colleges, including the student bodies.

In some places there is a local history society which collects and preserves the publications archivally. Where there is none, the public library should assume the responsibility. Both those organizations can operate successfully at grass-roots level, and when they do they relieve the larger libraries, including the state historical society libraries, of much difficult collecting.

The earliest house organ was *The Lowell Offering;* it was issued by the Lowell Cotton Mills in Massachusetts, beginning in 1842. Company magazines are still the best-known form, for internal use by the staff, for external use by customers and others, or for both purposes. Circulation figures for house organs can run into six digits, though for the typical one the circulation is relatively small. Some publications are quite important in their own right, e.g., *Endeavour*, which is published by Imperial Chemical Industries. There are countless employee magazines put out by organizations other than companies, e.g., by libraries. Almost from the beginning the New York Public Library has had a weekly, *Staff News.* The Library of Congress began its *Information Bulletin* as a staff magazine, but it has developed into an important library periodical, even though it still appears in near-print.

Limited Selection

Funds do not always permit the purchase of a back file when a subscription is placed after a serial has been in existence for a number of years. Commonly, when an established journal is ordered, the file is started with the preceding or following January, or at all events with the beginning of a new volume. Should the title be no more than two or three years old, the subscription ought to cover everything from volume 1, number 1, provided the issues are still in print. But for older titles acquisition of a complete back file usually has to be weighed carefully.

For some titles, mostly annuals and irregular publications, it may be necessary to subscribe to every second or third issue in order to conserve funds. Out-of-town city directories, e.g., may on occasion be acquired in this fashion without unduly reducing service, all the more so if complete files are maintained within reach. This expedient is acceptable when it adds to the resources of a library in a desirable way.

Microreproductions in Moderation

The philosophy which is developed in chapter 17 is that microreproductions are an invaluable aid to research but that they should be held down to a small proportion of the serial stock except, for the most part, in company libraries and in government research agencies. Particularly for periodicals, acquisition librarians should do their utmost to obtain print editions. Then the microreproductions which they must acquire will be accepted by readers without demur.

Back Files

Whenever possible an appropriate sum should be budgeted annually for the purchase of serial sets or parts of sets. In this way the resources of a community or library can be enriched as opportunity offers. For preference the fund should accrue from year to year. Strauss, Shreve, and Brown say:

> Files of periodicals constitute what may be the most important area of the library's resources, and immediate efforts should be made to acquire back files of those titles that will be needed without question. A few thousand dollars can be spent very quickly, particularly for long runs of the major journals. Moreover back runs are not always readily available when wanted so that it may take several

years to assemble all that are needed. Money should be set aside for this purpose.[22]

Evidence of the successful application of this policy is afforded by the experience of the Hampshire Inter-Library Center, cited in the section on cooperative acquisition earlier in this chapter. There is an *International Directory of Back Issue Vendors* (2d ed.; New York: Special Libraries Assn., 1968).

Piecemeal filling in of sets should be avoided as far as possible. There is a temptation to add parts which come by gift or in large-lot purchases; but unless a title is particularly important and scarce, or unless a crucial gap can be filled, it is better to restrict the rounding out of sets to the addition of at least a bound volume.

Brown makes the following comment:

> Almost all the scientific publications used and cited by research workers are classified as "serials." Back sets of these publications are referred to constantly. Thirty years ago complete sets of scientific publications could be purchased without too much difficulty and even odd volumes could be picked up at reasonable prices with the probability that missing volumes could be obtained later. Conditions changed very rapidly after 1930 and especially after 1940. Volumes lacking in a set are, in most cases, now extremely difficult to obtain. If odd volumes of a periodical are purchased, it is frequently found that the volumes obtained are the less important and that the volumes still missing are both the more important and more difficult to obtain.[23]

Monograph Series

As a rule all items in a series are wanted or only a few. There is an in-between situation, however, in which many items in the series would be ordered as individual volumes. In that event consideration should be given to the placing of a standing order for the whole series when it will enrich the resources of the area. Such an action

[22]Lucille J. Strauss, Irene M. Shreve, and Alberta L. Brown, *Scientific and Technical Libraries; Their Organization and Administration* (2d ed.; New York: Becker & Hayes, 1972), p.62.

[23]Charles H. Brown, *Library Resources in Selected Scientific Subjects at Louisiana State University* (Baton Rouge: Louisiana State Univ. Library, 1950), p.3.

would be in response to the sense of collecting responsibility which has come to the fore in the postwar years. As a bonus, the cost of acquisition procedures would be reduced somewhat, and the items would be available to readers faster than if each item had to be ordered individually.

Monograph series are very numerous. In 1969 the Serial Record Division at the Library of Congress reported that it had records for 81,933 of them. What Kamm and Taylor say of children's series is true of monograph series in general:

> This is the age of children's book series. Hardly a month goes by without a new one being launched. But for a publisher a series is more than a "brand name." He can publicise and sell the books in his series as a single unit, and the publication of new titles in a series tends to stimulate the older ones. Also, it is easier and more economic to design and produce books to a set formula. The printer knows what to expect, and economies can even be made by printing several books together at the same time. Thus it is that books in series can be cheaper than they would be if produced individually.
>
> From the buyer's point of view, it is reasonable to assume that if earlier titles in a series have proved reliable and suitable, later books on the same pattern will be equally suitable.[24]

Duplicate Holdings

When demand arises for extra copies of a purchased serial, a decision must be made as to whether it is wiser to duplicate or to spend the money on a title new to the collection. The answer is not so difficult in public and special libraries that emphasize service and the wide dissemination of selected titles, but elsewhere, particularly in university libraries, duplicate subscriptions are a matter of administrative concern.

The pressure for duplicate subscriptions is to provide service copies for current consultation and, in library systems, to accommodate both the main and branch or departmental collections. In special libraries it is frequently desirable, and may be necessary, to acquire service copies for journals that are routed to many people; otherwise readers may have to wait too long to see the latest issue of a journal which should be read promptly. The norm is often set at one copy of a periodical for each eight names on the routing slip. Service copies

[24]Antony Kamm and Boswell Taylor, *Books and the Teacher* (London: Univ. of London Pr., 1966), p.94.

are rarely bound, though issues from them may be utilized to round out a volume for binding. They may be held for several years to satisfy circulation needs or to provide reserve copies.

The Bailey report at Harvard University should stand as a warning against uncontrolled duplication other than the provision of service copies. Professor Bailey found that in 750 instances there was duplication in complete sets of long runs of periodicals in the botanical libraries at Harvard; in another 412 cases there was miscellaneous duplication. Altogether he found that there were approximately 30,000 excess duplicate volumes of botanical serials, estimated to be worth $130,000.[25]

Exchange and Gift

Since the budget for subscriptions is seldom adequate to serve all demands, at least in general libraries, thought must be given, as an integral part of the selection process, to the possibilities of obtaining each item by exchange or gift instead of by purchase. Collections can be enriched tremendously by judicious attention to these methods, which all too many libraries ignore.

Periodic Review

At regular intervals, possibly once every three years, all titles on the current checking records should be scrutinized to see whether, in the light of the serial program as a whole, they should continue to be acquired. Doubtful cases should be reviewed with a specimen copy in hand; it may even be desirable for the head librarian to pass on them. By means of a periodic check it is possible to eliminate titles that are no longer worth acquiring; duplicate subscriptions can be justified afresh or reduced in number; and cooperative aspects of collecting can be developed.

Systematic Selection

Serial selection is at its best when a systematic program is followed over the years. If such a pattern is not followed, a patchwork effect

25Irving W. Bailey, *Botany and Its Applications at Harvard* ([Cambridge, Mass.: Harvard Univ.], 1945), p.84–93.

is bound to occur, one that is very difficult to change. Fortunately, today the possibilities exist for the systematic development of serial resources. The fact that acquisition librarians were not particularly systematic in the past is no reason why their practices should persist into the future; they did excellently with the limited tools at their disposal. Now there are superior tools which should be exploited fully. Chief among them is *New Serial Titles—Classed Subject Arrangement.* And beyond that there are the annual book catalogs, such as *Serials and Journals in the M.I.T. Libraries,* which should constantly be checked to learn of a new title that a major library has already acquired and that another library should consider acquiring.

Bibliography

Davinson, D. E. "Acquisition Policy," in his *The Periodicals Collection; Its Purpose and Uses in Libraries,* p.103–11. London: Deutsch, 1969.

Grenfell, David. "Acquisition," in his *Periodicals and Serials; Their Treatment in Special Libraries,* p. 5–31. 2d ed. London: Aslib, 1965.

Rippon, J. S., and Francis, S. "Selection and Acquisition of Library Materials," in Wilfred Ashworth, ed., *Handbook of Special Librarianship and Information Work,* p.35–78. 3d ed. London: Aslib, 1967.

Strauss, Lucille J.; Shreve, Irene M.; and Brown, Alberta L. *Scientific and Technical Libraries; Their Organization and Administration,* p.144–52. 2d ed. New York: Becker & Hayes, 1972.

Reference counting for basic journals

Brodman, Estelle. "Choosing Physiology Journals," *Bulletin of the Medical Library Association* 32:479–83 (1944).

Brown, Charles H. *Scientific Serials; Characteristics and Lists of Most Cited Publications in Mathematics, Physics, Chemistry, Geology, Physiology, Botany, Zoology, and Entomology.* (ACRL Monograph, no.16) Chicago: Assn. of College and Reference Libraries, 1956.

Gross, P. L. K., and Gross, E. M. "College Libraries and Chemical Education," *Science* n.s. 66:385–89 (1927).

Raisig, L. Miles. "Mathematical Evaluation of the Scientific Serial," *Science* 2d ser. 131:1417–19 (1960).

Vickery, B. C. "The Use of Scientific Literature," *Library Association Record* 63:263–69 (1961).

Cooperation

Center for Research Libraries, *Annual Report* (Chicago, 1950–   ).

——*Newsletter* (Chicago, 1949–   ).

Hampshire Inter-Library Center, *Annual Report* (Amherst, Mass., 1952–   ).

——*Newsletter* ([Amherst, Mass.], 1955–   ).

6

Acquisition
Procedures

In the hands of experts serials are acquired and processed by efficient, businesslike methods. Every year the serial acquisition program can involve thousands, tens of thousands, even hundreds of thousands of serial issues. In the Library of Congress the figure has not fallen below a million pieces since 1945; the lowest number in that period was 1,111,551 in 1949, the highest 1,934,425 in 1967. What is involved, then, in most research libraries of various sizes and types is a mass activity which, when grasped as such, should ensure that all aspects of serial acquisition are made as simple and straightforward as they can possibly be.

Mass methods should always apply to the principal acquisition tool, which is the current checking record. Its manual operation is described in chapter 8, its computer operation in chapter 9.

Decision Slips

To formalize and systematize the different courses of action that should ensue once a serial starts to come regularly, many libraries, in the act of serial selection, employ printed or mimeographed decision slips (see figure 5), which can be attached to sample numbers on hand or held until the first issue arrives. Some libraries complement the decision slip with a card file to preserve the decisions that have been made, the reason being that over the years there would otherwise be no record of a decision not to acquire a title; this would give rise to the possibility that selection procedures might have to be repeated in some instances. Among other details the file may show: who recommended the acquisition or nonacquisition of a title;

NEW SERIAL TITLE

☐ Series   ☐ Subseries   ☐ Sub-subseries

Routing   Cleared

.... Selection Officer

.... For recommendation

.... Wanted for the Library .... Not wanted for the Library

.... Keep .....I.. sets .... Review before binding

.... Retain current issues only .... Retain this issue only

.... Acquire .... Back numbers .... Bound vols. only .... Continuation

.... By purchase .... By exchange or gift

......✓..... Recommendation review shelf, Ser. Rec. Div.   ....

.... Subject Cataloging decision shelf   ....

....✓.... Sets collected .... Sets monograph

.... Analyzed .... In full ......✓.... In part { ......✓.. This part

.... { .... Not this part

.... Not analyzed ....

............,. Serials Section, Desc. Cat. Div. for form card

......✓..... Cataloging Section, Ser. Rec. Div.

......①..... New Serial Titles Section, Ser. Rec. Div.   ....

.... Monthly Checklist of State Publications, E & G Div.   ....

.... Monthly Index of Russian Accessions

....

....

....

.... Exchange and Gift Division   ....

.... Order Division   ....

.... Copyright Office—for claiming

....②..... Card Division   ....

....③..... Preliminary Cataloging Section, Desc. Cat. Div.   ....

.... Shared Cataloging Division   ....

.... Serials Section, Desc. Cat. Div.   ....

.... Slavic Languages Sect., Desc. Cat. Div.   ....

.... Music Section, Desc. Cat. Div.   ....

....④..... Subject Cataloging Division   ....

....

....

Custody

⑤.....✓ Periodical R. R.   .... Law Library   .... Nat. Lib. of Med.

....✓.. G. P. R. R.   .... Orientalia Div.   .... Nat. Agric. Lib.

.... Slavic Room   .... Ser. Div. Sample File ____ ....

Searched in   ☐ SR   ☐ OC   ☐ FF   ☐ ULS   ☐ Newsp.

Author not established ☐ SR   ☐ OC   ☐ ULS

Author established ☐ SR   ☐ OC   ☐ ULS

Figure 5. Library of Congress decision slip

whether a sample copy is to be procured before the final selection decision is made; where the current file is to be located, and on occasion the period for which the file is to be current; whether a set is to be bound; whether a back file is to be acquired; whether earlier or superseded issues are to be discarded; and whether an annual is to be bought every second or third year instead of every twelve months. Since operational information about items that are acquired is eventually transferred to the checking records, the decision file becomes a catalog of negative decisions; it is one more place to check, one more file to maintain. If such a catalog is useful when a decision must be reviewed or for the avoidance of remaking decisions, then the cards should be kept, but just for a year or two, not indefinitely.

When standard-sized cards, bearing the initials of department heads and others, serve in place of decision slips, the decision file is composed of them. Otherwise the data on the slips must be transferred to cards. Should there be a serial catalog which complements the checking records, the cards are sometimes incorporated in it.

While many libraries of all sizes maintain decision files, most find that they can operate as well without them. A decision file does serve some purposes, though most of them are slight and negative. In general, it should be avoided unless there are good reasons for its existence.

Files of Sample Periodicals

Instead of discarding sample numbers for titles not to be acquired, acquisition departments often preserve them in a special file arranged alphabetically. Decision slips are attached to the items, or the information is written on the pieces themselves. The sample periodical collection can substitute for a decision file, yet, because it is not complete, both are sometimes maintained: the samples for possible bibliographical value, because so many of them are volume 1, number 1; the decision file as the comprehensive record.

When the sample file is old and extensive, as is the case at the Library of Congress, it can have a certain value for the bibliographer. In April 1971 there were 87,648 items in the Library of Congress collection; in 1949 the Harvard College Library had presented its accumulation to the Library of Congress. Harvard's file had grown for over a century, but it seemed wiser to add to the resource in Washington than to continue a separate one.

Order Records

It is advisable to keep the records for purchased serials entirely distinct from those for books and pamphlets, in manual as in automated systems. In particular, serials and nonserials should not be included on one and the same order sheet, and the serial order cards should be inserted in the checking records (see figure 6) so that there is just a single place to look for all current serials, whether on order or already being received. Regardless of how effective multiple-order forms may be for books, they are not the desirable medium for serials, which require, or should require, more clear space than is available on the typical multiple-order form.

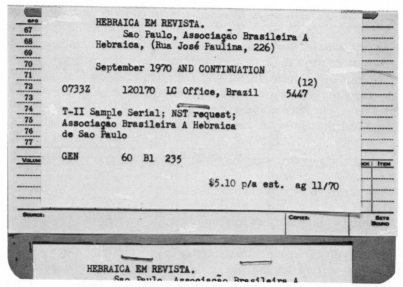

Figure 6. Acquisition data as recorded in the visible index at the Library of Congress. One copy of the acquisition action is stapled to the overriding slip for ready consultation. A second copy is stapled in such a way that the title of the serial appears in the visible margin of the basic entry card.

Book and serial orders are separated from each other partly for accounting and statistical purposes, but still more to characterize the ordering and receipt of serials as an operation which should be in the hands of specialized staff from the moment that the size of the undertaking warrants. The most compelling reason for separating the two, and an extremely important one, is that no serial should be requested by exchange, gift, or purchase without mention of a distinctive address which will take the issues on receipt directly to the checkers. Standing orders for annuals, monograph series, etc., should come under this ruling quite meticulously. In the past neglect of the single factor of a distinctive address for serials has made the handling of second-class mail burdensome and inefficient; the neglect will no longer be tolerable in the days ahead as the need for a coding in the mailing address becomes more and more apparent, a development which is explained in chapters 7 and 9.

Basically, then, the documentation which shows that exchange, gift, or purchase action has been taken should be in the visible index or its equivalent, with a sheet record as the supporting document. When this is so, and the dealer or publisher has been supplied with mailing address and coding, the checker can take immediate action on receipt of the first issue instead of setting the item aside to be investigated when the day's checking activities have been completed.

The Library of Congress has a flexoline visible reference index to outstanding serial orders. It gives author, title, order number, agent, number of copies ordered, and an abbreviation for the division in which current issues are to be housed (see figure 7).

In a relatively small number of libraries there is a complementary catalog of serial titles, the bulk of them being inactive. In the Harvard College Library this catalog is known as the S-Card (i.e., Serial Card) File (see figure 8); in the Library of Congress it is referred to as the Old Serial Record, though in the 1969 serial record sample the reference is always to the 3 x 5 file (see figure 9); and in the National Agricultural Library the name is the Alphabetical Serial File. Whenever it exists, serial librarians look on the complementary catalog as an invaluable bibliographical aid. It loses much of that

Title	Order No.	Vendor or agency	No. Copies	Address
Revista General de Marina. Mexico.	4796T	Rojas	01	OD
Revista Geografica.	5965T	EBSCO	01	OD
Revista Goaina de jurisprudencia e legislacao	5949Z	Leite	01	OD
Revista Gregoriana. SEE: Liturgia e Vida (2733x)				
Revista hispanica moderna	9766X	Stechert	01	SR
Revista horizonte.	8360T	Jose Porter	01	OD
Revista Iberica de Parasitologia	1248Z	Suarez	01	SR
Revista IMCYC. Mexico.	6169X	Porrua	01	OD
Revista Industrial. Mexico.	479T	Rojas	01	ATD
Revista Industrial y fabril	0465Y	Aguilar	01	OD
Revista Industriei alimentare - produce vegetale	0148W	Cartimex	01	OD
Revista interamericana de bibliothecologia.	2910T	Stechert (N. Y.)	01	OD
Revista internacional del notario	8067Y	Lajouane	01	OD
Revista invatamintului superior	0661Y	Cartimex	01	OD
Revista juridica.	6766W	Stechert (N. Y.)	01	OD
Revista juridica (Bogota)	0768Z	Camacho Roldan	01	OD
Revista juridica. Bolivia.	6120X	Arno Hermanos	01	SR
Revista juridica; dirigida por Bernardo Lucas	0467Z	Livraria Portugal	01	OD

Figure 7. Library of Congress flexoline entries

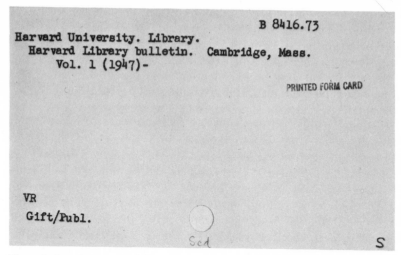

Figure 8. S-card from Harvard College Library. The tracing is on the verso of the
card.

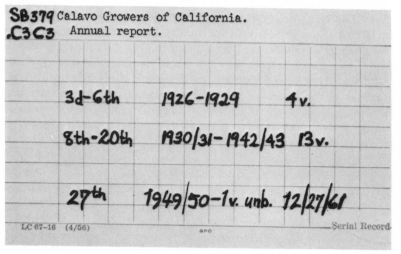

Figure 9. Card from the Library of Congress Old Serial Record

value, however, when there is a book catalog of current and retrospective serials, so that in the future the complementary record should be a book catalog.

International Standard Serial Numbering

Beginning with 1971–72 a system of international standard serial numbering (ISSN) has been developed by the R. R. Bowker Company as a parallel scheme to the International Standard Book Number and for similar purposes, i.e., as an identification symbol to be used in the ordering of serials through dealers and publishers. The initial display of the numbers occurs in the fourteenth edition of *Ulrich's International Periodicals Directory*, the third volume of which, entitled *Irregular Serials and Annuals, an International Directory*, contains an index to the entries in all three volumes. The system began with the assignment of numbers to some seventy thousand titles. Additional numbers will be assigned and published periodically as they are requested by abstracting and indexing services, libraries, and subscription agencies. It is hoped that an ISSN will appear on the cover of each issue.

Agents

The basic reason for acquiring serials through the intermediary of an agent, and not directly from the publishers, is that thereby the paperwork and accounting in an acquisition department are reduced. If hundreds or thousands of publishers had to be paid relatively small amounts each year, the advantages that derive in some instances from dealing with them directly might be more than offset. Paperwork in an acquisition department tends to be heavy; more should not be added if it can be avoided. Usually, though not always, an agent will pass on to the library the discount which some publishers allow or the special rate for multiple-year subscriptions.[1]

Service is by far the most important factor to be sought in choosing an agent. Prompt, regular, and reliable service is imperative if serial files are to be maintained without gaps. Each issue of the *Literary*

[1] On the relations between dealers and libraries see Edwin B. Colburn, "Mutual Problems of Serial Agents and Librarians," *Serial Slants* 1:20 (Oct. 1950); Albert H. Davis, "The Subscription Agency and the Library: Responsibilities and Problems from the Dealer's Viewpoint," *Serial Slants* 1:14 (Oct. 1950); and Ralph Lessing, "Subscription Problems as Seen by an Agent," *Serial Slants* 4:5 (1953).

Market Place gives a list of North American periodical agencies; Strauss, Shreve, and Brown have a selected list of both current subscription agencies and dealers in back files;[2] Grenfell provides a list of British booksellers who specialize in periodicals;[3] and the American Library Association publishes a directory of agents outside North America.[4]

Baer has stated the case for placing subscriptions through an agent. He says:

> The practice of direct subscription to periodicals with the appropriate publisher and renewal by the same method is probably no longer the predominant practice in libraries. The desire to lessen the clerical work load of the acquisitions department has led many libraries to utilize the services of a reliable agent whenever possible.
>
> Although there are serious drawbacks, primarily clerical work load, in dealing directly with all publishers of periodicals, some publishers offer attractive price reductions and good service in order to attract "till forbid" subscription business. The McGraw-Hill Publishing Company is an excellent example of a commercial publisher offering such a service. If the library currently subscribes to a number of periodicals published by them and in sufficient quantity to fall into the category of a large purchaser, McGraw-Hill can offer "till forbid" service, automatic billing and discounts which, though they vary according to the size of the order, are better than those that can be offered by any jobber. . . .
>
> The small industrial or public library must regard such attractive arrangements . . . with some caution. If the clerical staff level permitted by a budget is barely adequate to handle the clerical work involved in acquisitions, the advantage of placing all periodical subscriptions through an agent and foregoing the discounts quoted above may actually be the greater economy. . . .
>
> The utilization of a single agency through which to place all subscriptions which may be handled in this manner has two outstanding advantages. First, it reduces the amount of correspondence required for subscription, claim and renewal and usually permits it to be handled by routine utilization of forms. Second, any library, regardless of its size, becomes a "large order" library by joining its

[2]Lucille J. Strauss, Irene M. Shreve, and Alberta L. Brown, *Scientific and Technical Libraries; Their Organization and Administration* (2d ed.; New York: Becker & Hayes, 1972) , p.146–47, 151–52.

[3]David Grenfell, *Periodicals and Serials; Their Treatment in Special Libraries* (2d ed.; London, Aslib, 1965), p.200–201.

[4]American Library Association, Resources and Technical Services Division, *International Subscription Agents* (2d ed.; Chicago: The Association, 1969).

subscription business with that of many other libraries, large and small, handled by the agent.[5]

He goes on to say that great care must be exercised in the choice of an agent, the best method being to check with a variety of types of library nearby. He points out that a dealer will carry orders placed by the library on behalf of individuals in the organization and that it is advantageous to have the dealer supply a complete list of all subscriptions together with the renewal cost. The disadvantages of the system come from operating with an inefficient agent or from the inefficient use of a good agent.

Libraries expect to receive both discount and good service when they purchase books. Discount for serials differs from that for books; it is forthcoming on popular titles and on some multiple-year subscriptions. Two other types are described by Orne:

> Many institutions, like Washington University, subscribe to a considerable number of journals produced by a major source. We receive twenty or more journals published by the University of Chicago Press. We now have all the subscriptions to their journals on a "till forbid" basis, and receive an annual bill of 10 percent discount. . . . Some organizations and publishers are not only equipped but eager to take a standing order for all or specific publications, giving excellent service and good discounts. Thus *American Industries*, published in series at prices varying from $1.00 to $2.00, can be had at three for $2.50 on standing order. The American Council on Education in return for a stand-order assures a 20 percent discount on its publications. In some cases a membership is combined with a standing order, as in the case of the Modern Language Association of America. Our standing order for their *Monograph Series* comes at a 30 percent discount when placed direct.
>
> The field of library memberships deserves to be thoroughly reexamined from various points of view. Certain library memberships are very advantageous. Thus the Business Historical Society (Boston, Mass.) has a $10.00 membership fee which brings its *Bulletin* plus the *Harvard Studies in Business History*. By our count the *Studies* alone last year cost at list $14.00. An associate membership in the National Bureau of Economic Research at $5.00 brings three series, the Annual Reports, Occasional Papers, and Technical Papers, as well as a guaranteed one third off on any other publications. A membership in the British School at Athens costs less than $6.00,

[5]Mark H. Baer, "Serials and Out-of-print Titles," in Isabel H. Jackson, ed., *Acquisition of Special Materials* (San Francisco: San Francisco Bay Region Chapter, Special Libraries Assn., 1966), p.41–42.

and yields its *Annual* and a 50 percent discount on back volumes. The *Annual* alone if purchased through an agent costs $10.00. The *Transactions* of the American Philological Association sells for $5.00 through an agent. A membership including the *Transactions* costs $5.00 the first year, but $4.00 each year thereafter and allows special rates on any other publications.[6]

Baer adds:

The advantage of membership in national societies, institutions or associations, should be given serious consideration as a highly desirable method of acquiring serial publications which are often not readily available through an agent, or are available only on a membership rather than subscription basis. Most memberships provide substantial price benefits and frequently offer announcements, ephemera or even serial publications circulated only to members.

As an example of the price advantages to be gained, membership in the Institute of Electrical and Electronics Engineers (formerly two professional organizations, the American Institute of Electrical Engineers and the Institute of Radio Engineers, which merged in 1963) and its Professional Technical Groups enables the member to receive its *Proceedings,* all *Transactions* as well as its annual *International Convention Record,* at a cost of $143.10 per year. The price of these same publications to college and public libraries on a non-member basis is $384.65 per year. Non-member price to all other subscribers amounts to $612.50 per year.

Some highly desirable serial publications cannot be obtained by means other than corporate or individual membership unless the requestor falls into a special category. An example is the *Conference Board Record* (formerly the *Conference Board Business Management Record,* which merged two publications, *Management Record* and the *Conference Board Business Record*), a publication of the National Industrial Conference Board, Inc., a non-profit organization. This periodical is available only on a membership basis. In addition to this publication, the Conference Board publishes numerous pamphlets and ephemera which are sent to members. Possibly its most important publications are the series *Studies in Business Economics, Studies in Business Policy* and *Studies in Personnel Policy.* Management generally regards the quality of these monographs to be superior to most other publications in the same fields. The price of the monographs to non-members is generally 25 to 30 percent higher than member cost. In addition to this, members are supplied the first copy of each publication free with the membership and member price applies when ordering additional copies.[7]

[6]Jerrold Orne, "A Serials Information Clearing House," *Serial Slants* 1:12 (April 1951). The principles remain valid, even though the figures have changed since 1951.
[7]Baer, "Serials and Out-of-Print Titles," p.44–45.

Membership is often taken out by a library in the name of a professor or staff member when institutional membership is not possible, but sometimes the individual himself must join and be reimbursed by the library. It is virtually only *Chemical Abstracts* which considers the latter practice unethical. In addition to enabling the library to procure publications which would not otherwise be available or which would cost appreciably more, the practice confers an honor on the individual, who becomes a member of international and other bodies.

In addition to the factors of membership, multiple-year subscriptions, and special discount rates, a new element is causing a swing away from the use of agents. This is the service charge which agents are adding to subscription rates because the margin of profit is too small. In January 1968 the Hampshire Inter-Library Center reported:

> In an attempt to reduce operating costs, HILC has switched approximately one hundred and seventy-five subscriptions for scholarly journals or sets originating in North America from its regular agent . . . , either to subscribing directly with the original publisher, or to another agent. This was brought about chiefly when the . . . firm announced a ten percent surcharge on all such subscriptions, explaining that its costs and the costs of the publishers had risen. As of the latter, [the firm] said many publishers were allowing less discount to agents or jobbers, and suggesting either direct subscriptions with the original publishers—by-passing the agent but at no discount to the libraries usually—or surcharges to be imposed by the agents.[8]

Helen Tuttle, in discussing price indexes for American periodicals and serial services for 1970, says:

> An increasingly serious cost factor for libraries, one which these price indexes ignore, is the adding of service charges to subscription prices by periodical agents to cover their costs of operation. Some students of library problems are predicting that the agent of the future will approach libraries with contracts, offering to provide good periodical services for cost plus a service fee per title. Certainly, many serial librarians are finding that they can provide good service to their users only by placing subscriptions directly with the publishers, which suggests that subscription agents find the margin of profit too small to provide adequate staff for billing, record keeping, claiming, and reporting. If the present trend continues, serials li-

[8]Hampshire Inter-Library Center, *Newsletter* 13:6 (1968).

brarians will be doing some careful cost studies as they decide whether to put money into staff or into service fees.[9]

In the past the argument was generally in favor of working through domestic and foreign periodical agents except when: (1) it is necessary to order directly from the publisher, as is the case with the H. W. Wilson indexes; (2) institutional or personal membership is required for the acquisition of society publications; and (3) the publisher is able to offer advantageous terms for direct orders. The coming of the service charge has tended to obscure the argument; now each library should review the situation to see whether it will continue to work with an agent, place its orders directly with the publishers, or follow a judicious mixture of the two practices. At the moment, the service charge is by no means a universal custom, and much could be said in favor of service at cost plus a standard fee.

Price Indexes

At the congressional hearings on the appropriations for the legislative branch of the government, the Library of Congress has in postwar years made effective use of price-index figures for serial subscriptions. The figures show the substantial increases in costs by country and subject which year by year necessitate a larger budget for serials. All libraries which spend even a thousand dollars a year on serials should present similar evidence to their budgetary authorities. The price index for American periodicals and serial services is given annually in the *Library Journal;* the periodicals covered are those that are included in the services. The British price index appears each year in the *Library Association Record* and distinguishes among: (1) British periodicals, (2) Canadian and American, and (3) those of other countries.

Without the price indexes it is doubtful whether those in authority would realize that on the average subscription prices have exhibited a tendency to double over a ten-year period. Helen Tuttle makes the impact of the cost increases abundantly clear when she says:

> The average price of U. S. periodicals for 1970 made a phenomenal leap of $1.10 over the average price for 1969. In the dozen years since the base years of 1957–1959, the index for U. S. periodicals has risen to 211.6; that is, the price of subscriptions has more than

[9]Helen W. Tuttle, "Price Indexes for 1970: U.S. Periodicals and Serial Services," *Library Journal* 95:2427 (1970).

doubled, an average annual increase of 9.3 percent. The largest increases are the more recent ones. From 1960 through 1965, the annual increase in average price ranged from 29 to 39 cents. During the five years from 1966 through 1970, the increase escalated in the following sequence: 49, 58, 63, 66, and 110 cents.

To emphasize today's accelerated inflation two figures can be quoted. First, the percentage increase of 1970 prices (average $10.41) over 1969 ($9.31 average) is 11.8 percent, some 2.5 percent higher than the average annual increase for the past decade. Second, the index for 1970, if computed on the base years 1967–1969, is 120.2, while the 1960 index, computed on the base years 1957–1959, is only 108.1. That is, comparing the two years in terms of their three preceding years gives a 12.1 percent greater increase than 1960.

Serial services have followed the same path, with the 1970 index at 214.7, more than double the base figure. With the average price of the services at $85.44, the situation for libraries is indeed alarming.

Among periodicals the most spectacular leap this year was made by the Chemistry & Physics group, with an index increase of 68.3 points, the average price going from $26.60 to $33.45. The 1970 index for this group is 333.2; that is, the price of these periodicals has more than tripled since 1957–59. The next highest index is shown by the Mathematics, Botany, Geology, and General Science group at 288.8, followed by Medicine at 236.8. Children's periodicals, with an index of 133.2, show the lowest figure and were the same last year.[10]

The following is the ranking in terms of the average price per periodical according to the 1970 price-index figures:

1. Chemistry and Physics	$33.45	14. Sociology and Anthropology	$7.31
2. Medicine	23.44	15. Education	7.09
3. Mathematics, Botany, Geology, and General Science	18.11	16. History	6.90
		17. Political Science	6.72
4. Psychology	17.12	18. Journalism and Communications	6.36
5. Zoology	16.86		
6. Engineering	12.07	19. Literature and Language	6.15
7. Law	9.84	20. Philosophy and Religion	5.84
8. Business and Economics	9.03	21. Physical Education and Recreation	5.34
9. General Interest Periodicals	8.47		
10. Library Science	7.88	22. Agriculture	5.17
11. Industrial Arts	7.59	23. Labor and Industrial Relations	3.59
12. Home Economics	7.56		
13. Fine and Applied Arts	7.50	24. Children's Periodicals	2.65

[10]*Ibid.*

The base year for the British price index is 1965. The index shows an increase of 152.4 for the humanities and social sciences, 168.0 for medicine, and 183.6 for science and technology. The increase for all countries and subjects is 175.7. The general observation on the situation is: "There has again been a fairly steep increase in the prices. This is partly caused by publishers raising their prices to cover their costs, but in addition to this there is now a trend, especially amongst publishers of scientific journals, to produce extra volumes and supplements, thus increasing the cost of an annual subscription."[11]

There are no price indexes for other types of serials, but all of them have increased markedly in cost. Government publications have gained the least in price but, on the other hand, the number of free documents has declined steadily, so that today most government serials must be purchased. In addition to the rise in price for microreproductions, they are now on the market in ten different sizes: three each for microfiche and microfilm and four for microopaques. For *The Nation* in 1953 the cost per volume for microcards was $2.96, for microfilm $4.19; in 1970 the figures were $4.39 and $4.55, respectively, as well as $6.38 for microfiche. For reprints the history-of-science periodical *Isis* cost $14.00 per volume in 1953, $22.50 in 1970; and for secondhand sets, the art periodical *Kokka* cost $29.00 per volume in 1953, $63.00 in 1970.

Factors in the general price rise are manufacturing costs, postal rates, shipping charges, and storage fees. The answer to the ever-growing problem of budgeting for serials must be found in no small measure in the most skillful application of acquisition techniques. (1) Exchange and gift programs must be promoted and developed to their fullest extent. In the past many libraries have said that they have nothing to offer on exchange, and consequently they have no exchange program. If they are enterprising, however, they can as a rule find a number of serials, particularly those issued in the vicinity, which will provide advantageous terms for multiple subscriptions, and these can form the basis for a system of exchanges. (2) Cooperative collecting should be undertaken in metropolitan areas and other closely-knit communities. The objective should be enrichment of the resources of a locality; at the same time, harm should not be done to publication programs through drastic curtailments in subscriptions. (3) Duplicate serial sets should be offered directly to other libraries or to non-profit-making organizations such as the United States Book Exchange. Bound volumes and runs of sets should always be offered

---

[11]J. B. Merriman, "Comparative Index to Periodical Prices," *Library Association Record* 72:289 (1970).

directly, particularly to newly established or rapidly expanding institutions.

Bids

If there is any justification for securing bids before books are purchased, there is practically none in the case of serials. Discount is seldom available for serials other than monograph series. By contrast, the really important factor is service which leads to complete files year after year. It follows, then, that government regulations are a hindrance when they require libraries subject to their control to secure bids before subscriptions to current serials can be placed or renewed. It has been necessary for various federal agencies, the United Nations Library, and many others to win free of the restriction, but there are still a number of federal, municipal, school, and state libraries that are hampered by the system of bids. Actually, the number is decreasing and should disappear altogether.

The routine involved in the procurement of serials by means of bids is considerable. There is the labor of compiling multiple copies of the lists to be submitted to dealers; there is the paperwork that goes with sending out as many as eight lists; almost invariably there is telephone or written follow-up work to secure the necessary number of bids; and eventually there is the task of assembling and comparing the bids, if and when they are received. The net result of a bidding system is that delays in procurement occur unless a library can deal directly with a dealer or publisher, the cost of the operations is apt to outweigh any financial gain that might come from a low bid, and emphasis is placed on discount rather than on service. Bids tend to be penny wise and pound foolish by comparison with the results which can be obtained by alert acquisition librarians.

Dealers dislike the system just as much as librarians do. The dealer's point of view is as follows:

> A certain number of libraries—either due to regulations or by choice —ask for quotations before placing or renewing periodical subscriptions. This practice imposes additional work on libraries and dealers alike, and its merits are open to serious question.
>
> Periodical prices change constantly. For the last ten years there has been a steadily upward trend. Thus to protect himself against losses from possible price changes, a dealer will insert in his bid an "escalator clause" allowing him to make certain additional charges should the publishers raise the subscription rates. This clause is indispensable; for if a firm bid is requested, the bidder must raise

his prices sufficiently to insure against losses which he cannot pass on to the subscriber. And such higher bids, of course, defeat the purpose of the entire procedure and are costly to the library.

Concluding, therefore, that the "escalator clause" is beneficial to both parties, the library as well as the bidder, we encounter still another pitfall: the constantly rising prices of periodical subscriptions actually serve to penalize the best-informed bidder. Since he knows the latest (and hence the highest) prices, he will find himself *ipso facto* the highest bidder and will not be awarded the order. On the other hand, the most ignorant bidder may receive the order simply because his outdated prices are lower. Needless to say, this low bidder must eventually make a greater number of additional charges when he finds out the actual subscription rates than his better-informed competitor. . . .

We have, therefore, come to the conclusion that in evaluating bids two points must be constantly borne in mind:
1) Asking for firm bids, without an "escalator clause," forces bidders to increase the prices quoted.
2) The lowest bidder on a quotation may well prove to be the one whose prices are most obsolete, and the most expensive one after all additional charges are in.[12]

Some serials are simply not obtainable on any system of bids. The publications of the H. W. Wilson Company, e.g., which are sold to libraries on a service basis, must be obtained directly from the publisher.[13] And for some items institutional or personal membership is required.

The system of bids is less objectionable when the successful bidder keeps the subscriptions indefinitely. It is completely unacceptable when the subscription list must be submitted for fresh bids every year, or indeed whenever there is the risk that titles may be transferred back and forth from one agent to another, so jeopardizing both adequacy and continuity of service.

Exchange of Current Serials

When a library has significant serials of its own to offer, or when

[12]*Stechert-Hafner Book News* 7:20 (1952).

[13]This is not the place to discuss the merits of the service-basis charge for serials. The American Library Association and the Association of Research Libraries have debated the matter repeatedly. Among others, the Harvard Graduate School of Business Administration has investigated and justified the service charge. For a detailed study of the problem see John L. Lawler, *The H. W. Wilson Company; Half a Century of Bibliographic Publishing* (Minneapolis: Univ. of Minnesota Pr., [1950]), p.115–35.

it can readily draw on other items such as government documents or publications of university presses, it is in a strategic position to acquire many worthwhile serials and monographs on exchange. As a rule, exchange is the preferred method of procurement from those countries in which the book trade is not well organized. It may be the best way of guaranteeing the completeness of files. Both the Library of Congress and the National Agricultural Library have noteworthy exchange programs; the latter acquires something like 90 percent of its serials by exchange.

Since its inception in 1947 the *Unesco Bulletin for Libraries* has been the current medium for exchange possibilities. It is complemented by the systematic *Handbook on the International Exchange of Publications*, also issued by Unesco, which lists many individual titles of serials available on exchange. The most fruitful sources of exchanges are colleges and universities, government bodies, learned societies, libraries, and other societies and non-profit-making organizations. Periodicals and monograph series are particularly valuable items to be able to offer on exchange.

Once the exchange of a serial has been established, the record work in maintaining it is comparatively slight. For instance, for foreign exchange the Harvard College Library has numerous subscriptions to the *Quarterly Journal of Economics*. A bill is rendered and paid once a year for the multiple subscriptions; no further invoice or payment is required of any library, so the total transaction is economically advantageous.

Exchange programs for current serials operate at two levels. An officer must determine policy and initiate action, but thereafter the checkers take over. Correspondence should be held together as a unit, arranged by country, then by locality. For ready consultation there is generally a card index to the file, arranged similarly, which notes the names of the serials sent in each direction. For priced exchange the cost of each shipment received or sent is listed on the cards.

Subscription payments for outgoing current exchanges are made by the regular acquisition staff, preferably out of a special budget allocation. On the checking records the source of an incoming exchange is noted for follow-up purposes. Occasionally colored cards are employed to distinguish items which are received on exchange.

Exchange of Duplicates

The United States Book Exchange is the major American and international outlet for the exchange of publications. Its tremendous stock of serials makes it the largest resource in the world. Librarians may not select periodicals directly from the USBE shelves as they can books; instead they may submit their want lists for issues or runs just as they can check the lists of periodical titles, by country and subject, which USBE circularizes to member institutions. The director, Alice Ball, says:

> Most important of the unique characteristics of USBE as an exchange organization is the fact that member libraries can *order periodicals directly*, without waiting for their appearance on an exchange list. The direct-order and back-order system of USBE is made possible by the agency's pooling operation. Because of the number of periodicals in stock and in the daily receipts of USBE, this service offers one of the surest, as well as one of the most inexpensive, ways for a library to locate back issues of serials.[14]

Baer, speaking for special libraries, expresses the great value of USBE for building up and rounding out serial holdings when he says:

> Even with the adoption of a membership fee and the increase of material fees, libraries utilizing USBE to fill in back sets and issues will find the savings over most other methods more than offset the costs. Only if time is a primary consideration would the low cost offered by USBE have to be weighed against the desirability of ordering from a dealer whose catalog indicates immediate availability of the items desired.
>
> Since USBE must depend on contributions to maintain a stock from which to serve member libraries, it would seem that the likelihood of being able to obtain scarce and expensive items would be very small. Certainly they are not as available from this source as more recent or common titles, but, given time, many items of this type can be obtained from USBE. Some of the titles obtained by Ampex Corporation Technical Library during 1963 include the *Harvard Business Review*, volumes 2, 10, 11 and 14 for the years 1924, 1931/32, 1932/33 and 1936, issues of *Transactions* of various Professional Groups of the Institute of Radio Engineers (now Institute of Electrical and Electronics Engineers) published during the 1950's. Volumes of the *Harvard Business Review* for the years noted have appeared in dealer catalogs at $10.00 per volume, but were available from USBE at less than $5.00 per volume. Issues of the

[14]Alice D. Ball, "Exchange Supermarket," *Library Journal* 78:2059 (1953). See also her "Serials Acquisitions through the U.S. Book Exchange," *Serial Slants* 2:7 (July 1951), and "Costs of Serial Acquisition through USBE," *Serial Slants* 2:11 (April 1952).

Transactions for the years noted above vary in cost from $4.50 per issue to $12.50 per issue contrasted to the USBE price of $0.45 per issue.

With the exception of free exchange of duplicates between libraries, or the receipt of needed gifts, there are few methods more economical by which to strengthen the library periodical collection.[15]

At another level are the associations which act as intermediaries between libraries. Unlike the USBE, they hold no stock. They operate internationally, nationally, and locally. The British National Book Centre, which is in the National Central Library, functions both internationally and nationally, as does the highly successful Medical Library Association exchange. The latter has as its British counterpart the Medical Exchange, which is housed in the Wellcome Historical Medical Library. The Resources and Technical Services Division of the American Library Association conducts the Duplicate Exchange Union, which was formerly under the Association of College and Research Libraries. The American Association of Law Libraries and the American Theological Library Association both have exchanges. Williams has proposed that surplus stock from these and other systems should be sent to the USBE.[16]

The Special Libraries Association, both nationally and through its chapters, has successfully sponsored exchange work. Nationally the Metals Division and the Science-Technology Division have organized programs.

Baer expresses the philosophy of exchanges when he says:

> Apart from interlibrary loan, possibly one of the proudest examples of the spirit of cooperation and mutual assistance among libraries has been the widespread utilization of duplicate exchange aiding the enrichment of library resources throughout the nation. In spite of the physical and clerical labor involved in entering an active duplicate exchange program, even a small one, the rewards can be more than equal to the effort invested.[17]

[15]Baer, "Serials and Out-of-Print Titles," p.50–51. Similar valuable statements are made by Edmund G. Hamann, "Out-of-Print Periodicals; the United States Book Exchange as a Source of Supply," *Library Resources & Technical Services* 16:19–25 (1972).

[16]Edwin E. Williams, "Exchange between Exchanges," *Library Journal* 86:186 (1961). For the USBE as a whole see also his *A Serviceable Reservoir: Report of a Survey of the United States Book Exchange* (Washington, D.C.: USBE, 1959).

[17]Baer, "Serials and Out-of-Print Titles," p.49.

The exchange role of the Smithsonian Institution is the shipment of books and serials in bulk between American and overseas libraries.[18] An American library sends exchange publications to Washington, and the Smithsonian absorbs the cost of shipping them overseas. Large quantities of United States government publications are shipped abroad in this way.

Gifts

The routines for handling gifts have so much in common with those for exchanges that the two functions are commonly the responsibility of a single individual or unit. When a serial is to be acquired, a decision must be made on the means of procurement: by exchange, gift, or purchase. Items for purchase go to the order librarians, but items which are to be sought by exchange or gift are generally referred to the assistant or unit responsible for the activities.

John Shaw Billings, first director of the New York Public Library, believed that the library should grow as much by gift as by purchase. Consequently an active gift section was a feature from the beginning. In 1968/69 it was estimated that 38 percent of the current periodicals received by the library came from the publishers as gifts. Few libraries can approach that figure; yet the possibility of a gift subscription should always be weighed before setting out to purchase an item.

Many government publications should be requested as gifts. Since World War II the percentage of documents which must be purchased has risen sharply, yet there is still a large quantity of free material that may be obtained directly from the issuing body, through a congressman, or otherwise. Some libraries are designated as depositories to receive federal and other documents in part or in full. In the case of United Nations documents, many of the depository sets are exchanges rather than gifts. An advantage inherent in blanket schemes of this kind is that in the acquisition department the record work for documents is much reduced or, on occasion, eliminated.

As with exchanges, gift correspondence and records should be kept separate from the general acquisition files. Gifts may to advantage be distinguished in the visible index by means of cards of a distinctive color.

In smaller institutions, notably in small public libraries, there may be an administrative problem with periodicals published and supplied

---

[18]For the Smithsonian's contribution see "Smithsonian International Exchange Service," *Unesco Bulletin for Libraries* 3:166, 168 (1949).

gratis by pressure groups, propaganda agencies, and sects. It may therefore be better to decline them and leave their collecting to historical research libraries.

Transfers

Government libraries constantly transfer to the Library of Congress serials which have been weeded from the shelves or are otherwise surplus stock. Similarly, the main library of a university receives transfers from departmental libraries, just as the largest library in a community will serve as the repository for serials or parts of serial sets no longer wanted in smaller institutions. Since many of the titles are already held by the recipient library, the duplicates can become useful exchange material. In a university library there is commonly a prima facie case for holding in a storage collection the serials which are transferred from a departmental library.

Preliminary Sorting

Serials which are acquired in quantity by gift, large-lot purchase, or transfer should be screened before they are searched or otherwise acted on. Often it is possible to discard numerous items in the process of preliminary sorting and in this way reduce the quantity of publications which must be searched in the checking records, the card catalog, or elsewhere. Recent almanacs, college and university catalogs, obviously unwanted unbound issues of periodicals, who's whos that are certainly in the bookstock already, and many other items can be eliminated at this stage, particularly when they are scrappy or in poor physical condition. Good common sense rather than competence with serials is what is required to make the preliminary discards. As a matter of fact, a nonserial librarian may even save a certain amount of work by being somewhat more ruthless in rejecting material than would a serial specialist who could, e.g., be aware of the possibility of rounding out an extra set of a publication. Moreover, much of the work of preliminary sorting is done in connection with mixed lots of monographs, pamphlets, and serials. The serial publications must be separated from the monographs and pamphlets, and in the act of separating it is possible for a nonserial librarian to make discards from each group. As a safeguard, of course, a serial specialist could be asked to run through the discards set aside by the nonserial librarian to make sure that no mistake has been made.

When the serials under consideration are particularly numerous and bulky, it is commonly wise to have a copy of the *Union List of Serials* or a similar tool on hand during the preliminary sorting so that more significant runs can be discarded informally or offered on exchange to other libraries whose sets can be completed or rounded out appreciably. However, should a duplicate set be in excellent physical condition, it ought to be compared with the volumes on the shelves. The condition of the stack set might indicate that a second copy should be added to the collection or that some or all of the volumes on the shelves should be replaced by the new ones. Such comparison of serial sets is of increasing importance in research libraries because of the steady wear and tear on journals in particular. Because periodical runs are both expensive and scarce, the effects of constant use over each generation, particularly for basic titles, is perhaps the most worrisome aspect of bookstock conservation. Hence the substitution of fresh copies for worn stock or the addition of a second set can be a particularly rewarding experience for the librarian.

Searching

The items that survive the screening process are then searched in the current checking record, the serial catalog, or the card catalog in order to determine whether they are duplicates or not, in part or in full. Before they are searched, they commonly need to be arranged systematically to bring together in sequence all the parts of a set. It is generally best to search with the item in hand, but when sets are bulky, they can be listed on P-slips and then searched from the listing plus the latest volume.

Three groupings result from the searching process: items that can be added to existing files, duplicates, and titles new to the library. For each category the searcher makes appropriate notations to help the individual who must decide whether the items are to be retained or not and to help those who must add volumes to the collection. In the case of add-to-cards material the searcher often withdraws the main catalog card when it is not a one-plus entry so that it can be adjusted directly. When this is not done, a searching slip is filled out with the call number of the set and a statement of holdings. Additions to serial files should not be made automatically unless a substantial run can be added or a significant gap filled, or a really valuable work is involved. Duplicate unbound sets are usually discarded forthwith. It is better for the searcher to mark a searching slip with an expression such as "dup." than to write it on the duplicate piece or pieces. One reason for this preference is that the designation can go once on a slip, whereas it might have to go on many pieces; another is that the duplicates may have exchange or resale value which should not be diminished by library markings. The designation can also be written on a slip, which is inserted in the top item in a collection of miscellaneous unbound material, all of which is then tied up in a bundle for disposition. Titles new to the library should be carefully scrutinized to see whether they should be added to the collections or whether continuations should be acquired. As an aid to the librarian who must make decisions, it is often desirable for the searcher to check one or more union list and to report on other sets in the region.

The searcher may well be one of the serial checkers. Much of the unsolicited mass of serials which comes into a library, being more or less current, naturally passes through the hands of the checkers. A desirable element of variety is included in their routine when they are called on to search the older serials as well. Otherwise it is customary to have subprofessional assistants, who specialize in serial searching, check the noncurrent publications. These assistants can be made responsible for current acquisition searching as well: items listed in *New Serial Titles—Classed Subject Arrangement*, items in secondhand catalogs, items in United States Book Exchange lists, and so on. In general, serial and monograph searching should not be combined because of the specialized nature of serial records and routines. In many libraries the catalogers must do their own searching, but this is an uneconomical plan unless the staff is too small to permit specialization of functions.

Sorting

New titles disclosed by the searching process fall into two classes: current titles to be considered for acquisition and older works which are new to the library. In each case acquisition decisions must be made, and the decision making is time-consuming. When it is ruled that a title is not worth acquiring, the issue in hand may be consigned to the file of sample numbers or else be rejected outright. In addition to deciding that an item is to be acquired, it should be specified at the same time whether the method should be exchange, gift, or purchase. No current publications should ever reach the catalogers without word on their continuation. It is only in exceptional cases that current publications should be added to the bookstock without provision for their continuing receipt.

Sorting of noncurrent serials is based on judgments as to the value of the works to the library. A bound file is more apt to be retained than an unbound one because it does not entail binding costs and is not likely to have missing numbers. A complete set or a long run may well be kept at the same time that a broken file might be discarded, especially when it is unbound. Retention of a broken file has to be justified twice over because the recording, preservation, and servicing of sets which are riddled with gaps cannot be other than troublesome and therefore unduly expensive.

Economy is achieved by making a series of cataloging decisions during the sorting process. For monograph series it must be stated whether the monographs are to be scattered by subject or held together as a set on the shelves, also whether they are to be analyzed in full or in part. At times it may be decided to limit the analyzing to author or subject analyticals or to postpone it indefinitely, in which case a record should be made so that unanalyzed sets can come up for review from time to time. When it is ruled that current publications are to be analyzed in part, an instruction must be put on the checking records so that each item as it is received will be brought up for an individual decision. It must be specified, too, whether the material is to be shelved in a special location, e.g., a branch or departmental library, the reference collection, or even a storage library. Occasionally a decision will be made to keep a second set or to substitute part or all of a set for the volumes on the shelves. The binding or bundling of a work must also be indicated, at times with special instructions about the treatment of supplements or the advertising matter.

Collation

A further function that the searcher or another subprofessional assistant can and should perform is the collation of incoming serial sets, whether they are bound or unbound. Collation calls for administrative control in several ways; otherwise there can be much duplication of effort, as is shown in chapter 16. Checking for the nineteen special points which are listed in chapter 10, as well as for other data, can occupy a major part of the serial cataloger's time unless the checking and collating are delegated to a subprofessional assistant who has been taught to watch for, check, and record the various technical details that are supposed to be investigated and noted. The cost of collation can be reduced with this division of labor and the cataloger's production increased at the same time. The difficulty in setting up and maintaining such a program is that the conscientious serial cataloger feels impelled to do the collation himself, otherwise some detail may be overlooked or some unusual feature passed by.

Dr. Harvey Cushing had occasion, in an address at the dedication of the Allen Memorial Medical Library in Cleveland, to speak of the problems of collation. He said:

> Few more arduous and difficult tasks confront a curator of books than that of collating and getting bound the heterogeneous medical periodicals which comprise, it is estimated, about two thirds of the volumes in such a library as this. They vary to an incredible degree, and with no seeming rhyme or reason other than the fancy of the publisher, in their form, in their make-up, in their pagination, in their dates of issuance. There are "new series" and "old series," with changes in volume number, with changes in name, with changes in format. What was once a quarto becomes an octavo; volumes may cover irregular periods of time and have no relation to the calendar year; some use Roman numerals, some Arabic; there may be several sets of paging in the same volume; there may be separately paged supplements, serially paged advertisements and text. Journals may suddenly go out of existence with no obituary notice, or without publishing the banns they may intermarry and reappear hyphenated, scarcely recognizable in their new alliance.
>
> How librarians with any bibliographical conscience keep their sanity under these circumstances should be more a matter of surprise than that they should exhibit testiness when you or I, as privileged characters, walk off with an unbound issue and forget to return it. It will be a happy day for these long-suffering persons when Ostwald's *Weltformat*—the size of the *Index Medicus*—comes to be obligatory for all medical journals.[19]

Some of the workaday situations experienced in the John Crerar Library bring out still further the problems which can be encountered in collation. Miss Dickinson says:

> So many of the foreign journals delight in wheels within wheels;—periodical after periodical, all inside of the one which bears on its cover a simple name like *British Journal of Photography, Chemiker-Zeitung, Elektrotechnischer Anzeiger, Deutsche landwirtschaftliche Presse, Journal of Botany, Revista de Archivos, Bibliotecas y Museos* —and dozens of others. This method of publishing half a dozen journals together, under one cover, and books within periodicals, is one of the heaviest taxes on our time, patience and accuracy. For at

[19]Harvey W. Cushing, *Consecratio Medici, and Other Papers* (Boston: Little, 1928), p.258–59.

the Crerar, it must all start right from the periodical room, all the sections be separated, and sent in the right direction. The English *Journal of Botany*, for instance, has since 1902, issued twenty-two different booklets, as separate paginations in the *Journal*—a few pages at a time, a single book sometimes running for several years. You can easily comprehend the care needed to avoid mistakes.

Der praktische Maschinen-Konstrukteur of Leipzig had at one time five regular separate journals in its insides,—all cataloged with different call numbers. And as for the Spanish library journal *Revista de Archivos*—words fail me. I have already puzzled over twenty-seven different supplements, some of which have been running for sixteen years, and have neither beginning nor ending. Of course they did all *start* sometime, though owing to an unfortunate gap in our files, I can't tell *when;* and apparently some of them are never going to end.[20]

Some types of publication, newspapers and government gazettes,[21] for example, are particularly troublesome to collate. How can one determine the completeness of a set when there is no bibliographical checklist to specify errors in numbering, issues not published, supplements, editions, etc.? In chapter 21 the difficulties of attempting to assemble a complete set of League of Nations publications, for want of a definitive checklist, are pointed out. And it is far from easy to say what constitutes a complete file of a newspaper in view of the facts that there may be a number of editions of the paper each day; that large amounts of text, including important features, may appear in early editions and not in later ones, and the other way around; and that published newspaper indexes cover the contents of only one edition a day, usually the latest.

The matter of editions is one of the problems of collation that must be faced before a newspaper file, two or more sets of which have been deposited by different institutions, can be considered for discard

[20]Sarah S. Dickinson, "Idiosyncracies of Periodicals," *Catalogers' and Classifiers' Yearbook* 2:95 (1930).

[21]During the German occupation in World War II, when France was divided in two, each part of the country maintained its own gazette, with obviously different text but with the name and volume numbering of the original work. With the liberation of France a single publication was re-established under the same name and with continuing volume numbering. As if the normal problems of collating gazettes were not enough, libraries were faced with the task of arranging the twin sets for the war period. What was the proper procedure? Should one or the other set be preferred for the main file with the other shelved as though it were a supplement at the end, or should the two editions be interfiled, volume by volume? Whatever solution might be found, collation of the French gazettes for the war years was and remains a nice problem.

in a cooperative storage library. The New England Deposit Library has, e.g., long runs of newspapers which apparently duplicate one another. They were deposited in the 1940s by the Boston Public Library and the Harvard College Library. It is a policy of the New England Deposit Library to retain only a single copy of duplicated publications, but no action has been taken on the newspapers because of the extremely onerous task involved in collating them before a decision on discarding can be given. In a newspaper office, too, the bound file of the office's own publication is usually for only one edition, and that, as a rule, the final one for each day.

On occasion the problems of collation may be so knotty that even the expert bibliographer is hard pressed to provide an answer, as the quest for an original copy of the *Ulster County Gazette* for January 4, 1800, shows.[22] At least seventy-five different reprints of this particular issue, which was the first newspaper to announce the death of George Washington, have been recorded. Just two copies of the original issue are known; they are in the American Antiquarian Society and the Library of Congress. Every year libraries are asked hundreds of questions about the issue. For that reason the Library of Congress has a printed statement about it, just as it has no fewer than seventeen information circulars to help in distinguishing reprints from originals in the case of unusual newspapers that have at times been reprinted in facsimile. In a different area, the newssheet *The English Mercurie* of 1588, which ostensibly reported the defeat of the Spanish Armada, is a nineteenth-century forgery, as is *The Weekeley Newes* of 1606.

Consequently it is generally wise for libraries to aim at checklists of newspapers and other complicated items. As indicated in chapter 8, a sheet checklist may be the most serviceable internal device for libraries, since it permits clear display of long and involved statements.

Gap Records

Whenever Harry Miller Lydenberg was complimented because the New York Public Library had a much-needed but scarce item, he was inclined to temper his satisfaction by recalling items that the library lacked. More than once he commented that it is more important for the librarian to know what his library lacks than what it has. Such is the philosophy, the natural reaction, of the acquisitive librarian,

---

[22]See R. W. G. Vail, "The Ulster County Gazette and Its Illegitimate Offspring," *Bulletin of the New York Public Library* 34:207 (1930), and "The Ulster County Gazette Found at Last," *Bulletin of the New York Public Library* 35:207 (1931).

and those concerned with serials should be acquisitive librarians par excellence. In line with this philosophy, a few libraries have attempted to compile lists of their serial gaps. Not only is this a major undertaking, but it may be something of a losing battle, too. For one thing, a gap record constitutes one more place to be checked when lacunae are filled, so that it becomes a difficult file to maintain. Marjorie Plant speaks with enthusiasm, however, of the gap record in the British Library of Political and Economic Science:

> In the course of cataloging a loose-leaf register of gaps is compiled. From time to time sections of this list of wanted parts are stenciled and issued to likely donors, newsagents, and second-hand booksellers, sometimes with the happy result that the words "with gaps" can be deleted from the catalog and the entry in the register of gaps withdrawn.[23]

In manual situations the compilation of special lists of gaps can be undertaken whenever time and staff are available. One of the great advantages of the computer is that up-to-date gap records can be run off whenever they are desired. Lists are usually sent out to libraries with which exchange relations have been established, and may in fact accompany a list of duplicates offered on exchange. Periodic drives of this kind are effective means of keeping serial files reasonably intact.

Renewals

Once a library is on the mailing list for a gift or an exchange serial, the item can be expected to come for an indefinite time without requiring any further communication, any renewal of the arrangement year by year. But serials which are acquired by subscription must generally be renewed at stated intervals, usually annually, unless

---

[23]Marjorie Plant, "Periodicals Procedure in a University Library," *College and Research Libraries* 3:63 (1941). The fact that this library can carry out the program that Miss Plant describes demonstrates one of the advantages which a special library has, or ought to have, over the general library. There is a spirit of enterprise in special libraries which leads to undertakings like this. An example of general library use of the method is furnished by the Enoch Pratt Free Library, which has reported conspicuous success in filling gaps in its holdings of United States documents. Mimeographed copies of its list were sent to 231 state, university, and other libraries, with the result that thousands of items were supplied, practically all as gifts. See its *The Reorganization of a Large Public Library* (Baltimore, 1937), p.19.

dealers or publishers are ready to accept orders on a "till forbid" basis. Some serials, such as yearbooks, are treated by dealers as standing orders and are billed as each issue is supplied.

Subscriptions are usually paid in advance. When a subscription is to be renewed, the notice from a publisher or society, or the list supplied by a dealer, must be checked against the visible index or its equivalent to see that the renewal is in order, the number of copies is correct, and all issues which should have come on the previous year's subscription have been received. If the check of a dealer's list is to be thorough, it should be made with his previous list in hand; otherwise there may be no opportunity to catch up on titles which have inadvertently been omitted or to make an effective comparison of prices. A dealer's list is usually received several months before the end of the calendar year; in large libraries a considerable amount of time must be expended on the renewal list. For the treatment of renewals in computerized systems see chapter 9.

Billing Information

In many libraries the record of payments for subscriptions is in a special card file which is arranged by dealers' names. Maintenance of a separate file is difficult to justify; every payment posted in it represents an additional step. On the other hand, little extra time and labor are involved in adding the price in a multipurpose record when renewal notices and invoices are checked against it. Most libraries post the subscription payments as a matter of course. But why? How many of them put the data to any purpose? There is little justification in libraries that secure bids, because it is the total price which wins the bid; and there is little or no reason for recording billing information for titles ordered through dealers who specialize in serials as long as the library retains its invoices for a number of years. On the rare occasion when anyone wants to trace the cost of a periodical received through a firm like Ebsco or Faxon, whose name is noted on the checking records, it is a comparatively simple matter to go through the file of invoices for that firm. Whenever possible, therefore, billing information for serials should be restricted to the file of bills and vouchers which have been approved for payment.

Now that price indexes for serials are published annually, there is less reason than ever for posting subscription payments. The same applies to automated systems; there is no gain in cluttering up the computer record for a serial by adding the billing information title by title.

In the price-index era the really important matter is to provide a separate budget for serial subscriptions, in some cases too for the acquisition of back sets. Then it is possible from year to year to budget for inflationary trends, as well as for normal growth in the serial collection, and at the same time to avoid encroaching on other acquisition funds.

Disposal of Surplus Duplicates

The amount of space and time which a library can devote to the disposal of surplus duplicates will in large measure determine its policy. Sufficient duplicates need to accumulate before a list is made, and the items continue to take up space while the lists circulate. The preparation of the lists occupies much staff time because of the accurate detail that is involved.

The treatment of surplus serials takes on the following forms:

1. Many items are held in the periodical room or elsewhere as possible replacements for missing or mutilated issues, or else as extra copies for circulation or assigned reading. Many of these duplicates can be disposed of once the current volume has been bound.
2. Material of slight consequence should immediately be classed as waste paper for disposal. Minor government publications often fall into this category; other items are recent college catalogs, unimportant mimeographed publications, unbound newspapers, and many unsolicited gifts.
3. Certain items that union lists of serials indicate may be of value to another library should be offered to that institution. Likewise items in specified subject fields may by agreement be regularly forwarded to a special library in the vicinity: legal serials, whether duplicate or not, may be sent to a law library, medical publications to a medical library, and so on.
4. Selected items of some importance or extent may be held and listed for possible exchange.
5. When a library belongs to an exchange program, such as that of the Medical Library Association, all surplus duplicates in the subject field tend to be listed, the reason being that another library may be looking for just a single issue to complete a volume for binding.

6. Serials which are still on hand after these various procedures have been carried out should be sent to the United States Book Exchange for it to screen or add to its great repository.

In private institutions, e.g., college and university libraries, proceeds from the sale of duplicates and waste paper may generally be added to the book funds. In public institutions the money must as a rule be paid into the municipal, state, or federal treasury. Accordingly, public institutions have good cause to promote exchanges, since publications which are received in return will benefit the library directly, whereas funds that are paid into the treasury rarely result in gain to the library.

Statistics

Book funds should be divided in such a way that there is a separate budget and accounting system for serials. From an administrative point of view it is desirable to have controls over serial costs for: (1) current subscriptions, including loose-leaf and other services, (2) back sets and reprints, whether in bound or microcopy form, (3) binding, and (4) exchanges. Commonly the head librarian takes a special interest in these classes of expense and wants to see and discuss monthly reports on them for control and planning purposes. In particular he needs to watch closely the amount spent for serial sets so that the research collection can be developed to advantage year by year and funds will be on hand when opportunity presents itself.

The most useful nonfinancial figures for control are those that take the form of an annual count of serials by exchange, gift, and purchase. Anything more than that can occupy much staff time to compile and serve little or no practical purpose. The real basis for excellence is laid when the required financial and nonfinancial control figures are complemented by a book catalog which discloses the actual serial holdings of the library.

Most libraries compile an annual tally of the pieces which have been added to the collection. This is intended to serve as a very rough index of the work load, particularly of the serial checkers. The real value of the tally is a moot question, however. A "piece" may be a single current issue or a title page and index; it may be a single issue in a long, unbound set; or it may be a bound volume. The same volume which counts as only one piece when it comes into the library bound could have counted as twelve or fifty-two pieces had it come unbound. Accordingly the count of pieces is far from being a precise index of work performance. It always seems a sad waste of effort when an assistant sets about the task of counting every single piece in an extensive unbound serial, the sole aim of the operation being to add to the tally of pieces received. Since the annual figures are at best nothing more than a rough yardstick, the number of pieces in any large lot should merely be estimated rapidly, or else the count should be given in terms of the volumes that are represented. Unless a librarian feels that the figures for pieces serve some useful purpose in his institution, he should consider dropping them.

Bibliography

Baer, Mark H. "Serials and Out-of-Print Titles," in Isabel H. Jackson, ed., *Acquisition of Special Materials*, p.41–59. San Francisco: San Francisco Bay Region Chapter, Special Libraries Assn., 1966.

Davinson, D. E. "Acquisition Practice," "Donations," "Disposal," in his *The Periodicals Collection; Its Purpose and Uses in Libraries*, p.111–17, 118, 156–63. London: Deutsch, 1969.

Grenfell, David. "Acquisition," "Checking, Completing Sets, Disposal," in his *Periodicals and Serials; Their Treatment in Special Libraries*, p.5–31, 55–99. 2d ed. London: Aslib, 1965.

Rippon, J. S., and Francis, S. "Selection and Acquisition of Library Materials," in Wilfred Ashworth, ed., *Handbook of Special Librarianship and Information Work*, p.35–78. 3d ed. London: Aslib, 1967.

Strauss, Lucille J.; Shreve, Irene M.; and Brown, Alberta L. "Acquisition," in their *Scientific and Technical Libraries; Their Organization and Administration*, p.38–56. 2d ed. New York: Becker & Hayes, 1972.

7

Theory and Practice of
Serial Checking

From time to time it is important to review and be perfectly clear on the principles which underlie daily work with current serials; this procedure is especially necessary when major changes in technology are in prospect. It would, for instance, be fundamentally wrong if the new computer technology were to be called upon to do little more than has been accomplished with manual systems, yet at greater cost. The prospective changeover should lead to marked gains, preferably also to reduced costs, objectives which can be realized only when there has been complete rethinking and clarification of underlying principles. Actually it is rather appropriate that such rethinking should take place periodically because there is little that is static in the body of literature that must be brought under control. As Marietta Chicorel says: "Mobility is the hallmark of periodical literature. Probability of change in publication is equal to the responsiveness to changes in conditions which this literature is so well able to report. Its mercurial quality is evident in the periodical literature which we report from all over the world."[1] Similar mobility is therefore natural in thinking about control methods for serials. Above all, the mistake of expecting the computer to conform to patterns which have been successfully established for the existing medium must be avoided. Newly conceived patterns must be devised if progress is to be made, if computer technology is to come into widespread use for recording the receipt of current issues of serials.

[1]Marietta Chicorel, "Introduction," in *Ulrich's International Periodicals Directory* (12th ed., 2d annual supplement; New York: Bowker, 1967), p.ix.

Checking in Current Issues

On the surface it may seem superfluous to engage in a mass checking operation every single working day when the majority of serial titles reach libraries regularly without complication. Suppose, e.g., that a library discovers that its copy of the *Atlantic Monthly* has come like clockwork ever since the first issue appeared in 1857; should it continue to go to the trouble of recording the receipt of the successive issues month after month, year after year? Should it anticipate still another century of what, with hindsight, could well be regarded as wasted effort? Reflection on cases like this might lead to a system of checking that applied only to titles which at one time or another in their history had been delinquent, and a title would then be presumed to be innocent until it was proved guilty of nonreceipt.

This approach is generally unacceptable to libraries, more particularly to research libraries which want to preserve their serial sets intact more or less permanently. Experience and expedience have both pointed to the general need for recording each issue as received. Nevertheless, there is some practical value in debating the point, since a library ought to be fully aware of the ends which its checking records serve. Likewise it should determine those titles which can safely bypass the established routines because in certain instances it may be permissible to dispense with the checking operation for specific publications or classes of material, notably those newspapers and other items which are not preserved, as well as mimeographed items such as press releases which lack the kind of serial numbering that would guarantee the completeness of the set to be preserved. There are distinct possibilities of these kinds, even in research libraries, for which the completeness and preservation of files must be safeguarded by every possible means.

The following are some cases for study. In considering them, due allowance should be made for the fact that both reader demand and alertness on the part of the public service staff will provide a measure, possibly an adequate measure, of follow-up in instances of nonreceipt.

1. Do current issues of library tools, like the *Publishers' Weekly* and the cumulative H. W. Wilson publications, need to be posted in the current checking records? The staff would quickly be aware of their nonarrival, especially when multiple subscriptions come in a single shipment. In the case of cumulative publications, like the *Readers' Guide to Periodical Literature*, why record issues that will soon be superseded and accordingly discarded?

2. Each day in many libraries a local newspaper is put out for public use immediately on receipt. Should the paper be checked in first at the risk of delaying its availability to readers? If it were checked in, special handling might then be necessary to get it to its destination promptly, thereby increasing the cost of the operation.

3. In many cases libraries receive the *New York Times* daily and in addition subscribe to the microfilm edition, discarding the actual papers when the microfilm is received. Is there any reason then for checking in the expendable daily issues?

4. Is it necessary for a library to check in the expendable issues of journals it acquires on the University Microfilms or the microcard plan whereby current numbers are no longer retained once a microreproduction has been received?

5. Popular titles, such as the *New Yorker*, are sometimes acquired in duplicate, one copy for current use, the other laid aside to constitute the file for binding and preservation. In such circumstances is there any point in entering each current issue in the checking records?

6. Quite often libraries are on mailing lists to receive marginal material such as press releases and propaganda. Regardless of whether the items are added to the permanent bookstock or not, should the cost of processing marginal material be increased by checking it in regularly? Note that items in this category may be weak serials in the sense that they lack the control elements by means of which the completeness of a set can be determined or follow-up work undertaken with any degree of certainty. In such cases the checking amounts to a mere tabulation of issues in the library.

7. When there is clearly little or no difficulty in securing a replacement copy, for the periodical room or for binding, is there any point in posting the receipt of current issues? Examples are a library's own publications, e.g., a staff bulletin, or those of a parent institution. Here the reaction might be a mixed one: issues of minor serials might go unposted whereas issues of major ones should be posted, in part because the library accepts the primary responsibility for reporting changes of title and other details to *New Serial Titles*.

Obviously there are individual items as well as classes of material whose titles can merely be listed in the current checking records but which do not have to be posted when issues are received. New York Public Library practice for these titles, applied somewhat less now that checking functions have been decentralized, is to mark the records with the instruction "Stamp and shoot"; i.e., once the instruction has been noted, the checker stamps the piece with the library mark of ownership and forwards it to its destination without further action. In 1951/52 what is now the National Agricultural Library eliminated the posting of service copies. Accordingly consideration should be given to the possible elimination of posting procedures for items such as: (1) current issues of cumulative publications which will eventually be replaced by bound volumes for permanent preservation; (2) expendable items such as daily newspapers that are not preserved, as well as newspapers and periodicals which according to plan are not retained once a microreproduction for them has been received; (3) a library's own minor publications or those of the institution to which it is attached; (4) professional tools that are not retained for preservation; (5) service copies; (6) titles for which an extra copy for binding is acquired and set aside; and (7) weak serials, i.e., items such as press releases and unnumbered monograph series whose notation does not permit firm follow-up procedures. Restriction of the practice is indicated whenever there is a positive answer to any of the following questions: Does the library have a sense of responsibility for the primary reporting of this title to the *Union List of Serials*? Is it difficult to obtain a replacement copy for an issue, either currently or when the volume is being prepared for binding? Is there reader pressure to know when an issue of the particular title is likely to be received?

While posting can be dispensed with in approved instances, titles should almost invariably be listed in the current checking records. The reasons are that there may be checking instructions which should be noted when an issue is received; for statistical purposes titles can readily be tallied among the serials received by exchange, gift, or purchase; accounting information may have to be recorded; and from a reference point of view it is desirable in a library to have a single listing of all current serials. In the emerging computer practice the listing is increasingly taking the form of a book catalog; all current serials should definitely be in that catalog.

The great majority of current issues should definitely be posted in the checking records. A basic reason for the maintenance of detailed checking records can be found in the word "control." The Library of Congress says: "The control of acquisitions in serial form has been one of the principal problems of the Library of Congress and, indeed, of all large research libraries, during the past 10 years."[2] Serials, except weak ones, by their very nature lend themselves to control measures. Apart from the types which have no fixed periodicity or seriality whereby the completeness of a file can be determined, in general the integration of a serial file received seriatim can be controlled by checking in each issue by date or serial number. By means of its checking records, then, a library can tell almost at a glance whether its files are complete or whether follow-up action should be taken. Should the checking records be dispensed with altogether, it would be much more troublesome, if not almost impossible, to reconstruct the story from the pieces themselves, scattered as they are throughout the collection, in use, at the bindery, and so on.

Pressure of reference demands is another reason why detailed checking records should be kept. Each working day in the Library of Congress, for instance, the Serial Record Division answers an average of two hundred telephone inquiries about the receipt of material or about the library's holdings of a given title; in fact, the service is so exacting that portable telephones, which can be plugged in at various points along the visible-index setup, have been in operation for many years. Whenever there is a heavy amount of reference consultation, there is an extremely strong argument for a book catalog of serial holdings, as well as for a computer system which can be tapped by both the reference staff and the serial checkers. A major finding of the West Virginia University Library is that reference pressure is taken off the serial record by the annual publication of a computer-generated list of all serial holdings in the university. Since the list is widely distributed, most readers already know what is available. Accordingly the serial record is consulted by the public service staff only when a problem arises. The first step, then, to relieve reference pressure on the checking records is to compile an annual list of all serials; the second is to install a computer checking system with access at various points in the library.

The handling of multiple copies that come from different sources or go to two different locations represents another reason why checking records are necessary. Then, when copy one is received, it is checked off and sent to its destination; later, when copy two arrives,

---

[2]*Annual Report of the Librarian of Congress* 1951 (Washington, 1952), p.80. The following comment is made on p.16 of the same report: "Serial publications (*i.e.*, periodicals and other repetitive publications) present a special problem because they are by far the most numerous publications the Library receives, and they are also the type of publication most used in defense-related research."

it too follows its appointed course and is neither discarded as an unwanted duplicate nor misdirected. Whenever unwanted duplicate issues appear from various sources, they can safely be discarded on the evidence of the records. On the other hand, replacement copies which have been ordered, especially to allow a volume to be bound, do not run the risk of being discarded as unwanted items because the records are specially marked to show that the replacements have been requested. Lastly, the current checking record constitutes the most businesslike way of verifying serial bills for payment.

These arguments in support of checking procedures are borne out by an experiment conducted in the Library of Congress, which showed that nearly two-thirds of the serials in the experiment could safely dispense with posting.

> In 1962 a study of the routing problem was undertaken, primarily to ascertain the feasibility of forwarding serials without checking them into the Record. It had been proposed that incoming serials could be handled more efficiently by having two types of serial records: 1) a Flexoline record giving title and disposition of the serial to be used for serials which were routed and then discarded; and 2) the Serial Record 3x5 card file to be used for all other material. A small sample of 1287 titles from the visible file was studied with respect to retention, source, and routing. The conclusion of this study was that 62.8% of the sampled records could be handled with a Flexoline Record. However, other considerations such as possible impaired reference service, increased cost, and the need for extra staff to maintain the Flexoline Record led to the abandonment of this proposal.[3]

Of all the reasons why libraries maintain, and should maintain, current checking records, two are of paramount importance. The first is that the records exist for control purposes: just as far as is practicable libraries must ensure that every single issue of a serial publication is received, and that prompt and decisive follow-up action is taken whenever an issue fails to materialize in the first instance. The second is that there must in many cases be written instructions about the way an item is to be treated once it has been received: to whom it is to be routed; what its current location or its call number is; whether it is to be analyzed; whether superseded numbers are to be discarded; and a whole series of other operational details.

[3]Library of Congress, *Serial Record Sample* (Washington, 1969), p.47.

Three Stages of Development

Many, but by no means all, checking systems have passed through two stages of development in the interval since the visible index was introduced. Most general libraries resisted the second stage, leaving it largely to special libraries to pioneer. Even so, rather surely, checking systems are about to enter into a third stage which in the course of time may well become as universal as the first one was.

The tendency was to adopt the cataloging form of name for the entries when the first visible indexes were installed in libraries in 1913. That form presented no particular problems as long as comparatively simple titles predominated, especially for English-language publications, and serial collections were relatively small. But in special and other research libraries difficulties arose as foreign-language titles increased in number and corporate entries multiplied. The latter tended to be troublesome in inflected foreign languages such as German. The difficulties were even greater when alphabets other than the roman were encountered, so much so that serials in Arabic, Chinese, Cyrillic, and other characters were commonly relegated to special files which were operated by language specialists. On many occasions the professional staff had to help the checkers by saying what the technical entry might be.

There is a certain advantage in utilizing the catalog form of heading on the visible index because it is common to the work of practically all parts of a library. One can go from the card catalog to the visible index and vice versa without complications when the headings agree, as for the most part they do in general libraries. From the standpoint of the checker, however, there are three significant handicaps in attempting to work with catalog entries in what is, after all, a mass operation.

1. Visible-index cards must be typed before the serials can be cataloged. This is true even in the age of first-issue cataloging, which for many libraries such as the Library of Congress came into being in 1971. Some libraries have put temporary entries in the visible index which must serve until the catalog cards have been made. Then, should the temporary and catalog entries disagree, the visible-index card must be changed. At the Library of Congress it is estimated that "such adjustments ... do not occur in

more than about ten percent of the entries set up."[4] From 1948 to 1968 the Library of Congress averaged 15,616 new entries a year in its visible index, so that the adjustments affected some 1,562 entries annually, or about 6.5 a working day. In 1968 the annual addition was 29,685, or 12.5 a working day.

2. Even though the catalog and visible-index entries are thus made to agree, it does not take long for differences to occur. Changes of heading or title occur faster than the serial catalogers can handle them, and on many occasions the catalogers have purposely waited before changing an entry to see if the new name is really stable. Yet the visible-index entry must naturally be maintained under the latest name. The tempo of work at the index, as in the current periodical room, is such that changes must be made immediately, not months or years later when the catalog may eventually be adjusted. The 1967 catalog code has helped in this respect by authorizing an additional catalog entry in place of recataloging whenever there is a change of name or title. The revised ruling increases the problem in (1) above, so that reliance on the catalog entry really calls for very prompt cataloging.

3. In any event the catalog entry is frequently too technical for efficient and rapid sorting of the second-class mail and for checking. Almost invariably the checkers are clerical assistants, not library school graduates who are versed in the intricacies of the catalog code. In many cases their language equipment is not of the best, and yet they are called upon to apply technical rules for entry to items in a wide variety of languages. Supervisors may fret over wasted time when they see their assistants fumbling for a technical heading, particularly one in a foreign language. Rather fortunately, there are not too many periodicals whose main title consists of a numeral, but how many checkers could find the entry for the French periodical *2000* without wasting time? On occasion the supervisors themselves have trouble in locating a heading when an assistant asks for help.

Take the case of a checker who does not know German, yet in the course of a day's work must check in a serial whose title is *Berichte*

[4]Paul L. Berry, "Library of Congress Serial Record Techniques," *Serial Slants* 3:15 (1952).

der Deutschen botanischen Gesellschaft. The checker may look under "Berichte" and "Deutschen," and from the latter be led on to "Deutscher" and "Deutsches" before backtracking to "Deutsche." To the trained librarian the form "Deutsche botanische Gesellschaft. Berichte" is perfectly clear and obvious, but the cataloging entry may not be so clear and obvious for the title *Berichte des geobotanischen Instituts der eidgenössischen technischen Hochschule, Stiftung Rübel, Zürich,* which the checker is supposed somehow to find under "Zurich. Eidgenössische technische Hochschule. Geobotanisches Institut. Stiftung Rübel. Berichte."

Part of the problem is, of course, the inordinate length and complexity of some corporate headings. A checker is inevitably delayed in his work when he must read through as many as four lines of the heading, and there is always the danger of recording an item on the wrong card when complex or verbose headings require careful examination in order to distinguish one title from another.

So the presence of technical entries in the visible index constantly interrupts the steady progress of the checker's work as he goes through the alphabet or his part of the alphabet. Undoubtedly technical entries nullify some of the advantages of the preliminary arrangement of serials, intended to facilitate the checking process. Also, when a checker's responsibility is for part of the alphabet only, items may have to be passed from one person to another because the technical entry was not correctly anticipated; and there can be interruptions to the work of the supervisory staff as they are called on to help in figuring out the cataloging entry.

In order to avoid this type of problem, some libraries entered on a second stage in the evolution of serial checking practice. For the most part these were special libraries, which as a group are more sensitive to direct methods than general libraries. They did not hesitate to deviate from the catalog entry whenever a more convenient or more natural form would help the checkers at the visible index. The following noteworthy practices at Standard and Poor's Corporation Library in New York City show how the entry is based not so much on the catalog entry as on the form which serves best in the daily routines: (1) A title entry may be preferred to a corporate entry, e.g., *Glass Containers*, supplemented by the name of the main series, the cataloging form being "U.S. Bureau of the Census. Glass containers." (2) A catchword, e.g., "Railroads," may be employed to group together all the publications of a given type. The entry can therefore be "Railroads—Revenue Freight Loaded & Received." This is neither a direct title entry nor the cataloging form, which is "Association of American Railroads. Car Service Division. Revenue freight loaded and received from connections." (3) Because they are a feature of Standard and Poor's Library, corporation reports are in a separate checklist, with various titles on the card for a corporation. Thus a single card with multiple listings suffices for advance reports, annual reports, income accounts, and press releases, whereas conventional systems would call for four cards or four overriding slips for these different titles.

Among the publications of corporate bodies the case for entry under title is strongest for periodicals, and especially for those periodicals which are commonly referred to by initials. The matter has been discussed by medical librarians on a number of occasions. In a medical library the individual who speaks of JAMA is apt to look for the catalog entry under *Journal of the American Medical Association*, rather than under the corporate entry, and many medical libraries list their periodicals in this way, both for cataloging and for the visible index. A somewhat similar plan has been followed in the British Library of Political and Economic Science, where

> title entry is adopted for all periodicals other than government publications (which are entered under the name of the country in alphabetical order of issuing departments). The *Journal of the Institute of Bankers*, for example, is so entered, with a reference from the name of the institute. As the only exceptions to this rule, "Report" and "Annual Report" are avoided as entry-words; the library contains several hundreds of bank reports alone, so that to concentrate *all* reports in one section of the catalog would probably cause the reader to turn away in despair.[5]

When a visible index was first installed in the Harvard College Library in 1939, it too followed direct and natural entries. The basic principle was that the form of entry should follow the wording as it occurred on the serials themselves. Thus "Bulletin of the New York Public Library" was preferred to the corporate entry because that was the wording on each issue. On the other hand, the *Bulletin* of the Association of Former Russian Naval Officers in America, Inc., was listed under the corporate name, not the title, because the name of the organization appeared first on the pieces, followed by the title. Accordingly the checker no longer had to struggle with grammatical constructions in foreign languages but quite readily found the entry under a form such as "Berichte der Deutschen botanischen Gesellschaft." Two exceptions were made to the general practice: United States federal documents were for the sake of convenience listed un-

[5]Marjorie Plant, "Periodicals Procedure in a University Library," *College and Research Libraries* 3:63 (1941).

der "U.S." followed by their titles, and annual (but not monthly or quarterly) reports went under the word "Report." When a difference existed between the catalog and visible-index entry, the cataloging form was put on the back of the visible-index cards; correspondingly, cards in the serial catalog gave variant visible-index entries, and in these ways it was possible to pass from one type of entry to the other with almost no inconvenience.

Note that under this pattern the checkers are no longer concerned with capitalization, punctuation, or other details that may weigh heavily with the cataloger but are out of place in a tool such as the visible index. The whole approach to the entry becomes an essentially practical one: the result is a heading in a hard-used work record, made as clearly, concisely, and naturally as possible for effective and efficient checking, which, after all, is the primary purpose of the visible index. This is the philosophy that applies, or should apply, whenever checking is a mass activity.

It is a matter of regret that the Library of Congress, which began along experimental lines when its visible index was installed in 1942, decided ten years later to revert to cataloging entries. In a memorandum on the editorial project in the Serial Record Division, dated 20 November 1953, the change of direction was justified as follows:

> Policy as to cataloging rules to be followed in setting up entries in the Serial Record has varied widely since the setting up of the Serial Record. This variation has resulted in inefficiency of recording information in the record and in getting information from the record. In some cases, information as to bound holdings on 3 by 5 cards is under one heading and information as to unbound holdings is under other headings in the visible file. One of the primary objectives of the project is to bring all the Serial Record into conformity with the A.L.A. rules of entry and thus into conformity with the other catalog controls of the Library.[6]

One serious consequence for the Library of Congress was that cross-references had to multiply. In 1969 there were no fewer than 46,180 references in the visible file, a record which ought to be able to function with virtually no cross-references.[7]

---

[6]Some of the changes that were made in the Serial Record can be found in *Serial Slants* 2:22 (Jan. 1952); see also the Library of Congress, *Departmental & Divisional Manuals* 20:55 (1952). *Serial Titles Newly Received*, the predecessor to *New Serial Titles*, had also embarked on experimentation; for the changes in it compare the introduction to the issue for December 1951 with that for January 1952.

[7]Library of Congress, *Serial Record Sample*, p.62.

However, the whole question of entry disappears in the third stage of development. Instead of a catalog or natural entry, a coding is preferred. The proposed Standard Serial Number is not the coding that should be adopted; it is too easy to transpose digits, and the SSN is not meaningful. While much remains to develop *Coden for Periodical Titles*, which is published by the American Society for Testing and Materials, its notation is short and meaningful and can be successfully applied to either manual or computer systems. The notation for *Berichte der Deutschen botanischen Gesellschaft* is BEDB-A; for the *Berichte des geobotanischen Instituts der eidgenössischen technischen Hochschule, Stiftung Rübel, Zürich* it is BGBI-A; for *Glass Containers* it is GLCO-A, and for the *Journal of the American Medical Association,* JAMA-A; for the *Library Quarterly* it is LIBQ-A; for the *Publishers' Weekly,* PWEE-A. When it comes to Cyrillic or other nonroman characters, the coding is a further simplification; e.g., it is TUGM-A for *Trudy Ukrainskogo Nauchno-Issledovatel'skogo Gidrometeorologicheskogo Instituta,* for which the catalog entry is "Ukrainskii Nauchno-issledovatel'skii Gidrometeorologicheskii Institut, Kiev. Trudy."

Considerable savings are possible, even in a manual checking system, when codings are added to the mailing addresses because the time-consuming process of alphabetizing the second-class mail and sorting out the nonserial segments is greatly simplified. Incoming serials can then be arranged by the codings on the wrappers, thus eliminating any guesswork about what the entry might be. At the same time cards in the visible index are arranged by the codings, not by the entries which have been customary in either of the earlier stages, but the coding should be followed by one or other type of heading for the sake of verification. In an automated system the savings are much greater because the alphabeting process is dispensed with altogether; input can be completely at random when codings are in effect, as is explained in chapter 9.

Typical mailing addresses can take a form such as:

Serial Record Division BGBI-A   Serial Record Division TUGM-A
Library of Congress   Library of Congress
Washington, D.C., 20540   Washington, D.C., 20540
U.S.A.   U.S.A.

In most libraries mailing addresses have been extremely unsystematic. Serials come addressed to the present director of libraries or acquisition librarian, as well as to their predecessors and anyone else who may have signed the original exchange, gift, or purchase correspondence; to the library in general or the acquisition department in general; to any section, e.g., for exchanges or gifts; and so on. It is no exaggeration to say that serials come into all too many libraries with a dozen or more different addresses on the wrappers; and mixed up with it all there can be professional journals for staff members and others, as well as all manner of items in no way connected with serials, e.g., books, prospectuses, and secondhand catalogs. The daily work of the entire acquisition department can benefit by the fullest use of codings.

When a serial is not already covered by *Coden for Periodical Titles*, or when a newly published title is to be acquired, libraries write to the American Society for Testing and Materials to find out what the coding is or will be. Then the official form of address for the library, complete with coding, can be included in all requests for serials by exchange, gift, or purchase.

For serials which bypass the posting procedures a number can be substituted for the letter coding, preferably in the series 9000–999. The figure 9000, e.g., could mean "stamp and shoot to the periodical room"; 9010 could mean "stamp and shoot to the reference desk"; and so on. Numbers can also be employed for items which come in bulk shipments, e.g., for United States federal documents—that is, until such time as the *Coden* designation is printed on the cover of the documents. In any event, the adoption of coding for the mailing address and the checking cards will simplify and speed up manual checking procedures, just as it can be a major factor in making automated systems competitive in cost with the visible index.

Two non-mnemonic alternatives to *Coden* came into operation in the 1970s. One is the International Standard Serial Number for booktrade use, which was mentioned in the previous chapter and which has been endorsed by the Resources and Technical Services Division of the American Library Association. The other is the eight-digit Standard Serial Number which the Library of Congress, beginning with 1972, is assigning to all items in the National Serials Data Program on the recommendation of the Standards Committee, Z39, of the American National Standards Institute. The argument for the SSN is that arabic numbers are more nearly universal than are alphabetical codings. However, neither the ISSN nor the SSN is suitable for manual or computer checking systems because they are longer, not mnemonic, and on both scores much more prone to error, as has proved to be the case with the International Standard Book Number for monographs. Insofar as *Coden* is mnemonic to a high degree, in addition to being desirably shorter, it tends to have its own correction devices and is in general apt to be comparatively error-free. Very definitely *Coden* is the system to use for checking purposes and to aid in developing, not ISSN or SSN; and since it is clearly superior in the checking function, it is preferable for all library operations. It is something of a calamity that three codes are in use for library work with serials when one would serve adequately.

Arrangement of Entries

Since the visible index is a heavily used work record, its entries in either the first or second stage of development should be filed in such a way that they will most effectively serve the requirements of the people who work with it extensively. The more simple and natural the arrangement can be, the better. Most libraries do as the Library of Congress does: they arrange the visible-index entries according to the filing rules for the card catalog. Those rules are more technical than is desirable in a work record which is operated by clerical staff; they should be adjusted so that the mass operation of checking can be expedited.

Several special breakdowns may be desirable.[8] Should serials be received in bundles as well as individually, a special section at the end of the alphabet saves time and effort as the items in the bundles are checked in. Some overseas dealers, e.g., in Germany, Great Britain, and the Netherlands, accumulate current periodicals and forward them to a library in weekly packages. When the bundles are opened, it is convenient to record the items in a tray or trays under the name of the dealer instead of going all through the alphabet for a relatively small number of pieces. In this way both items and bills are checked off rapidly and renewal lists are handled extremely simply. For consultation purposes there should be a reference from each title to the dealer file, either in the main alphabet or in a supplementary record such as a title-a-line visible reference index.

In a university which has an extensive publication program time can be saved for the checkers when the university's serial publications are held together under its name, regardless of whether they

[8]In the original visible-index installation in the Harvard College Library the main alphabet was supplemented by the following breakdowns: Allen (Great Britain), Harrassowitz and Koehler (Germany), Harvard University publications, the Organization of American States, Slavic titles, Stechert-Hafner, United Nations documents, and United States federal serial documents.

would normally be cataloged under the name of the institution or under their own titles. Frequently there are multiple copies of the publications as well as a number of locations to which they are sent; there can be personal contacts and special arrangements associated with their procurement; so for these and other reasons it may be desirable for one staff member to be responsible for the handling of all the university's publications, and that person's work is facilitated when the records are held together as a unit.

In some libraries Slavic serials in the Cyrillic alphabet are listed as a group, even though the entries are transliterated. Such serials are more generally interfiled in the main alphabet. There is a stronger argument for segregating titles in Oriental languages because language specialists are more commonly called upon to check them in. For titles in special language breakdowns it is not necessary to put references in the main part of the alphabet or a supplementary file.

The biggest question of arrangement is whether to interfile document and nondocument serials or to keep them independent of each other, with document specialists in charge of the document file, which is in another location. In almost every instance there is nothing to gain and much to lose when documents are segregated from nondocument serials. A common staff that must keep all the work on a strictly current basis, regardless of type, and organized so that one person can step in when another is absent will maintain the checking operation more satisfactorily in every respect than a divided staff can possibly do. These observations apply even when a library maintains an uncataloged collection of government documents; the serial documents must still be checked in issue by issue, and the regular checkers can perform that function better, often on better equipment, than the document staff can do, more particularly when the latter is composed of part-time help.

Third-stage codings are arranged alphabetically and are followed by the numerical listings. The key to the arrangement is the alphabetical list of titles in *Coden*; but since they are not necessarily in cataloging form, some skill will have to be employed in consulting the list. It is possible that libraries with manual systems should interleave and annotate their copies so that they can always have ready access to the catalog entry, but of greater value will be the widespread production of book catalogs of serials which will include the *Coden* symbols. In automated systems it is possible at frequent intervals to run off printouts arranged by the codings, then once a year to produce a printout in the form of a book catalog which is arranged by author and title.

References

Since space in a visible index is at a premium, references are and should be held down to a bare minimum. Otherwise they can easily occupy a fourth of the space and become a factor in overcrowding of the trays. They tend to remain in a visible index long after their usefulness has passed. Their multiplication is clear evidence of the overfrequent choice of ineffective headings, many of them being for older titles which under the 1967 cataloging code would no longer be under a technical form of entry.

The existence of a book catalog for serials dispenses with the need for references in the visible index because the book catalog can readily supply any needed references. It is possible to fill the top tray in each visible-index cabinet with title-a-line strips which provide the references. Another method is to have on top of every second cabinet a title-a-line "Insite Index" with the references that relate to each pair of cabinets.

Enumerative Statements of Holdings

There are two ways of characterizing serial holdings on visible indexes: one is the enumerative statement, by means of which each individual issue is registered seriatim; the other takes the form of a summarized statement of the same data. The enumerative statement lets readers and staff know precisely how many issues there were for each volume; the summarized statement lets people assume the completeness of every volume, a completeness which the checking records could substantiate by virtue of their enumeration of the parts.

The checking records for the first four volumes of *Serial Slants* demonstrate the nicety of enumerative records, but at the same time they show how much easier the summarized statement is for ordinary and rapid comprehension.

v.1,	1950.	1/July	2/October
	1951.	3/January	4/April
v.2,	1951.	1/July	2/October
	1952.	3/January	4/April
v.3,	1952.	1/July	2/October
v.4,	1953.	1/January	2/April
		3/July	4/October

The enumerative statement makes it clear that volume 3 was complete in two numbers, a fact which the summarized statement "v.1–4" takes for granted. There are numerous similar cases of irregularities in the publication program for which the detailed checking records afford the only means of establishing the number of issues which make up a complete volume. There are also cases in which the original serial numbering or date was printed on the spine only and was lost when the volumes were bound, leaving the checking records as the sole source of evidence, insofar as they still survive.

An axiom of serial checking is that the records should be so compiled currently that in later years they can be relied upon implicitly. The time to determine that volume 1 is complete in seven issues, volume 2 in ten, and volume 3 in eleven is when the relevant issues are first handled. The later history of the library file of a serial, the investigations of a future bibliographer, have to depend on the authoritativeness of the primary checking records.

Data on Visible-Index Cards

In many libraries it is customary to type the heading and other key information in the visible margin on both the face and back of the checking card. Thereby the details are visible at a glance as soon as a tray is opened, regardless of whether the cards are lying in their

The visible index in the Library of Congress, the largest library installation in the world. More than a million pieces are processed annually, and a system of portable telephones is necessary to answer some two hundred requests for information daily.

normal position or are turned back for consultation. This duplication is desirable when postings of any kind must be made on the back of the card; it should be avoided when no checking details go on the back of the card. Herein lies one of the advantages that accrue from the use of overriding slips; only rarely when they are employed must information of any kind go on the back of the permanent card, and hence there is no occasion for typing the heading on the back of the card for finding purposes.

Since the number of characters that can go in the visible margin is relatively small, abbreviations may be freely adopted in transcribing the entry as long as they are perfectly clear. It is in order to contract some words, to use the ampersand, to omit most subtitles, and to eliminate unnecessary words and virtually all marks of punctuation. For instance, "SEATO" should by all means be preferred to "Southeast Asia Treaty Organization," "UNESCO" to "United Nations Educational, Scientific, and Cultural Organization," and "UN" to "United Nations."

The information given on visible-index cards in the Library of Congress represents the widest range of data usually recorded. It includes the following items, not all of which are needed by most libraries:

1. The basic-entry cards give:
   a. The heading or title by which the publication is identified in the Serial Record Division; since 1952 this has been the cataloging entry, but prior to that date it was a direct heading, so that differences between the two headings were indicated on the basic-entry card.
   b. The record of serial titles which are not retained by the Library, with an indication of their disposition.
   c. Sufficient bibliographical information to distinguish similar titles from one another; the place of publication usually serves to distinguish between homonyms.
   d. The essential bibliographical history of the item.
   e. The number of sets which are retained in the permanent collections.
   f. The call numbers for the permanent sets and the location of service copies.
   g. The custodial division which services unbound issues or volumes.
   h. The next routing station for processing, e.g., the Binding Division, Labeling Unit, or Preliminary Cataloging Section; also any intermediate stations for entry in accessions lists.
   i. Treatment decisions for monograph series.
2. Bound holdings that are permanently retained are recorded on special overriding slips.

3. The checking overriders show:
    a. The posting of issues or volumes currently received, whether bound or unbound.
    b. The sources from which copies are received.
    c. A record of binding progress.

   When an overriding slip is full and all items on it have been bound, the statement of holdings is consolidated on the special overriding slip mentioned in (2), and the full checking slip is then destroyed.[9]

Checking Practices

In the first two stages of development the second-class mail should be opened on a long counter or table when it is at all extensive. Wrappers should be slit open by means of a paper knife if the title of the serial is not evident at a glance; the wrappers should be inserted in the pieces and not discarded until the issues have been checked off, otherwise essential checking information may be lost. For preference the checkers themselves should open the wrappers and do the preliminary sorting, though in bigger installations other acquisition assistants may help with the operation in order to expedite matters.

Items for individuals and special destinations should be sorted out and sent along for delivery. Letters about serials, renewals, etc., should be set aside for action after the daily checking process has been completed. Rush items should be collected for priority checking; a list of them can be compiled and posted for ready consultation, though of course in third-stage coding a symbol can be employed to indicate that a serial should be given priority treatment. Bundles from dealers should likewise be segregated and accorded priority.

In the preliminary arrangement items are sorted by first letter of the entry only. Resultant groupings can then be placed beside the relevant cabinets so that the checkers can carry out the precise arrangement while sitting in position. Wrappers can now be cut for items which did not need to be opened earlier.

The posting of rush items and serials which come in bundles should precede the strict alphabetizing of the nonrush material. Among the rush items may be current newspapers which bypass the checking activity, as well as national bibliographies which should go to selection officers without delay. Bundles should be accorded priority be-

[9]For Library of Congress checking practices in general see its *Departmental & Divisional Manuals* 20:44–63 (1952). Note, however, that this manual was compiled before the Serial Record Division reverted to the cataloging entry for its visible index and before the editorial project was begun.

cause they can be checked off rapidly in their own tray and because they should be held together as units so that the source of no item is left uncertain. Apart from rush items and bundles, checking should proceed in the normal alphabetical sequence without backtracking until the main job has been completed. In general it is better to defer action on items that prove to be out of order; the correct entry should be jotted down and a fresh alphabetical arrangement should ensue.

In manual systems in the third stage of development the codings on the wrappers are utilized for the rapid arrangement of the serials for checking. However, the opening of the pieces can be left for the checkers to do as they post the items. In computer systems which operate with codings on the wrappers the preliminary arrangement is eliminated because serials can be processed at random.

Checkers usually stamp and mark each piece as it is posted. On the other hand, stamping can be done more economically as a separate operation after the checking process has been completed; but it may be better for the checkers to do the stamping so that the job, when it is done, does not become monotonous and therefore careless. The checkers prepare or insert riders and routing slips when necessary, and all the checking directions on the visible-index cards are carried out precisely.

When the checker has been once through the alphabet, or his part of the alphabet, the serials may be in four groupings:

1. Pieces which have normally been posted, stamped, and otherwise marked are ready to go to their destination.
2. Items that were out of order in the initial posting are now alphabetized and checked off or passed on to another checker.
3. Unwanted duplicates are accumulated for a decision on their disposition.
4. Titles which are not listed in the visible index must, after the checking process has been completed, be checked against the decision file, the old serial record, or the official or public catalog, or else be sent to the appropriate officer for a selection decision.

Should gaps be noted, claims are made out immediately by the checker. In some libraries the checker jots down the details and passes them on to a clerk-typist after making a record of the claim on the visible index. There are two advantages in having the checker make the claims: first, addresses can be taken from the piece in hand, since its address is almost surely correct; and second, there is then no risk of delay in an operation that all too often suffers from neglect.

Checkers should have pads on which to note points that arise in the course of their work. These include: changes of name or title which require adjustments on the basic entry card as well as refiling, the conversion of a temporary to a permanent record, and full overriding slips to be replaced or replacements to be made for full checking cards. All such matters, with the exception of gap work, should be attended to after the orderly process of checking has ended. The process should not be interrupted for details that can be cared for later because the principal objective of the checkers is to get the mass of new serial issues to their destination as rapidly as can be. Material that does not originate in the mail—large gifts, transfers, etc. —can also be left for the clean-up period since it does not have to be processed rapidly; so too can letters, renewal notices, and other miscellaneous items. Quite generally the checker makes a tally as the work proceeds so that the number of pieces added to the library can be recorded.

Methods of posting in the Library of Congress are as follows:

> When recording serials in the Visible File the accessioner normally enters the issue on the checking sheets rather than on the basic entry card. The method of recording used by the accessioner is largely determined by the checking pattern originally established by the Serial Record catalogers. Serials are recorded by the most important sequence indicia, which commonly are numbers or dates. It is at times advisable, however, to record material by both numbers and dates, e.g., official gazettes. The checking sheets are designed either for number or date checking, with several varieties for each ... but these sheets may easily be adapted for checking by both number and date. In the method of checking by number *or* date, a check mark ($\sqrt{}$) is placed beside the number or in the date box; where checking is by *both* number and date, a date is placed beside the number or a number is placed in the date box. The checking pattern is planned to give sufficient information for proper identification in as economical a manner as possible.[10]

This practice is well conceived. The last sentence of the quotation should be the guiding principle for all checking systems. The posting procedure is simplified and speeded up when a simple check can take the place of an issue number. Subseries should be recorded regularly, but the main series can usually be overlooked; only in rare instances do both need to be noted. When two or more copies are received simultaneously, they can be checked off as one. However, should multiple copies be received at different times and from various

[10]Library of Congress, *Departmental & Divisional Manuals* 20:50 (1952).

sources, it is necessary to insert a check for each. Two or three checks are clear enough, but numbers should be preferred when there are more than three copies. Alternatively, extra overriding slips or even checking cards can be pressed into service, each copy being posted completely separately, but this practice is desirable only in unusual circumstances.

Because it is of the utmost importance in research libraries to guarantee that files of serials are complete, and because enumerative statements are not always easy to peruse, it is highly advisable to add a symbol to the checking record once a volume has been completed, title page and index and all. A red check by the volume number or year or a ring around either can act as this quickly interpreted convention; or a special column can be provided in which a red C, for "complete," can be inserted. Such a symbol can save much time and add a measure of assurance whenever a complicated slip or card is scanned for gaps or holdings. In itself the symbol is an adjunct to follow-up work, just as it is an aid when the summarized statement is being brought up to date on the permanent records. Attention to this one small detail in the course of the day's work will prove in the long run to be a valued labor saver.

Some libraries, particularly special libraries, like to record on the visible index the date of receipt for each issue, even though the pieces themselves are stamped with the date. The day and month (but not the year) are generally given, usually in the form 2/24; they are written in the checking squares. The reason for doing this is that the date can answer occasional requests for the approximate time a new issue may be expected. Much extra work is involved in adding the date of receipt to tens of thousands of postings annually; accordingly it should be added only for low-frequency serials, e.g., quarterlies and annuals, though possibly monthlies too. General libraries should avoid the practice, and it is unnecessary in any visible index equipped with a progressive tab system. Checking slips and cards are very much clearer when they are not cluttered up with the date of receipt in each square, and there is real gain in having clear, simple records, especially for follow-up or scanning purposes.

One other detail that can go in the checking squares is the report on the receipt of analytical cards for monograph series which come on standing orders from the Library of Congress. When the regular posting is done in black with pen or pencil, a good convention is to post the arrival of the cards in color, possibly red. Should the cards come after the piece to which they relate, they can be written up and filed immediately in the card catalog; should they come before the piece, they can be filed in a special tray and activated when the item arrives. In the latter case the system can function as a follow-up device so that the dealer will be prompted to supply a work which the Library of Congress has already received.

With automated systems there has been a tendency to add greatly to the checking practices. The actuality should be the very opposite; otherwise the cost of the operation mounts and the printouts become difficult to read. Computer practices and principles are discussed in chapter 9.

Follow-Up Systems

The two fundamentals of a good checking system are completely reliable records and a vigorous and enlightened follow-up program. General libraries frequently experience great difficulty in training the checkers to institute prompt and systematic follow-up. Sometimes the difficulty results from overelaborate acquisition routines that hamper claiming and replacement work; sometimes the cause is simply pressure of work, a state of affairs that is all too common; and sometimes it is fatigue or neglect on the part of the staff. Supervisors must constantly remind their staff that incomplete serial files are a burden to a library at every turn: they inconvenience the reference and circulation services; prevent volumes from being bound on schedule and may even bring about physical damage or further loss to the unbound parts; increase the cost of acquisition work because of the measures that may eventually have to be taken to try to obtain a missing item; and make the cataloging more expensive than need be because of broken records, as well as additional processes such as bundling.

Follow-up work can be based on a system of tabs attached to the checking records, or it can be relatively informal. Tabs come in two basic styles: those that clip on and those that slide along the visible margin. The clip-on tab is intended chiefly for nonvisible records. It acts as a signal to show that a missing number has been written for and that further action may be necessary if the gap is not filled within a reasonable time. These tabs are generally made of metal for longer life. For visible indexes, however, transparent plastic signals are preferable so that the data in the visible margin which they may cover will not be obscured. Sliding tabs may specify either the date when the last issue arrived or the date when the next one is due.

The real motive for installing a visible index in the British Library of Political and Economic Science was to be able to tell at a glance when follow-up action should be taken. According to Marjorie Plant:

> This has been achieved by a simple system of tabbing: not, of course, by the old-style tab which took the clumsy a minute or more to

fix in place, but by one held in a transparent groove and flicked to its new position in a matter of two seconds. The bottom edges of the marking-off cards have a blank space at each end but are otherwise divided into twelve monthly divisions and five weekly divisions (as there may be five Tuesdays, say, in any one month). In one of the monthly and one of the weekly divisions of each card a green tab has been fixed. In the space at the extreme right a tab of another color signifies a particular year. Taken together these three tabs show, correct to the nearest week, *not the date of issue* of the periodical part last received nor of the next one due, *but the date when the next part is due to reach the library.* A black and white striped tab at the extreme left of the card signifies that, owing to irregularity of publication, this date may be uncertain, while the insertion of an orange one shows that, the periodical in question having become overdue, action has been taken.[11]

Special libraries generally favor the use of tabs on their visible indexes, while general libraries are more inclined to frown on them. Despite Miss Plant's "two seconds," the general library is apt to consider them an expensive device to operate. When the New York Public Library installed its visible index in 1919, it decided against a signaling system because it estimated that the equivalent of one full-time checker would be required to manipulate the tabs.

There must at least be informal, productive follow-up when tabs are considered to be too time-consuming. When the task is done informally, the checkers, or special follow-up assistants, go through the entire visible index at stated intervals looking for overdue items. If at all possible, with this method the file should be completely checked every quarter. In most cases more frequent checks are not thought to be necessary because the regular checking procedures tend to disclose most run-of-the-mill gaps; that is, if in recording receipt of the June issue it is noticed that the May number has not been checked in, then follow-up action is naturally taken. In any event each library must determine for itself the time interval that is to elapse before action should be started on overdue publications of various frequencies. The interval for overseas publications is appreciably longer than for domestic ones and depends on the part of the world from which the item in question comes. Also for high-frequency serials, e.g., a weekly, the time interval should be shortened, just as it should be lengthened for low-frequency ones.

The heart of the matter is to see that steps are really taken to

[11]Marjorie Plant, "Periodicals Procedure in a University Library," *College and Research Libraries* 3:60 (1941). Miss Plant goes on to give several examples of how the signaling system operates. For a special study of signaling procedures see R. M. Jacobs, "Focal Point: A Composite Record for the Control of Periodicals Using a Visible Signalling Device," *Journal of Documentation* 6:213 (1950).

procure missing or replacement copies, whether on evidence derived from daily routines or from a periodic review. The advantage of a signaling system is that the checker is never allowed to forget the need for prompt follow-up action.

When the checkers are responsible for follow-up action, they should have on hand a supply of postal cards that can be filled out quickly and simply on the basis of evidence on the checking records. The cards should be filled out and dispatched with as little formality as possible, preferably with none, because claim procedures should be automatic.

There should be similar procedures for copies to replace items that have been lost or mutilated in the periodical room or elsewhere. Acquisition department routines should be streamlined to permit essential ordering of this kind to be carried on in a routine fashion. The periodical room staff should begin action by filling out a postal card, which must be routed through the checkers so that the replacement action and its date can be noted on the visible index; in this way the replacement copy can be sent to its proper destination when received. If these procedures are not followed, there is the risk that a replacement copy will, on arrival, be discarded as an unwanted duplicate. A symbol in the appropriate checking square, denoting that a replacement has been requested, can serve as a rule. The symbol should preferably be in a distinctive color. An alternative is to clip or otherwise attach a P-slip or other memorandum to the checking record.

So important is it for a research library to have a trustworthy follow-up system that in larger institutions thought should be given to the possibility of having a part-time or full-time assistant whose responsibility is to read the files continuously looking for items on which follow-up action should be taken. The follow-up procedure is reminiscent of the way in which shelves are read to keep the book-stock in order. In too many instances such a follow-up operation has been considered a secondary function of serial librarians who, if the truth were known, are so fully occupied with their primary tasks that talk of secondary functions is academic. Yet ways must be found of making it a primary function, just as it is when signaling systems are in operation. Without doubt special libraries devote more attention to follow-up activities than general libraries do; nevertheless all libraries ought to be able to say with Marjorie Plant: "The checking for overdues is carried out weekly; the whole process occupies only a few minutes."[12] Achievement of that goal is in the offing because one of the great advantages of an automated system is that the computer can be programmed not only to note delinquent items but also to write out the follow-up notices.

Preparing Checked Serials for Use

Once the pieces have been checked in, they should be treated according to a general plan or according to the directions which are on the visible index. The library's stamp is put on the front cover of unbound serials or on the verso of the title page of bound items. The stamp is often combined with the date of receipt; sometimes even the hour is specified. The stamp should be designed as attractively as can be, and it should be applied with care so that the result is neat and text or illustrations are not encroached upon. When multiple copies are received, some of which are service copies, it may be desirable to apply distinguishing marks so that service copies do not eventually find their way into the permanent collections. A simple device is to add "copy 1," "copy 2," etc., to the permanent copies and "copy A," "copy B," etc., to the service copies.

Riders may be inserted in the pieces to serve a variety of purposes. They may be mimeographed or printed, especially when they convey routing instructions, or they may be blank slips on which the checker writes or stamps the information. Their most common uses are to indicate that an item should circulate to an individual or a number of individuals and to convey cataloging data, particularly for monographs in series. A rider may also indicate that leaves are to be cut. It is unwise to circulate serials with uncut leaves because readers are apt to damage the pages when they themselves do the cutting, usually without the benefit of a paper knife. In some libraries unbound serials are sent to the bindery to have their edges trimmed by machine. More often leaves are cut by periodical room attendants or by attendants in various parts of the library whose duties are light enough so that they can undertake a certain amount of busy work of this kind.

Some items go through the end processes that are described in chapter 12, e.g., bound volumes that require analyzing, bookplating, lettering, shelflisting, etc. The checkers add the call numbers to annual reports and other publications that are to go into manila-rope bundles, pamphlet boxes, or other containers in the stacks; and on occasion a new container must be supplied, usually when a report from the stack says that the existing container is full. Call numbers are as a rule not added to items which are to go to a periodical room, but shelving symbols may be put on the pieces when the current periodicals are arranged in broad subject groupings.

¹²*Ibid.*, p.61.

Binding Records

In a multipurpose system the dates when volumes are sent to and returned from the bindery are added to the visible-index cards or slips. The alternative listing is usually in the binding-records section or the circulation file. In the Research Libraries of the New York Public Library a special file was formerly maintained in the General Research and Humanities Division to show when volumes were sent to the bindery and returned from it; in this way readers would not be sent to the Periodicals Division for issues that were no longer there. That file no longer exists; the reference librarians obtain the information for readers by calling the Central Serial Record.

Notes from Dealers and Publishers

The following are some of the notes that libraries list on the checking records as part of the bibliographical history of a set:

> The issue for June 1971 completely o.p.
> No. 273 misnumbered 278.
> v.1, no.3 never published.
> v.6 complete in five numbers.

The notes are usually documented by addition of the name of the dealer or other source, followed by the date of the communication. Not infrequently the information comes in response to a follow-up inquiry. Some of the notes are duplicated on the catalog cards; sometimes the information disappears altogether when the checking records are discarded.

Bibliography

Berry, Paul L. "Library of Congress Serial Record Techniques," *Serial Slants* 3:14–18 (1952).
Library of Congress. *Order Division.* (Departmental & Divisional Manuals, no.20) Washington, 1952.
———*Serial Record Sample.* Washington, 1969.
Plant, Marjorie. "Periodicals Procedure in a University Library," *College and Research Libraries* 3:57–63 (1941).

Manual Methods
of Checking

In the early years of the century catalog cards which measured
7.5 x 12.5 centimeters or 3 x 5 inches were the common medium for
recording the receipt of current issues of serials. The cards were
printed in appropriate forms to match the frequency of issue; they
were housed in small catalog cases, about a thousand cards to a
drawer. The system worked reasonably well because at that time the
number of issues received each day was not great by contemporary
standards. It broke down as the number of current titles multiplied,
but it lasted as late as 1939 in the Harvard College Library and even
several years longer at the Library of Congress. The National Agricultural Library employed it until 1971, thanks to a remarkably fine
series of adaptations. Almost all of the card systems were superseded
by the visible index, which remained as standard equipment right into
the computer period and still can hold its own with most computer
programs, at least in terms of economy and checking efficiency.

Several libraries installed visible indexes in 1913, soon after the
equipment came on the market. Two types were exhibited at the
American Library Association Conference held in Washington, D.C.,
in 1914. They gave rise to the following comment:

> It would be extremely hazardous to predict that the standard size
> card would ever be forced to give over to any other indexing device
> any of the ground it has gained as an essential feature of library
> equipment. There seem to be, however, very good possibilities that
> the visible indexing devices manufactured by the INDEX VISIBLE
> COMPANY and by the RAND COMPANY may come to fill an
> important place in library equipment, supplementing the card
> index. Many large business offices have recognized the importance
> of these devices, enabling them to index long lists of names in very

small space in such a way that any name on the lists can be quickly and conveniently found. Both the INDEX VISIBLE and the RAND VISIBLE INDEX are made in many sizes and styles, adapted to so many purposes that they seem to give good promise of satisfactory adaptation to library purposes.[1]

The Committee on Library Administration, under the chairmanship of Arthur E. Bostwick, which sponsored the exhibit, added:

> The committee will not undertake to say what the future possibilities of these indexes in library service may be, but it would seem as though the devices were of sufficient interest and offered sufficiently good possibilities for adaptation to library service at some time in the near future, if not at present, to justify their inclusion in the exhibit and to make it worth while for librarians to give them careful consideration.[2]

Since 1913 a number of firms have manufactured visible indexes. The Index Visible Company, which was established in New Haven, Connecticut, in 1912 by Professor Irving Fisher, merged with Remington Rand in 1925. The differences among the products of the various firms are not as great as might be anticipated, due in some measure to the fact that one company may hold a patent which another arranges to use. The basic difference is between the Kardex type, which sets the checking card into a pocket and thereby limits the capacity of a drawer, and the Acme type, in which the card hangs independently from a wire or other attachment. Some manufacturers carry both models. Among the leading American makes are Acme, Globe Wernicke, Kardex, Postindex, Victor, and Yawman and Erbe.

Over the years libraries have adapted three varieties of visible-index equipment to work with serial publications: (1) the title-a-line form, mostly employed for quick-reference work; (2) book units that hold the checking cards and slips, often found in small libraries; and (3) the type most generally installed in libraries, with the checking cards or slips lying flat in shallow trays in small cabinets. When a library has both a visible reference index (1) and a visible index (3), there may be some difficulty in distinguishing between the two by name when generically they are both visible indexes. Since the visible

---

[1]American Library Association, *Descriptive Catalog of the Exhibit of Labor-Saving Devices and Library Equipment* (Washington, D.C.: American Library Assn., 1914), p.26–27.
[2]*ALA Bulletin* 8:81 (1914).

reference index is more strictly an index, it is better in the circumstances to apply another term to the checking records. So the Library of Congress refers to the checking records as the "visible file," while the Harvard College Library employs the expression "visible record." For tracing purposes the latter uses VR for the checking records and VI for its rotary reference file. Throughout this book "visible reference index" refers to the title-a-line reference type, "visible index" to the checking records.

Visible Reference Indexes

Readers and staff members often wish to find the call number of a serial quickly, particularly when they have drawn their references from an abstracting or indexing service. They are helped when a library's periodicals, or preferably its serials without regard to type, are listed on a title-a-line visible reference index. They can check that record rapidly without having to hunt through the card catalog in a time-consuming way.[3] Commonly the information on the visible reference index is limited to the title, call number, and an indication of the location of current numbers when they are not housed in the periodical room. The reasons for limiting the information are that the visible reference index is not a posting record and that an attempt must be made to confine all the data for a given title to a single line six to eight inches long.

Frequently the strips in a visible reference index have no protective covering. It is better to enclose them in plastic tubes to prevent them from becoming soiled through constant fingering or from being marked with pencil or ink. The tubes can accommodate either a single-line entry or a multiple entry, for example, for the publications of a corporate body, which takes up two or more lines.

Multiple entries serve a number of purposes. When a library has two or more publications of a corporate body, space is saved by listing the name of the body only once; hanging indention then effectively sets off the titles of its publications. A similar scheme can be followed for the different parts of a serial, for example, for the historico-philosophical and the mathematico-physical sections of the proceed-

[3]Printed and mimeographed checklists and catalogs serve a similar purpose. In some libraries the lists of periodicals indexed by abstracting and indexing services, often in the front of the volumes, are annotated with the call numbers to provide the same type of convenience.

ings of a learned society.[4] In chapter 7 attention is called to the fact that equipment of this kind has been effectively employed in the Library of Congress as an index to outstanding serial orders.

Fusion of Reference and Checking Functions

In a few libraries the visible reference index has been made to do double duty as a combined reference and checking record. This effect is achieved by installing regular checking forms in the panels in place of the title-a-line strips. There are proportionately more panels in the double-duty file because of the buildup, but otherwise what is seen at a glance is to all intents and purposes the same as if one were looking at a standard visible reference index. Should anyone want to know more than that, e.g., whether the library has received the latest issue of a periodical, all that is necessary is to open up the checking record and scan it. The checker, however, is not as well served; it is not possible to operate as conveniently as it is when one is seated at a cabinet-type visible index located behind the scenes. The posting of issues must be done on the vertical panels instead of on a flat surface, that is, unless the checker is ready to detach the panels one by one as needed. Also the checker must compete with others for use of the file, since it is a public as well as an official record. The Science Reading Room at Massachusetts Institute of Technology has installed a dual-purpose system of this kind.

An alternative practice is to locate the regular visible index where it may be consulted by readers. In the Wellesley College Library, e.g., the visible index is adjacent to both the public catalog and the current periodicals collection, which is housed on open shelves. In that library the public catalog contains main and secondary cards for serials purchased on a standing order, subscriptions placed on an "until forbid" basis, and serials, including periodicals, received as gifts. When only a very occasional volume is received by the library, the title is omitted from the visible index, but holdings are added in pencil on all catalog cards. Otherwise the cards disclose gaps in the file, when holdings began, a "to date" statement, and the stamp

---

[4]On p.86 of the first edition of *Serial Publications* a segment of entries from the visible reference index in the Harvard College Library was reproduced. The segment illustrated the kind of practices described above. The title-a-line rotary file has now been discontinued at Harvard because of the old age of the equipment. There has been some talk of producing computer lists of important serial titles to take up the slack.

"Kardex." The visible index provides the checking record for current issues for the last five or ten years—or longer than that for annuals— depending on frequency of issue. It shows the location of current issues and back files. The rest of the information on the checking records is much more for official use: the source, fund, the name of the department which ordered the item, whether analyzed, whether added to the series, a code letter identifying the bindery to which a complete volume will be sent, whether to tie or bind, the last bound volume on the shelves, the bindery charge and date of a volume sent to the bindery or held in the Serials Department awaiting a missing issue which has already been claimed, and a record and date of the claim for a missing issue. Beyond this, the Wellesley College Library maintains a title-a-line visible reference index, which is located on the study table in the periodical-indexes alcove of the Reference Room. It covers current periodicals only and shows where current issues and back files may be found.

At the Babson Institute Library, where the visible index is available for consultation as at Wellesley College, there are no duplicate entries in the card catalog. The checking records serve also as the cataloging records. A similar practice was adopted when the Linda Hall Library was founded. By 1963, though, it was apparent that the Kardex could no longer serve the reference staff, the interlibrary loan staff, and the public, and still be used as an administrative instrument for the Serials Department. After due consideration the Linda Hall Library began work on a book catalog of its serial holdings; it now issues a cumulated revision of the book catalog annually, which has become in effect the basic reference list for serials in the library. The records for noncurrent titles have been removed from the visible index to an inactive file. They are returned to the Kardex only when there is some change between printings of the book catalog, e.g., when a volume or issue is added, when a volume is charged to the bindery, or when an error is detected which must be corrected. The Kardex is therefore a current check-in record, a housekeeping record for the Serials Department (order records, payments, special notes, etc.), and a supplement to the book catalog. When an asterisk appears in the book catalog, the statement of holdings can be found only in the visible index, and the record of bound volumes is either there or in the inactive card file of noncurrent titles.

The fusion of checking and reference functions in one way or another can be seen in a number of special libraries where ready and full access to serial files is of paramount importance. And in libraries in which journals are received and checked in the periodical room, as at the University of California, the intention is to make data on the checking records accessible to readers, not directly, but through the periodical room staff.

Visible versus Blind Files

When a drawer in a standard cabinet is opened, the cards constitute a blind file because, except for the guide cards, no heading can be seen, whereas in a visible index the eye finds the right place so that the very entry that is wanted is seen at a glance. Eye finding constitutes such an advantage that librarians who converted from a blind file to a visible index were almost without exception happy with the results. At the British Library of Political and Economic Science the verdict was: "The time saved by using a visible index has in itself fully justified the initial expenditure."[5] At Los Angeles in 1932 the reaction was: "It is difficult to restrain undue exuberance in contemplating the benefits of this visible system. . . . It is believed that the expense is justified by efficiency in operation."[6] The consolidation of records was one of the causes for congratulation at Los Angeles, as in many other instances. Until the visible index was installed:

> Periodicals and newpapers had been ordered and checked in the Periodical Department; documents in the Catalogue Department; continuations in the Order Department. In all of these departments chief interest was centered on their major tasks which were not concerned particularly with the keeping of these specialized records. Therefore, finding the various unions more and more incompatible, finally a complete separation has been achieved, and a more equable and decorous combination permitted, bringing into being the Serials Division of the Order Department.[7]

The situation in the Library of Congress as late as the early 1940s was even more complicated than that in Los Angeles before 1932: "At that time, in order to check on Library of Congress serial holdings, it was necessary to consult records in 14 different locations and in some of these locations there was more than one catalog to be consulted—a total of some 32 separate files."[8]

[5]Marjorie Plant, "Periodicals Procedure in a University Library," *College and Research Libraries* 3:60 (1941).

[6]Los Angeles Public Library, Serials Division, *Workbook of Serials Procedure* (Los Angeles, 1932), p.7–8.

[7]*Ibid.*, p.2.

[8]*Annual Report of the Librarian of Congress* 1952 (Washington, 1953), p.84–85. Chapter 8 of the report tells the story of how the visible index was developed and installed at the Library of Congress.

The benefits of consolidated records should be appraised apart from any question of the merits of the visible index. At Yale, for example, it was reported in 1948 that "seventeen separate card files have been eliminated or consolidated; others are under consideration,"[9] a task for the Serial Department completely dissociated from installation of a visible index.

A number of separate files existed in the Harvard College Library prior to the changeover to a visible index in 1939. The files were for government publications, Hispanic material, nondocument serials in general, serials of all kinds in the field of education, and Slavic titles. Obviously there was much overlap between the records. The file for nondocument serial publications contained approximately a hundred thousand cards. It consisted of two fifty-tray units, each drawer of which was uncomfortably full. The live titles, some three or four thousand in number, were distributed throughout the catalog. In seeking each current title, the serial assistants had to contend with twenty-five or so inactive ones.

Some idea of the physical labor involved in a day's checking in the former Harvard file can be gathered from the fact that a full drawer weighed about eight pounds. If a checker had an entry to make in each of the hundred drawers and lifted another twenty-five drawers in backtracking because the desired entry was not in the first location tried, she would have lifted a ton in the course of a single day's operations: half a ton in lifting the drawers down and half a ton in replacing them. With the expenditure of so much physical energy, fatigue was bound to set in, to retard the checking process or to lead to errors. Moreover, the drawers were not adequately guided, so there was much finger work in trying to find an entry. Often, too, although printed form cards were employed, data were not in a standard place because the cards filled up so rapidly. For many years a change to a visible index had been desired. In 1935, in a memorandum to the director of the library, T. Franklin Currier had said:

> So far as the advantage of a visible record system is concerned as against the present antiquated card system, there is no need to take time to debate, for it is already unquestionably recognized as a necessary feature in well-managed libraries, and it makes greatly for prompt service and economy. Moreover, the concentration of information about all current periodicals at one station in the Library

[9]Yale University, *Report of the Librarian* 1947–48 (New Haven, Conn., 1948), p.15.

will be a distinct addition to the service we now give and will notably help those who use the Library.

Naturally, when the visible index was finally installed, it was a welcome change to the staff because it involved so much less sheer labor.

These details are recounted because it is important to point out that the change from a number of poor blind files to a consolidated visible index freshly contrived ought to lead to rejoicing, but the comparison is not a fair one. What ought to be compared is a good blind file and a good visible index. If the live entries in the main Harvard checking record had been segregated and consolidated with the live entries in the other files, and if new cards with adequate space had been provided, there would have been less objection to the former system. Space cannot be afforded in the visible index for completed or inactive serial records; neither should it be allowed in a blind file. Add to the reduced but consolidated catalog a really good system of guide cards and space the cards generously in each drawer—perhaps in a tub tray—and the result could be something to vie with the visible index, as was demonstrated in the National Agricultural Library not long afterwards.

One feature of the older Harvard system was excellent and was retained. For newspapers and for certain complicated serials—for instance, the *Mercure de France*, which ran from 1672 to 1820 and from time to time appeared in parallel editions in various cities—sheet records had been preferred, with appropriate references in the card file. The loose-leaf sheet records, on typewriting paper, provided in an admirable way for long and involved statements of holdings. There are serials which do not lend themselves to listing on cards; in particular, newspaper holdings can be checklisted well and clearly on sheets. For many years the sheet records served Harvard as a clear, straightforward, efficient tool, convenient to consult and easy to handle. Put the same records on standard-size cards, or even on 4 x 6-inch cards, and a complete contrast would be achieved.

Careful thought was given in the Harvard College Library in 1939 to the possible retention of the old blind file, rearranged and improved so that it would have a maximum of effectiveness. Retention would have meant that most checking cards would be typed afresh. Many of the earlier ones had manuscript headings, and it is certainly more efficient to have the entries typewritten. Reconstruction of the file would have cost much less than the sum in hand for the conversion of the records to go on a visible index. But there were three major objections: (1) a 4 x 6-inch card is much superior to the standard-size card for checking purposes; (2) overriding slips to extend the life of the checking records could not have been adopted; and (3) the records would have been too concentrated for the convenience of all who needed to consult them. Accordingly a visible index was installed, a consolidated record spread out so that a number of people could work at it simultaneously.

The visible index was not settled upon, however, until experiments had been carried out with other types of equipment. The Electrofile and the Wheeldex were set up and studied under working conditions. In the Electrofile, by means of a keyboard and a system of coding, the appropriate card can be made to jump up at random; it can be removed for posting and put back in the file without regard to alphabetical arrangement. Despite these real potentialities, there were drawbacks. The coding presented obstacles, but they could have been surmounted. The real trouble lay in the fact that the keyboard controlled only one tray at a time. Likewise the Wheeldex, a rotary file, seemed to offer attractive possibilities, especially the model set in a desk at which the checker could work with several thousand records comfortably at hand and with clear space in front of her. At that time neither the Wheeldex nor the Cardineer, another rotary file, had been electrified, a development which might have affected the result. But in all tests the visible index was first in speed and efficiency, just as its employment of overriding slips guaranteed economy in maintenance.

Side by side with the Harvard experience must be set the contrary findings in the National Agricultural Library. There a change was made from a visible index to a blind file. The former Victor visible index had 3 x 5-inch cards, about three-fourths of them in trays intended for 4 x 6-inch cards. Other people besides the checkers consulted the record intensively:

> The current files are in constant use not only by the periodical checkers, but also by the permanent serial records assistants who answer all requests for information on holdings, by Acquisition Section assistants for searching purposes, and by Division of Bibliography assistants for information of value in the preparation of new bibliographies. The permanent serial records assistants alone account for about 2000 uses a month.[10]

Because of the heavy nonposting consultation, the twenty visible-index cabinets were put on swivels, two units to a swivel. Normally

[10]Bella E. Shachtman, "Current Serial Records—An Experiment," *College and Research Libraries* 14:241 (1953).

the files faced the checkers, but when someone else wanted to consult a file, it was swung around to face the other side of the desk.

The checkers worked at the files all day long. "We wondered how much time was being used just to pull out and push back trays, thereby lessening the amount of time available for recording material. And how much was fatigue toward the end of the day lowering the output of the checkers?"[11] So as an experiment part of the alphabet was rearranged in a standard file, a relatively simple task because the headings were already typed at the top of the 3 x 5 visible-index cards.

> We asked the checker responsible for this part of the alphabet to separate her publications, so that she could record publications part of the day in what remained of her visible files and the other part of the day on the cards in the 3 by 5 tray. Four hours were spent working with the 3 by 5 tray and the checker averaged handling seventy pieces per hour; four hours were spent working with the visible files and the same checker averaged forty-one pieces per hour, showing an increase of twenty-nine pieces per hour in using the 3 by 5 tray.[12]

The experiment was so successful that a twenty-tray cabinet was designed, four trays high. All trays were then within normal arm's reach, in contrast to the situation that prevailed when some of the visible-index units were twenty trays high. There were sixteen inches of filing space in each new tray, and there were pulls and label holders at each end to permit people on both sides to get at the cards readily. Soft wood was used for the front, sides, and back of each tray and composition board for the bottom to hold the weight down and reduce the risk of fatigue from handling many trays in the course of a day's work.

[11]Bella E. Shachtman, "Simplification of Serial Records Work," *Serial Slants* 3:10 (1952).

[12]*Ibid.* Pearl H. Clark, in *The Problem Presented by Periodicals in College and University Libraries* (Chicago: Univ. of Chicago Pr., 1930), p.27–29, reported on time studies for the posting of three hundred periodicals, two-fifths of which were in foreign languages. Identical records were set up in a blind and a visible file. Two individuals checked the periodicals in groups of fifty titles at a time, first in one file and then in the other. For experimental purposes the periodicals were not arranged alphabetically. The average time was 17.4 minutes for the posting of fifty titles in the visible index, 23 minutes in the standard file. Mrs. Clark cautioned against taking these figures at their face value, since different results might have been obtained under ordinary library conditions. Because of the marked discrepancy between Mrs. Clark's figures and Miss Shachtman's, there is evidently room for an extensive time-and-motion study of work at blind and visible files.

You can imagine what this meant to our checker. In the first place, the trays she now used were lighter than any trays she had previously used. Secondly, instead of pulling out and pushing back eighty-nine trays for her part of the alphabet, she now used only seventeen 3 by 5 trays. Lastly, with her file set up in front of her within easy reach, she had much more work space available on her desk, without using part of another desk as she had had to do with the visible files.[13]

Production records were kept for several months. The statistics covered work at the visible index, the blind file, and in two cases work at the visible index after a spell at the blind file. The following table shows the results obtained.

PERCENTAGES OF WORK EFFECTIVENESS

	VISIBLE INDEX	BLIND FILE	RETURN TO VISIBLE INDEX
First checker	85	109	103
Second checker	95	98	99
Third checker	110	118	

The evidence shows that although there is a gain in production in each case when the 3 by 5 files were used, over the production in using the visible files, a comparable drop is not shown upon returning to use of the visible files, and in fact, production may continue to show an upward trend. The old management principle seems to be proven anew—motivation and training play the most important part in producing high worker efficiency regardless of the equipment used. The motivation in this experiment came from the enthusiasm of each checker in participating in the experiment and her interest in the results. Further motivation came from each checker's desire to stop working with visible files from which she had to pull out and return so many trays in comparison to the number worked with in the experimental file.[14]

As a consequence of the experiment the National Agricultural Library gave up its visible indexes and reverted to a blind file. Ten double visible-index units were replaced by six specially designed cabinets,[15] and eight desks have been replaced by six. Apart from the

[13]Shachtman, "Simplification of Serial Records Work," p.12.

[14]Shachtman, "Current Serial Records," p.242. For an explanation of the percentages of work effectiveness see her "Simplification of Serial Records Work," p.11.

[15]In the new installation the cabinets were somewhat modified. The free filing space per drawer was reduced to fourteen inches, and the cabinets were designed for fifteen drawers in three rows, so limiting the height of the cabinets to sixteen inches, which, by coincidence, is the height of the recommended thirteen-tray visible-index unit.

gain in space, the following were the advantages of the new system:

1. Accessibility of most of the file to the checker while part of it is being consulted by others.
2. Better morale by improvement in the appearance of the section.
3. Easy insertion of new titles with no need for shifting cards as is necessary in the visible index.
4. Handling of fewer trays by the checker, thereby lessening fatigue.
5. Informational letters can be interfiled with the cards temporarily.
6. Use of guide cards at quarter- to half-inch intervals simplifies finger finding.[16]

In weighing the evidence presented by Miss Shachtman, a number of factors must be taken into account. Most visible indexes are devoted overwhelmingly—95 percent or more—to the daily routine of posting incoming serials, and the reference use is to a considerable extent through the checkers themselves. In the National Agricultural Library the checking and reference functions were fairly evenly divided, so it was proper to organize the file to serve both groups of people equally. Nor did the checkers open and arrange the mail. In most libraries the incidental duties provide variety in an otherwise monotonous operation. The visible-index equipment in operation before the changeover was not the best. Units were twenty trays high instead of the normal thirteen; the needless extra height not unnaturally tired the arms.[17]

The style of checking card designed for the National Agricultural Library was unusual. The 3 x 5 card was possible because it was intended to last no more than three years, after which it would be renewed photographically. The name and address of the publisher were typed in a strategic location and photographed in such a way that claims for missing issues could then be inserted in an open-faced envelope ready for mailing. The success of the operation can be gauged by the fact that an annual workload of nineteen thousand claims was possible.[18] But by 1971 the system of blind files and

[16]Shachtman, "Current Serial Records," p.242.

[17]At one stage the problem of reaching for trays was solved in the Johns Hopkins University Library by rearranging the visible-index trays so that the alphabetical sequence became lateral. Before working on a given part of the alphabet, the checker pulled out all the trays in a row. The trays were returned to position before those in the next row were pulled out.

[18]See Ralph R. Shaw, "Photoclerical Routines at USDA," *Library Journal* 78:2064 (1953). The routine for claims is illustrated on p.2069. See also his *The Use of Photography for Clerical Routines* (Washington, D.C.: American Council of Learned Societies, 1953), especially p.14, 55, 57, 61–63, 68, and 70, where comparative figures are given for claiming and other serial operations.

photographically reproduced cards had been superseded by a computer program.

Alternatives to the Visible Index

For a while the John Crerar Library worked with edge-punched cards for its checking records; a few of them still remain in the check-in files. Actually the punching feature was never utilized. In a file of up to fifteen thousand titles, where daily postings are necessary, it is not feasible to needle, separate, tabulate, disorder, and refile the records in order to derive information of a secondary nature.

The University of Texas Library has employed IBM punched cards in an auxiliary capacity.[19] In general, though, punched cards belong only in a fully automated system.

Formerly much hope was held out for rotary files as an alternative to the visible index. Swarthmore College Library for a while had a rotary file for its continuations together with an old visible index for checking in periodicals. It decided to have uniform equipment for continuations and periodicals. Since it had already come to the conclusion that a visible index is easier to use than a rotary file for a large number of records, it gave up the rotary file and acquired Acme visible indexes for the total operation (see figure 10). The former Wheeldex entries were illustrated in the first edition of *Serial Publications* (p.99–100). On the new forms the box for frequency has been dropped; "Accession?" has been added to cover volumes issued in parts; "Estimate" is for budget purposes; "Source" has been changed to "Publisher," since the source is given in full on the back of the card; while "S.O.-L.C. Cards" is still on the form but all standing orders have now been cancelled, since the library now subscribes to Library of Congress proofsheets. An asterisk is still used in the visible margin to show that previous cards for the entry are in a dead file. The clips which were formerly attached to the side of the card as a signaling system are no longer employed.

Temple University gave up its rotary file as unsatisfactory. The cards fell off it; the staff found it bulky and troublesome. It was replaced by a Kardex.

The University of California Library has been devoted to its rotary file from the inception. It was a Herring-Hall-Marvin Record File, a type that is no longer being manufactured. When it was no longer

---

[19]Alexander Moffit, "Punched Card Records in Serials Acquisition," *College and Research Libraries* 7:10 (1946).

VOL. & NO.	DATE RECEIVED	PRICE	INVOICE DATE	VOL. & NO.	DATE RECEIVED	PRICE	INVOICE DATE	VOL. & NO.	DATE RECEIVED	PRICE	INVOICE DATE
1	9.5.68	21.05	7.15.68								
2	10.15.68	45.00	9.16.68								
3	11.4.68	18.00	10.28.68								
4	12.1.68	28.57	12.2.68								
5	1.2.70	43.05	1.26.70								

CIRCULATE? Yes	FUND Mod.Lang–Ling.	ACCESSION? Yes	ANALYZE? No	S.O.-L.C. CARDS No	ESTIMATE $50.- '71
PS25 .S4 v.	PUBLISHER Mouton				
	TITLE Current trends in linguistics				
	ENTRY Sebeok, Thomas Albert				

Figure 10. Visible index entry for a continuation, from Swarthmore College Library

possible to add to the twelve units already in operation, two wheels were acquired from another manufacturer, later followed by one of a third make. Neither of the two is liked, and the library wishes that it could find some secondhand Herring-Hall-Marvin equipment.

Rotary files are quite compact by comparison with visible indexes. At the University of California it was found that the capacity of a wheel is 4,200 cards of the stock that libraries require. That is the equivalent of three and a half thirteen-tray visible-index cabinets with three-sixteenths of an inch visibility. The compactness is satisfactory when only one person works at the files or when space is limited, as at California. It is less satisfactory when a number of people must consult the file constantly and simultaneously.

Electrical models are more suited to library work than manual ones. The feature offers little or no gain in systematic checking, but it does facilitate reference consultation. Segments can be removed from the electrical models without throwing the wheel off balance, whereas removal of a segment from a manually operated model impedes checking because the wheel is no longer in balance.

Rotary files, especially when motorized, are much pleasanter to operate than other nonvisible files, cost somewhat less than visible indexes, and, in some makes, lend themselves to efficient follow-up work. But they are based on the principle of finger finding rather than eye finding, and they incur a heavy burden of retyping because of their inability to take overriding slips. They serve larger institutions better than small ones; in fact, a library should have at least two thousand serials before it considers purchase of a rotary file.

Predominance of the Visible Index

Clearly, until automation takes over, the visible index has established itself as the standard equipment for use in checking current issues of serial publications. This much is obvious at any rate: eye finding is faster than finger finding—otherwise there would be no occasion for guide cards in a catalog drawer—so the visible index, which is based on the principle of eye finding, has a head start on any nonvisible system.

Specifications for a Visible Index

When a serial collection is quite small, or when for any reason the records should be portable, the checklist may be in book form. The Kardex book unit holds up to 128 entries which measure 4 x 6 inches. In the Acme style the maximum is 168 entries for 4 x 6 cards and three-sixteenths of an inch visible margin, 126 when the margin becomes a quarter of an inch. In some Commonwealth countries the Kalamazoo visible index, which is in book form, is still in use in libraries (see figure 11). Much work is entailed in shifting entries, so the Kalamazoo should not be adopted for a library that has a growing or large collection of serials.

For the metal cabinets duplex units, in which two rows of cards are visible at a glance, are preferable to single ones. Although all manufacturers do not build duplex trays, these offer real advantages to most libraries. It is possible to have 188 cards measuring 4 x 6 inches in a duplex tray with three-sixteenths of an inch visibility or 142 with quarter-inch visibility; consequently only half as many trays must be opened or closed in the course of a day's work. The Library of Congress, however, prefers the single units because they tie up less of the file at any given moment; it also feels that duplex trays may be a little harder to pull out and push back.

Cabinet height should be limited to twelve or thirteen trays. Then the checker does not have to reach far for any tray. Obviously with that height limitation the cabinets will spread out rather widely in an installation that must provide for five to twenty-five thousand

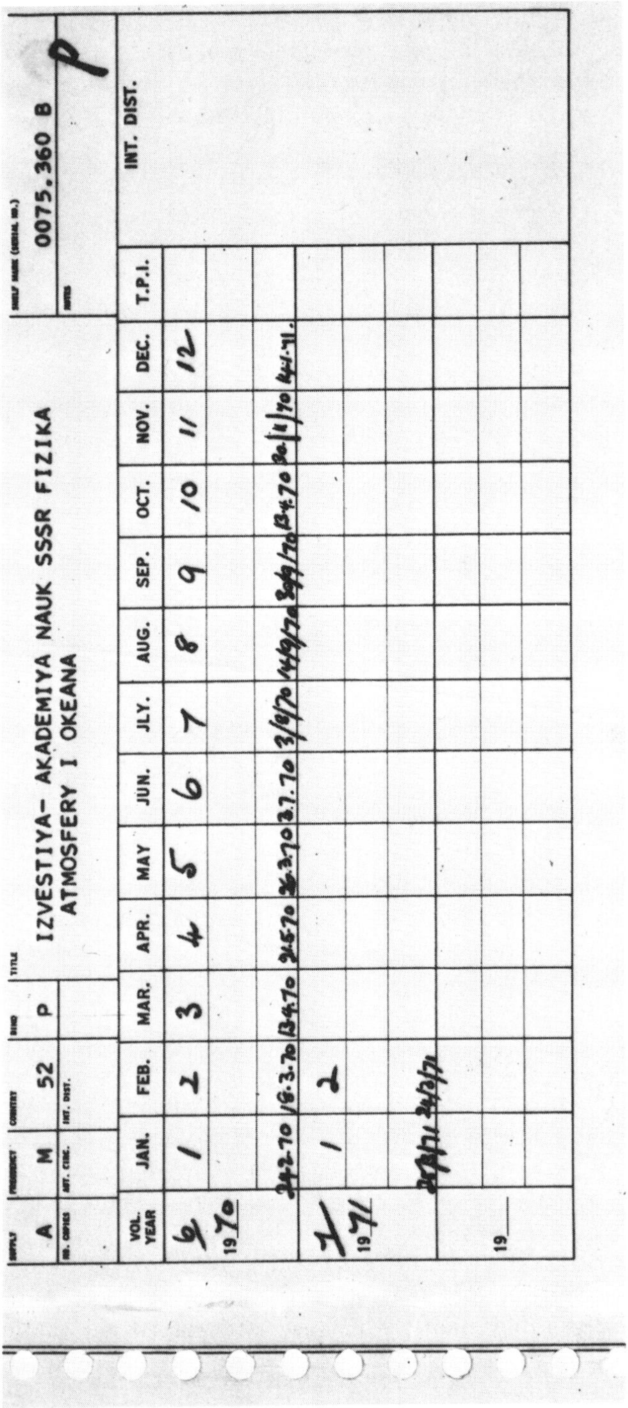

Figure 11. Kalamazoo entry as used in the National Lending Library at Boston Spa, Great Britain

entries or more. But the spread has its advantages: it allows for working space at regular intervals where serials may be piled up before and after checking, and it permits checkers to work close to the records without blocking them for others who need to consult them.

In general, visible-index cabinets should not be placed on work desks, at least in larger installations. The reason for this is that, except when it is almost exclusively the province of one person, the visible index should be looked on as a utility record available to all staff members. So desks or other work space should be provided for the checkers elsewhere in the vicinity where they can perform a variety of ancillary tasks. Further, it is better to place the cabinets on work tables rather than stands. When cabinets are on stands mounted on wheels, they can on occasion be moved around conveniently, but they do restrict the checker's work area and generally require it to be augmented by a book truck to hold the serials that are being checked. When stands are favored, they should be equipped with sliding work shelves; otherwise the bottom tray in each cabinet must be replaced by a slide, thus reducing the capacity of the unit. The advantage of work tables is that they produce superior working conditions. They should therefore be preferred whenever the records are devoted preponderantly to checking. At least one extra table should be on hand for the receipt and sorting of the day's mail, for mail baskets, and for the *Union List of Serials*, which is a commonly consulted work tool. Adequate shelf space should also be available when there is much material to be dispatched to different parts of the library, including branch and departmental libraries.

A visible margin of three-sixteenths of an inch is all that is required for serial records. With so small a margin the working capacity of each tray is increased by 25 percent. Some trays have pulls that are hard on the fingers of the checker. Larger pulls can be obtained, and they should be covered with rubber.

For Acme-type cards a bottom-line card holder should be acquired as an aid in typing the information that goes in the visible margin. No such aid is needed for Kardex-type cards, since they have perforated stubs which help to hold the cards in place in the typewriter and which can be torn off once the typing has been done.

It is possible to buy cabinets that can be locked. Locks are not required for ordinary library purposes, however, nor are fire doors. Locked cabinets are, however, desirable to house the records for security-classified technical reports.

Cards and Slips

The checking records may consist of single or double cards, folded forms, or cards combined with overriding slips. Early library installations depended on single cards, but today the multiple forms with their greater capacity are preferable; a major disadvantage of nonvisible checking systems is that they cannot utilize multiple card forms and overriding slips. Overriding slips in conjunction with basic entry cards, such as are in the visible index in the Library of Congress (see figure 12) are the most effective device for prolonging the life of checking records and of greatly reducing the burden of retyping when the records become full. The slips can be single or double, but experience has shown that a number of single slips are more effective than double slips. Checking details are given in pencil.

Cards and slips can be bought from the firms that supply visible indexes. Standard forms suffice, but many libraries prefer to have individualized forms printed for them to accommodate a variety of local circumstances. The common experience in libraries has been that it is more economical to have the forms printed locally, at least after the initial printing supplied by the manufacturer of the visible index. This is especially true in universities and other institutions which have their own printing plants.

The number of kinds of forms should be restricted to approximately four to six. Except in unusual situations there is no point in having more because a form may be able to serve two or more serial frequencies equally well. The most common forms are for weeklies (see figure 13), monthlies (see figure 14), irregular publications (see figure 15), and annuals or numbered series (see figure 16). When newspapers are checked in, there must be a form for dailies (see figures 17–18); on the other hand, the monthly form generally suffices for microfilm editions (see figure 19). Blank or ruled cards can fill a number of utility roles. They can be used for irregular publications, outstanding orders, references, and unnumbered series. They may also serve as dummies when it is necessary to remove a card from the file, e.g., to change the heading in some way. Colored stock may be desirable for dummies, outstanding orders, and references; the color can signal at a glance that there is no point in opening up the file to look for checking information.

The typical single card for weeklies lasts four years, for monthlies, ten. At the expiration of that time the card must be replaced by a fresh one, onto which all the essential data from the superseded card

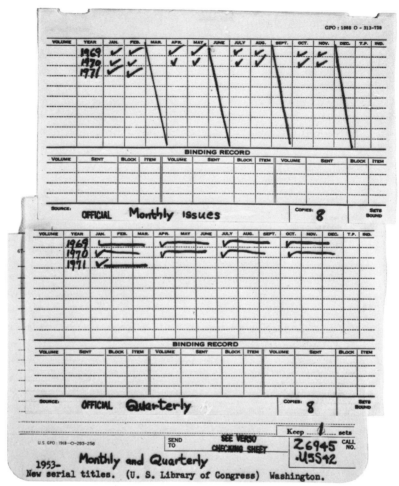

Figure 12. Overriding slips and their basic entry card, from the Library of Congress visible index

have been copied. Under this system the serial staff must plan for a large retyping job at the end of every four and ten years, with a certain amount of retyping going on continuously. The process would be almost prohibitive for libraries in which periodicals for branches are checked in centrally, because the cards would expire much too rapidly. For these libraries double cards or folded forms provide four times the normal checking space. Folded forms fill out the tray to some extent, but unless they create too much buildup this is not serious, and a moderate amount of buildup makes it easier to turn up the cards at a desired spot.

By far the most successful device for overcoming the necessity for periodic replacement of entries due to full records is the overriding slip in conjunction with a basic entry card. As many as five or six of these auxiliary slips can be attached to an entry successfully. The Library of Congress has at times added as many as ten, but that number seems to result in excessive buildup.

Under the system of basic entry cards and overriding slips the cards bear the permanent information: details of entry, call number, checking directions, summarized statement of holdings, billing data,

Deutsche Nationalbibliographie

Earlier record on Sed   ACME 27390-6

	JAN.	FEB.	MAR.	APR.	MAY	JUNE	JULY	AUG.	SEP.	OCT.	NOV.	DEC.	T. P.	IND.
1970	1	6	10	14	18	23	27	31	36	40	45	49	Jan-Mar	
	2	7	11	15	19	24	28	32	37	41	46	50		
	3	8	12	16	20	25	29	33	38	42	47	51		
	4	9	13	17	21	26	30	34	39	43	48	52		
	5				22		35		44					
1971	1													
	2													
	3													
	4													

Reihe A. Neuerscheinungen des Buchhandels   Ref 622.13

	JAN.	FEB.	MAR.	APR.	MAY	JUNE	JULY	AUG.	SEP.	OCT.	NOV.	DEC.	T. P.	IND.
1970	1	3	5	7	9	11	13	15	17	19	21	23	Jan-Mar	Apr-Jun
	2	4	6	8	10	12	14	16	18	20	22	24		
1971	1	3												
	2													

Reihe B: Neuerscheinungen ausserhalb des Buchhandels   Ref 622.13.3

Figure 13. Overriding slip for a weekly, from Harvard College Library. Actually this is the form for a monthly. Series A shows how five lines must be allowed for a weekly; series B shows how a work issued twice a month can be entered. The two overriding slips require only a single basic entry card.

Harvard library bulletin — Call no = RR 58.20

v.1-14 (Winter 1947- Autumn 1960) complete — ACME 27390-6

Vol.			JAN.	FEB.	MAR.	APR.	MAY	JUNE	JULY	AUG.	SEP.	OCT.	NOV.	DEC.	T. P.	IND.
15		1967	1			2			3			4				
16		1968	1			2			3			4				
17		1969	1			2			3			4				
18		1970	1			2			3			4				
19		1971	1			2										

Figure 14. Monthly overriding slips used for a quarterly, from Harvard College Library. Earlier, as illustrated in the first edition of *Serial Publications*, p.106, a ruled slip was preferred for this title. Checking slips for monthlies and quarterlies normally last for twenty years. When the summarized statement is simple, it is given at the top of the slip; there is a reference to the S-card when the statement is complicated.

Aequationes mathematicae — Call no = Sci 870.19

Vol.	No	Date		
1	1/2	1968		
	3	1968		
2	1	1968		
	2/3	1969		
3	1/2	1969		
	3	1969		
4	1/2	1970		
	3	1970		
5	1	1970		

Figure 15. Ruled overriding slip, from Harvard College Library. The capacity of the slip has been increased by the provision of three columns.

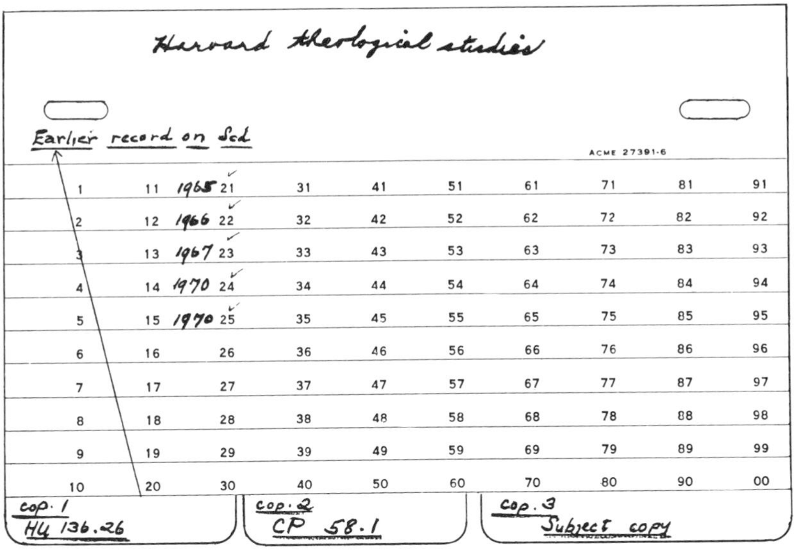

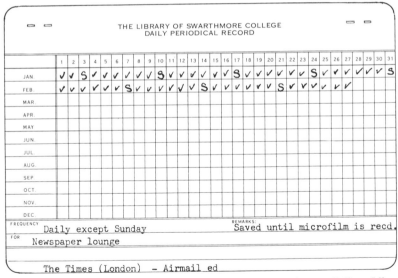

Figure 16. Overriding slips for an annual or a numbered series, from Harvard College Library. Note how the margin has been cut away so that the three copies can be visible at a glance.

Figure 17. Visible index entry for a newspaper, from Swarthmore College Library. The letter *S* in the checking squares stands for "Sunday" and helps to show at a glance that the file is complete.

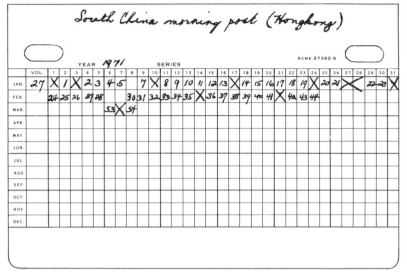

Figure 18. Overriding slip for a newspaper that is posted, from Harvard College Library

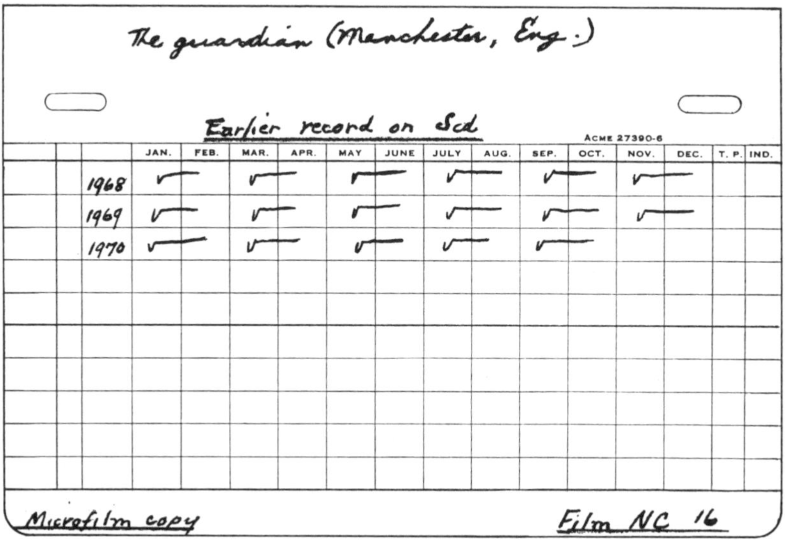

Figure 19. Overriding slip for a newspaper on microfilm, from Harvard College Library. Only the microfilm copy is posted. The original issues are "stamped and shot" to the Periodical Room without record. Missing issues are not claimed. When the microfilm arrives, the Periodical Room is notified that the corresponding issues can now be rejected. The Harvard College Library keeps very few newspapers in the original edition. Daily issues are either replaced by microfilm copies or rejected after a year, the records being marked "Current year only kept in this library."

etc. The whole of the card, both front and back, is free for these notations, though usually only the front is required. Ruled cards suffice for all these purposes, but special forms may be preferred. The overriding slips are the printed checking forms for weeklies, monthlies, etc. They are expendable and can be used on both sides by turning the slips over when the first side is full; in this way they double the life of the checking records. When both sides are full, the slip is removed and a substitute added with a minimum of effort. When the substitution is made, the summarized statement of holdings on the permanent card should be adjusted—a routine which must be carried out much more frequently under other systems—and there may be other data as well to add to the new overriding slip.

Multiple overriding slips serve when there is more than one publication under the name of a corporate body or when copies of a serial come from different sources or go to different destinations. In these circumstances the checking directions go on the overriding slips, not the basic entry card. At times it is helpful to cut away part of the bottom margin of multiple overriding slips so that the headings on the slips underneath may be partly or wholly visible.

The Library of Congress destroys its superseded checking records. Some libraries like to preserve them for the sake of the detailed information they can in rather rare instances provide, but from an administrative viewpoint there is no reason for preserving superseded checking records once the summarized statement of holdings has been updated on the basic entry card or the permanent serial records. There is a better case for preserving the superseded records when the visible index itself is the permanent serial catalog. In that event the next-to-latest checking record may be preserved, since it is unlikely that still earlier records will ever be consulted.

Optimum Size of Visible-Index Cards

Early checking records for serials generally conformed to the international size, 7.5 x 12.5 centimeters, or else measured 3 x 5 inches. Experience soon taught, however, that cards of those sizes were too small for efficient work. Larger cards up to 5 x 8 inches were therefore adopted. The most common size was 4 x 6 inches, and these are the dimensions that are now recognized as standard for serial checking records. A 4 x 6 card allows for a reasonably large visible margin, even with three-sixteenths of an inch of visibility, in which to write the name of the serial plus certain other information, principally the call number. The checking squares are big enough to carry several types of information, among them the issue number, checks for multiple copies, date of receipt when that is required, and checks for Library of Congress cards for analyzed series. Elsewhere on the front or back of the card there is space for checking directions, billing records, cataloging information, statements about issues that were not published, the summarized statement of holdings, etc. Cards that are larger than 4 x 6 inches preclude the utilization of duplex trays, make the file more extensive and costly than need be, and yield far less checking space than is provided by overriding slips on 4 x 6 cards. Legibility and accuracy may be sacrificed on 3 x 5 cards, or some data may have to be kept in supplementary files.

Title Inserts

When a change of title has to be made in a Kardex-type visible index, the new heading can be typed on a thin strip called a title insert. The new heading can then be inserted in the plastic covering that protects the visible margin. For Acme-type visible indexes there are slip-on sheaths, also known as visible-margin protectors, that can be attached to any card to permit the addition of a title insert. A simpler method is to type the new heading on plain paper, which is then pasted on the card or stapled to it. As was shown in figure 6, the Library of Congress makes temporary entries in its visible index by stapling reproductions of purchase requisitions onto blank cards.

Plastic covers over the visible margin are a somewhat doubtful asset in general. As the National Agricultural Library found, they give rise to glare, which can be a factor leading to fatigue on the part of the checkers.

Bibliography

Bennett, Fleming. "A Multi-Purpose Serials Record," *College and Research Libraries* 9:231–37 (1948).

Berry, Paul L. "Library of Congress Serial Record Techniques," *Serial Slants* 3:14–18 (1952).

Grenfell, David. "Accession and Other Records," in his *Periodicals and Serials; Their Treatment in Special Libraries,* p.32–54. 2d ed. London: Aslib, 1965.

Jacobs, R. M. "Focal Point: A Composite Record for the Control of Periodicals Using a Visible Signalling Device," *Journal of Documentation* 6:213–28 (1950).

Keller, Alton H. "A Flexoline Record of Serial Holdings," *Library of Congress Information Bulletin* 21–23 (16 Jan. 1950).

Litchfield, Dorothy H. "Paleolithic Practices in the Checking and Cataloging of Periodicals," *Library Journal* 60:58–61 (1935).

Shachtman, Bella E. "Current Serial Records—An Experiment," *College and Research Libraries* 14:240–42, 248 (1953).

———"Simplification of Serial Records Work," *Serial Slants* 3:6–13 (1952).

Shaw, Ralph R. "Photoclerical Routines at USDA," *Library Journal* 78:2064–70 (1953).

9

Computer Methods
of Checking

In chapter 7, which is concerned with the theory and practice of serial checking, only passing attention is paid to principles which should underlie the emerging computer technology. The reason for this is that a new medium should not be devised and operated on the basis of the theory and method developed for another one; in particular, the use of flow charts, embedded in former usage, often holds advances back through disregard of this insight. The danger is greatest for a new medium with as much potential as the computer has. Consequently, computer methods of checking should be allowed the fullest freedom to evolve within the ambit of their own theoretical foundations. In that way the full strength of the computer can be called into play at the same time that economical and efficient performance becomes possible. Above all, preconceived ideas must be set aside, at least until hypotheses can be fully tested and a new theory established. Deficiencies in the theoretical foundations have undoubtedly been responsible for the fact that up to 1970 only a relative handful of libraries have ventured into automated methods for checking in the current issues of serial publications.

Theory of Entry

While the computer is a powerful instrument of tremendous potential, it is also an expensive one to operate unless information is fed into it concisely and compactly. For checking purposes it follows then that, because of their length and complexity, conventional forms of entry must be completely rethought and most likely avoided. Whether one likes it or not, headings such as the following should be out of the picture if checking systems are to be automated:

174

Massachusetts Institute of Technology. Center for Materials Science and Engineering, Annual report on research in materials science and engineering.

Nederlandse Centrale Organisatie voor Toegepastnatuurwetenschappelijk Onderzoek. Commissie voor Hydrologisch Onderzoek, Verslagen en Mededelingen.

Texas. Agricultural and Mechanical University, College Station. Dept. of Oceanography and Meteorology, Contributions in oceanography and meteorology.

In the computer-generated *Serials and Journals in the M.I.T. Libraries* the name "Massachusetts Institute of Technology" is always reduced to "M.I.T.," though for the sake of economy "MIT" would be better; the abbreviation is filed as though the name were spelled out in full, however. Likewise, "A and M University" is preferred to "Agricultural and Mechanical University," although "A&M U" or preferably "A&MU" would suffice. There can be no justification for inserting place names such as "College Station" in the computer heading, since they are vestiges of card cataloging practices which are nonessential, even for cataloging, except in the case of identical names. This is where *Coden for Periodical Titles* comes into force. Its code symbols are permissible for manual checking systems, but they are imperative for computer programs because they can make a computer checking system viable, a state of affairs that did not exist formerly. With *Coden* in operation the entries given above are replaced by mnemonic codings: MTMR-A, CHOV-A, and TAOC-A. These concise listings produce three highly important effects: (1) the checkers can operate by means of random access to the computer record; (2) the process of alphabetizing the second-class mail disappears once the coding is included on the mailing wrapper, as indicated in chapter 7; and (3) reference consultation of the record from various points in the library becomes very rapid and is no longer in competition with the checking process.

The alphabetical listing of titles in the published volumes of *Coden for Periodical Titles* is only one of the possible indexes to the codings. The American Society for Testing and Materials also supplies the service in the form of magnetic computer tapes and punched and printed IBM cards. There is a monthly updating subscription service for the punched cards, the tapes being updated annually. With the aid of one or other of these services it is possible for a library to create its own local index to the *Coden* symbols it employs, but undoubtedly many libraries will prefer to make their own punched cards in order to substitute cataloging or stage-one entries for the *Coden* listings, which are stage-two titles—i.e., they are based on the wording as given in the caption or else on the cover or title page, wording which sometimes puts the corporate name first and the title second and sometimes puts them the other way around. In addition to these indexes, future book catalogs and union lists of serials can serve in a similar capacity by including the codings with the entries.

It goes almost without saying that a coded entry simplifies the checking procedures greatly, all the more so when the codings are included systematically on the mailing wrappers. It is on the reference side that codes may be considered somewhat more sophisticated than entries in either stage one or two, although it must be admitted that some cataloging entries have been so sophisticated that it has been difficult for readers and staff to find them. This has certainly been the case with many headings made under former cataloging codes; it is less true of entries prescribed under the 1967 code, so that if a library wishes to retain cataloging headings when it converts to an automated system, it ought to follow the 1967 rulings and not perpetuate the former style. However, reference consultation can be rapid and effective once the coding is freely available in a variety of indexes; in fact, it will be more rapid and effective than with any other system, including the card catalog. Moreover, in a fully online checking system, consultation can be performed at any time a library is open, so that access to the checking records will be much greater than it is with manual checking systems.

Symbols in *Coden for Periodical Titles* may be entered as a five-character or six-character field. The purpose of the fifth letter is to indicate which of a number of four-letter grids the code belongs to; that is, the capacity of the system is twenty-six times greater than the present allocations, all of whose symbols are in the "A" series. A check letter has been devised to control possible errors in the application of the system, e.g., the inversion of letters. If the coding is entered as a five-character field, then a check character is generated and added as a sixth character; if it is entered as a six-character field, a check character is generated from the first five and matched with the sixth. Thus for the *Journal of the American Chemical Society* the complete *Coden* with check character is JACS-AT. Check characters to minimize errors are already in use at the Chemical Abstracts Service and should be incorporated in library systems. Accordingly, the addresses on the mailing wrappers, as recommended in chapter 7, should for an automated system take a form such as:

Serial Record Division JACS-AT
Library of Congress   or
Washington, D.C., 20540

Copyright Office JACS-AT
Library of Congress
Washington, D.C., 20540

Identification Numbers

In almost all systems serials are assigned an identification number. It is generally five to eight digits long, but one or two letters may be substituted for the first digit or digits. The purpose is both identification of the item and fitting it into its proper alphabetical sequence in any printout. The University of California at San Diego employs an accession number and leaves the alphabetical arrangement to the computer. With the use of *Coden* symbols the identification number becomes superfluous as long as computer sequencing is acceptable. With serials the problem of automated arrangement is much simpler than it is with the totality of entries in a catalog of books and serials combined. But, in any event, it is possible to program elements of editorial practice into the computer so that there can be adjustments as desired to the straightforward computer sequencing.

A Divided Record

The objective toward which libraries have been working in their visible indexes has been a multipurpose record that provides a single place in which to look for serial information of various kinds. With the computer, however, this trend may well have to be reversed. A major reason for saying this is that only the checking function needs to be online. That function does not have to be online continuously, though it can be to advantage; essentially it requires that facility just for the period immediately following receipt of the second-class mail each day. But for reference consultation it will undoubtedly pay to have the service online daily for as long as the library is open.

Among other functions, e.g., accounting, binding, and holdings information, there is quite definitely no call for similar priority and expense. They therefore should be separate records which can be activated merely at those times when they are wanted. In a sense this is the same type of organization that is found on a multipurpose visible index, because on it the checking information is in the most accessible position, with the other data being relegated to less convenient locations on the cards or overriding slips. Also, batch processing for accounting, binding, and holdings serves manual and automated systems equally well, whereas posting is a mass activity which is carried out every single working day.

A number of libraries have already automated their acquisition procedures for controlling funds, issuing lists on which to obtain bids, ordering new titles, paying invoices, and renewing subscriptions.[1] As a consequence, there is no occasion for including subscription rates in any form in the automated checking system; it would be mere duplication to do so. Further, there can be no gain in amalgamating the two records. The one real point of connection stems from the practice of making sure that all issues to date have been received before paying a subscription in advance. But when an automated system has a follow-up control, that procedure becomes superfluous because note will already have been made of any delinquent items.

The function of the binding, holdings, and shelflist records for serials requires clarification. All three are very similar in scope, and there are slight differences in form. The binding record and the shelflist are expressed in terms of the physical units on the shelves, but the latter includes unbound issues in bundles, envelopes, etc., which the former does not. The record of holdings is not concerned with the physical form on the shelves; quite often it takes on a one-plus formulation, but that is not essential. It is possible, therefore, to design a system that will serve all three purposes. The form for a monthly might be: 1–6, 7^{2-11}, 8–24 1947–70, with no break in the dates to correspond with the breaks in the issue numbering. Superior figures for the parts of a volume are already a common device in libraries; inferior figures could be introduced as the device for showing that a bibliographical volume is on the shelves in more than one physical volume. Hence 1–5, $6–12_2$, $13–20_3$ would mean that the first five volumes are bound individually, 6–12 are bound one volume in two, and 13–20, one volume in three.

The troublesome factor in attempting to correlate binding, holdings, and shelflist records is that in many cases the binding record becomes something more than a list of volumes that have been bound. In an automated system it then produces a list or slip to notify the staff that issues should be gathered from the current-periodical shelves; it generates a binding slip with the instructions for the binder, as well as a shipping list if that is desired; and it makes a

[1]For details of these procedures and pertinent forms see International Business Machines, *Library Automation—Computerized Serials Control* (White Plains, N.Y., 1971), p.60–67.

punched card to be read by the computer when the bound volume is returned from the bindery, so updating the binding record. When these procedures are desired, the data should be stored separately and be activated once a week by prestored binding dates on the checking records. Otherwise a prestored date can produce a simple instruction to prepare issues for binding; but when there are large serial holdings, this device is of value chiefly for items, such as annual reports, which are on the stack shelves. It can very well be that items on the current periodical shelves are best handled by traditional manual methods, particularly because they are adequate for the periodical room staff, who can judiciously select the items to go to the bindery over a period of time in such a way that it will not be swamped and hold volumes for an undue period. On the whole it seems wise to suggest that only smaller libraries, and chiefly special libraries, should engage in anything more than notification by means of a prestored binding date.[2]

The general finding, then, is that insofar as a binding-instruction record is maintained in the computer it should be offline, activated perhaps once a week by means of prestored dates, arranged by *Coden*, and should be a list which excludes items that do not go to the bindery, e.g., serials that come bound, like the cumulated issues of the Wilson indexes; volumes that are not preserved for more than one or two years; and works which are sent to a storage collection. Should this decision be reached, it is possible to develop a program which will in effect amalgamate the binding, holdings, and shelflist records. In that event the shelflist itself is modified along the lines set out in the section on shelflisting in chapter 12.

The greatest activity in the field of serial automation has occurred in the production of lists of holdings. The style of the lists is very varied; standardization has not yet begun to appear.[3] Pioneer work is being done in institutions such as the Linda Hall Library, the Medical Library Center of New York, Massachusetts Institute of Technology, the San Francisco Public Library, the University of California at Los Angeles Biomedical Library, and the University of California at San Diego.

The amount of detail which is given in computer-generated book catalogs differs appreciably, but the principle underlying all of them is that the data adequate for the checking records are adequate for book catalogs. This is a sound principle and is in contrast to the

---

[2]For automated binding practices see IBM, *Library Automation*, p.87–91.

[3]For the production of lists of holdings and a series of samples see IBM, *Library Automation*, p.42–60.

MARC program, which originally considered the inclusion of 278 data elements and ended with eighty.[4] Half of the MARC data elements are for subject cataloging. Book catalogs are generally content with one or two controls for subject cataloging: either the call number alone or the call number and the location.

The range of information included in book catalogs is exemplified in the following entries from the Linda Hall and Massachusetts Institute of Technology libraries.

LINDA HALL LIBRARY	M.I.T. LIBRARY
AIBS bulletin. (American Institute of biological sciences) Washington. 1(1951)–13(1963) ‖ → BioScience.	A.I.B.S. Bulletin (American Institute of Biological Sciences) (Current title is Bioscience) SCI (QH.B624) V.1,1951–V.13,No.6,Dec 1963
American journal of mathematics. Baltimore. v1(1878)– * Index: 1–50(1878–1928); 51–75(1929–53)	American Journal of Mathematics SCI (QA.A512) V.1,1878 +
Combustion [1929–]. (In-ce publishing corp.) New York. v1(1929/30)–2 (bd w/v20(1929) of unrelated title, Combustion [1919–29]); 3–4; 5 n1,5,7–12; 6–8; 9 n3,6–12; 10(1938/39)– *	Combustion ENG /V.1,1929–V.4,1933/ +
Isis; journal of History of science society. Cambridge, Eng.; etc. v1(1913)–<32–35>; 36(1945)– Subtitle varies. *	Isis HAYB (Q.I81) V. 1, 1913 + HUM Current Nos.
Journal of symbolic logic. (Association for symbolic logic) New Brunswick, N.J. v1(1936)– Incl. "Index of reviews" in even numb. vols. Index: 1–25(1936–60)(publ. as v26)(alcove)	Journal of Symbolic Logic SCI (QA.J87) V. 1,No.1, Mar 1936 +
Norelco reporter. (North American Philips co.) Mount Vernon, N.Y. v1(1953/54) n2–3,6–8; 2(1954/55)–	Norelco Reporter SCI (QD.N834) V.1,No.1,Sept 1953 +

[4]The list of eighty data elements can be found in Library of Congress, Information Systems Office, *Serials, a MARC Format* (Washington, 1970), p.25–31.

Nuclear engineering abstracts. London. v1(1960)–2; 3 not publ.;
4(1963) || •-D

Nuclear Engineering Abstracts
SCI   (ZTK.N964)
        V.1,No.1,July 1960+

RCA review. (RCA laboratories)
Princeton, N.J. v1(1936)–

R.C.A. Review
ENG   V.1, 1936+
MAT   Latest Two Years Only
SPC   V.25, No.2, 1964+

The examples given above show that the Linda Hall Library does not classify its serials, but uses location symbols: * to signify that current numbers are on the current shelves and • to indicate the bibliography shelves. The M.I.T. location symbols are ENG, Engineering Library; HAYB, Hayden basement stacks; HUM, Humanities Library; MAT, Materials Center Reading Room; SCI, Science Library; and SPC, Space Center Reading Room.

There are numerous differences in descriptive detail. Linda Hall uses capital letters much less than M.I.T. does, and for the computer the fewer capitals there are the better. Linda Hall also gives more punctuation than M.I.T. does, though the latter inserts periods in acronyms, and again there is a computer saving in omitting punctuation whenever possible. Subtitles are not recorded by M.I.T., a satisfactory procedure in general. *Isis* is as good an entry as *Isis; Journal of History of Science Society.* It is true that there are other periodicals of the same name; but today most people want the history-of-science periodical and not the German nineteenth-century journals, which can for the sake of convenience be listed after the modern *Isis.* The alternative would be to follow Linda Hall's practice of adding a date in brackets to distinguish the names, though with the dates arranged in inverse chronological order. Further, M.I.T. adds the publisher's name and the place of publication only when it feels that the information is of value: it says *Engineer* for the New York periodical of that name and *Engineer (London)* for the old-established British journal. The M.I.T. practice of distinguishing when necessary seems a sound policy, especially for the computer, for which the guiding principle should be to omit all nonessential data. That principle applies to the abbreviations for volumes and parts of volumes; union lists almost invariably omit these expressions, and about half the book catalogs do. The difference between the em dash and the plus sign is of long standing; the only solution to that problem is to give up open entries and supply information through the last bound volume instead. Split years for dates of issue give rise to varying practices, but the differences involved do not seem significant. If a reader wants the first issues of the first volume, is it necessary to specify anything other than "volume 1" and the year in which the serial began publication? One library says that volume 3 of *Nuclear Engineering Abstracts* was not published and that the work ceased publication with volume 4; very likely both pieces of information should be included in the entry. Linda Hall lists cumulative indexes, M.I.T. does not, and again the information is probably worth listing.

All such differences deserve study and attention. They are evidence of profitable experimentation out of which can come the practice of the future. As Hammer says:

> One of the most significant advantages of a machine system is the continuous updating and expansion of serials catalogs and lists. Cumulations of holdings can be made in almost any combination of time periods and subjects. For example, a physics library may receive a weekly cumulated list of serials acquired in only the field of physics, or it may receive a monthly cumulated union catalog of all serials obtained throughout the university library system.
>
> The lack of just such a rapid and inexpensive method of updating was responsible for the demise of the old book catalog. The advent of the computer and its superb ability to accomplish the necessary data manipulations has returned the book catalog to its former importance and has begun the demise of the card catalog. The cycle has now been completed.[5]

Bosseau makes a similar observation:

> The library users, faculty, students, and librarians, are quite happy with the system. In fact, it has been noted that when users want serial information they seldom refer to the card catalog even for call numbers. Most users have never had direct access to the serials holdings information before and they have in general become enthusiastic supporters of the printed book catalog type of serials holdings information.[6]

Checking Systems

While book catalogs of serials have multiplied and made their mark, automated checking systems are still comparatively few in number. The reason is that manual systems are still functioning well; also, automation has not reduced the cost of the checking operation.

[5]Donald P. Hammer, *Automated Serials Control in the Purdue University Libraries* ([Lafayette, Ind.: The Library, 1965]), p.3.

[6]Don L. Bosseau, *The University of California at San Diego Serials System: Past, Present and Future* (La Jolla, Calif.: [The Library] 1968), p.22.

There is almost no sign of any breakdown in work with well-planned, well-maintained visible indexes. The Library of Congress may constitute an exception; a breakdown may be in the offing for its visible index, judging by an observation made by the chief of the Serial Record Division in a memorandum dated 22 July 1970. He says:

> The internal handling of serials in the Library, check-in, claiming, routing, binding, etc., will soon be approaching a crisis stage. These functions are performed and controlled by the Serial Record file. Because of the diverse functions performed by this file and the large bulk of material passing through it daily, access to the manual file is becoming increasingly more difficult.
>
> Most of the functions required for internal control of serials are of a repetitive and clerical nature and thus lend themselves to automation. While the Library's problem in serials handling seems to be unique, this uniqueness is due to the great bulk of material received. For some years we have side-stepped the issue, deploring the state-of-the-art and citing astronomical cost figures necessary to completely automate the entire Serial Record. The cost would be high if one envisions a turnkey operation, but this will not be the case. More than any other library function, the automation of serials processing must be an experimental and evolving operation. The state-of-the-art, while not yet able to produce ultimate utopian solutions, is more than adequate from which to begin some developmental work.

Since 1913 the visible index has served libraries excellently, and in general it should not be given up in favor of an automated system until there is clear evidence of the superiority of automation in terms of economy and efficiency. Until then a library is on sound ground when it has a visible index complemented by a computer program for accounting and renewals and for lists of holdings. More harm than good is done by indicating that manual methods suffer from serious deficiencies and therefore should be replaced by computer methods. The proper approach is to say that the visible index has served and is serving libraries well, and that when there is a wholesale changeover to automated methods it will be because their lower costs and their greater effectiveness characterize them as devices that will serve libraries even better than the visible index has.

Verity has listed what he considers to be deficiencies in the visible index,[7] and the points he has made have been reproduced in IBM, *Library Automation.* The deficiencies are said to be: (1) a visible

[7]John B. Verity, *Automated Serial Records, an Oblique Look at the State of the Art* (UCRL–71729 [Livermore, Calif.: Lawrence Radiation Laboratory, 1969]).

index is not portable, and this is an inconvenience for most users; (2) it cannot be reproduced readily; (3) the cards and overriding slips are nonregenerative, they wear out and sometimes become unintelligible; (4) the record cannot be manipulated, so a copying task is necessary before related records can be set up; (5) posting data and consulting them are mechanically awkward and hence inefficient; (6) the checking process is personnel-dependent; and (7) visible indexes are susceptible to ambiguous, though not necessarily erroneous, input.

> These deficiencies, usually described in different terms, have long been recognized by librarians. But, other than improving a library's visible files somewhat by adding movable signals, getting improved holders, slides, drawers, etc., and redesigning the forms, the librarian could do little to improve the situation. The advent of punched card equipment, however, gave the librarian tools enabling him to do much of his serials processing and, hopefully, to overcome many of the deficiencies and handicaps of his existing manual serials system.
>
> The deficiencies of the existing manual systems have handicapped librarians in accomplishing tasks they wanted done. As the number of serials increased, without a proportional increase in the work force, certain functions had to be set aside, often permanently. As a result, both service and control deteriorated, and new demands for services could not be accommodated.[8]

Most of the seven points are inconsequential, untrue, or else apply equally to an automated system. Service and control have not deteriorated unless a visible-index system has been allowed to run down. Advances will not come by taking a negative aspect; they will follow from the design of an automated system that is superior in every respect. Hammer has described the present situation as follows:

> While many areas of library operations can be improved or even radically transformed by automation, the one area that probably stands to gain most, and needs the most help, is serials. . . .
>
> Some librarians and some computer people have already expended much effort in the development of automated serials systems, but to date, as fine as many of the efforts are, they, like the computers they use, are only in the horse and buggy stage of automation. What the future holds no one can be sure, but without a doubt much greater sophistication in input methods and in mass data storage will be among the first improvements necessary before the automation of serials can be considered a problem solved.

[8]IBM, *Library Automation*, p.3.

Very few libraries have developed a major serials automation program and most of those that presently operate machine systems are small libraries. A few important research libraries, perhaps half a dozen, have made significant advances in serials automation. The vast majority of libraries are waiting for someone else to solve the problems. While this is understandable, it is not very constructive. The problems of serials, automated or otherwise, require the total effort of the library world and not just that of a few brave and steadfast souls who are strongly motivated toward research. This reluctance to become involved has resulted in very spotty automated serials developments across the country.

Since most publishers cannot or will not make an effort to correct the bibliographical wrongs of their colleagues, perhaps the united efforts of librarians can persuade the recalcitrant and indifferent publishers to accept at least the national standards for periodical format (USASI Z39.1-1967) and the internationally used identifying code, CODEN.[9]

There are a number of statements in print which say that the cost of computer checking approximates that of manual procedures; there are statements in proposals for automation which say that fewer staff members will be required, that there can be a staff reduction of 40 percent. A safer guide is the estimate prepared for the conversion of Linda Hall's 11,257 current serials to computer form: "The estimated cost of operating this computerized system would exceed the present budget by less than $800 per month, and ... the total cost of detailed system design, data conversion and system implementation would not exceed $40,000."[10] It would be unwise to ignore Locke's cautions about computer costs, however. He says:

> We know how to do inventory control; we know how to do data retrieval; but we don't know how to do information retrieval in any sophisticated sense. We have almost no hard facts about costs in large operations. We can afford as much inventory control as can be handled within present budgets, plus normal increases.[11]

[9]Donald P. Hammer, "Serial Publications in Large Libraries: Machine Applications," in Walter C. Allen, ed., *Serial Publications in Large Libraries* (Allerton Park Institute, no.16 [Urbana, Ill.: Univ. of Illinois Graduate School of Library Science, 1970]), p.120–21.

[10]James R. Green, *Feasibility Study of Computerization of Serials Functions for Linda Hall Library of Science and Technology* (Kansas City, Mo.: [The Library], 1970), p.2.

[11]William N. Locke, "Computer Costs for Large Libraries," *Datamation* 16:74 (1970).

Add to this Hammer's graphic expression that some "libraries have courageously squared off with the major dragon and devised check-in systems."[12] The checking records and procedures in reality do constitute "the major dragon" which must be confronted in automating work with serials, though the day is not far off when the total cost and efficiency of a computer checking system will be at least as economical, perhaps more economical, than manual operations are, at the same time that they achieve more and better results.

Beginning in 1959, experimentation was under way in several centers. Then in 1962 the University of California at San Diego installed and began to operate the first computer checking system. It was offline, and the basic principles established for it have remained standard practice, though with a number of variations. A record was stored in the computer under a short title, but giving the frequency of publication or the expected date of arrival for the serial. Then, at the start of each month, the computer produced what is known as an "arrival card" for each issue expected during the month. The arrival cards were filed in a tub tray, from which they were removed by the checkers by finger finding. When the arrival cards were forwarded to the data processing center, they were read into the computer, the record was updated, and a daily list of receipts was printed.[13]

In the Biomedical Library at the University of California at Los Angeles the arrival card is generated when the entry for the previous issue is fed into the computer. This pattern is followed in the Oak Ridge National Laboratory for foreign and irregular serials, but arrival cards for domestic publications are generated monthly.

Two problems have to be faced with arrival cards. One is the receipt of issues for which there is no card on file; the other comes about because of changes in the established pattern; in both cases new cards must be punched. In some libraries new cards are created for up to 15 percent of the issues received.

There is considerable variety in the methods that have been devised for predicting the date of receipt for a serial. The successful range for prediction is from 80 to 90 percent. Domestic publications can be predicted more satisfactorily than overseas ones, as can European and North American serials in either direction. But serials traveling between other continents, particularly to and from the Southern

---

[12]Hammer, "Serial Publications," p.122.

[13]Specimen arrival cards are reproduced in IBM, *Library Automation*, p.69–71; arrival lists are reproduced on p.75–78. Checking procedures in general are covered on p.67–83. Since this is an exceptionally fine state-of-the-art publication, I shall not duplicate the basic procedures here.

Hemisphere, are not easy to forecast. Mail and shipping services are the most critical factor to be reckoned with, followed by the efficiency of publication programs in various countries and institutions.

Instead of arrival cards some libraries prefer to print a list of expected serials, with full titles and with arbitrary numbering, which is also on a prepunched card. When an issue is received, the checker finds the entry on the list and selects the numbered card, which is then forwarded to the data processing center. At the University of California at San Diego it was found that the list method is nearly twice as fast as the arrival-card system.

A number of different patterns are in operation for updating the computer record. Most libraries prefer to have daily updating with daily lists of receipts; some incline to every other day, still others to weekly runs. In the San Francisco Public Library there are daily runs which are cumulated weekly and monthly; consequently, branch librarians no longer want their own checking systems.

Decentralization of checking is entirely possible with automated systems, especially for departmental libraries in universities. A departmental library can send its arrival cards to the main library for action, or it can use the same transaction number for a serial that is in operation centrally. A similar system is possible between libraries, especially when a common subject field applies or when there are in a community a number of libraries with fairly similar programs.

Online checking, which is the desideratum, is in effect in only a few institutions, notably in the Biomedical Library at the University of California at Los Angeles, Laval University in Canada, and the Milton S. Hershey Medical Center Library at Pennsylvania State University. Arrival cards are not needed in an online system; the computer record is updated immediately and can be consulted through any terminal. The problem is, of course, the cost of online service, and if that cost is to be met, then without doubt data must be fed into the computer as concisely and compactly as possible.

Follow-Up Work

Although the computer can spot gaps and write out claims automatically, this procedure has not worked out satisfactorily. Dealers have reacted unfavorably to the system, which does not allow for strikes and other delays. Accordingly, arrival cards which have not been activated and computer-generated lists of various kinds are reviewed by a librarian who uses his judgment about instituting a claim or not. When a claim is to be made, the computer can prepare it, or else a manual practice can be followed. The value of the computer claim is that second and third notices can ensue automatically, to be followed by a notice to a serial librarian to take special action.[14]

Routing of Current Issues

A two-digit code on the arrival or checking card can tell the checker that the table of contents of an issue is to be reproduced for circulation to staff members so that they can know what is in an issue and request it to be sent to them. Or the computer can provide routing slips to be attached to an issue so that it will be circulated to one or more people. When a number of readers wish to see the current issue and the library wants the item to be returned after each consultation, it is possible to have carbon copies of the routing slip held at the circulation desk and used for each later circulation. Commonly the computer prepares a list of periodicals that each individual needs to see; each person is asked to review the list and to note any titles that he no longer desires to see currently. The feeling is that the practice tends to tighten up the system and to improve service to those who really are keen on seeing current issues regularly.[15]

Statistic

The computer can be programmed to give the number of issues received annually as well as the number of titles which come by exchange, gift, or purchase. This is about as far as the keeping of statistics should go. Some libraries, however, have the computer provide a wide range of figures; the San Francisco Public Library, e.g., maintains a computer record of thirty-three different sets of figures. Some of the data may have value while a program is in the experimental stages, but overdesigning the statistical program should be avoided, just as overdesigning the computer system in general is a danger to be avoided.

The Computer Program

The desirable starting point for a library's automated program for

[14]For follow-up procedures see IBM, *Library Automation*, p.84–87.
[15]Routing procedures and examples of routing slips are given in IBM, *Library Automation*, p.92–96.

serials is a holdings list that should be reproduced at least annually. That program can pay for itself quickly because it can and should carry with it the cessation of card cataloging for serials. Accounting procedures should be automated when acquisition accounts in general are computerized. From an administrative point of view, binding records may be retained on a manual basis unless there is good and compelling reason for automating. The last serial function to be converted should be current checking. The change should not be made unless a library is ready to make the fullest possible use of *Coden,* so that there can be an online system which operates as concisely and compactly as can possibly be, and unless the library is ready to substitute a holdings list for conventional cataloging. If these conditions are not acceptable, automated checking should be left to the handful of libraries that are ready to underwrite the expense of experimentation, either because the computer is available to them without cost or because other aspects of the serial program, e.g., the building up of resources, can be sacrificed.

In any event much experimental work remains to be done. For one thing, the best equipment to use still has to be determined. Hammer, for example, says: "I personally consider the cathode ray tube as the most satisfactory method by far. It is, unfortunately, also the most expensive, but the results gained far surpass those gained from any other system."[16] It may well prove to be, however, that with the use of *Coden* it will be better to have a computer printout of the checking instructions for each title, so that the cathode ray tube will from that point of view be less satisfactory than a regular terminal. Certainly the whole range of possibilities that *Coden* presents, including elimination of the identification number, must be fully explored experimentally before judgments of this kind can be substantiated.

Bibliography

The literature on automated systems for serials up through 1970 is adequately covered in International Business Machines, *Library Automation—Computerized Serials Control* (White Plains, N.Y., 1971), p.99–106. An excellent state-of-the-art study, this document should be carefully read because it provides a summary of the findings that have been established in the course of the pioneer experimental work.

16Hammer, "Serial Publications," p.127.

3

Cataloging and Classification

10

Theory of Descriptive Cataloging

Precisely the same retrograde sentence opens the chapter on serials in the North American text of the *Anglo-American Cataloging Rules* as was written into the 1949 *Rules for Descriptive Cataloging in the Library of Congress*. The sentence reads: "The general principles for cataloging serials are the same as those for cataloging monographic publications; wherever suitable, the rules for the cataloging of monographs are to be applied to serials."[1] The British text is much more to the point. It says: "Periodicals, continuations, and works published frequently or regularly in new editions (such as guide books, who's whos) of which the library holds several parts, either simultaneously or successively, are described as serials according to the rules which follow. . . . The general principles and rules for cataloguing monographs are applied wherever there are no specific or appropriate rules for serials in this chapter."[2] The British statement fits in with the dictum by Miss Ditmas, quoted in chapter 2, that the serial has attained the right to be treated *sui generis* and not as a poor relation of the book, whereas the North American statement is in sharp contrast to the dictum, just as it is an oversimplified approach to a difficult and technical field.

The major points of connection between monograph and serial cataloging are: (1) the products of the two have had to mesh in a unitary card catalog, a situation which is undergoing a change as more and more libraries produce a serial catalog in book form; and

[1]*Anglo-American Cataloging Rules; North American Text* (Chicago: American Library Assn., 1967), p.231. The identical wording occurs in *Rules for Descriptive Cataloging in the Library of Congress* (Washington, 1949), p.51.

[2]*Anglo-American Cataloguing Rules; British Text* (London: The Library Assn., 1967), p.183.

(2) the corporate entry is common to both types of cataloging. Even with the corporate entry the dominance of book cataloging has led to some undesirable results. For example, there has been a tendency to catalog many serials under the corporate name when entry under the title would be more appropriate, and added entries have been made for some corporate bodies when their role is simply that of publisher.

Beatrice Simon has been outspoken about the differences that ought to exist between the two types of cataloging. She says:

> No one can seriously maintain that a serial is like a book in any but the most superficial aspect, and yet we have never ceased to try to force serials into the techniques and routines evolved for books. Look, for instance, at the absurd way in which some of us try to get the statement of a badly broken set onto the card form designed for the bibliographical notation of a book. The resulting confusion presented to the user of the catalog is enough to send him away in disgust at our inefficiency. Look, too, at the way in which many libraries scatter periodicals throughout a classification by the reckless addition of .05 at any given point in the scheme. Surely it is time to admit frankly that, excellent as were the principles laid down by our illustrious predecessors for the acquisition, arrangement and cataloging of books, the rules are not adequate for the reality of a library bulging with serials. It is no reflection on these people to acknowledge that they were not gifted with second sight and so did not provide for this contingency. It *is* a reflection on our own intelligence if we continue to make use of their inadequate methods and do nothing constructive to improve them.[3]

Whereas monograph cataloging is for the most part static, since the typical book or pamphlet is a unit complete in itself, serial cataloging must to a large extent be dynamic to provide for publications which may persist for centuries before they are complete and may undergo a series of major and minor changes during their lifetime, for example, new name, place of publication, publisher, scope, and volume numbering. The cataloging of monographs is comparatively straightforward; serials run the gamut from the straightforward to the wayward, if not the downright perverse, as the case studies in chapter 11 illustrate. Many serials lie directly across a second big problem area, that of the corporate entry. Accordingly, the serial cataloger must be versatile and patient enough to wrestle

[3]Beatrice V. Simon, "Let's Consider Serials Realistically," *Library Journal* 71:1296 (1946).

with a combination of two of the toughest problem areas in all cataloging. As Miss Goss says of the vast domain of serials: "The Pilgrim who enters this field must be prepared to flounder through the Slough of Despond, to struggle up the hill Difficulty, and, with Hopeful to cheer him on, make his progress toward the Celestial City of Truth."[4]

In 1949 the Library of Congress listed seven ways in which, it said, serial cataloging differs from book cataloging; in 1967 the North American text of the *Anglo-American Cataloging Rules* increased the number to ten. There is no corresponding list in the British text because of its basic philosophy. The ten differences are:

1. A serial which changes its title, or which is entered under a corporate heading for a body that changes its name, is cataloged as a series of entries, one for each segment that goes with a title or name. In the 1967 code there are footnotes on pages 22 and 232 which state that the Library of Congress does not follow this ruling. In 1971, however, it decided to use successive entries, as provided for in Rule 6D.

2. Under earlier practice a serial publication was cataloged from the latest volume, with notes for variations in earlier volumes, while a set of books is cataloged from the first volume, with notes for variations in later volumes.

3. The subtitle of a serial is frequently omitted from the catalog entry altogether, or it may be given in the form of a note; the subtitle of a book is given in the body of the catalog entry.

4. When needed, the author statement for a serial is given as a note, not in the body of the entry as for a book.

5. Likewise the editor statement occurs in a note, not in the body of the entry as for a book. The reasons for the serial practice are that the prominent position on the catalog card after the title of the work can then be devoted to the important statement of the library's holdings and that when editors change it is more convenient and economical to add to an editor statement which takes the form of a note.

6. When the catalog entry for a serial does not disclose the full extent of a library's holdings, it is customary to in-

[4]Edna L. Goss, "The Cataloging of Serials," *Catalogers' and Classifiers' Yearbook* 2:73 (1930).

clude on the catalog card a form statement which refers
the reader or staff member to the current checking record
or the shelflist for a statement of the library's holdings.
For books the statement of holdings is always on the
main-entry card at least, if it is not on all catalog cards.

7. Because serials are issued periodically, the frequency of
publication should be noted.

8. When the statement of holdings does not indicate the
duration of a serial, it should be noted on the catalog
card along with suspensions and resumptions of publication.

9. Note should be made of the fact that a serial is the organ
of a corporate body, either for a period or throughout its
history.

10. Serial publications from time to time have special numbers of one kind or another which must be described.[5]

This list of ten differences fails to note, or to emphasize as the most
important difference of all, the fact that there are complementary
and supporting records for serials, while for the most part the catalog
records for books stand entirely on their own. There is no reason in
theory or practice why serial cataloging for current publications
should stand on its own. No approach, then, to serial cataloging is
satisfactory which does not make due allowance for the role played
by the current checking records, whether they are manual or computer; by the *Union List of Serials* and *New Serial Titles*; and by
other serial records, which today include what is bound to grow in
extent and importance, the library's own serial catalog in book form.
It is accidental, and accordingly immaterial, that the supporting
records generally are not located in the catalog department or in the
card catalog, that they may be in the acquisition department, the
periodical room, or elsewhere. They must at all times be considered
as joint records, serving all parts of a library fully and equally. It is
a sound principle of library administration that serial records, no
matter where they are located, must not be looked on either pos-
sessively by the department which houses them or extrinsically by
another department; in other words, they must be prevented from
becoming the victim of the kind of departmentalization which tends
to turn into compartmentalization.

[5]*Anglo-American Cataloging Rules; North American Text*, p.232. For the original list of seven differences see *Rules for Descriptive Cataloging in the Library of
Congress*, p.51–52, or the first edition of *Serial Publications*, p.121. The additional
items in the 1967 listing are (1) and (3–4).

There are, of course, serials which require few if any supporting records within the library itself. They are the titles which have ceased publication and for which the library has a complete file. The catalog entries for "complete and dead" serials have much more in common with the entries for monographs than do the current items; but for the active titles—the continuing and the incomplete runs— the record can and should be divided between the current checking system and the card catalog or its equivalent. The two types of record should not be permitted to duplicate each other beyond a bare minimum. In order to justify their existence, they must be complementary; otherwise the cost of serial cataloging, already high, is bound to be excessive.

A simple illustration of the duplication of effort which ensues when the principle of complementary records is ignored is afforded by the statement of frequency which, for unexplained reasons, both the Library of Congress and the North American text of the *Anglo-American Cataloging Rules* specify as "an important feature for the characterization of a serial, and occasionally for its identification."[6] But, in theory or practice, is frequency a cataloging feature, let alone an important feature, for a current serial? What purpose does the information serve on a catalog card? The current checking records have no alternative; they must pay attention to frequency so that the correct form for a daily, weekly, monthly, or annual will be selected for checking purposes and the follow-up period for claims for missing numbers can be determined. Should a weekly turn into a monthly or a quarterly, then a new form must be substituted for the old one. As Beatrice Simon says: "We are only interested in the periodicity of the *current* issues, and that information is readily available on the checking-in record."[7] When the frequency statement for current serials is confined to the current checking records, costs are held in line; but when the serial checkers must report changes in frequency to the catalogers so that they can adjust the statement on the catalog cards, costs are increased appreciably. Also, adjustment of the catalog cards is generally a slow process.

Three technicalities have to be observed in making the cataloging statement of frequency. (1) When the title of the publication specifies

[6]*Anglo-American Cataloging Rules; North American Text*, p.232. Introduction of the concept of identification is somewhat misleading. When a weekly edition must be distinguished, for example, from a monthly edition, the edition statement constitutes part of the body of the entry; as such it has nothing to do with the frequency statement.

[7]Beatrice V. Simon, "Cataloguing of Periodicals," *Ontario Library Review* 33:242 (1949).

the frequency, as in the case of *Library Quarterly*, the frequency statement in the collation or in a note is omitted. (2) When the frequency can be expressed by an adjective or a brief phrase, the statement becomes an extension of the collation, e.g.,

> v. illus. 21 cm. annual.
> v. illus. 21 cm. monthly (except July and Aug.)
> v. illus. 21 cm. semimonthly (during the school year)
> v. illus. 21 cm. 3 no. a year.

(3) A note is employed when a more extended statement is required than under (2), e.g.,

> Four no. a year, 1931; 5 no. a year, 1932–34.
> Issued several times a week.
> Monthly, accompanied by a midmonthly supplement.
> Monthly, 1901–June 1904; quarterly, Sept. 1904–

When more than three changes in frequency are involved, the Library of Congress covers them by the note "Frequency varies."[8] There are inconsistencies between (2) and (3) because "Frequency varies" and "Issued several times a week" are shorter than "semimonthly (during the school year)"; but the real weaknesses consist of making the reader look in three different places on the catalog card to find information that ought to be integrated, and of including the statement in an open entry at all.

It cannot be said too often or too strongly that in a library the current checking records are the foundation on which every other serial record should be built. When the current records are sound and adequate, all later work can depend on them. They are official records, not just for the department in which they are housed and administered, but for the institution as a whole. There can be no doubt about it: the current checking records have as much validity as any cataloging records do, regardless of the facts that they are compiled and maintained by clerical, not professional staff, and that they generally are not under the control of the serial catalogers. It is unfortunate that comparatively few libraries have taken advantage of the principle of complementary serial records. Yet much economy

---

[8]These details about the frequency statement are from *Anglo-American Cataloging Rules; North American Text*, p.236–37, which in turn took them unchanged from *Rules for Descriptive Cataloging in the Library of Congress*, p.56.

can result from the full realization of the principle, since it is clear that the cataloging of current serials does not need to be anywhere near as detailed and technical as the cataloging code has made it under the influence of the Library of Congress.

In 1951 Trotier made a case for the principle of complementary serial records. He pointed out that in the University of Illinois Library:

> The record of holdings of serials in the Acquisition Department files is largely duplicated in the official shelf list, the public shelf list and the general card catalog maintained by the Catalog Department; and the record of bound serial volumes found in the Binding Department is duplicated, for the most part, in the two shelf lists as well as in the card catalog.[9]

After proposing the formation of a central serial record, he went on to say:

> Fundamental to the program I have in mind is the acceptance of two propositions, namely, that the visible files of the central serials record should be the basic record for current serials, whereas, in the case of serials which have ceased publication, the standard entries in the card catalog should form the complete and authoritative record. For current serials the record in the catalog can then be kept down to the bare essentials. Beyond the most important subject entries only those secondary entries will need to be made as will enable the user to establish that the library has the publication he wants.[10]

Why Serials Are Cataloged

The reasons for cataloging serials are brought out by an analysis of the conditions that prevailed in the United Nations Library until 1949. In the formative years of the library the catalogers could not keep pace with the intake of publications, particularly of serial publications. These serials were numerous; they contained a large admixture of government documents; they were in many instances of fundamental importance to the delegations and the Secretariat of the United Nations.

[9]Arnold H. Trotier, "Some Persistent Problems of Serials in Technical Processes," *Serial Slants* 1:7 (Jan. 1951).
[10]*Ibid.*, p.9.

All library functions were adversely affected by the shortcomings in serial cataloging. The Acquisition Unit, instead of devoting full time to its normal activities, had to take up much of the slack. It had to maintain a file that listed all items which had been received in the library. It had to assign class marks to numerous serial titles in order to know where to send successive issues as they arrived. In other words, it had to do a considerable amount of temporary cataloging. The Cataloguing Unit and the reference staff wasted much time trying to locate items requested by readers. The Circulation Desk had to struggle with a charging system arranged by author and title, since arrangement by call number was out of the question when so many items lacked one. A given serial title might be recorded in the charge file in a variety of ways because complicated corporate entries and titles, as well as a wide range of languages, often made it difficult to bring charges for the same serial together under a common heading; discharging was even more troublesome, as was the locating of a volume which another reader desired. Care of the stacks suffered because of the extensive assortment of uncataloged and unbound material on the shelves and also because service copies regularly found their way to the stacks along with permanent copies, the shortcoming here being that the shelflist did not control the flow of publications into the stacks. Clearly it was necessary to get the serials cataloged, and cataloged promptly, to allow all parts of the United Nations Library to function normally.[11] Thus it can be seen that serials are cataloged for the following basic reasons, over and above the age-old one of bringing order into a mass of material:

1. To provide a certain amount of essential data for use in the serial checking records, e.g., the call number, particularly for works such as annuals, directories, and who's whos.
2. To afford a uniform medium for the arrangement of serial entries in the charging system in those libraries which circulate serial publications and do not use transaction numbers.
3. To facilitate the shelving of material in the stacks, especially when changes of corporate author or of title occur.
4. To allow serials to be bound systematically, and more particularly types such as annual reports which tend to be

[11]The principles and practices of serial cataloging developed for the United Nations Library in 1949 are given in detail in its *Manual of the Cataloguing Unit* (Lake Success, N.Y., 1950), p.36–42.

held in the stacks in unbound form. In some libraries it is considered to be the responsibility of the catalog department to get them bound at appropriate intervals.

5. To permit all departments in a library to concentrate on their normal functions without let or hindrance caused by the existence of unrecorded serials.

6. To promote a maximum of self-service on the part of readers who consult the card catalog before going to the shelves.

Another reason for serial cataloging is that it facilitates cooperative undertakings such as *New Serial Titles* and the *Union List of Serials*. All these reasons are evident and practical; there is nothing esoteric about them. If they are weighted heavily on the administrative side, that is because service to readers depends to a high degree on the catalog record. In so far as any of them do not apply in particular circumstances, e.g., in a public library branch that does not preserve its periodical files, the cataloging can be simplified or even dispensed with entirely. The Linda Hall Library and the National Lending Library for Science and Technology have both functioned smoothly from their foundation without catalog records or classification. The former employed its visible index as a catalog; the latter developed highly successful self-cataloging methods. Both eventually came to book catalogs, however.

The great range and extent of serial cataloging practices which exist among libraries of comparable size and service requirements must be accounted for on the basis of subjective rather than objective reasons. Often the justification for what a library does is to be found in decades of ingrown usage; often it will be found in the influence of overelaborate cataloging codes. Much of it can be traced back to the Library of Congress, whose serial cataloging has not changed very much from the days of Miss MacNair[12] and Miss Pierson,[13] the cousins who for a major part of their lifetimes were dedicated to serial cataloging in that library. From 1951 to 1967 the Library of Congress followed simplified rules for less important publications,[14] but the 1967 cataloging code erased that advance.

[12]Mary W. MacNair, *Guide to the Cataloguing of Periodicals* (3d ed.; Washington, 1925).

[13]Harriet W. Pierson, *Guide to the Cataloguing of the Serial Publications of Societies and Institutions* (2d ed.; Washington, 1931).

[14]*Rules for Descriptive Cataloging in the Library of Congress: Supplement 1949–51* (Washington, 1952), p.16–19.

History Cards

Authority cards for serials are chiefly the history cards which are made for corporate bodies. These cards are sometimes useful enough to readers and staff members so that they are developed into information cards to go into the public as well as the official catalog. The Library of Congress has printed a number of information cards; libraries frequently find them well worth acquiring for their own catalogs. A few catalog departments make history cards for periodicals, but that is surely a supererogatory task.

Miss Pierson has recorded some of the story of history cards at the Library of Congress.[15] She gives an idea of the massive effort that went into the making of history cards for society publications prior to the introduction of "no-conflict" cataloging in 1951. Administrators who are concerned about the cost of cataloging should read her article and reflect on it. So much time can be expended on the making of history cards that libraries should determine whether they need to continue such records. Many libraries of all kinds and sizes operate satisfactorily without them, except for an occasional information card, so their value is open to question.

A development of note is the application of the principle of "no-conflict" cataloging to history cards, which has led to the idea of "limited search" in making the cards. New York Public Library practice, adopted in 1952, is as follows:

> *a. Purpose.* All corporate names used as authors or subjects are "established" in order to insure consistency of entry in the catalog and to relate the various forms of such names appearing in the catalog.
>
> *b. Information recorded on authority cards.* Information regarding corporate bodies is generally not made available in the public catalogs. Information recorded on authority cards is restricted, therefore, to data which can be used for purposes of cataloging to distinguish one body from another and as a basis for cross references. The following data are considered to be useful:
>   1) name
>   2) date of founding, establishment, incorporation, etc.
>   3) changes of name
>   4) affiliation or union with other bodies
>   5) date of dissolution
>   6) headquarters

[15]Harriet W. Pierson, "The Forest of Pencils; Adventures in Corporate Entry," *Library Quarterly* 4:306 (1934).

The inclusion of additional data on authority cards is not authorized.

c. "Limited search" principle used in establishing corporate names.

1) In establishing corporate names, the principle of "Limited search" is to be applied. This principle is used for corporate names in much the same way as the "no-conflict" principle is used for personal names, the idea being that it is unnecessary to search for, find, and record information which does not have *direct* bearing on the form of entry.

2) Whenever possible, corporate names will be established using the material at hand for both form of entry and information about the entry; in other words, *it is unnecessary to verify such information in other sources*. In cases where the material at hand does not answer such questions as are enumerated above, outside sources should not be consulted unless the information sought is essential in making a decision as to the *form of the entry proper*. It is not necessary to consult outside sources in order *merely* to discover the date of founding, headquarters, etc.

3) It is recognized that there are times when consultation of a familiar reference work offers a quicker means of finding facts of the kind which may be required for entry establishment than does extensive reading of the text of the material at hand.[16]

Title-Page Cataloging

One of the accomplishments of *Studies of Descriptive Cataloging*[17] was the freeing of the catalog entry from the tyranny of the title page. In serial cataloging the title page never held sway as it did in the cataloging of books; one reason is that many serials lack title pages; another is that the successive title pages for a serial may pass through numerous transformations. Yet undesirable elements of title-page cataloging persist with serials, although the 1949 Library of Congress statement has been somewhat modified in the 1967 code. The 1949 ruling began: "The data given in the body of the entry, with the exception of the record of holdings, are taken from a single source as far as possible." The 1967 ruling requires only that the title and imprint be taken from a single source. The rest of the ruling is very much the same in both codes:

If the publication has no title page, the title is taken from the cover, caption, masthead, editorial pages, or other place, the order of pref-

16New York Public Library, Preparation Division, *Technical Order* 64–3 (1964).
17Library of Congress, Processing Department, *Studies of Descriptive Cataloging* (Washington, 1946).

erence being that of this listing. The source of the data is specified
if it is not the title page, cover, caption, or masthead. However, if
there is no title page or cover, and the caption or other titles differ
the source of the title used is specified and the other titles are
noted.[18]

Without doubt great latitude is needed to make the most of individual
circumstances, especially if the transposition and integration ad-
vocated in *Studies of Descriptive Cataloging* are to be meaningful in
serial cataloging.

For long the most serious practical consequence of the title-page
approach to serial cataloging was that the majority of descriptive
and subject catalogers were reluctant to catalog a periodical from the
first issue. They preferred to wait until the first volume was complete,
happily with a title page and index. For the sake of this theory they
were ready to face the extra work and cost entailed.[19]

Of less significance are the technical details which sometimes pay
scant attention to the title page and sometimes cling to it. A short
title may be adopted when by this device minor variations in the
wording on different issues can be disregarded. Subtitles are omitted
unless they are necessary for identification purposes or to specify
the scope of a publication, and when a subtitle is both necessary and
long, it is given as a note in order to leave space after the main title
for the statement of holdings. Many libraries, and particularly special
libraries, omit from the titles of reports the adjectives that denote
frequency; e.g., "Financial statement" instead of "Monthly financial
statement"; and "Report," not "Annual report" or "Biennial report."
Serial numbering that is included in the title is omitted in the
transcription; so "Report of the annual meeting," not "Report of the
first annual meeting." On the other hand, expressions on the title
page which accompany the serial numbering are retained in the
catalog entry (though no longer on bindings), regardless of whether
retention of the wording facilitates or retards comprehension of the
entry. Thus "Aviation equipment red book. 1944–   ed." is the
Library of Congress form, in which the word "edition" has been
retained merely because it occurs on the title page, not because it
has any value whatsoever on the catalog card. A simpler entry that
would satisfy all serial demands would be: "Aviation equipment red
book, 1944–   ."

[18]*Anglo-American Cataloging Rules; North American Text*, p.232. The earlier
ruling is from *Rules for Descriptive Cataloging in the Library of Congress*, p.52.

[19]For the 1971 changeover to first-issue cataloging, see the section on temporary
cataloging in chapter 12.

The use of brackets shows a further confusion in theory. The ruling is:

> The data in the statement of holdings are not enclosed in brackets when ascertainable from the issues being cataloged even though they do not appear on the title page or title page substitute which forms the basis of the catalog entry. Brackets are not used to enclose the "v." or comparable designation if it appears in a later volume of the publication.[20]

Thus the interpretation of the entry "Housing index-digest. v. [1]–4, no. 3" is that volume 1 was not designated as such anywhere in the volume. The other volumes are numbered somewhere, but not necessarily on their title pages. The practice differs from monograph cataloging, where brackets indicate data taken from a source elsewhere than the title page. Very unfortunately, the practice does not coincide with the use of brackets in the *Union List of Serials* and *New Serial Titles,* in both of which they signify an incomplete volume.

Description of an Incomplete Set

The normal supposition would be that a library with an incomplete set would catalog exactly what it has and nothing more. This is precisely what happens in book catalogs and what ought to happen in computer listings. Oddly enough, however, some libraries prefer to catalog, not what they have, but a complete set. Having cataloged a complete set, and this without having had recourse to a definitive bibliography, they then make a note at or toward the end of the entry specifying the gaps in their file, hoping that readers and staff will be patient enough to read through the whole entry to discover that, after all, the library does not have what it started out to say it had. The ruling is:

> If the library does not have all of the volumes that have been published, the extent of the complete set is recorded, provided the information is available; the volumes that are lacking are specified in a supplementary note. If essential data are not available, the statement of holdings consists only of the data relating to the first issue.

[20]*Anglo-American Cataloging Rules: North American Text,* p.235. The statement does not occur in the British text.

> If information about the first issue is not available, no record of holdings is given.[21]

The ruling does not appear in the British text. Nevertheless Hamilton believes that it applies in Great Britain, saying: "The entries for serials are entries for a bibliography, as well as a record of what is in the library."[22] This is an echo of the old theory of bibliographical cataloging that was repudiated in the survey of the Library of Congress in 1940. In a comment on Hamilton's statement, it was said: "There had been an intriguing discussion on when one should catalogue something one had not got: the answer being, when it is a serial; though it was rightly pointed out that this could be confusing to the user; and it might be very costly."[23]

Practice in the Yale University Library is as follows:

> *Yale's set complete or nearly complete* (no statement cards required).
> a. When Yale has a complete set of a serial which has ceased publication or lacks only one or two volumes, the set is cataloged as a closed entry; *i.e.,* the holdings statement following the title gives complete information as to volumes published.
> 1) If available evidence indicates that Yale has a complete set but there is no definite proof of this, a note is added to the history card as follows:
> No more published?
> 2) If Yale's set lacks only one or two volumes, cataloger indicates in pencil under call number on history card which volumes are wanting; *e.g.,*
> wanting: v. 9, 12
> b. *Exception.* For monograph series which are analyzed, statement cards listing the authors and titles must always be made so that there is a listing of the analytics.
>
> *Yale's set incomplete* (statement cards required).
> a. When Yale's set lacks more than two volumes or consists of a scattered file and information about the title is available, the set is cataloged as a closed entry, cataloger writes under the call

[21]*Ibid.,* p.233. A footnote states that the principal sources that should be checked for the complete statement of volumes published are the *British Union Catalogue of Periodicals, New Serial Titles,* and the *Union List of Serials.* It goes on to say that the extent of the complete set need not be given when the library's holdings are very fragmentary.

[22]G. E. Hamilton, "Serials (Rules 160–168)," in J. C. Downing and N. F. Sharp, eds., *Seminar on the Anglo-American Cataloguing Rules (1967),* (London: The Library Assn., 1969), p.58.

[23]Downing and Sharp, eds., *Seminar,* p.88.

number on history card in pencil "Incomplete," and makes a statement card listing the volumes which Yale has, as for open entries.

1) Cataloger makes a note on the statement card of the final volume and/or date of publication of final volume. This goes on the line following that which lists the last volume published or, if Yale lacks the last volume, the line that would list it if Yale had it. The note reads:

Ceased publication with v. 6, no. 7, Jan. 1922.

Ceased publication with 1956.

2) If statement card does not allow for all volumes in set, ceased publication note is added in pencil at bottom of last card used so that it can be erased and moved to another card if necessary; *e.g.*, if set closed with v. 66 and last volume in Yale set is v. 46, which would be on statement card 3, the ceased publication note is added in pencil at bottom of statement card 3.

3) If the date of the final issue is uncertain, such a note is followed by a question mark; *e.g.*,

Ceased publication with v. 5, 1956?

b. When Yale's set lacks more than two volumes or consists of a scattered file and information about the title is not available, the set is cataloged as an open entry.[24]

Although the 1967 cataloging code makes it clear that the details of a complete set must be easily ascertainable, much routine is involved in attempting to catalog what is not on hand. Nor can the results be at all satisfactory, for bibliographies of serials are noted for their practical value rather than their definitive bibliography. The *British Union Catalogue of Periodicals, New Serial Titles,* and the *Union List of Serials* are tools of inestimable worth, but their details have never been submitted to the bibliographer's close scrutiny. Actually the search is wider than these three tools, judging by the example in Rule 167D which reads: "Began with Apr. 1943 issue. Cf. Willing's press guide, 1944." The serial cataloger who relies on nondefinitive aids may be guilty of poor bibliography. Moreover, readers can easily be misled by descriptions of complete sets which are not locally available. This is all the more possible because the statement of holdings is prominent by comparison with the note at the end of the entry which records gaps.

The only sound practice for a library is to describe what it has. This should be axiomatic; it is a principle of economy. It does not

[24]Yale University Library, *Cataloging of Serials in the Yale University Library* (3d ed.; New Haven, Conn., 1969), p.20–21.

result in questionable bibliography, and it does not confuse readers. Fortunately the practice just described will end with the coming of book catalogs for serial holdings.

Entry under Successive Titles

The serial cataloger is constantly confronted with two troublesome variables: the title of a serial may change, and so may the corporate entry or its subdivision. For the first seven decades of the century catalogers waged a losing battle trying to keep up with the endless changes, even though they kept their spirits high, as Miss Pierson has recorded:

> As societies multiply and the number of books increases, we sometimes ask ourselves, where will it end? This mass of human experience, discovery, achievement, must be preserved, the records must be kept clear, the tangled threads of changing titles must be patiently straightened out; but to the thoughtful person it is an inspiring task, for enfolded in those pages which, perchance, few but the cataloguer will ever see in their unbroken sequence, is the history of modern civilization, the written result of organized human effort, the panorama of life itself. The cataloguing of it is not, after all, a science, but an art—a plastic art, if you will—and *art is long*; is there not proof of this in the memoirs of a well known academy whose first volume appeared in 1756 and whose second volume followed one hundred and twelve years laters, in 1868?[25]

Over the same period British practice was the direct opposite of the American. In order to avoid the interminable recataloging brought on by changes of name and title, British catalogers preferred to make the cataloging entry under the earliest title, a practice that was no more satisfactory.

In 1967, however, the British and the North American texts of the Anglo-American cataloging code decided to abandon both the former systems and to make a separate entry for each change. For several years the Library of Congress held back on the new Rule 6D, but, beginning in 1971, it too is following the practice of entry under successive titles.

[25]Harriet W. Pierson, "The Gay Science—the Cataloguing of the Publications of Learned Societies," *Proceedings* of the Catalog Section, American Library Assn., (Chicago, 1929), p.144. The memoirs are those of the Academia de Buenas Letras de Barcelona.

Entry under Title?

Since the serial cataloger is constantly confronted with two elements which are subject to change, the title and the corporate name, it is natural to ask whether the two should not be reduced to one. This could be accomplished by cataloging serials under their titles with an added entry, when necessary, for the corporate body. At least one library, the British Library of Political and Economic Science, follows this practice for the majority of its serials, and in both texts of the Anglo-American cataloging code title entry is authorized for almanacs, biographical dictionaries and who's whos, directories, indexes, monograph series, periodicals, serially published bibliographies, and yearbooks. This is a wise easing of the rules because added entries under variant forms of names for corporate bodies can be multiplied freely without occasioning recataloging. So a title entry *Bibliography of Agriculture*, as now authorized, would not have required recataloging when the Department of Agriculture Library became the National Agricultural Library.

There is an exception to the rule, however. When the main title includes the name of a corporate body or its acronym, or when the title consists solely of a generic term such as "Contribution," then entry under the corporate name ensues. At least the first part of the exception is unfortunate; it gives rise to needless technicalities. Accordingly, the *Harvard Business Review* and the *National Geographic Magazine* continue under their titles because the corporate names are not present in full, but the *University of Detroit Law Journal* must go under "Detroit. University. Dept. of Law" because the name of the university is given in full.

The Statement of Holdings

Early in this century the common practice was to maintain the statement of holdings on the main, added-entry, and subject cards in all catalogs: departmental, official, and public. So great was the burden of add-to-cards work that gradually the information was maintained on main cards only. Secondary cards were stamped with a reference to the main entry. In other libraries it was decided that the statement of holdings could be eliminated from the main cards as well. When this practice is followed, the cards read "v. 1– ," "v. 1 to date," "1902– ," etc. The British cataloging code authorizes use of the plus sign in place of the dash if desired, a wise course of action since the plus sign is the conventional union list symbol for an open entry; and actually, in library parlance, "v. 1– " is known as a "one-plus" entry. While many libraries keep adding to a "v. 1– " entry, most do not. At the Enoch Pratt Free Library, catalog cards for serials currently received show the date of Pratt's first issue and are stamped "to date." When a serial is no longer received, the stamped words are removed and the holdings statement is closed. While it is still received, the record of serial holdings is maintained in the Serials Unit of the Processing Division.

The one weakness of the simple one-plus system is that readers and staff may be misled as to library holdings when files have not been kept up to date. For this reason Dorothy Litchfield spoke of "the exasperating and often misleading 'v. 1–date.' "[26] Most book catalogs use the one-plus entry, e.g., the annually produced *Serials and Journals in the M.I.T. Libraries,* which favors the plus sign, and *Serial Holdings in the Linda Hall Library,* which inclines to the dash.

Open entries which do not specify holdings are possible in institutions in which readers and staff take it for granted that the library has reasonably complete files, at least of more recent volumes. They are clearly indicated in any type of library for reference works such as *Who's Who in America,* the latest volume of which will be on the reference shelves far more rapidly than the catalog records could be updated. Beyond that, however, is it necessary for a library to show in its card catalog the latest bound volume of the *Atlantic Monthly,* the *Library Journal,* or the *New York Times?* And if a one-plus entry is satisfactory in book catalogs and union lists, is it not equally satisfactory in the card catalog?

Libraries are increasingly recognizing the wisdom of the philosophy expressed by Beatrice Simon, who says of the statement of holdings:

> My experience is that the public does not use the information. It is the staff who find it helpful, and as long as the people who answer the questions have easy access to the record that is all that matters. It is an expensive and time-consuming routine to keep the public catalogue up-to-date. It involves the filing of temporary cards when the original is out having the entry corrected. Large libraries have worked out elaborate systems of triplicate travelling cards for this purpose so that there is always a full record in the catalogue and not just a title saying "Card temporarily removed." These are complicated and expensive to install and administer. Unless you place the burden on your library user of determining, through the cataloguer, that the library has the volume or issue which his ref-

[26]Dorothy Litchfield, "Paleolithic Practices in the Checking and Cataloging of Periodicals," *Library Journal* 60:60 (1935).

erence calls for, then I think it unnecessary to have more than the title represented with a note telling the user to consult the Serials Record for detailed holdings.[27]

Considerations of this kind indicate the importance of putting the effort into avoiding gaps in serial holdings rather than into making detailed catalog cards. The expensive records and files for the catalogers to maintain and service are those for incomplete sets.

Hanging Indention

One of the numerous technicalities in serial cataloging is the employment of hanging indention for title main entries (see figure 20). In the preparation of copy for printing or duplicating it may be necessary to switch from one style of heading to the other. When the cataloger chooses a corporate body for the heading which the reviser alters to a title entry, or vice versa, the change in heading usually calls for retyping of the copy. The technicality disappears in book catalogs because all the entries in them tend to take hanging indention.

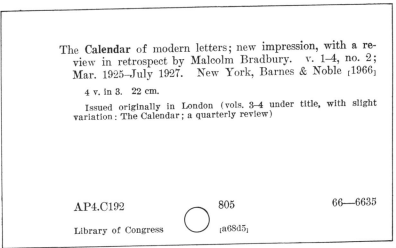

Figure 20. Example of hanging indention. For examples of cataloging forms in general see Laura C. Colvin, *Cataloging Sampler, a Comparative and Interpretive Guide* (Hamden, Conn.: Shoe String, 1963), especially p.157–76.

[27]Simon, "Cataloguing of Periodicals," p.241.

Until 1949 hanging indention was also applied by the Library of Congress to the editor, imprint-varies, and title-entries note on serial entries in order to give special emphasis to them. Other notes followed paragraph indention. But from 1949 on paragraph indention has been the rule for all notes.

Simplified Rules

The Library of Congress introduced simplified rules for the cataloging of serials in 1951, but these were unfortunately not incorporated in the 1967 code. Yale still has its simpler rules for serials destined for the storage collection; for lack of space, though, little if anything is being added to the resource. Harvard has virtually allowed its simplified rules to lapse. It is sad to have to report these developments as long as card cataloging persists. Research libraries do collect and catalog numerous titles of slight consequence and, as Professor Peterson has indicated, they should acquire more. For example, there are all too many entries in *New Serial Titles* for which no file is preserved in North American libraries. And, since serial cataloging at best is expensive, economical methods of processing less significant serials are highly desirable.

Need for Revision of Serial Cataloging Rules

Perhaps the saddest comment which was made on the North American text of the 1967 cataloging code was: "The American rules seem at times almost haphazard in their arrangement, and are very clearly based on the provisions of the LC 1949 rules, without the benefit of rethinking."[28] The rules were not the work of the Catalog Code Revision Committee, and they are to a high degree taken from *Rules for Descriptive Cataloging in the Library of Congress*. Hamilton went on to say:

> We should recognize that the rules for descriptive cataloguing are guides and not mandatory instructions. They set out the procedure for constructing entries which contain every conceivable piece of information about the publication, and there are, of course, libraries in whose catalogues the full history of the publications in the library should be recorded. . . . Other libraries, particularly the spe-

[28]Hamilton, "Serials (Rules 160–168)," p.59.

cial libraries, which serve a known readership whose demands can to a considerable extent be anticipated, are in a position to decide how much of the specified information is relevant and useful in their particular case. . . . In my own library, for example, we never record information about size or illustrative matter in serials. Or, if a library's policy is to retain only the current issue of directories, for example, what useful purpose, in terms of exploitation of that library's stock, is served by giving details about the previous titles or imprint variation?[29]

Some technicalities cannot be avoided in view of the complex materials that must be recorded, but all rules should be scrutinized closely to see whether they are necessary, particularly in the light of the limitations that must apply in book catalogs and computer listings. One problem is that details tend to snowball when they are given in the body of the entry, the imprint, collation, and notes. Changes occur in every part of the catalog entry, and once they do, there is a temptation to list them.

Notes in particular are troublesome and expensive, yet curiously they seldom find their way into book catalogs. The 1967 code lists nineteen types of notes taken from the 1949 *Rules for Descriptive Cataloging in the Library of Congress*, all of them subject to some measure of change. They are:

1. Frequency of publication, the details of which are given at the beginning of this chapter.
2. Report year, when the period covered by an annual report is not the calendar year:
   > Report year ends June 30.
   > Report year for 1928–30 ends June 30.
   > Report year irregular.

   For reports which are not annual:
   > Fourth report covers period Mar. 1942–Dec. 1943.
   > Period covered by reports ends Mar. 31.
   > Period covered by reports is irregular.
3. Duration of publication when not specified in the statement of holdings:
   > Ceased with v. 4, no. 4 (Aug. 1935?) Cf. Union list of serials.
   > Published 1820–64. Cf. Union list of serials.
   > "Published . . . since 1909."
4. Suspension of publication:
   > Suspended during 1919.

29*Ibid.*, p.61.

Suspended 1923–31.

Suspended with Dec. 1942.

Suspended with v. 11.

5. Irregularities and peculiarities of numbering unless they occur within a volume number: combined issues or volumes, confusion in the use of series numbering or whole numbers, double numbering, numbering that does not begin with volume one, the publication of preliminary editions not included in the regular series, etc.:

An introductory number called v. 1, no. 0 was issued Nov. 30, 1935.

Issues for 1892–1902 called v. 2–12; 1903–Apr. 1906 called v. 1–4, no. 4; May 1906–July 1910 called v. 1–5, no. 3.

Issues for Feb.–Mar. 1939 have no vol. numbering but constitute v. 1, no. 1–2.

Vol. numbers irregular: v. 15–18 omitted; v. 20–21 repeated.

Vols. 1–7 not published.

Sarah Dickinson tells of some of the "strange twists and combinations" among irregularities and peculiarities of numbering. "A minor, but a bothersome, trick, is to skip numbers when the issues are not published. The *Proletarian* of Chicago is one illustration. Dozens of numbers have been omitted, but hope springs eternal in that man's breast, and he is always thinking he may fill the gaps. So when I receive no. 5, May, and then no. 9, September and claim, he answers, 'We skipped 6 to 8.' Why under the sun not call the next issue 6, even if it was published in September? . . .

"The most remarkable example of this kind of thing was the *Altruist* of St. Louis. We started out with it bravely in 1903, paid our agent, but though it was a monthly, numbers 1 to 6, and 12, were not published. The next 4 out of the 12 came; the next 3 out of the 12; but always numbered as though the others had come out. And when I claimed and claimed, the same answer would come: 'I called it no. 10, because it would have been, if numbers 1 to 9 *had* been issued; I still hope to catch up.'

"But alas, a record of 14 years showed that out of 204 due, only 89 arrived. But who can blame that publisher? The price was first 10 cents a year, then 25 cents—postage from St. Louis included."[30]

---

[30]Sarah Dickinson, "Idiosyncracies of Periodicals," *Catalogers' and Classifiers' Yearbook* 2:94 (1931).

6. Connection with prior publications:

> Continues News letter issued by the society under its earlier name: Society of American Bacteriologists.
>
> Formed by the union of Serial slants and the Journal of cataloging and classification.
>
> Published during the suspension of Zeitschrift für Fischerei und deren Hilfswissenschaften.

7. Titles absorbed:

> Absorbed L'Art décoratif, Jan. 22; Les Échos d'art, Jan. 1932; L'Architecte, Jan. 1936; Le Décor d'aujourd'hui, May/June 1958.
>
> Absorbed Metals technology and, in part, Mining and metallurgy.
>
> Absorbed Proceedings of the Pacific Northwest Library Association in Oct. 1937 and became the association's official organ.

8. Organ of a society unless the fact is evident from the heading.

> Journal of the Minnesota State Medical Association and of other medical societies of Minnesota.
>
> Official organ of the Interne Council of America, 1938–41; journal of the Association of Internes and Medical Students, 1942– .
>
> Official publication of the Peace Officers Civil Service Association of California and, 1930–37, of the California Academy of Police Science.

9. Minor variations in title, mostly covered by notes such as "Title varies slightly" and "Subtitle varies"; but if they contribute to the identification of an item:

> Binder's title, 1930– : Anuario Córdoba.
>
> Cover title, July 1920– : The Flame.
>
> Running title, 1940–Jan./Feb. 1942: The Canadian Red Cross dispatch.

10. Issues with special titles:

> Each vol. has also a distinctive title: 1939, Government, the citizen's business.—1940, Exploration in citizenship.—1941, Self-government under war pressure.

11. Issuing bodies:

> Published by Pergamon Press for the American Geophysical Union and the Pergamon Institute, 1957; translated and published by the American Geophysical Union, 1958– .
>
> Published by the Westinghouse Club (called 1904–May 1910 Electric Club)
>
> Vol. 1 published by the students of the Claremont Colleges and La Verne College; v. 2– by the students of Pomona College.

Vols. for 1925–Jan. 1933 issued under the auspices of the New Mexico State Highway Dept. (with the Dept. of Game and Fish, July 1931–Jan. 1933)

12. Editors for whom added entries are made and whose names are apt to be better known in relation to the work than the exact title of the work itself or who have been associated with a major publication for a notably long period:

Edited by A. Alonso.

Editor: 1939– H. L. Mencken.

Founded and for some years edited by O. Janke.

Beatrice Simon says: "Elaborate notes concerning editors and changes in commercial publishers are, in my opinion, a complete waste of time. The rare person who needs this information finds it by going to the journal itself. Furthermore, his need of the information is usually in connection with some serious piece of work and, believe me, he will not take *your* note as his authority. He will verify at the source. Anyone who is interested in knowing that a library has a copy of the Tatler, knows who the editor was. If he is discovering this fact for the first time, he will discover it in a much more pleasant way than by plowing through the added entries in a library catalogue."[31]

13. Variations in imprint, covered by "Imprint varies" when there has been only one change of place and publisher:

Imprint varies: 1870–81, Leipzig, L. Voss.—1882–96, Hamburg, L. Voss.—1897–1920, Berlin, R. Friedlander.

Published in Rotterdam by Nijgh & Van Ditman, 1916–40.

Vol. 3, no. 2, published by J. Debrett.

14. Connection with later publications:

Absorbed by Monumental news-review.

Continued by its The Colombo plan technical co-operation scheme.

Superseded by the publication with the same title, published since May 1965.

Superseded in 1962 by Schriften, issued by the library under its later name: Bibliothek für Zeitgeschichte.

15. "No more published?" used to express doubt about what really is the final issue. The expression is placed last or next to the last when contents are given.

Miss Pierson observes wistfully: "It may take hours of research to establish the truth of the distilled statement

---

[31]Simon, "Cataloguing of Periodicals," p.242.

'No more published' (it takes 150 pounds of rose-leaves to yield less than an ounce of attar of rose!) "[32]

16. A brief contents note, characterizing a work as a whole, designating the parts of a set, or justifying added entries:

> Includes "Bibliography of Northwest materials."
>
> Issues for 1922–31 include section: "The Woman voter," official organ of the National League of Women Voters.
>
> "A preliminary investigation into the state of the native languages of South Africa, by C. M. Doke" (with bibliographical appendices): v. 7, p.[1]–98.

17. Supplements. These may be monographic or serial in character and may be treated in several ways:

> Blätter für Volksbibliotheken und Lesehallen. 1.– Jahrg.; Jan./Feb. 1900–
> Leipzig, Harrassowitz.
> > v. 24 cm. bimonthly.
> ———Ergänzungshefte. 1.– Leipzig, Harrassowitz, 1905–
> no.   24 cm.
> Ceased publication with no. 5 (1915) Cf. Union list of serials.
> The Oregon state bar bulletin. v. 1– Dec. 1935–
> Portland.
> > v.   26 cm. bimonthly (except Aug. and Oct.)
> Vols. 1– issued as a suppl. to the Oregon law review.
> Unnumbered and undated supplements with title Bollettino accompany each number.

18. Indexes to more than a single volume, displayed in tabular form or noted if the tabular form is impracticable; a note may be used for a single index to a serial that has ceased publication:

> Includes index.
>
> Indexed in the index of v. 1–25 of the Mennonite quarterly review.
>
> INDEXES:
> > Vols. 1–9, 1881–90, *with* v. 9.
> > Vols. 10–15, 1891–96. 1 v.
> > Vols. 1–20, 1881–1901, and suppl. v. 1–8, *with* index to v. 10–15.
> > Vols. 21–40, 1902–21, *in* v. 40.
> > INDEXES:
> > Author index.
> > > Vols. 1–6, 1915–21 (Suppl. to v. 6) *with* v. 6.
> > Subject index.
> > > Vols. 1–6, 1915–21 (*Its* Bulletin no. 14) 1 v.

[32]Pierson, "Forest of Pencils," p.308.

General index.
Vols. 1–10, 1915–24. 1 v. 28 cm.
19. The record that an item is bound with another:
Vols. 1–2, no. 1 bound with its Bulletin on relief in France,
no. 1–54, its Bulletin on refugees abroad and at home, no.
1–18, and its Bulletin on relief in England, no. 1–17.

The seeking out and recording of detailed information for these nineteen points, as well as for other technicalities, is a time-consuming, expensive process. It can take from a day to a week to check up on all points in a long and involved set, and the information is sought not by clerical assistants as a rule, but by the serial catalogers themselves. In the days of Miss MacNair and Miss Pierson it was possible to enjoy the patient and thorough investigation of serials. Today the burden on catalog departments, in terms of arrearages, budget, and work load, is generally so great that the coming of book catalogs and computer controls is a promise of relief from the over-elaboration of the past.

Book Catalogs for Serials

The emerging book catalog for serials is mechanically or computer-produced so that annual editions can appear. The M.I.T. catalog has been issued yearly since 1959 as a computer product. It includes titles that are being received currently, as well as many serials that have ceased publication or that are no longer received regularly. Each entry gives: (1) the complete title; (2) holdings by volume, number, date, etc.; (3) the location of the set or sets; (4) the specific location, e.g., on the reference shelves, within certain libraries; (5) call numbers for the set or sets; and (6) references in parentheses to earlier or later titles. Notes cover only the obvious essentials: e.g., current title; formerly; last 2 years; last 10 years; latest only kept. Special symbols are: the plus sign, which means "and later numbers to date" (/1962/+ means that a few numbers are missing from the file for 1962); half parentheses, which mean that the current numbers are in a different location from the main set, e.g., HAYB (V. 12, 1946+ , ENG (Current Nos., is an indication that the back file is in the basement of the Hayden Library while the current numbers are in the Engineering Library; and a star, which directs attention to footnotes for terms such as "bulletin" and "journal" where it is explained that the first word of the entry may also be found under names of societies, institutions, or geographical locations. Typical entries are:

N. L. L. Translations Bulletin
(Formerly L. L. U. Translations
  Bulletin)
ENG v. 7, No.1,Jan1965+
HUM (REF Z 1033.T7N11)
    V. 1, 1959+

Serial Slants
(Current title is Library
  Resources and Technical Services)
HAYB (Z.S485)
    V. 1, 1950–V. 7, 1956

The Linda Hall Library began with the idea that its visible index would serve as the catalog for its serials. But by 1963 it became apparent that the visible index could no longer serve the public, the interlibrary loan and reference staffs, and still be used as an administrative instrument for the Serials Department. After due consideration work was begun in 1965 on the program for a book catalog, and a trial edition appeared the next year. A cumulated revision is now issued annually and is distributed throughout the country and overseas to nearly five hundred institutions. Copies are available throughout the library, at every service point and in every department, so that staff and public have easy access.

Under corporate entries the Linda Hall Library catalog uses em dashes as a sort of ditto mark. In the first position the dash serves to repeat all information up to the first period of the nearest entry, where the information is given in full; in the second position it stands for the information up to the second period; and so on. Thus:

Akademiia nauk SSSR. Doklady.
——. Izvestiia.
——. Botanicheskii institut. Flora SSSR.
——. ——. Trudy.
——. ——. ——. Seriia 1.

The last line can then be interpreted as "Akademiia nauk SSSR. Botanicheskii institut. Trudy. Seriia 1."

Quite a number of symbols are employed. A double bar indicates that a serial has ceased publication. A double stroke separates the parts of series: e.g., ser. 1 vl (1880) –10 (1899) // ser. 2 vl (1911) – . Angle brackets signify microreproductions: simple angle brackets, a microfilm; angle brackets which include the words "fiche:" a microfiche; and angle brackets with "card:" a microcard. The abbreviation

"Tr:" stands for a reference to a cover-to-cover translation which is in the library and which is almost always in English; an example is:

> Radiofizika. Moscow. v1(1950)– Tr: Radiophysics.

The interpretation of the reference is that *Radiophysics* is a full translation of *Radiofizika*. An arrow pointing to the left indicates that the serial continues an earlier publication which is also in the library, and an arrow pointing to the right indicates that the serial is continued by, or was absorbed into, a later publication in the library's collection. Except for November, all months are two-letter symbols. Several entries follow:

> ACCESS quarterly. (Chemical abstracts service) Columbus, Ohio. v1970n1 (Oc/De 1969) — Suppls. 1969 edition of ACCESS, for which see Card catalog: Z5523.A3 1969 qto.   Ref. desk

> Bibliographie der deutschen zeitschriftenliteratur. Osnabruck. v1 (1896) —128 (1964) ‖ v95–96 not publ. Index: author 34–35 (1914); author 43–46 (1918/20) ; 66-75 (1930–34) ; (indexes [34–75] in stack) ;

> 97–113 (1947–56) (incl. v30–39 of Bibl. der fremd. lit.). Also as Internationale bib. der zeitschriften lit. Abt. A. →Internationale bib. der zeitschriftenlit. aus allen gebieten des wissens.

Note that, for the sake of clarity, a break is made between each group of lines making up an entry.

> Harvard university.
> ——. Library.
> ——. ——. Harvard library bulletin. v1(1947)—   publ. suspended 1961–66. Index: 1–10 (1947–56) bd w/10; 11–14 (1956–60) bd w/14.

> Journal des scavans. Paris. 1741; 1790; 1792 Ja →After 1792 Journal des savants.
>   Rare book room

Linda Hall serials are neither cataloged nor classified. A few serials have been cataloged, and the book catalog refers to the card catalog for the statement of holdings in those cases.

The future very definitely lies with book catalogs of serial publications, not with card catalogs. Attention should no longer be focused on revision of the card-cataloging rules for serials; instead it should be on the ideas, the style, the symbols, the total program for the production of book catalogs. They provide the cross-references that are needed for the current checking records; they facilitate the work of the person who finds his citations from abstracting and indexing services and who then requires the call numbers or the locations; they are available at all service points and in all departments, with the consequence that reference consultation of the current checking records declines sharply. Quite importantly, they reduce the cost of cataloging because they require only essential information.

Computer Cataloging of Serials

The elements for computer cataloging are much the same as for book catalogs; computer cataloging likewise should concentrate on only the essential information. But because computer operations are expensive, the data should be fed into the system concisely and compactly. For conciseness it is necessary to work out a dictionary so that common terms like "bulletin" and "journal" are reduced to simple symbols which can be printed out in the concise form or in full, whichever is desired. The biggest problem is the development of subject codes, because Library of Congress classification symbols and subject headings do not lend themselves to computer operations. Key libraries should undertake the responsibility for preparing subject lists of serials akin to the medical ones described in chapter 19.

MARC has aimed at perpetuating the card-cataloging practices. It began by listing 278 variables which should be recorded for serials. Following a survey by the Nelson Associates the number was reduced to 80. But for MARC to be successful in the field of serial publications, it will have to abandon card methods and to think much more in terms of the emerging book catalog techniques.

Bibliography

Anglo-American Cataloging Rules: North American Text, p.20–23, 231–46. Chicago: American Library Assn., 1967.
Anglo-American Cataloguing Rules: British Text, p.17–21, 183–90. London: The Library Assn., 1967.
Dunkin, Paul S. "Problems in the Cataloguing of Serial Publications," in International Conference on Cataloguing Principles, *Report,* p.191–98. London, 1963.

Franck, Marga. "Some International Differences in the Cataloging and Bibliographical Listing of Serial Publications," *Serial Slants* 2:1–10 (Oct. 1951).

Hamilton, G. E. "Serials (Rules 160–168)," in J. C. Downing and N. F. Sharp, eds., *Seminar on the Anglo-American Cataloguing Rules (1967)*, p.55–66. London: The Library Assn., 1969.

Library of Congress. *Descriptive Cataloging Division.* (Departmental & Divisional Manuals, no.8) Washington, 1950.

———*Subject Cataloging Division.* (Departmental & Divisional Manuals, no.3) Washington, 1950.

Lubetzky, Seymour. "The Cataloging of Publications of Corporate Authors, a Rejoinder," *Library Quarterly* 21:1–12 (1951).

———"Serials," in his *Code of Cataloging Rules, Author and Title Entry*, p.80–84. [Chicago]: American Library Assn., 1960.

Pierson, Harriet W. "The Forest of Pencils; Adventures in Corporate Entry," *Library Quarterly* 4:306–13 (1934).

———"The Gay Science—the Cataloguing of the Publications of Learned Societies," in *Proceedings* of the Catalog Section, American Library Assn., 1929, p.136–44. Chicago: American Library Assn., 1929.

Simon, Beatrice V. "Cataloguing of Periodicals," *Ontario Library Review* 33:237–45 (1949).

Taube, Mortimer. "The Cataloging of Publications of Corporate Authors," *Library Quarterly* 20:1–20 (1950).

Yale University Library. *Cataloging of Serials in the Yale University Library.* 3d ed. New Haven, Conn., 1969.

11

Six Case Studies
of Serials

In the course of the text it has been stated several times that only the experienced serial librarian has any real insight into the intransigent nature of serial publications. The complexities that can arise totally unexpectedly have to be known to be believed. In a sense there is a parallel between serials and medicine: certain diseases and operations in a small hospital may be accounted as rare, whereas in a big city hospital the identical situations are encountered regularly enough for the staff to take them in stride. It is much the same with serial publications: what is considered to be a rare occurrence in a small library is looked on as part of the day's work in large institutions. Naturally in any library the mass of annual reports, government documents, periodicals, and so on, goes along without let or hindrance day after day. But no one should be misled by the routine character of most of the publications: by no manner of means do serial irregularities occur only as rare events, only in exceptional situations. On the contrary, they are met with so persistently, especially in large research libraries, that serial specialists are quite accustomed to their ways.

However, the half dozen cases which follow are not intended for the specialist. Their aim is to give nonserial librarians and beginners some idea of the problems that continually arise and of the solutions that are found to the problems. The six cases are far from being the most troublesome that could be experienced; they are rather run-of-the-mill. All have been taken from the daily work of the serial catalogers in the Harvard College Library.

1. *Archivio di filosofia*. Harvard College Library has volumes 1-11 of this quarterly periodical; they were published from 1931 to 1941.

Volumes 12–13 are lacking. There is a note on the S-card[1] which reads: "Beginning with anno 14 (?) ceased to be a quarterly periodical and became a monograph series with some volumes numbered, others unnumbered." Because of uncertainty over the nature of volumes 12–13, a manuscript note was added: "If 12–13 ever rec'd, give to Ser. Cat. If they are periodicals, add to cat. cards & remove ? after anno 14 on S cd note. If 12–13 are monographs, correct S cd note to read: Beg. with anno 12 (or 13) ."

The bibliography, and hence the treatment, of wartime casualties is often uncertain. Naturally, the periodical part of the publication should be held together, and for that reason the monograph series would almost certainly have been kept together as a set if it had been numbered throughout. But with the mixture of numbered and un-numbered volumes, the only wise course of action was to scatter the monographs by subject. The decision at Harvard was to remove the entry from the visible index and to record on the S-card that the monograph catalogers were to call for an added entry for each monograph under the heading *Archivio di filosofia* in the official as well as the public catalog. The added-entry cards were filed after the entry for the periodical itself, a card which says: "anno 1–11 (1931–41), For later years, see separate cards following."

2. *Bibliographic Bulletin of the Linda Hall Library.* The series consists of mimeographed bibliographies, numbered consecutively. In a university many of these items belong in departmental libraries; yet if the whole set were scattered and each bibliography were cataloged separately, the entries under Linda Hall Library would multiply at an undesirable rate.

Accordingly, a decision was made to keep all Widener Library issues together as a set which would be bound incomplete and have slips inserted at appropriate places to indicate the departmental libraries in which the missing numbers were located. An instruction was put on the visible index for the checkers to submit each issue as received for a decision on location and for them to see that stack issues were bound whenever ten accumulated. Further, the instruction specified that the bibliographies were to be indexed by subject only.

The record ended with number 15 and with a note: "No more published?" *Serial Holdings in the Linda Hall Library* did not exist at the time; now it is possible to discover from it that the publication began with number 1 in 1950 and continued through number 15 in 1958; there is no indication, though, that the work has ceased publica-

---

[1]The S-card was described in chapter 6. It is an entry in the Serial Card File, which is an official serial catalog for older works.

tion. This is only one of countless cases in which libraries do not and cannot know whether future issues will ever appear.

3. *Canadian Journal of Research.* Volumes 1–12 were published normally, and a cumulative index was issued for them. The two Harvard sets are in the Chemistry and the Farlow departmental libraries. Volumes 13–21 were divided into four sections but issued in two parts: section A/B for the physical and chemical sciences, which are in the Chemistry Library; and section C/D for the botanical and zoological sciences, which are in Farlow. The pattern changed again for volumes 22–28, each of which was issued in six parts. These parts, with their Harvard locations, were:

Section A, physical sciences	Chemistry Library
Section B, chemical sciences	Chemistry Library
Section C, botanical sciences	Farlow Library
Section D, zoological sciences	Zoological Museum Library
Section E, medical sciences	Medical School Library
Section F, technology	Widener Library

Then with volume 29 each section became an independent journal with a title of its own. However, the new journals began their numbering not with volume 1 but with volume 29. The titles of the independent journals were:

Canadian Journal of Botany
Canadian Journal of Chemistry
Canadian Journal of Medical Sciences, which, with volume 32, became the *Canadian Journal of Biochemistry and Physiology,* then with volume 42 split into the *Canadian Journal of Biochemistry* and the *Canadian Journal of Physiology and Pharmacology*
Canadian Journal of Physics
Canadian Journal of Technology, which with volume 35 became *Canadian Journal of Chemical Engineering*
Canadian Journal of Zoology

It is by no means easy to make a clear series of catalog entries for so complex a set. Undoubtedly a book catalog makes the task much simpler, and it could be that the Linda Hall Library, whose catalog entries follow, has hit upon an exceptionally fine way of telling the complicated story. In these entries the symbol → indicates that the serial was continued by or was absorbed into a later publication which is in the library's collections; the later work will be found under the entry that follows the arrow. The symbol ← indicates that the serial continues an earlier publication, also in the library's collections; the exact entry for the earlier publication follows the arrow. The five-pointed star symbolizes the fact that the latest issues are on the current shelves. The double bar means that the serial has ceased publication and that the last issue listed was the last one published.

Canadian journal of research. (National research council of Canada) Ottawa. v1(1929)–7; 9; 10n6(1934) → After v12(1935) in sections below.

——. Section A. Physical sciences. v13(1935)–28(1950)|| ← Canadian j. of research (without sections). – Canadian j. of physics. ANNEX

——. Section B. Chemistry. v13(1935)–28(1950)|| v13–21 bd w/ its Sect. A. ← Canadian j. of res. (without sections). → Canadian j. of chem.   ANNEX

——. Section C. Botany. v13(1935)–28(1950)|| ← Canadian j. of res. (without sections). → Canadian j. of botany.   ANNEX

——. Section D. Zoology. v13(1935)–28(1950)|| v13–21 bd w/ its Sect. C. ← Canadian j. of res. (without sections). → Canadian j. of zoology.   ANNEX

——. Section E. Medical sciences. v22(1944)–28(1950)|| → Canadian j. of medical sci.

——. Section F. Technology. v22(1944)–28(1950)|| → Canadian j. of tech.   ANNEX

Canadian journal of biochemistry. (National Research Council of Canada) Ottawa. v42(1964)–   ← Canadian j. of biochemistry and physiology.

Canadian journal of biochemistry and physiology. (National research council of Canada) Ottawa. v32(1954)–41(1963)|| ← Canadian j. of medical sci. → Canadian j. of biochem. *and* Canadian j. of physiology and pharm.

Canadian journal of botany. (National research council of Canada) Ottawa. v29(1951)–   ← Canadian j. of research. Sect. C.

Canadian journal of chemical engineering. (Chemical institute of Canada) Ottawa. v35(1957)–   ← Canadian j. of technology.   *

Canadian journal of chemistry. (National research council of Canada) Ottawa. v29(1951)–   ← Canadian j. of research. Sect. B.   *

Canadian journal of medical sciences. (National research council of Canada) Ottawa. v29(1951)–31(1953)|| ← Canadian j. of research. Sect. E. → Canadian j. of biochemistry and physiol.

Canadian journal of physics. (National research council of Canada) Ottawa. v29(1951)–   ← Canadian j. of research. Sect. A.   *

Canadian journal of physiology and pharmacology. (National research council of Canada) Ottawa. v42(1964)–   ← Canadian j. of bio-chemistry and physiology.

Canadian journal of technology. (National research council of Canada) Ottawa. v29(1951)–34(1956/57)‖ ← Canadian j. of research. Sect. F. → Canadian j. of chem. eng.

Canadian journal of zoology. (National research council of Canada) Ottawa. v29(1951)– ← Canadian j. of research. Sect. D. *

4. *Le disque vert.* The Harvard holdings for this monthly literary review, from 1922 through 1941, are:

> Année 1, no. 1–6 (mai–oct. 1922)
> Année 1, sér. 2, no. 1–4/5/6 (nov. 1922–avril 1923), entitled Écrits du nord (fusion du Disque vert et de la Lanterne sourde)
> Année 2, no. 1–3 (oct.–déc. 1923)
> Année 2, sér. 3, no. 4/5 (1924) and num. spécial (1924)
> Année 3, sér. 4, no. 1–3 (1925) and unnumbered issue (1925) entitled Le cas Lautréamont
> Unnumbered issue (1934) entitled Au disque vert
> N. s. année 1, no. 1 (15 juillet 1941)

An issue "hors série" appeared in December 1952, entitled *Hommage à Marcel Proust.* In October 1952 the dealer reported: "Your set is complete." Then the periodical came to life once more with année 1, no. 1 (avril 1953). Because of the confusion in the periodical's numbering, the catalogers decided to give the issues beginning with April 1953 a separate book number.

The binding of such a periodical presents considerable difficulties, all the more so since this particular title adopted three different formats during its career. The solution, once the dealer's report had come, was to bind the numbered and unnumbered issues chronologically. There are now on the shelves bound volumes for 1922–23, 1924, 1925, 1934, 1941, and 1953, the single issue for 1941 being in a pamphlet binder.

A number of the items had to be analyzed, among them being whole issues devoted to Charlie Chaplin, Freud, and Max Jacob.

5. *Internationale Zeitschrift für Erziehungswissenschaft.* Harvard has volumes 1–13 Heft 4/5, April 1931 to August 1944, of this journal, plus volumes 4–6, 1947–[51]. This is a complete set despite the gap in years and the volume numbering. Volumes 1–3, 1931–34, were published in Cologne under the editorship of Professor Friedrich Schneider. A Nazi editor took over with volume 4, 1935, and the place of publication was changed to Berlin. At the same time the title was modified to *Internationale Zeitschrift für Er-*

ziehung. The work of the Nazi editor ended in August 1944. Then in 1947 Professor Schneider resumed publication under the original title, this time in Salzburg; but because he did not recognize the Nazi volumes, he designated his revival volume 4, that is, the fourth under his editorship, instead of volume 14. Thus there are two volumes 4, 5, and 6, although in each case the two represent different years.

Harvard decided to treat the set as a single work, arranging the volumes on the shelves chronologically. The *Union List of Serials,* which entered the first thirteen volumes under the Nazi title, made a separate entry for the revival, but noted that volumes 1–3 were published in Cologne in 1931–34.

6. *Oxfordshire Record Society.* This monograph series lacks a title, so it was cataloged as [Oxfordshire record series]. It represents a problem in binding and analyzing. Each part is numbered consecutively which would be well and good if every monograph were complete in a single issue. Unfortunately, the monographs may run through several issues not numbered consecutively. For example, Sir Samuel Luke's *Journal,* volumes 1–3, appeared in volumes 29, 31, and 33 of the series, and volumes 1–4 of *The Church Bells of Oxfordshire* were published in volumes 28, 30, 32, and 34. Before the problem was realized, much of the set had been bound up consecutively in serial sequence, several issues to the volume. Thereafter the parts of monographs were bound together, with the same class mark but a separate book number. Incidentally, the Library of Congress call number for Sir Samuel Luke's *Journal* is "DA670.09A3 vol. 29, etc." The use of "etc." in the call number is a very poor device from the point of view of reader and stack service, even when, as happens on occasion, the full list of numbers for a single monograph can be quite long.

Most libraries have erred in making volumes of serials too large. The difficulties with the Oxfordshire Record Society's publications were increased because each volume was not bound as a unit. If each volume had been bound as a unit from the start, it would have been much easier to rationalize the set in the interest of service to readers. But once the multiple physical volumes were on the shelves, there was a natural reluctance to tear the bindings apart, even in a good cause.

12

Descriptive Cataloging
Procedures

The degree of complexity which attaches to serial cataloging procedures is directly related to the policies which every library determines or should determine for itself. A decision ought to be made on the value of each procedure in relation to the program of the library as a whole as well as to the cataloging budget and situation. Yet, for one reason or another, such a basic review is seldom undertaken. At the very least, a considerable amount of detailed work is inescapable in dealing with serials, but practices and procedures naturally become much more burdensome when rules are highly technical and are strictly applied.

How far afield established practices can lead is illustrated by Miss Pierson's description of the way in which hours and days were spent on the single task of making the history card for a minor association: "The pursuit of information concerning this association led through encyclopedic articles and substantial volumes, through involved sentences, false trails and wordy jungles, to emerge finally in the Congo Free State."[1] The introduction of the no-conflict principle for the establishment of names produced no ill effects, and other procedures can likewise be reduced or simplified to advantage. The greatest gains are possible when catalogers give recognition to the contributions of other serial librarians, notably those who are working with the current checking records and in the periodical room. In some cases, usually found in special libraries, recognition of the principle of division of labor has resulted in elimination of serial entries in the card catalog, total reliance being placed on the check-

[1]Harriet W. Pierson, "The Forest of Pencils; Adventures in Corporate Entry," *Library Quarterly* 4:308 (1934).

ing records. In other cases skeleton form cards have been adopted (see figure 21) ; they give merely the call number, author/title, and a reference to the checking records for further information, should it be required. Nowadays the trend is toward book catalogs for serial holdings, and entries for serials can be safely omitted from the card catalog altogether whenever a book catalog is reissued periodically. In all three situations many procedures are eliminated, e.g., the cataloger's search, volume by volume, for peculiarities and irregularities in issue and volume numbering.

Sci 1560.81.45

U.S. National Labor Relations Board.
   Annual report. Washington.
      Vol. 1 (1935/36) -

**For a full record of the Library's holdings apply to
the Reference Desk or the Serial Division.**

O

Figure 21. Form card from Harvard College Library

General Cataloging Procedures

At one time catalogers made work slips for serials which were assigned to them, not only for current publications but also for items which would be set aside for future cataloging. They kept the records at their desks as aids in locating a title that might be requested.[2] Today it is generally recognized that individual finding lists, kept on or in a cataloger's desk, are not satisfactory for the work of the cataloging department as a whole. It is now customary to record current serials without delay in the visible index or its equivalent; to list noncurrent purchased sets, including reprints, in the outstand-

[2]An individual "cataloguer's finding list of entries" is briefly described by Mary W. MacNair in her *Guide to the Cataloguing of Periodicals* (3d ed.; Washington, 1925), p.19.

ing order file or the automated order record; and for the rest to make no temporary listing, particularly of items which come in large-lot exchanges or as gifts, purchases, or transfers.

When the cataloger is ready to catalog a serial, the first step is to study the information which has been provided by the acquisition staff, information which is often set out on a decision slip. When a set has not already been collated, the cataloger goes through the publication carefully, making notes about points that will come up in the preparation of the catalog entry. P-slips are commonly placed in the set to mark any point to which the cataloger may wish to refer back; such points are the occurrence of cumulative indexes, new series, supplements, and other features which will be noted on the catalog card. Some matters may require investigation, and reference is often made to the *Union List of Serials* to see whether it provides the answers. After the problems have been resolved and forms of names have been determined or established, a draft catalog entry may be necessary to arrange all the manifold details in proper sequence. It is not needed for form cards or for short and concise catalog entries, but whenever the cataloging details are long or involved, the draft entry is an invaluable aid in the final preparation of the cataloging copy. Its most sophisticated form was found in the planning sheets which were in force in the Research Libraries of the New York Public Library prior to the introduction of computer cataloging.[3]

Since the subject cataloging of serials is generally so broad that it is comparatively simple, it is customary to have the serial catalogers, unlike the monograph catalogers, classify and subject-head their own material. This practice is becoming more desirable as subject headings disappear with the coming of book catalogs for serials, all the more so because in classification there are comparatively few places into which serials fit. In those libraries in which the subject catalogers, not the serial catalogers, are responsible for this phase of the work, routines must be set up for the serials to be transmitted to the subject catalogers once the descriptive cataloging has been done and then returned again for completion of the cataloging copy. In addition to the extra handling that is entailed, the disadvantage of this system is the delays that inevitably occur. Subject catalogers tend to give first priority to books; as a rule, they deal with serials only once a week at the most.

When the catalog entry has been prepared, the cataloger must

3An example of a planning sheet can be found in the first edition of *Serial Publications*, p.148–51.

pass on to other units the information they require for their records. The checkers in the acquisition division, the staff in the periodical room, and perhaps others must be apprised of the call number, correct entry, and any other details they require. At the Library of Congress the shelflisters transmit this type of information to the staff in the Serial Record Division. If the end processes are not performed by serial assistants, the preparation-for-shelves staff must be given any special instructions there may be about shelflisting, binding, or otherwise preparing the material for use.

There may also be other matters to attend to, such as the actual preparation of the visible-index card or the title-a-line strip to go on the visible reference index. There may be an acquisition entry to be canceled once the catalog cards have been filed. Statement cards may have to be prepared or written up, and traveling cards may have to be prepared as exact duplicates of the official main-entry cards. Book cards are on occasion made by the serial catalogers or under their direction; more commonly the preparation-for-shelves staff attends to them when they must be provided for items which go directly to the stacks or for volumes just returned from the bindery. The special report forms for *New Serial Titles* must be made and dispatched by contributing libraries,[4] and attention must be given to various *Union List of Serials* activities.

Serial catalogers must initiate action on Library of Congress standing orders for monograph series so that analytical cards will be supplied as soon as they are printed. Receipt of the cards, however, is best handled through the checking records, as described in chapter 7.

Volumes added to existing sets, which originate in the periodical room or elsewhere, often pass through the hands of the serial catalogers instead of being processed exclusively by clerical assistants. The reason why catalogers in some libraries want to see added volumes is that they feel impelled to watch for changes in any of the variables which they record on the catalog cards; otherwise they are dependent on reports from the serial checkers or periodical-room attendants. Cresap, McCormick and Paget, in their 1951 survey of cataloging in the New York Public Library, recommended that the serial catalogers there forego handling added volumes because serial adding is largely a routine which need not be organizationally

---

[4]Examples of the report forms as filled out by contributing libraries are given in A. F. Kuhlman, *A Report on the Consumer Survey of New Serial Titles* ([Washington, D.C.: Library of Congress], 1967), p.83–84. Included are several examples of short-title reports as well as of change-of-title notifications.

related to professional cataloging. In any event, as data on open entries are simplified in deference to the contributions made by the checking records or as they are eliminated because of the existence of a book catalog of serial holdings, there is little or no occasion for routine additions to be handled by the catalogers.

Temporary Cataloging

Some libraries have followed the policy of cataloging periodicals, as well as other serials which are received issue by issue, when the first number is received. Others have preferred to postpone cataloging until a completed volume is ready for binding or bundling. In the latter case the catalogers hope that a title page will be on hand by the time they do the regular cataloging. They are ready, therefore, to go to the extra routine of making a temporary entry for the catalog which will disclose the presence of the title and serve until the permanent entry can be substituted for the temporary one.

A case described by Miss Dickinson shows the reasoning behind the cataloging preference for working from a completed volume rather than the first issue. She says: "I remember I cared for the *Army and Navy Journal,* of Washington, for a full year, all records under that name, to be much surprised to have the title page, when it arrived, read *American Army and Navy Journal*; and consistency obliged me to make a number of changes."[5] Subject catalogers likewise have preferred to operate with a completed volume in hand because, although their class marks and subject headings must of necessity be quite broad for the typical serial, they feel that the first issue may not define the scope of a work sufficiently for their purposes.

The temporary entry gives the location of the current issues—in the periodical room or elsewhere in the library system—not the call number, which will be inapplicable for a year or more. However, unless the call number is eventually added to the temporary card, there can be an awkward interval in which there is a volume on the shelves in the bookstacks, yet the call number is not disclosed in the catalog until the permanent entry is filed some time later. On the other hand, it must be generally understood that permanent entries made from the first issue give the call number, not the location of the current issues, even though there will be no volume in the bookstacks for twelve months or longer.

5Sarah S. Dickinson, "Idiosyncracies of Periodicals," *Catalogers' and Classifiers' Yearbook* 2:95 (1930).

In first-issue cataloging the information is taken from the cover or caption. It is realized that a title page may never appear, and that when one does, it rarely alters the entry materially. It is also realized that subject cataloging can be undertaken just about as effectively from a single issue as from twelve or fifty-two, one reason being that the first number often contains an editorial statement about the scope of the new publication.

In the opening section of chapter 5 it was seen that periodicals must be cataloged from the first issue if they are to secure prompt listing in *New Serial Titles* and *New Serial Titles—Classed Subject Arrangement*. In 1969 the Library of Congress made a start with first-issue cataloging when it reported that many English-language serials were now being treated in that way;[6] in 1971 it changed over to first-issue cataloging completely.

The practice of first-issue cataloging is in the common good. It reduces the cost of serial cataloging, just as it eliminates the delay that formerly intervened between the periodical room and binding, a delay that often made trouble for readers and staff, especially when citations had been taken from current periodical indexes. From now on all libraries should make their permanent catalog records as soon as the first number of a periodical or periodical-like publication has been received.

Add-to-Cards Procedures

Catalog maintenance is not a great burden to serial librarians when cards are one-plus entries or refer to the serial checking records for details of holdings. Maintenance can be quite burdensome, however, when year after year the catalog cards must be updated to disclose the latest volume which has been added to the classified shelves or the most recent change in any of the nineteen or more matters of serial detail which are subject to variation.

There are sundry ways of adding to existing records in the official and public catalogs, as well as in departmental catalogs.[7] The simplest

---

[6]*Annual Report of the Librarian of Congress* 1969 (Washington, 1970), p.28.

[7]Some idea of the extent of the problem of maintenance can be gauged from the fact that what is now known as the Research Libraries of the New York Public Library has at least 102 catalogs to maintain, according to the 1951 survey by Cresap, McCormick and Paget. They are located in twenty different divisions, not all of which have serial entries that are kept up to date; but the catalog-maintenance load in that library, as in other libraries with subject departments, has been heavy, so much so that it was a major factor in causing the library to freeze its card catalog and to turn to computer cataloging.

procedure is to have the serial cataloger adjust the main official card; then a clerical assistant copies the changes onto the appropriate cards in the different catalogs, taking the official card as a model. When there is no official catalog, a clerical assistant should remove the main public card, leaving a dummy in its place, and give it to the serial cataloger for updating; thereafter for departmental catalogs the procedures are the same as before. At an earlier time all cards in a set were adjusted; nowadays it is customary to stamp the secondary cards with a reference to the main card for full details, and in that way the cost of add-to-cards work is held down. The full sets may have to be adjusted when changes affect details other than holdings; if so, the nineteen variables carry an extra cost with them whenever any one has to be updated.

Add-to-cards assistants can operate directly at the catalogs, making changes in pencil for the statement of holdings; in this way no dummies have to be written for the entries on which they are working, and therefore there are no cards to be refiled. Naturally, when there are changes that require typing, the cards must be removed from all catalogs, and dummies must be inserted in place of main entries; eventually all cards must be refiled and dummies canceled.

The traveling card, sometimes called the return-duplicate card, is an extra entry made for current serials. When not in operation, it is filed either immediately behind the official card to which it relates or else in a special supplementary record. At the time that new holdings are added to the official card, they are put on the traveling card as well, whereupon the filer substitutes it for the main card in the public catalog. The latter then becomes the traveling card and is held until the next transaction takes place.

The system of traveling cards has the advantage that the cataloger sees the changes which are made in both catalogs. But there are a number of disadvantages. The traveling card is not always forthcoming when it is wanted: the issues of some serials follow so rapidly on the heels of one another that there is scarcely time to complete the cycle before the next part arrives; and it happens once in a while that a serial addition with the traveling card in it is set aside for further investigation or work, the net result being that catalogers may have to wait for weeks or months before the card comes to light again. Also, the traveling card can easily be misfiled because of the presence of numerous duplicate entries which complicate the filing. At times, then, a substitute traveling card must be made in order to keep the process moving. A few libraries have even gone to the extent of making not only traveling cards—of which there were approximately sixty thousand in the New York Public Library

—but a permanent file of typed dummies as well, all ready to be dropped into place whenever a traveling card might be removed to institute a transaction. But what can be more fatuous than to see a cataloger make a substitute dummy to go in the permanent file of dummies because the original one cannot be found?

In 1952 the New York Public Library gave up the traveling-card procedure which it had formerly used for its document serials. It adopted tabulated cards for all its open-entry serials and established a routine for photocopying the official cards once they had been changed. The photocopies were substituted for the main cards in the divisional, public, and shelflist catalogs, the replaced cards being thrown away. What was distinctive about this practice was that only a single tabulated card was authorized per title; should the card become full, then a fresh one was made with a summarized statement of earlier holdings followed by a conventional checklist for later holdings.

The tabulated card, which many libraries favor, is a device for separating the catalog entry from the enumerative statement of the library's holdings (see figure 22). Essentially it is a checklist card which is tied or otherwise attached to the catalog card so that the two in conjunction contain the full record without overcrowding.

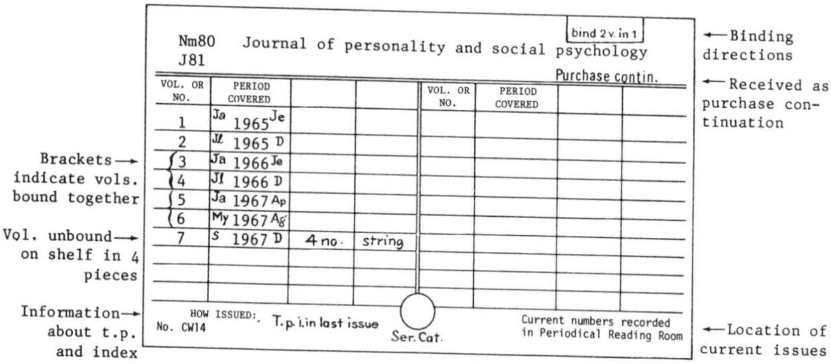

Figure 22. Tabulated card from Yale University Library

Yale University practice for tabulated or statement cards is as follows:

> A. Yale uses the following types of statement cards: annual, 1–50; monthly, 51–100; daily, 1–100; monograph, copy 1–4; film.
>
> No rules can be laid down as to which kind to use for various types of publications. Experience with them gradually develops in the cataloger a basis for judging.

B. In making statement cards the following points should be kept in mind:

1. Heading on statement card (author and title or title alone) is the same as on the history card, *not* shortened. *Exception*: When title is in a non-Roman alphabet, the romanized title is given on the statement card.

2. Whatever designation (volume, year, etc.) appears in the *first* left hand column on the statement card is the designation by which the volumes *must* be marked. (a) If set has a volume numbering which is not used for marking, this numbering must be given in the third or fourth column on the statement card, not the *first* column. (b) If marking of columns varies in any way from the listing in the left hand column (*e.g.*, if volume listed as v. 5 is issued in two parts and marked 5:1 and 5:2, or if the publication is issued in several series [marked II:1 or III:1, etc.]), the marking is indicated at top of card at right of call number in pencil so that serial assistants will know how to mark future volumes.

3. If the serial has more than one kind of numbering, the various numberings that appear on the volumes are given on the statement card, if possible; *e.g.*, set may have volume numbering and continuous, or whole, numbering for each issue throughout the set. The numbering by which volumes are marked is given in the first column on statement card and the other numbering in the third or fourth column.

In marking volumes, preference is given to volume numbering rather than whole numbering.

4. *Abbreviations for months.* On statement cards Yale uses shorter abbreviations for months than the standard ones. They are: Ja., F., Mr., Ap., My., Je., Jl., Ag., S., O., N., D.

5. *Imprint dates.* If the imprint date in a volume varies more than one year from the period covered, it is recorded in the third column on the statement card. *Reason*: This gives a clue as to when the next volume may appear.

6. The statement card must show the number of physical pieces there are on the shelf if more than one.

a. If the volume entered on a line is bound in 2 volumes, that is indicated; *e.g.*,

Vol.	Period covered	
1	1945	2v.

b. If volume is in several parts unbound on the shelf, the number of pieces is indicated *even though the volume is complete*. This is done in pencil so that it can be erased when volume is bound.

1) If complete, the number of parts is given; *e.g.*, 12 no. (rather than no. 1–12, which indicates that there are more numbers than 12 in the volume).

2) If incomplete, the card states in pencil the numbers which Yale has, *not* what Yale lacks; *e.g.*, no. 1–3. *Reason*: Often we do

not know what constitutes a complete volume—there may be a supplement or special numbers. Therefore, it is better to specify what we have.

7. If from the order slips in the volumes it is ascertained that the serial is to be received as a continuation, the statement cards are marked to indicate this on the right side just above the line: Purchase contin., Exchange contin., Gift contin., Depository, PL 480.

If continuation has been ordered or requested as an exchange or gift but the continuation has not yet been established, cataloger, instead of stamping card, writes in pencil: Purch. contin. ord. [date], Exch. contin. req. [date], or Gift contin. req. [date]. This is erased and card stamped when the continuation has been established.[8]

Whatever plan of add-to-cards work for serials is adopted, the task of keeping serial open entries up to date is costly. Libraries must reckon up the cost of the program in terms of service. Do the returns justify continuation of the practices? Is it necessary, e.g., to tell readers and staff through the medium of the card catalog that the recent bound volume of the *Journal of Near Eastern Studies* may now be sought in the bookstacks? What is being done is continuing card-catalog practices inaugurated before the *Union List of Serials* came into being, but now that it does exist as a valued tool, would not its one-plus type of entry suffice in card catalogs too? Would it not be better to free the serial catalogers as far as possible from the burden of catalog maintenance so that they could keep up more easily with essential activities? Note that none of the systems which have been described helps in the frequently troublesome interim period when a volume is in the transition stage between the periodical room, the bindery, the cataloging department, and the bookstacks.

Fortunately, there is now a solution to the problem. When a library produces a book catalog of its serial holdings at annual or other fairly frequent intervals, the problem disappears, at the same time that service to readers and staff is increased and catalog-maintenance costs drop. Notable examples of such catalogs are *Serials and Journals in the M.I.T. Library*, which in 1969 was in its eleventh edition, and *Serial Holdings in the Linda Hall Library*.

Shelflisting

In the typical library the shelflist is the control record for material which has officially been added to the collections; it serves also for the assignment of book numbers and for the occasional inventory of the bookstock. Naturally, the shelflist is less significant in libraries which arrange their periodicals in one alphabetical sequence, house their serials in vertical files, prefer class marks to call numbers, or take no inventory. In a branch public library, for instance, no shelflist entries are required for expendable periodicals, and small special libraries may operate without a shelflist record for their serials.

Some serial librarians think that there is no need for a statement of holdings on the shelflist card, provided the listing in the checking records or other serial lists is accurate and sufficiently full. They consider the addition of serial holdings to the shelflist to be a time-consuming duplication of effort. As for inventory, advocates of this policy feel that it is not necessary to take stock of the individual volumes of a set. When the shelflist card shows that a title should be on the shelves, what is needed is to see that all volumes are in order and that no extraneous material has crept in among unbound issues. This kind of shelfreading may not disclose the fact that an unbound issue is missing, but it is justified on the score that when anyone wants a missing item, its absence will be discovered. In an age when microfilm copies can be obtained readily, there is much to be said for this course of action.

The planning behind the multipurpose serial record at West Virginia University Library took advantage of this philosophy:

> The serials record was to be both checking record and shelflist record in alphabetical order. It was realized that a shelflist record arranged alphabetically by author and title was a new departure, and would not be universally sanctioned. However, its practical merits far outweighed those of a classified arrangement. The latter, it was felt, would be completely justified only at inventory times, the intervals between which at West Virginia University Library are so great as to present no serious objection to the alphabetical arrangement. It was believed that, for inventory purposes, the cards in a single tray could be removed, arranged in classified order, rearranged after checking against stack holdings and location file, and replaced within a day's time. . . .
>
> To prevent duplications in assigning call numbers it was determined that referral cards bearing call number, author, and/or title, and stamped with the legend, "For Holdings See—Serials Record," would be inserted in the shelflist.[9]

---

[9] Fleming Bennett, "A Multi-Purpose Serials Record," *College and Research Libraries* 9:232 (1948). Over the years the only substantial change in the central serial record at West Virginia University Library has been the recent addition of

The checking records must be developed somewhat more fully when the shelflist is bypassed or reduced to skeleton form. In particular, binding information must be included, and the summarized statement of holdings should then be set out in shelflist form, i.e., as a record of the physical, not necessarily the bibliographical, volumes on the shelves. The situation is different in an automated sytsem, however. There the shelflist record can be dispensed with because the computer can readily supply a classified list of serials to facilitate the assignment of book numbers or to serve inventory purposes.

Here again is a problem for the library administrator to think through. In how many places in a library should permanent serial information be recorded? In automated checking systems the answer should surely be: one. In manual systems the visible index and any supporting serial catalog must be maintained; but what about the public and official catalogs, and what about the shelflist? It has already become clear that, with the trend toward book catalogs of serial holdings, card-catalog records can well be eliminated, with at the most a referral card under the name of the piece, though even that is not necessary.[10] For the rest, the philosophy of the future may well be that it is better for a library to put every effort into a single multipurpose serial record, in preference to scattering its energies as in the past. It was in this spirit that the National Agricultural Library decided on the "limitation of permanent serials-holdings records to the basic inventory record, which is the Alphabetical Serial File."[11]

Nonetheless, many libraries feel that the shelflist is the definitive record of their holdings, so much so that in a few cases it is kept in a fireproof safe for insurance purposes. Naturally, for these libraries the shelflist ranks with the current checking records: the shelflist reflecting the way in which the serial units appear physically on the shelves, the checking records concentrating on enumerative and summarized statements of holdings. For these libraries both types of information must be maintained meticulously because between them they carry the official account of the institution's serial resources.

---

dealer, payment, and other acquisition-department information, which previously had been maintained on a separate visible index.

[10]A piece of supporting evidence for this statement is that the *National Union Catalog* and the *Union List of Serials* are to a high degree complementary records, and there are no references in the *National Union Catalog* to union-list entries, yet recourse to each tool is made without any real difficulty.

[11]National Agricultural Library, *Report* 1953 (Washington, 1953), p.3.

The convention for the shelflist is that the statement of holdings is made in terms of physical units: bound volumes, bundles, envelopes, or other types of container. In effect the shelflist entries take the form of an extended summarized statement; thus "v. 1–4, 5–8, 9–12" means that the twelve volumes are bound in the three groupings indicated. In order to avoid ambiguity, a ligature is often used with the inclusive numbers for volumes that are bound in one; so "v. 1–48, 49–50, 51–80" means that volumes 49 and 50 are bound together, while all other volumes are bound individually. At times, too, the statement of holdings is not given in summarized fashion but is spread out seriatim to allow the date of each inventory to be stamped under the volume number to which it relates. These expanded statements require many shelflist cards per title. The Research Libraries of the New York Public Library gave up the practice in 1952.

At times a rubber stamp is added at the end of the holdings statement to indicate that current issues in the periodical room or elsewhere have not yet been shelflisted; but that is not a shelflist function, because the record is intended to cover items in one location only at a time. Some libraries omit the record of all unbound parts, thereby making inventory difficult for a class of material that tends to be disarranged and to have missing numbers. Sometimes the shelflist card carries a statement of the source from which the publication was received; but unless a serial has come constantly from one or two sources, it is a counsel of wisdom to omit the statement, otherwise one or more cards can easily be filled up with a rather valueless listing.

Either the shelflist or the checking records, and generally the former, must serve as the basis for the number of serial volumes added to the collection each year or withdrawn from it, this for the annual count of the library. A tally is kept, usually by broad classes, as each item is added or canceled. The tally should be maintained strictly, especially in the largest libraries, which are less and less likely to take inventory in the future because of the size and cost of the undertaking.

There has been much debate, especially in the Association of Research Libraries, about the proper way to count the bookstock. Should the count be based on the physical units on the shelves, or should it take bibliographical units into account? The latter method gives a truer picture of the extent of a library, enlarging the count to allow for monographs which are bound by series in collective volumes and reducing it for bibliographical volumes which are split into two or more physical volumes through binding exigencies.

However, compilation of figures based on bibliographical units is more complicated and more difficult to maintain than a count of physical volumes. In any circumstances a truly accurate count of serials is hard to procure because bundles, envelopes, etc., are constantly being removed from the bookstacks for readjustment, commonly for binding. With much traffic in both directions, errors are difficult to avoid. For this reason the New York Public Library found it expedient for a number of years to subtract an appreciable arbitrary figure annually; in 1931 the figure was 7,500. Thereby the decennial recount of the actual bookstock came out more consistently with the running annual figures.

End Processes

Material for the end processes is derived from three main sources: (1) serials in publishers' bindings are forwarded by the checkers; (2) freshly bound volumes come from the bindery, in big quantities in large research libraries; and (3) newly cataloged works stem from the serial catalogers. In addition, some items are received from the catalogers or a service unit when changes or corrections are to be made.

The following items are included in the end processes:

1. Bookplates are pasted on the inside of the front cover unless library-bound volumes have special endpapers with the library's seal woven in. Such endpapers can obviate the need for bookplating, provided that no book fund or gift requires a specific bookplate.
2. Book pockets or date-due slips may be inserted in serials which circulate. Sometimes the process is omitted on the score that the publications will not circulate sufficiently to justify the labor involved.
3. Bound volumes are marked with the library's stamp, which sometimes includes the date of accessioning or acquisition. The stamp and call number are added to each piece which goes to the stacks in unbound form.   ·
4. Call numbers are lettered on the spine, also as a rule on the inside of the front or back cover. Volume numbers should be incorporated in the call number, although some libraries do not include them when they occur clearly elsewhere on the spine.

5. Leaves are cut when necessary in bound volumes, as well as in unbound items which are not destined immediately for the bindery.
6. Title pages are embossed with the name of the library. Perforation, which at one time was a common practice, has generally been abandoned.
7. Unbound serials which, for the present at least, will not go to the bindery are inserted in manila-rope bundles, envelopes, or other types of container unless there is already a unit on the shelves into which they can fit.

Manila rope is fairly expensive, especially when it is bought in precut sizes, but it gives good support to unbound serials. It must be lettered and then tied with tape or lawyers' pink pulls, never with string, which is much harder to untie. Occasionally boards are inserted in the bundle to give added support to an oversize volume.

Manila envelopes and manila-rope bundles have proved to be more satisfactory than boxes and metal containers, which admit dust and do not lend desirable support to the items that are stored in them, so that physical deterioration tends to take place in the pieces. Patent binders with spikes, staples, etc., which damage the serials, should be avoided; at the most they should be employed for expendable material only. Portfolios afford protection for unbound newspapers, which are sometimes bundled in brown paper instead, as are other items which will eventually be stored. At times thin serials, annual reports for instance, are put in pamphlet binders, especially when there is little likelihood of other numbers coming along to help in constituting a volume for binding.

End Processes for Storage Material

Chapter 10 mentioned the decline of simplified rules for the original cataloging of serials destined for a storage library, but end processes are generally simplified whenever new acquisitions are sent directly to storage. At Harvard and Yale there is no statement of holdings in the shelflist. Unbound material is often bundled or placed in envelopes to save the cost of binding. Subject classification is dispensed with in most cases; call numbers can consist of a mere size designation followed by a running number. The Harvard College Library has employed numbered slips, which otherwise would have been used for monograph series in the visible index, as an aid in assigning the running numbers.

Analyticals

Libraries analyze the component parts of as many of their monograph series as they can justify. Analyticals are always made when the volumes of a set are dispersed by subject. The Library of Congress has printed analyticals for the contents of many thousands of unlisted monograph series, as well as for more than seven thousand which it formerly recorded in its *List of Series of Publications for Which Cards Are in Stock* (4th ed.; Washington, 1932). The list will not be updated because the Card Division feels that it is more practical for subscribers who are interested in standing orders for specific series to submit their requests on individual order slips to discover whether a series has been analyzed. It is customary for libraries to place standing orders with the Card Division so that they can acquire the analytic entries automatically, just as soon as the cards are printed. The H. W. Wilson Company and other card suppliers print analyticals which are particularly designed to suit the needs of smaller public libraries.

Once the serial routines have been established for the treatment of monograph series and are in operation through the visible index or otherwise, the making of analyticals is mainly the responsibility of the monograph catalogers. Nevertheless the serial staff must continually: (1) record decisions on whether a set is to be analyzed and post receipt of cards that come on standing orders; (2) indicate the heading that is to go on the series added entry; (3) supply the call number for items in kept-together series; (4) specify that a set is scattered; (5) notify the catalogers when no series entry is to be made;[12] and (6) question whether duplicate copies are to be kept for subject.

Most college and university libraries analyze too few government serials, even though Library of Congress cards are available for them. Instead they tend to rely on printed indexes, including the analyticals in the Library of Congress book catalogs. In general, far more monograph series could be analyzed than most libraries attempt. Even the Library of Congress has not analyzed all of the more than seventy thousand monograph series which it has. The *Handbook of Card Distribution* says: "There are many other series that have not been covered, having been passed by in recataloging in order to deal

---

[12]The checking records should not be allowed to serve as a substitute when it is deemed that series added entries are not worth making for the card catalog. There can be justification for recording on the checking records the author, title, and call number of a sample volume in a series, but a complete tabulation ought to be avoided.

with the general books more promptly or because they were of a composite character (*i.e.*, made up of numerous short papers) ."[13]

Mention should be made of the fact that analytical entries are often made for a *Festschrift* when one is discovered in a serial publication. The checkers must be alert to catch commemorative issues as they occur. A few libraries analyze plays found in incoming serials; although this is a questionable policy, it is followed because printed indexes to plays are neither prompt nor inclusive. An uncommon type of analytical is mentioned by Miss Pierson, namely a subject entry for a feature brought out on a serial catalog card.[14]

Series Entries

An additional catalog entry is commonly called for under the name of a monograph series when its parts are analyzed. Such added entries are of most value for scattered sets; they have little value for kept-together series, and so should be avoided because the volumes on the shelves tell whatever story may be needed.

Earlier some libraries maintained a manuscript contents book to provide readers with a list of items in series. A reference card in the catalog drew attention to the place in the contents book where the list for a particular series could be found. Some library book catalogs made a fine reputation for themselves for the quality and extent of their series entries, e.g., the *Catalogue* of the Peabody Institute of Baltimore, which was published from 1883 to 1905. The book catalog of the Library of Congress is increasingly valuable on this account, particularly for the contents of government monograph series, as can be seen from the entries for the *Bulletin* of the United States Geological Survey and the *Technical Paper* of the United States Bureau of Mines.

Today most series entries are unit cards, at the top of which is added the name of the series and the volume number, if any. Such cards are called series added entries. The principal alternative, the typewritten consolidated series card (see figure 23), is steadily giving way to the unit card; e.g., in 1952 the New York Public Library gave it up because the unit-card system was felt to be better, even though it takes up much more space in the card catalog. At that time it was estimated that a complete changeover to unit cards would add

13Library of Congress, Card Division, *Handbook of Card Distribution* (8th ed.; Washington, 1954), p.9.

14Harriet W. Pierson, *Guide to the Cataloguing of the Serial Publications of Societies and Institutions* (2d ed.; Washington, 1931), p.62.

Vol.	Imprint date	Author and title
		A Series of monographs on applied chemistry Classed Individually No statement cd. In public cat. Ser. a.e. v. 1
1	1928	Wheeler, E. The manufacture of artificial silk.
2	1929	Hilditch, T.P. Catalytic processes in applied chemistry.
3	1942	Britton, H.T.S. Hydrogen ions. 3d ed.
4	1946	Durrans, T.H. Solvents. 5th ed.

HOW ISSUED
NO. CW2   ser.cat

Figure 23. Consolidated series entry as used at Yale. In this case the consolidated card is in the official catalog; added entries are preferred in the public catalog.

about 3 percent to the size of the public catalog. By contrast with the unit series card, which is largely the responsibility of the monograph cataloger, consolidated series cards are usually the concern of the serial cataloger. In either case it is necessary to set up routines so that information is supplied by one group to the other, but it is rather disconcerting to find that the procedures tend to be disproportionately expensive.

The monographs in some series are so numerous—e.g., the Columbia Teachers College *Contributions to Education* comprise 974 titles —that the product of either system is costly and space-consuming. Each of the items cited above from the Library of Congress book catalog runs to over a hundred cards, not cheap to buy. The unit cards for some monograph series can fill a whole catalog drawer, while a fifth of a drawer can be filled with consolidated series cards, an awkward quantity to tie and hold together. Alternatives in the circumstances are to hold the set together and make no series added entries of either kind or else to refer to a printed list of the volumes in a series such as Baer has provided.[15] In fact, the appearance of Baer has made the existence of series entries completely superfluous, at least as far as pertinent monograph series are covered in her work. Space can be created in card catalogs by canceling the series cards

[15]Eleanora Baer, *Titles in Series, a Handbook for Librarians and Students* (2d ed.; Metuchen, N.J.: Scarecrow, 1964–70). 3v.

for all titles included in Baer's *Titles in Series,* a work which can be annotated with the call numbers before the cards are scrapped. Similar observations apply to the catalog entry for monograph series which a few libraries make and place in front of the series added entries. The only possible justification for such a procedure is that the catalog entry permits the making of subject cards for the series. But would it be a loss if there were no cards in the catalog for the Teachers College *Contributions to Education* under the subject headings "Education—Collections," "Education—Societies, etc.," or "Education—Periodicals and society publications"?

Recataloging

In libraries with large serial holdings recataloging has been a major function of the serial catalogers. It has originated more from changes in the name or title of a serial than from discovery of faulty records. Hence recataloging in the ordinary sense has not been a particularly serious problem. In the past serial catalogers have had to devote as much as a third of their time to making over the records in a futile attempt to keep pace with changes of name or title. Miss Pierson says that "there is record of one society which changed either its name or title 41 times in 14 years."[16] This is an extreme case, but it does point up the folly of trying to keep the main entry under the latest name or form of name, just as it explains why serial catalogers often wait to see whether a change is stable before adjusting the records. Cresap, McCormick and Paget say: "It is reported that the average corporate issuing body undergoes a change of name every 15 to 20 years, and that this frequency of change requires the vigilance now exercised in cataloging new material."[17] Over a ten-year period statistics had shown that the ratio of recataloging in the New York Public Library was not far from one to two. In the circumstances it was fortunate that, of the items recataloged, eleven out of twelve could be cared for by correcting existing records, not making them over completely.

Spalding describes the situation at the Library of Congress at about the same time as follows:

16Harriet W. Pierson, "The Gay Science—the Cataloguing of the Publications of Learned Societies," *Proceedings* of the Catalog Section, American Library Association 1929 (Chicago, 1929), p.137. Unfortunately, in later years Miss Pierson was unable to recall the name of the society or its publication.

17Cresap, McCormick and Paget, *Survey of Preparation Procedures, Reference Department, New York Public Library* ([New York, 1951]), p.11 of ch. 6.

In fiscal 1953 the Descriptive Cataloging Division did original printed card cataloging for 5,383 titles and it recataloged 1,927 titles. When the figure of 1,927 titles recataloged in one year is related to the estimated 50,000 printed open entries for serials now in the catalogs the rate of recataloging may be expressed as 3.9 per 100 title-years. Thus it will be seen that the problem is not so much the result of the frequency of changes in serial entries as of the volume of changes that results when a large number of serials is active and subject to even infrequent change. It is estimated that it takes 50 percent longer to recatalog than to catalog originally and if this is so, then about 35 percent of the time spent in the descriptive cataloging of serials for printed cards was devoted to recataloging operations and 65 percent to original cataloging operations. The work of the subject catalogers in recataloging serials is usually slight but shelflisters require the same amount of time for work on recataloged entries as for original shelflisting if the call number is not changed, and twice as much time if the call number is changed. (At the present time the call number is changed only when there is a change in corporate entry and a long run of earlier volumes is not involved.)[18]

Fortunately the amount of recataloging in all libraries has been sharply reduced by the change in the cataloging code whereby items are not recataloged when the name or title alters; instead an entry is made under the new name or title. So the *ALA Bulletin* did not have to be recataloged when it became *American Libraries*; a new catalog entry was made under the latter title. This saving is quite significant, though the saving can be still greater when a book catalog for serials replaces the catalog entries.

A special type of recataloging that occurs from time to time consists of the conversion to serial form of what was originally taken by the catalogers to be a book. When these presumed books first appear, they are sometimes called editions, although the word "edition" applies equally well to serials and to monographs; witness the annual *Handbook of Private Schools*, whose 1970 volume was called the fifty-first edition. Sometimes the "books" are pseudoserials which are now being accorded serial treatment. Miss Goss has provided some effective illustrations of the borderline area which exists between books and serials. She says:

When is a periodical not a periodical, but an individual author's

[18]C. Sumner Spalding, *Certain Proposals of Numerical Systems for the Control of Serials for Their Application at the Library of Congress* (Washington, 1954), p.2–3. He explains the term "title-years" as follows: "100 title-years means 100 titles for one year, 1 title for 100 years, 10 titles for 10 years, etc."

work? No rule can solve these problems and I should like to mention here several examples which have come to our attention recently. The *Female spectator*, by Mrs. Eliza Haywood, was evidently considered a periodical by the Library of Congress, and included in the *Union list*. In 1928 the card was revised and the entry changed to Haywood, with a note "Originally issued in monthly parts, April, 1744–May, 1746, ostensibly by a club of four women."

Mykologische hefte . . . Hrsg. von Gustav Kunze und Johann Carl Schmidt, 1–[2] heft, Leipzig, 1817–23, is in the *Union list*, credited to one library only, and in Bolton's *Catalogue of Scientific Periodicals* (v. 1 only), but the preface to the second number which appeared six years after the first states that it has lost the character of a periodical, although it was started as such.

Another example is *Nordische miscellaneen*, 1–28, 1781–91 and the following *Neue nordische miscellaneen*, 1–18, 1792–98, entered by the Library of Congress under the name of the author, August Wilhelm Hupel. Both are in the *Union list* under title and yet this was not recognized at first as a serial by catalogers at Minnesota and was almost overlooked for the *Union list* supplement.[19]

Similar cross-classifications have been repeatedly encountered by librarians as they checked their catalogs in order to report to the *Union List of Serials* or a similar work. The problem is troublesome enough to warrant the suggestion that author series ought to be treated as serial publications whenever they take on serial form, an added entry being made for the "author."

Serial recataloging is the most expensive form of cataloging that there is. It can take a week or more to recatalog a serial set. Hence the importance of reducing the number of titles which are to be recataloged and the value of the new rule which permits cataloging under the new name or title, instead of attempting to bring entries up to date by means of recataloging.

Bibliography

Cresap, McCormick and Paget. *Survey of Preparation Procedures, Reference Department, New York Public Library.* [New York, 1951].

Goss, Edna L. "The Cataloging of Serials," *Catalogers' and Classifiers' Yearbook* 2:73–92 (1930).

New York Public Library. Preparation Division. "Cataloging and Adding of Serials," *Technical Order* no.53–83 (1953).

Yale University Library. *Cataloging of Serials in the Yale University Library.* 3d ed. New Haven, Conn., 1969.

[19]Edna L. Goss, "The Cataloging of Serials," *Catalogers' and Classifiers' Yearbook* 2:82 (1930).

13

Subject Cataloging

Technical problems in the subject cataloging of serials do not compare in difficulty or extent with those encountered in descriptive cataloging. Just the same, subject cataloging has remained very much of a backwater all through this century as far as serials are concerned, so that practice today is almost the same as it was fifty years ago and more. In this time the descriptive cataloging of serials has undergone a series of close investigations through catalog code revision, but there has been no corresponding scrutiny of subject-cataloging theory and practice, in general or in particular. This is apart from the fact that there are perennial problems for which really satisfactory solutions may never be found, one of them being the determination of the best plan for assigning book numbers to serials whose names or titles change.

As a rule, the subject cataloger looks at serials with a quick glance and a generous appraisal, such being the nature of this aspect of his work, but his colleague, the descriptive cataloger, has always examined them closely with a wary eye. The reason for this state of affairs is that in the past classification and subject headings for serial publications have not been particularly important. A library can function excellently without any classification for its periodicals, as most special libraries do; some operate successfully without subject headings, e.g., the Linda Hall Library and the National Lending Library for Science and Technology. In the comparatively near future, as book catalogs for serial publications multiply, subject headings as they have been known may well be abandoned. When that happens, there will be little loss, because the really important subject work with serials is to be found for the most part in the abstracting and indexing services.

Yet there can well be a demand for a new type of subject control in libraries to serve computer purposes.

When at the turn of the century the Library of Congress began to formulate its subject-cataloging program, there were comparatively few abstracting and indexing publications in existence. Among indexes the Royal Society's *Catalogue of Scientific Papers* began publication in 1867, the *Index Medicus* in 1879, and the *Engineering Index* in 1892. Abstracting services, at least in English, came somewhat later; e.g., *Science Abstracts: Physics and Electrical Engineering* in 1903, *Chemical Abstracts* in 1907, and *Biological Abstracts* in 1926. In the circumstances it is not surprising to find that the abstracting and indexing program of the day made little or no impression on the thinking of those who planned the subject-cataloging programs for libraries. But today's terms of reference, being so very different, call for a review of the situation, now that there are numerous computer systems designed for subject control in addition to several thousand abstracting and indexing services.

Subject Headings for Serials

In the assignment of subject headings the serial character of an abstracting service, directory, periodical, or yearbook is brought out as a rule by a distinctive form subheading. For other serials there may be a nondistinctive subheading, no subheading, or even no subject heading, but contemporary Library of Congress policy is to give an appropriate subheading to most serial publications and to treat government serials like nongovernment ones.

The principal subheadings for serials employed by the Library of Congress from 1971 on are:

Abstracts—Periodicals	Directories
Collected works	Periodicals
Collections	Societies, periodicals, etc.
Congresses	Yearbooks

The subheading "Collections," which is also applied to books, covers monograph series in the humanities and social sciences; in science and technology "Collected works" is preferred in order to avoid the suggestion of a collection of objects. "Congresses" relates to the serial or nonserial proceedings of conferences, congresses, symposiums, workshops, and other meetings, though formerly, when publications were limited to the texts of papers presented at a session, the subheading "Addresses, essays, lectures" was favored. Since most directories are considered to be serial in nature, the subheading "Directories" is not further subdivided to indicate frequency, but stands for any directory, whether it is a serial or not.

Subject to certain limitations, the subheading "Periodicals" is now assigned consistently by the Library of Congress to serial publications of all types which are issued more or less regularly, up to and including annuals. This was not the case in the past, however; the subheading "Societies, etc." was a frequent substitute. Until very recently the Library of Congress attempted to characterize serial society publications as such by means of that subheading. The custom has been discontinued. Therefore, in this sense, the three expressions "Societies," "Societies, etc.," and "Society publications," all of which were extensively applied in the past, have become obsolete as form subheadings. Actually, "Societies, etc." is still in vogue, but only as a topical subdivision. Consequently the normal form subheadings for serials should in the future apply to serial society publications as well, i.e., "Collections," "Periodicals," "Yearbooks," and so on. Only one exception is made in the case of society publications: when they merely contain information about the affairs of the organization, they receive no subject heading at all, because in the Library of Congress the main or added entry for a society serves to cover the subject also.[1]

Earlier Library of Congress practice drew distinctions among the following subheadings:

> *Societies*: for collections, memoirs, reports, transactions, etc. of societies under the name of the subject or subjects of which they treat; e.g., "Botany—Societies."
>
> *Societies, etc.*: for publications of museums, universities, and other institutions, as well as of certain commissions, none of which was regarded as a society in library parlance.
>
> *Societies, periodicals, etc.*: for publications which relate to individuals; e.g., "Dickens, Charles—Societies, periodicals, etc." is the heading assigned by the Library of Congress to *The Dickensian; a Magazine for Dickens Lovers.*

---

[1]For the cross-references which the Library of Congress makes in this connection see David J. Haykin, *Subject Headings, a Practical Manual* (Washington, 1951), p.17. Other libraries avoid, and should avoid, this type of reference because of the length of the lists and the large amount of work that is entailed in maintaining them.

Society publications: for works on subjects where the connotation of the expression "Societies" might be ambiguous; e.g., "Ants—Society publications;" "Fungi—Society publications;" and "Insects—Society publications."[2]

As could have been expected, the distinction between a periodical and a society publication was often a nice one. At times two headings had to be assigned to cover both aspects. So for the *Journal of Dental Research* the Library of Congress gave both "Dentistry—Periodicals" and "Dentistry—Societies." The reason for the duplication was that in 1934 the periodical became the official organ of the International Association for Dental Research and included its proceedings as well as those of other organizations.

Of the four subheadings beginning with "Societies" or "Society," only one is still in operation for serials, namely, "Societies, periodicals, etc." Its sole application is under the name of an individual as a form subheading for all serial publications, including those of societies, which are devoted to the study of that person, e.g., "Shakespeare, William, 1564–1616—Societies, periodicals, etc." It may also be applied as a topical subheading.

The subheading "Yearbooks" is assigned to publications: (1) which appear annually, and (2) whose individual volumes summarize the accomplishments or events of the year which occurred in the particular subject field or discipline. Annual publications which do not summarize receive the subheading "Periodicals." Of two annuals, *The Journal of Pacific History* and *Journal of Palynology*, the former takes "Pacific area—History—Yearbooks" because it summarizes events in that area, the latter "Palynology—Periodicals" because, although it is an annual, it consists of individual contributions to knowledge.

The subheading "Abstracts" is no longer applied to serials. So in the Library of Congress the publication *Nuclear Science Abstracts*, which formerly took the two headings "Atomic energy—Abstracts" and "Atomic energy—Periodicals," now carries the single subject heading "Atomic energy—Abstracts—Periodicals." Likewise the former policy under which certain specific subject headings could not be subdivided by form headings is generally no longer in effect. Under that policy headings were often doubled. For example, the *Journal of Experimental Medicine* took the two headings "Medicine, Experimental" and "Medicine—Periodicals"; but now in the Library of Congress it carries the one subject heading "Medicine, Experimental—

2*Ibid.*, p.109–10. Cf. also Harriet W. Pierson, *Guide to the Cataloguing of the Serial Publications of Societies and Institutions* (2d ed.; Washington, 1931), p.61–63.

Periodicals." There are many examples of the former policy in that library's catalogs and on its printed cards, but newly cataloged or reprinted material follows the present policy. Still further, the custom of not subdividing names of places by subheadings is no longer applicable. The *Journal de la marine marchand et de la navigation aérienne*, whose name was formerly *Journal de la marine marchand et de l'Empire français*, earlier took the headings "Merchant marine— France" and "Merchant marine—Periodicals." Now it takes the heading that was not possible before, "Merchant marine—France—Periodicals" as well as "Shipping—Periodicals." Actually, the new headings in part probably represent a subject cataloger's compromise for a difficult situation, since the publication consistently contains material on: (1) the French merchant marine, (2) French shipping, (3) the world merchant marine, (4) world shipping, and (5) less than a page per issue on French and world commercial aviation combined.

These changes are all moves in the right direction. It would have been better if an exception had not been made in favor of "Societies, periodicals, etc." Other libraries have long used "Periodicals and society publications" as an inclusive subheading. That has been the custom in the Research Libraries of the New York Public Library. Still others have been content to use simply "Periodicals," which is undoubtedly the wise course of action and the one which the Library of Congress is approaching. Many years ago the Harvard College Library adopted the subheading "Periodicals and other serial publications" on guide cards to cover all types of serials indiscriminately, but the form on the subject cards has been just the abbreviation "Period."

In 1971 the Library of Congress gave up abbreviations in the tracing; e.g., "Bibl." for bibliography, "Direct." for directories, and "Period." for periodicals. Although many libraries had not followed the Library of Congress in these abbreviations, the usage is wise and really should be followed by all libraries. Headings are printed at the top of Library of Congress cards, but other libraries must type the headings on; every superfluous character typed over and over again, thousands and tens of thousands of times a year, costs money that could be turned to better advantage.

Examples of Subject-Cataloging Practice

The Library of Congress author and subject catalogs in book form, i.e., the *National Union Catalog* in both the current and retrospective editions, afford excellent case studies for serials under terms like

"Bulletin," "Journal," "Society," "United Nations," and "United States." The following items, drawn for the most part from recent issues of the two publications, are designed to give some insight into the ways in which subject headings are assigned to the principal classes of serial publications.

Abstracts

Australia. Commonwealth Scientific and Industrial Research Organization. C.S.I.R.O. science index.
1. Research—Abstracts—Periodicals.   2. Research, Industrial—Abstracts—Periodicals.   3. Translations—Bibliography.

Bulletin signalétique.
1. Science—Abstracts—Periodicals.   2. Science—Bibliography—Periodicals.

Almanacs

France. Almanach national.
1. Almanacs, French.   2. France—Registers.

Information please almanac.
1. Almanacs, American.

Annual reports

No form subheading is assigned to annual reports. In many instances they take no subject heading.

Florida. Division of Correction. Report.
1. Prisons—Florida.

Massachusetts Institute of Technology. Libraries. Report of the director of libraries.
No subject heading.

Ohio. Dept. of Education. Annual report of the State Superintendent of Public Instruction.
1. Education—Ohio.

Bibliographies

The Booklist and subscription books bulletin.
1. Bibliography—Periodicals.   2. Books—Prices.

Gt. Brit. Stationery Office. Daily list of government publications.
1. Gt. Brit.—Government publications—Bibliography.

Book reviews

The New York review of books.
1. Books—Reviews—Periodicals.

City directories

London and suburbs trades' directory.
1. London—Commerce—Directories.

Polk's Washington suburban directory of Maryland and Virginia towns adjacent to the District of Columbia.
1. Washington, D.C.—Suburbs—Directories.   2. Prince George's Co., Md.—Directories.   3. Montgomery Co., Md.—Directories.   4. Arlington Co., Va.—Directories.   5. Fairfax Co., Va.—Directories.

College and university catalogs

Announcements, bulletins, and catalogs take no subject heading.

Directories

Directory [of] scientific resources in the Washington, D.C. area.
1. Research—Washington, D.C.—Directories.   2. Research—Maryland—Directories.   3. Research—Virginia—Directories.

Government publications

Great Britain. The London gazette.
1. Gt. Brit.—Politics and government—Periodicals.

Massachusetts. Metropolitan Area Planning Council. Housing Metropolitan Boston.
1. Housing—Boston metropolitan area.

New York (State) Division of Educational Management Services. School business management handbook.
1. Public schools—Business management.

U.S. Dept. of Agriculture. Economic Research Service. Balance sheet of agriculture.
1. Agriculture—Economic aspects—U.S. 2. Agriculture—U.S.—Statistics.

Handbooks

The Lawyers' pocketbook.
1. Lawyers—Africa, South—Handbooks, manuals, etc.

House organs

The Index. The New York Trust Company.
1. U.S.—Economic conditions—Periodicals.

The Telephone flash. United Telephone Publications.
1. Telephone—U.S.—Employees.   2. Trade-unions—Periodicals.

Indexes

The New York Times index; a master-key to all newspapers.
1. Newspapers—Indexes.   2. Indexes.

Library catalogs

Quite often library catalogs are provisional serials. They begin as sets and continue as serials. They can also be pseudoserials with one edition succeeding another, generally on an annual basis. The former tend to be for larger libraries, the latter for smaller libraries as well as for special resources such as serials in larger institutions or for departmental holdings.

>Columbia University. Libraries. Avery Architectural Library. Avery index to architectural periodicals.
>—— —— Supplement.
>1. Architecture—Periodicals—Catalogs.

>U.S. Library of Congress. Serial Division. Newspapers currently received and permanently retained in the Library of Congress.
>1. Newspapers—Bibliography—Catalogs.

Monograph series

The form subheadings for monograph series, including technical-report series, are either "Collected works" or "Collections." But often the regular subject heading has sufficed.

>Australian Association of Adult Education. Monograph.
>1. Adult education—Australia.

>Smithsonian Institution. Smithsonian contributions to zoology.
>1. Zoology—Collected works.

>U.S. Environmental Science Services Administration. ESSA professional paper.
>1. Geophysics—Collected works.

Periodicals

Although a work exhibits periodicity or has a word such as "journal" in its title, it is not necessarily treated as a periodical from a subject-heading point of view. Also, the heading "Law—Periodicals" is subdivided by country.

>Federación Argentina de Colegios de Abogados. Revista.
>1. Law—Periodicals—Argentine Republic.

>Journal of African and Asian studies.
>1. Africa—Periodicals.   2. Asia—Periodicals.

>Journal of Asian and African studies.
>1. African studies—Periodicals.   2. Oriental studies—Periodicals.

>Journal of Korean studies.
>1. Korean studies—Collections.

Journal of modern literature.
  1. Literature, Modern—20th century—History and criticism—Periodicals.

Journal of programmed instruction.
  1. Programmed instruction—Collections.

Journal of reading behavior.
  1. Reading—Addresses, essays, lectures.

New York University. School of Education. Education quarterly.
  1. Education—Periodicals.

Statistics

South Africa. Bureau of Statistics. Statistical yearbook.
  1. Africa, South—Statistics.

U.S. Atomic Energy Commission. Statistical summary of the physical research program.
  1. Research—U.S.—Statistics.

Symposiums

Very few symposiums have been accorded serial treatment, even though they recur periodically. The papers and proceedings generally take the form subheading "Congresses"; but the subheading "Collected works" is also employed, and on occasion no subject heading is assigned.

Agricultural Symposium, Atomic Energy Centre, 1966. Proceedings.
  1. Agriculture—Congresses.

Symposium (International) on Combustion. [Papers.]
  1. Combustion.

Telephone books

Telephone directory, London.
  1. London—Directories—Telephone.

Treaties

United Nations. Treaty series.
  1. Treaties—Collections.

Union lists

Access.
  1. Chemistry—Periodicals—Bibliography—Union lists. 2. Chemistry—Bibliography—Union lists.

Who's whos

The standard subheading for who's whos of given localities is "Biography—Dictionaries." But many works relate to professions and other groups, and they take the expression for the category followed by the subheading "Directories."

Eminent educationists of India.
  1. India—Biography—Dictionaries.

Gannon, Francis Xavier, Biographical dictionary of the left.
  1. U.S.—Biography—Dictionaries.

Official talent and booking directory.
  1. Music trade—U.S.—Directories.   2. Musicians—U.S.—Directories.

Who's who among students in American junior colleges.
  1. Junior college students—U.S.—Directories.

Who's who in Brazil.
  1. Brazil—Biography—Dictionaries.

Who's who in guidance in Indiana.
  1. Personnel service in education—Indiana—Directories.

Who's who in Japan.
  1. Japan—Biography—Periodicals.

Who's who in philosophy.
  1. Philosophy, Modern—20th century—Bio-bibliography.   2. Philosophers, American—Directories.   3. Philosophers, English—Directories.

Who's who in show business.
  1. Entertainers—Directories.

Who's who in the Gorton government.
  1. Cabinet officers—Australia.

Yearbooks

Advances in biophysics.
  1. Biological physics—Periodicals.

Advances in primatology.
  1. Primates—Collected works.

Annual progress in child psychiatry and child development.
  1. Child study—Periodicals.   2. Child psychiatry—Periodicals.

Annual survey of Commonwealth law.
  1. Law—Commonwealth of Nations—Yearbooks.

The British antiques yearbook.
  1. Art dealers—Gt. Brit.—Directories.

Columbia University. Institute of Cancer Research. Scientific report.
  1. Cancer research—U.S.—Yearbooks.

Indian Cancer Research Centre. Progress report.
1. Cancer—India.

International auction records.
1. Art—Catalogs—Yearbooks.

There are three problems which call for study and action in the field of subject headings for serials. (1) Subject catalogs and the tracings on pre-1971 Library of Congress cards which are acquired by libraries in the future should be reviewed in order to bring together in the catalog all the items which under the old and new practice should be interfiled. (2) The coming of book catalogs may require certain new policies; e.g., when the Library of Congress assigns no subject heading because of its special system of references, its subject catalog in book form commonly supplies a subject heading. The *Graduate Journal* of Boston University's Graduate School received no subject heading on the catalog card, but in the book catalog it was entered under "Boston—Learned institutions and societies." Likewise the *International Student Bulletin*, which calls for no subject heading in the tracing, is listed under "Education—Societies, etc." in the book catalog. On the other hand, most book catalogs of serial publications pay no attention to subject listings. Evidently the old system is no longer adequate; does the future call for no subject headings for serial publications or does it require a new system designed for machine manipulation? (3) Clearly the Library of Congress subject headings for serials are cumbersome for computer activities. They were not planned with such a prospect in mind, so it is not a criticism of the system to say that it would be extremely difficult, as things stand, to have the computer compile a list of American who's whos on the basis of the subject headings. And yet this is the kind of task that should now be possible with the computer. Consequently thought must be given to a new pattern of subject control for serials, a pattern that will facilitate computer searches.

Form Headings

In most libraries entries are not made for individual journals under form headings such as "Periodicals" or "American periodicals." As can be seen from MacNair[3] and Pierson,[4] the Library of Congress

[3]Mary W. MacNair, *Guide to the Cataloguing of Periodicals* (3d ed.; Washington, 1925), p.13–14.
[4]Pierson, *Serial Publications of Societies*, p.62–63.

early in the century made added entries under the headings "Periodicals"[5] and "Societies," as well as under the name of a place followed by the subheading "Learned institutions and societies." These practices could be revived in computer listings, but their value is doubtful. In the analysis of its serial holdings the Library of Congress recorded eleven forms which had more than ten thousand entries. They were:

Periodicals	81,281	Directories	15,650
Annual reports	50,411	House organs	14,831
Statistics	29,558	Conference proceedings	13,243
Trade journals	25,480	College catalogs and	
Yearbooks	19,657	bulletins	11,287
Society publications	18,681	Law publications	10,998

No listing was made by country, but the publications in seven languages were in excess of ten thousand:

English	359,277	Russian	21,506
German	63,375	Italian	17,274
Spanish	49,583	Dutch	10,815
French	42,927		

Form headings were abandoned in the card catalog. Can they be justified on the computer in view of the magnitude of the undertaking?

The United Nations Library decided to adopt a form heading "Periodicals" subdivided by the name of the country from which the publication came; it was intended to cover serials of all kinds, and the particular interest was in receipts from smaller countries. Some periodical rooms, for example in the Research Libraries of the New York Public Library, keep a card file arranged by country of origin as an aid to readers who want to know what periodicals are on hand from a particular country. When that type of record is not maintained, it may be difficult to respond to readers' requests except perhaps through dealer lists in the acquisition department.

[5]Julia Pettee in her *Subject Headings* (New York: Wilson, 1947), p.91–92, says: "The general form heading Periodicals is quite uncalled for. Why should a library assemble in one list all of its periodicals when it keeps a serial file and we have the Wilson *Union List of Serials*?" At one time, too, the Enoch Pratt Free Library made form headings like "Spanish works—Periodicals" for journals in foreign languages. See its *Catalog Department Manual* (Baltimore, 1940), p.58. But it no longer makes such entries.

Form headings are assigned to works about nonindividual serial publications, and duplicate headings are made for works about the serials issued by ethnic groups. So, for a work about German newspapers published in Switzerland, the headings would be: "1. Swiss newspapers (German). 2. German newspapers—Switzerland." For a work about periodicals in the English language published in Ireland the headings would be: "1. Irish periodicals (English). 2. English periodicals—Irish." An exception to this practice is made for works about magazines and newspapers published in the United States in languages other than English. An illustration of this type of heading is "Swedish-American periodicals," with references from "American periodicals, Swedish" and "Swedish periodicals."

Subject Indexing of Periodicals

In addition to the analytical entries described in the preceding chapter, some libraries make a feature of including in their catalogs index cards for significant periodical articles. The objective is to supplement the published indexing services, not to duplicate them. Whenever extensive subject indexing of this kind is undertaken, the library's list of subject headings must be expanded, because periodical articles require finer headings than books do.

An instruction on the checking records directs the staff to route selected titles to the officers, who will indicate the items that are to be indexed. Most articles are indexed by subject only, but some are indexed by author or by author and subject. The subject catalogers supply the headings, and after that has been done, the cards can be typed.

Index entries are made according to the current name of the serial in exactly the same way that the indexing services operate. Difficulties can arise when a reader asks for the item which, under the conventional system of serial cataloging, is still represented in the catalog and the shelflist, as well as on the shelves, by the former title. With closed stacks, attendants may report that there is no such title, so the call slip must be verified. The problem can occur as long as the journal is in the periodical room or at the bindery, in fact until the catalogers have made an entry under the new name. The answer to the problem is to make the change in the catalog entry at the same time that it is made on the checking records; there is no justification in waiting for a volume to be completed before the catalog records can be adjusted.

In the Research Libraries of the New York Public Library the divisions send issues to the Searching Section to have the indexing undertaken. That section maintains a control file which provides the cataloging form of entry and the call number. Items are posted there, so there is an indication of the stage they have reached. The actual indexing is done in the Monograph Cataloging Section. Non-current items which should be indexed are routed to the Searching Section by the Adding Section on the basis of instructions on the Central Serial Record.

Several libraries have established an excellent reputation for index entries. Notable among them are the National Library of Medicine, the Research Libraries of the New York Public Library, and the Peabody Museum Library at Harvard University. At the first two of these institutions the program was inaugurated by Dr. Billings. The genesis of his thoughts on indexing has been described in these terms:

> The *Index-Catalogue of the Surgeon-General's Library,* called by Dr. William H. Welch "America's greatest gift to medicine," was conceived out of the need of a young medical student, John Shaw Billings. Mindful of his toilsome search through the literature of medicine preparatory to his doctor's thesis, he determined years later, when in charge of the Surgeon General's Library, to gather the books and journals of medicine in adequate numbers, to catalog them, and to index their contents, so that future generations would neither have to go to Europe to see the books nor handle the thousands of volumes which had heretofore been required for any thorough review of a subject.[6]

In Washington Dr. Billings aimed at a printed bibliography. But in New York he had the index entries filed in the public and divisional catalogs. Three quarters of a century later those catalogs afford a truly splendid starting point for research because of the blending of the book and periodical literature on a great variety of subjects. Julia Pettee, after describing Dr. Billings' contributions in Washington and New York, added: "The catalog of the New York Public Library deserves a place by itself not only because of its importance as the largest and most fingered catalog in the country,

---

[6]From the unpublished appendixes to *The National Medical Library; Report of a Survey of the Army Medical Library,* by Keyes D. Metcalf and others (Cambridge, 1944), p.66. The published part of the survey (Chicago: American Library Assn., 1944) contains two chapters on the *Index-Catalogue.*

but because in its history are combined the various elements that have gone into the development of our standard dictionary form."[7]

The alphabetico-classed catalog in the Peabody Museum of Archaeology and Ethnology makes a similar contribution to knowledge in the field of general anthropology and its subdisciplines prehistoric archeology, ethnology, and physical (or biological) anthropology. So important was this catalog considered to be that for a number of years the American Anthropological Association had wanted to have it published. It did appear in 1963, together with the list of subject headings used in its compilation, and supplements are keeping the work up to date.[8]

Subject Classification for Serials

There are five standard ways in which serial sets are arranged in the bookstock. (1) Files of periodicals are often not classified by subject but are arranged in a simple alphabetical sequence. Special libraries follow this plan very generally. (2) Serials are classified quite broadly, without regard to any subject breakdowns in a field. (3) Close classification is applied; hence serials are distributed among the books so freely that large clusters of serial publications do not often occur. (4) Annual reports, directories, lists of members of organizations, society publications, etc., are commonly classified apart from the periodicals. (5) The bound volumes for recent years, especially the last ten years, may be shelved apart from the rest of the set which, since the volumes are not consulted so frequently, may be located in a less convenient place, possibly even in a storage collection.

Marie Prevost made the classical statement on the nonclassification of periodicals. She said:

> The vague class number on a periodical has never been of use. It is not needed when a library splits into departments. Walk along the line glancing at the last volume of each title. Chalkmark it E for Education, A for Art, the mind working automatically. Withhold decision on doubtful titles until departmental urge appears.
>
> The only inlet to periodical use is through indexes to their articles. The remedy for an unindexed periodical is not classifying but

[7]Pettee, *Subject Headings*, p.44.

[8]*Catalogue of the Library of the Peabody Museum of Archaeology and Ethnology, Harvard University* (Boston: G. K. Hall, 1963), 54v. First supplement (1970), 12v.

getting it indexed. Even if classified, recourse must be had to its own index.

Moreover we have with us an all important situation produced by the fact that the people who have done the most intensive work on checklists and indexes, giving us our prime tools (witness Gregory and Wilson) both list and refer to a periodical by each of its successive titles during the period in which that title is in force. This knocks the bottom out of our long-cherished habit of forcing them together by a call number; but it works with the least possible friction. A tyro shelves them correctly; the public find them under the expected name; the reference staff send directly to the shelves for the title given in checklist or index without recourse to catalog for call number or ancient title.

May I outline what I, myself, consider the ideal way of recording periodicals?

All periodicals, current and bound, the entire responsibility of the periodical division.

All periodicals to be shelved by title current at date of publication, without call or accession numbers.

All holdings for a given title to be shown only on a Kardex card in its "visible" file. A new card for each change of name. This means that all bound volumes, note of volumes in bindery, the receipt of unbound issues including today's,—will appear in this spot only. (Newark has a card printed in this form.)

A card to be placed in the book catalog under each name of each periodical, and under each subject desired, with note: "For holdings see entry in Kardex record." Where change of name has occurred, the note will read: "This periodical has appeared under the following titles: . . . For holdings see entries in Kardex record." The titles to be listed chronologically but without dates. These cards *never* to be out of the catalog, a new one to be written at name change and substituted as the old one is removed,—a full time service impossible when periodicals are accessioned and classified.

Compared with the classifying method the above means: great speeding up of service at all points; much reduction in labor; complete and exact information always available at a single location; no laboriously kept-up, eternally incomplete cards for bound volumes to mislead the unwary into believing the file stops a year or two back at best.[9]

Broad classification is really only a variation on the alphabetical plan. The system can be illustrated by saying that in Dewey all

[9]Marie J. Prevost, "Why Classify Periodicals?" *Wilson Library Bulletin* 15:85 (1940).

philosophy journals would go in 105. The *Journal of Symbolic Logic* would go there and not in 160.5 (journals in the field of logic) or 164.05 (journals in the field of symbolic logic). Likewise *Ethics* would go in 105 and not in 170.5 (journals in the field of ethics). In these cases 160.5, 164.05, and 170.5 would never be used. The Harvard classification is very much along these lines.[10] In the class for economics periodicals, for example, the following assortment of titles occurs: *Afro-Asian Economic Review; Agricultural and Industrial Progress in Canada; American Economic Review; American Review of Soviet and Eastern European Trade; Australian Journal of Statistics; Business Week; East African Management Journal; Economic History Review; Finnish Trade; Fortune; Indian Statistical Series;* and *Pakistan Development Review.* In a close classification each of these twelve journals would be in a different class, just as the *Journal of Symbolic Logic* would be in 164.05 in Dewey.

The classification of nonperiodicals is a fairly complicated matter. In special libraries annual reports and financial statements are commonly arranged alphabetically and housed in vertical files, but in general libraries they are usually classed with the institution to which they relate. Directories also tend to be classed by subject in all types of library. Many libraries prefer to treat the proceedings of societies as though they were periodicals. Dewey has the form number 06 for society publications, but as far as serial publications are concerned it is better to put as many items as possible into 05; otherwise there are constant debates as to whether an item belongs in 05 or 06.

When space is at a premium, particularly on the open shelves and in many special libraries, it is customary to divide sets of periodicals, keeping the recent years close at hand. At Enoch Pratt Free Library the dividing date between stack and main-floor serials is the same for all departments; the current and three preceding years of bound volumes are shelved in the departments, earlier volumes in the stacks. There is an exception to this in the case of about 350 frequently used titles for which runs of twenty-one years are shelved together on the first floor rather than in the stacks.

Beatrice Simon has suggested a sixth plan for the arrangement of serials. She advocates neither an alphabetical nor a classified scheme, but groupings by form, e.g., government documents, periodicals, serials issued by corporations, and society publications. Only in the general library of a university would she consider a classified arrange-

---

[10]Harvard University Library, *Periodical Classes: Classified Listing by Call Number, Alphabetical Listing by Title* (Widener Library Shelflist, no.15 [Cambridge, 1968]).

ment; there she says the classification should be broad, and books and serials should be separated. She points out the difficulty of classifying a publication like the *Canadian Journal of Economics and Political Science* so that both the economists and the political scientists will be happy. She observes: "I have seen several librarians start out with the alphabetical arrangement, and then change—not to a subject arrangement but to one which gathers forms together."[11]

In the long run, the answer to the question whether to classify— and if so, how—or not to classify serials may prove to be more of a practical issue than a theoretical one. And the crux of the matter may well be as Marie Prevost suggested: "The remedy for an unindexed periodical is not classifying but getting it indexed."

Subject Classification for Government Documents

The United States government has a network of depository libraries which receive all or a selection of the federal documents distributed through the Superintendent of Documents. The list of depositories is published annually in the *Monthly Catalog of United States Public Documents*. It includes college, public, state, teachers' college, and university libraries—even several school libraries. Numerous institutions therefore have had to decide whether to classify the material or not. The alternative to incorporating the publications in the classified bookstacks, as the Library of Congress does, is to set up a documents collection as a unit in itself.[12] In chapter 4 in the section on the organization of the document collection, this practice is described as substandard whenever the collection is not as well located, organized, or serviced as the current periodicals are. Often it is located in one of the more remote parts of the bookstacks, available for relatively short hours, and the responsibility of non-

[11]Beatrice V. Simon, "Cataloguing of Periodicals," *Ontario Library Review* 33:244 (1949). This article should be studied carefully for the light it sheds on the whole problem of the classification of serials. See also her earlier article, "Let's Consider Serials Realistically," *Library Journal* 71:1296 (1946).

[12]The chief protagonist of this type of organization is Ellen P. Jackson. See in particular her *Administration of the Government Documents Collection* (ACRL Monograph no.5 [Chicago: Assn. of College and Reference Libraries, 1953]). See also Ruth M. Erlandson, "The Organization of Federal Government Publications in Depository Libraries," in Anne M. Boyd, *United States Government Publications* (3d ed.; New York: Wilson, 1949), p.569–79. An older study which is still of value is Thomas P. Fleming, "The Organization of Work with Public Documents in University Libraries," in *Public Documents* (Chicago: American Library Assn., 1936), p.101–27.

professional staff whose tasks are to check the receipt of current documents, shelve them, and help in finding material when necessary.

Government documents are on an equal footing with other serials in the Library of Congress and the Research Libraries of the New York Public Library; witness the important bibliographical work produced in each of them. For example, since 1910 the Library of Congress has issued the *Monthly Check-list of State Publications,* and the editorial offices of the Public Affairs Information Service are in the Economics Division of the New York Public Library. The acquisition and reference programs in those libraries are exceptionally fine.

The collection of federal documents that comes nearest to completeness is under the direction of the Superintendent of Documents. Its catalog is a shelflist arranged by issuing bodies. The classification, i.e., the notation developed for the publications of the issuing bodies, is given in the *Checklist of United States Public Documents, 1789–1909,* and since July 1924 in the *Monthly Catalog of United States Public Documents.*[13] On the classification of depository sets Eastin says:

> Classification systems vary throughout the depository libraries. Sixty-eight do not use any classification system for depository collections. The greatest number make use of the Superintendent of Documents classification system, a total of 174 libraries preferring this system. Fifty-four others use the Superintendent of Documents system in combination with the Dewey decimal system. The Dewey system alone is employed by 111 depository libraries, while 8 others partly use the Dewey, and 15 more combine the Dewey system with department and bureau treatment. The last-mentioned department and bureau system is used exclusively by 32 libraries. Various other systems, such as Cutter, Library of Congress, subject treatment, and 23 individual or specialized classification systems are also used.[14]

Ethelyn Markley criticizes the Superintendent of Documents classification on six grounds:

> 1. There are often delays of months in assigning numbers to ephemeral or declassified items.

---

[13]For a loose-leaf edition of the schedules see Mary E. Poole, *Documents Office Classification,* compiled in North Carolina State College Library, Duke University Library, Virginia Polytechnic Institute Library ([Ann Arbor, Mich.: J. W. Edwards, 1946]).

[14]Roy B. Eastin, "Let's Use Public Documents!" *Library Journal* 73:1556 (1948).

2. Since the classification is by issuing body, awkward situations develop when titles are transferred from one issuing body to another.

3. The works of agencies which publish in the same or closely related field are not brought together on the shelves.

4. Numbers that were assigned from 1909 to 1924 are hard to obtain unless they are taken from the unofficial schedules compiled by Miss Poole.

5. The notation is often long; it is difficult to read because of inferior and superior numbers; and it results in a fixed rather than a relative location for the publications of a department.

6. Direct access to the shelves by subject is precluded; an intermediary aid is required, such as an alphabetical author file or the *Monthly Catalog of United States Public Documents*.[15]

Accordingly, she prefers Ellen Jackson's notation which is applicable to all types of government publications,[16] though she also speaks well of Swank's scheme for state and local documents, which is intended to complement the Superintendent of Documents system.[17]

Most special libraries and many university libraries, as well as the Library of Congress and the Research Libraries of the New York Public Library, have felt the need for the subject approach which a regular classified arrangement of government publications affords. They catalog and classify documents as they do other material; they know that four out of five federal documents are serial in character, so follow normal channels; and they make use of the Library of Congress cards which are available for all but municipal documents. In other words, they make no distinction between government and nongovernment publications so far as the organization of their bookstock is concerned. This policy is especially desirable in library systems where large quantities of documents are required both centrally and in departmental libraries. The demand may be such that at times holdings must be duplicated between the two. The duplication is natural because few departmental collections could operate

[15]A. Ethelyn Markley, *Library Records for Government Publications* (Berkeley: Univ. of California Pr., 1951), p.18–19.

[16]Ellen P. Jackson, *A Notation for a Public Documents Classification* [Stillwater: Oklahoma Agricultural and Mechanical College], Library Bulletin no.8 [1946].

[17]Raynard Swank, "A Classification System for State, County, and Municipal Documents," *Special Libraries* 35:116 (1944).

without government publications, least of all those whose fields are business, law, public administration, and science and technology.

The serials which the Library of Congress classifies in J 1-999 are an exception to any plan of scattering government publications by subject. They include the "congressional set" of federal documents, which is arranged by arbitrary numbers assigned to the publications of the fifteenth and later Congresses.[18] The current numbers are obtained from the *Numerical Lists and Schedule of Volumes* issued by the Superintendent of Documents. Since there is an interval before the numbers are made public, there is always an assortment of un-numbered volumes at the end of the set waiting for numbers to be assigned. Much valuable material is to be found in the congressional set. For instance, Commodore Perry's *Narrative of the Expedition of an American Squadron to the China Seas and Japan, Performed in the Years 1852, 1853 and 1854* was published as a House of Repre-sentatives document. Clearly it should be analyzed to make it readily available to the historian, just as it should be shelved in the rare-book collection.

Minor government publications form excellent material for co-operative acquisition and storage. The Center for Research Libraries has made a feature of gathering them in. One disadvantage inherent in the self-cataloging documents collection is that minor serials are held in the main stacks when they could properly go into a storage collection.

In theory there is no objection to dispensing with subject classi-fication for minor government serials, any more than there is for nonserials. The objection comes when standard publications, which should be readily accessible to readers and staff, are buried in un-cataloged and unclassified collections, and surely it is an anomaly to find the publications of the Freer Gallery of Art in such a resource. The consequences of discriminating against government publications are all too apparent from the *List of the Serial Publications of For-eign Governments,* which disclosed that there are only two really strong documents collections in the United States: one at the Library of Congress and one at the Research Libraries of the New York Pub-lic Library.

The Library of Congress has developed its classification scheme especially to provide for government publications of all kinds. By con-

---

[18]An explanation of the serial numbers is given in Laurence F. Schmeckebier, *Government Publications and Their Use* (2d rev. ed.; Washington, D.C.: Brookings Institution, 1969), p.161–66.

trast, the document sections in the Dewey Decimal System are among its weakest parts, so much so that in libraries with extensive document holdings many adjustments in the scheme need to be made.

Form Symbols in the Notation for Serials

Stack service in research libraries demonstrates that a mnemonic device in the call number helps to disclose that an item is a serial. On their call slips readers may fail to mention the volume number or other essential information; stack attendants are then unable to find desired items. But omission of essential data can be detected at the time call slips are presented when there is a mnemonic element in the call number. The Dewey form number 05 for periodicals is valuable in this respect, as is the class AP (general periodicals) in the Library of Congress scheme; not so, however, the class AS (academies and learned societies), which includes both monographs and serials.

There is no consistent pattern in the Library of Congress classification; the treatment of serials varies even within a class. The following variations occur in Z (bibliography):

SHORTHAND

Z53P	General periodicals	Z54Y	Yearbooks
	English shorthand	55	Societies
54	Periodicals		

PALEOGRAPHY

Z108	Periodicals, societies, congresses

BOOK INDUSTRIES AND TRADE

Z119	Periodicals	Z120	Societies, trade unions
119.5	Yearbooks		

BINDING

Z267	Periodicals	Z268	Societies

BOOKSELLING AND PUBLISHING

Z284	Periodicals, societies

LIBRARIES

Z671	Periodicals	Z673	Library associations

GENERAL BIBLIOGRAPHY

Z1007	Periodicals	Z1008	Societies, congresses, etc.

The Dewey form number 06 (societies) includes monographs as well as serials, though the serials really should be minor ones. Both here and in many parts of the Library of Congress classification the problem encountered in subject headings is to some extent repeated: what is the difference between a periodical and a society publication? In subject-heading practice the question can be straddled by the use of duplicate headings, but in classification the issue must be faced squarely. One guiding principle could well be that in cases of doubt the number for periodicals should be favored. In any event a choice must be made between dividing the periodicals from the periodical-like publications on a subject or dividing the publications of a society. On all counts the distinction between periodicals and society publications causes trouble. It could well be a false distinction that should be abandoned, or if not abandoned altogether, at least redefined more realistically. As an example of the problem, three publications of the American Library Association can be taken: *American Libraries,* which was formerly the *ALA Bulletin,* the proceedings of the annual conferences, and the annual list of members. It could well be that the first should classify in 020.5 or Z671 and the third in 020.6 or Z673. But what about the second? Because there is some doubt, should it not go in 020.5 or Z671 also?

Assignment of Book Numbers

As a collection grows, the assignment of book numbers that keep publications in strict alphabetical order becomes an increasingly formidable task. For titles that begin with words such as "art," "music," and "science," as a noun or an adjective, in English or any other language which has cognate forms, the Library of Congress has led the way in attacking the problem. It spreads or otherwise skillfully manipulates the book numbers to provide an effective arrangement instead of "grafting"[19] them on to a narrow base. But no classification scheme yet devised has provided the extremely broad base required for headings such as "Great Britain," "New York," or "United States." In 1969, for example, the Library of Congress had 9,762 titles on its visible index for United States documents; it had another 9,764 on its Old Serial Record. In 1900 no one envisaged how the entries would multiply under a heading such as "United States." In the cir-

[19]To use an expression of Anna C. Laws, *Author Notation in the Library of Congress* (Washington, 1930), p.12.

cumstances today it is questionable how far strict alphabetical arrangement on the shelves ought to be retained, particularly in the trouble spots. It could well be that alphabetical sequence will have to give way to accession order within each letter of the alphabet.

Library of Congress procedures for assigning book numbers to serial publications are:

Periodicals, Documents, etc., present certain problems which are best solved by keeping materials in these forms together in larger groups, either at the head of a given class or in special numbers at the beginning of a block of class numbers covering a broad subject. Typical of the latter is the following sequence under Anthropology:

GN
1	Periodicals.
2	Societies. Institutions.
3	Congresses.
	Collections.
4	Collections by several authors.
6	Collected works of individual authors.
8	Minor collections of papers, essays, etc.
11	Dictionaries and encyclopedias.

Where a form sequence is needed for a single class, variants of the following are used for subclass arrangement:

.A1	Periodicals and Societies
.A2-4	Documents in series.
.A5	Documents in monographic form.
.A6-Z	Monographs.

Yearbooks, congress reports, and society publications are treated analogously. In each instance, the Shelflist must be consulted carefully because of the great variation in treatment between different parts of the classification schedules. They are frequently arranged by content, that is, the publications are assigned book numbers on the basis of their logical sequence and importance rather than upon the vagaries of their titles.

The book number having been determined, the shelflister then writes the full call number on both cards, leaving the copy as a temporary card in the shelflist, later to be replaced by the printed cards. Returning to his desk, the shelflister inscribes the call number in the book, on the verso of the title page, and prepares other copies of the master card for various records, using the fluid-process cards wherever possible.

For all materials in those categories where the Serial Record Division has maintained the record of holdings since 1942, the shelflister must prepare for that division an extra copy of [a preliminary catalog card on which the assigned call number is recorded.][20]

Occasionally an unnumbered series is classed together. Arbitrary numbering must then be devised. And special schemes must be developed for the publications of complex bodies such as the Organization of American States, which produces editions in several languages.

A temporary shelflist card should not be made and filed, to be replaced later on by the permanent card, as in the Library of Congress practice described above. Instead the card should be made in advance of the assignment of the book number, preferably at the same time that the preliminary cards are made. Then the serial cataloger can add the statement of holdings, and the shelflist card can be dropped into place as soon as the book number has been determined. The more complicated the statement of holdings which goes on the shelflist card, the more desirable is it to follow this practice; otherwise the details must be copied onto the permanent card when it is forthcoming, and the copying and filing add to the work load. The practice is particularly desirable for libraries which use tabulated cards.

Should a serial set be recataloged because of a change of name or title, much labor can be involved in altering the book numbers, since all call numbers inside the volumes and on the spines must be corrected, and shifts in the bookstacks may be necessary to accommodate the set in its new location. If book numbers are not adjusted, publications which become well known under a later title will continue to be shelved under less-known earlier titles, to the inconvenience of those who consult the shelves directly. The alternative of shelving the segments of serials in accordance with each change of name or title is not altogether a happy plan, particularly in large research libraries where, e.g., there can be cumulative indexes which do not fit in with the plan of splitting up sets. And, after all, *Ethics* is still the same publication as the former *International Journal of Ethics*. Whether they like it or not, most large research libraries retain the original book number through all the vicissitudes in the life of a serial. The number is altered for the most part only when a change is of such magnitude that a new work has in fact emerged. So classification tends to be somewhat conservative in holding serial sets together.

[20]Library of Congress, *Subject Cataloging Division* (Departmental & Divisional Manuals, no.3 [Washington, 1950]), p.35–37.

Monograph Series

In the act of sorting or classifying, decisions must be made about keeping monograph series together as sets or scattering them by subject. Often it is difficult, even extremely difficult, to predetermine the best course of action; hence decisions have to be reviewed as trouble develops, whereupon it may be decided to keep part of a set together and to scatter the rest. Should duplicate sets be available, the first copy is generally held together and the second scattered by subject. The *Loeb Classics,* e.g., are valuable in both ways: the kept-together set for the person who asks for a volume in the *Loeb Classics,* the scattered set for those who are working with an individual author. Likewise, when a volume of a monograph series which is held together comes in as a gift, it is generally marked "keep for subject" and recorded as an added copy on the main entry for the analytical, not for the monograph series.

When a complete set is on hand or on order, the presumption may be in favor of keeping a series together in the following circumstances:

1. Government documents such as the congressional set or geological-society publications.
2. Items whose parts are not regular bibliographical units, e.g., the *Cambridge History of the British Empire.*
3. Near-print, e.g., technical reports.
4. Pamphlet series which obviously do not need to be scattered and whose parts might otherwise end up in pamphlet volumes. Many German series belong in this category.
5. Publications with continuous paging.
6. Series on a narrowly defined topic, e.g., Byzantine art.
7. Sets whose parts might prove difficult to classify, especially when the monographs are written in Latin or any of the less common languages.
8. Unanalyzed series, even when the analyzing is merely postponed.
9. Well-known sets which are likely to be asked for as such, e.g., *The Harvard Classics.*
10. Works for which a cumulative index is issued, e.g., the *Skrifter* of the Norsk Folkeminnelag, which has an index covering v.1–49.

When a library does not intend or need to acquire a complete set, the individual volumes on hand should almost invariably be scattered by subject. When a complete set is on hand or on order, the presumption may be in favor of scattering the volumes by subject in the following circumstances:

1. General series, like *Everyman's Library,* which cover many subjects.

2. In institutions which are connected with storage libraries, those series which have items that should go directly to storage instead of to the classified shelves.

3. In library systems, notably university library systems, those series which contain volumes that ought to be located in the main as well as branch or departmental libraries whenever the acquisition of duplicate copies cannot be justified. Conversely, a branch or departmental library should always scatter the volumes of a series unless all of them are in its subject field.

4. Items whose name or title is apt to change, the evidence being taken from the prior history of the organization which publishes the series or from the set itself when it has been acquired after there has been at least one change of name.

5. Loosely connected series on a diversity of subjects, e.g., the *Publications of the University of Manchester.*

6. Publications which include items on poor paper, since such items will sooner or later cause gaps to occur in a set unless they are preserved under special conditions.

7. Publishers' series, e.g., the *College Outline Series.*

8. Series that clearly should be scattered by subject, e.g., the *University of Minnesota Pamphlets on American Writers.*

9. Sets whose component parts look like ordinary monographs and are generally regarded as such, e.g., the *Rivers of America* series.

10. Special library holdings, except when the institution is a historical-research library or when the total set falls within its subject field; also the holdings of school and small public libraries, but this does not apply to complete sets of works such as the *Farmers' Bulletin* and the *Pageant of America.*

11. Titles which include reference books in the narrow sense of the term, e.g., *Carnegie Institution Publications,* of

which volume 353 is Tatlock and Kennedy's *Concordance to the Complete Works of Geoffrey Chaucer and to the Romaunt of the Rose.*

12. Unnumbered series to which factitious numbering is not to be supplied.

Most decisions on scattering or keeping together are made from the announcement of a new series or from the first volume in the series. When volume 1 of the *Cornell Studies in English* appeared, it was clear that the series should be scattered because the first item was Northup's *Bibliography of Thomas Gray.* Likewise it was obvious from the start that the *Useful Reference Series* should not be held together. But the prospectus for the *Victoria Histories of the Counties of England* seemed to indicate that the set should be kept as a unit; for one thing, the size of the volumes is such that they would generally be found on the oversize shelves and constitute very much of a set there. And the *Reference Shelf,* although the subjects are miscellaneous, from the start suggested itself as a kept-together set because it was announced as a series of works for debaters.

Hard and fast rules cannot be laid down. The way in which one library treats a monograph series may not be the right way for even a similar institution. Certainly the way in which the Library of Congress proceeds is no indication of the way in which a university library should act. There are multiple copies for 18.45 percent of the monograph series in the national library, duplication of a magnitude which no university library could afford; and the Library of Congress does not have the decentralized collections which are found in numerous buildings on a university campus, both close at hand and at a distance.

Divided Holdings

Oftentimes part of a serial is shelved in one place and part in another. The reference collection in particular is responsible for much splitting of sets. The latest volume of a serial may be on the reference shelves: a city directory, a college catalog, a who's who, or a work like the *Statesman's Year-book*; the next-to-the-latest volume may go to the acquisition or catalog department to save an extra subscription; and the back file may be in the bookstacks. Periodical runs are also divided in institutions which like to have the bound file for the last ten years or so on the reference shelves or in another convenient location, the theory being that the greatest demand is for more recent volumes. Lack of space is the motive for division of another kind:

relief from overcrowded shelves is often obtained by transferring the earlier part of a set from departmental libraries to the main stack collection or from the stacks to a storage library. In a large library system the serial staff may spend a considerable amount of time handling transferred sets, both complete and partial.

Separate shelflist cards should be made for each location. The shelflist for the reference collection should show only the items shelved there. One reason is that a hard-worked reference collection should be inventoried annually, since relatively more items are lost from the reference shelves than from the bookstacks.

The catalog records should be marked in such a way that the disposition of a set is clear (see figure 24). Double or triple call numbers may be necessary to disclose that the latest volume is in the reference room, its predecessor in the catalog room, and earlier volumes in the stacks, or to show that the last ten years of a periodical are in the reference collection or a departmental library, while the rest of the set is in the bookstacks.

```
                          Latest = RR 1011.12; Ref 600.150
                                   Catal.Rm.; Lamont
                          Earlier = LSoc 5.17
        The World of learning.  London
           1st ed. (1947) and later years




                                    ◯
```

Figure 24. Method of indicating multiple locations, from Harvard College Library

When items are susceptible of being transferred from one location to another after they have been superseded, the serial checkers can help by listing the successive locations on the verso of the title page of the incoming volumes. This device permits reference librarians and others to tell at a glance where earlier volumes may be found, and it facilitates the transfer of items from one location to another. Such a listing for the *Statesman's Year-book* might be:

R305.S8
Catalog Rm
305.S8

The former location is lined out as each transfer takes place.

Deposit-Library Holdings

A few American libraries have adopted a classification by size for the serials which they house or intend to house in deposit libraries. The scheme devised at Yale is:

WO up to 22.5 cm.
WP 22.5 to 26 cm.
WQ 26 to 32 cm.
WS 32 to 45 cm.
WT 45 cm. and over.

At Harvard College Library a distinction has been made between current serials and back files. The current publications go in KS, which is an active class; volumes may be added to KS from year to year as they are acquired. Back files more commonly go into the size classification for monographs, even though the remainder of a set may be transferred to the New England Deposit Library at some time in the future, and the two parts will then be in different locations. The letter *A* has now been included in the size notation; the subclasses are used for serial sets which are seldom added to, as well as for works in parts.

The W material at Yale is shelved in the main stacks, ready to be moved to a storage library should occasion arise. For the time being, little is being added to the collection. At Harvard part of the material is in the New England Deposit Library and part is in the bookstacks awaiting erection of a second unit in the storage building. Experience has proved that there is a certain advantage in holding newly cataloged items for a year or so in the bookstacks before transferring them to storage; for instance, the catalogers may wish to refer to the publications while the records are still in progress.

Bibliography

Haykin, David J. *Subject Headings, a Practical Manual.* Washington, 1951.
Library of Congress. *Subject Cataloging Division.* (Departmental & Divisional Manuals, no.3) Washington, 1950.

4

Housing
   and Servicing
Serial
Publications

14

Reading Rooms
for Serials

Whenever the size of an institution or of its serial collection warrants, separate reading and storage facilities are provided for one or more of the several classes of current serials which must be assembled and serviced before they can be bound, serials which are then not good stack material in the first instance. Current periodicals are the first and most natural type of serial to be given a room of their own. The room may include current newspapers in its scope, especially in college and university libraries; it may even assume some measure of responsibility for current government serials. In the past a newspaper room was often installed in public libraries, and in the bigger ones it cared for both current issues and bound files. But there are fewer newspaper rooms today, especially now that microfilm has to a large extent replaced the bound files of papers. When government publications are not distributed by subject throughout the bookstock, it is customary to have a special room for both current issues and back files. It is uncommon to find special rooms for current serials of any kind in school libraries or in smaller public and special libraries; display racks for current periodicals are much more usual in them.

The organization of current serials at the Library of Congress is particularly interesting because since 1944 government publications, newspapers, and periodicals have been for administrative purposes consolidated in a Serial Division, although each retains its own reading room in different parts of the main building. While the name is reminiscent of the self-contained serials department which has been the goal of some serial librarians, the Division is strictly a reference unit; processing duties are incidental because the checking functions are carried out in the Serial Record Division in the annex. The scope of the Serial Division is somewhat unusual, as the concluding part of the following statement discloses:

> The function of the Division is to have custody of certain groups of materials "which require, or for reasons of convenience are given, reader and reference service prior to their addition to the general classified collections." Insofar as they are not allocated to other divisions, the following groups are included: periodicals and general serials, learned society publications, government serials, pamphlets, books in parts, and ephemera of various sorts.[1]

The Periodical Room

Some small libraries have periodical rooms which house, display, and service their current journals; the rooms become fairly common in medium-sized institutions, and they are the order of the day in large organizations. In big establishments there may be subject divisions which draw the current journals in their fields away from the general periodical room;[2] there are upwards of twenty in the Research Libraries of the New York Public Library.

When current periodicals are displayed in the reading room, they naturally come under the jurisdiction of the reference staff. Then, when a periodical room emerges, it is just as naturally considered to be part of the service to readers, even though the periodical librarian spends an appreciable amount of time on occasion checking in the issues as they are received in the library, and regularly preparing volumes for transmission to the bindery, filling out requests for replacement copies for worn or mutilated issues, and doing other processing work. The advantages of constituting the periodical room as a reference unit are: (1) reader services can be coordinated advantageously, (2) circulation procedures can be standardized, and (3) processing units are left desirably free of custodial duties.

Davinson disapproves of the periodical room as such because it separates books and journals, which he feels should constitute a unity. He says:

[1]Library of Congress, *Serials Division* (Departmental & Divisional Manuals, no.9 [Washington, 1950]), p.7. The name was originally Serials Division; it is now Serial Division.

[2]The standard organizational patterns in public libraries are described in *A Survey of Libraries in the United States* (Chicago: American Library Assn., 1926), v.2, p.145–49; those of college and university libraries are described in v.2, p.217–20.

There is a great deal of interest and enjoyment to be had from browsing through a large, general, collection of current periodicals. Such a thought might well have been the motivation behind the creation of separate rooms for the display of periodicals so that they could be enjoyed in comfort and quietness away from the bustle of a busy library. If this was the motivation it is as laudable as it is misguided, as misguided as the more probable reason for the separation—the feeling that because the format differed from that of books the purpose also differed. Whatever the reasons, the segregation of the two media, books and periodicals, into separate rooms is not to be recommended. If a library periodical collection is selected, as it should be, to complement the bookstock, then there is no justification for segregating the current display of periodicals from the bookstock.[3]

There is a substantial amount of truth in Davinson's observations. But in big, busy institutions where streams of readers pour into the periodical room, e.g., in the Research Libraries of the New York Public Library, the focus must be on handling people quickly and efficiently, not on the interest and enjoyment that comes from browsing. Actually Davinson's idea can and should be carried out in large open-access libraries, notably in universities, where the periodical room is frequently converted by students into an additional study area. The coming of freestanding stacks in multitier bookstacks has made it possible to create oases at various intervals in which there can be easy chairs for readers who wish to browse among the new books, current periodicals, and reference books in their subject. Decentralization of the traditional periodical-room function was originally planned for the new bookstack at the University of Sydney so that the classicists, historians, philosophers, and others would each have their own browsing area.

The treatment accorded current issues varies greatly. Sometimes they are merely laid on shelves or tables, or placed in pigeonholes of one kind or another; increasingly today they are put in plastic covers of differing types. Springbacks and other patent binders, as well as a number of less expensive covers, including manila rope, were formerly utilized. They are still employed in some periodical rooms; e.g., the Library of Congress puts some six hundred of the titles most in demand in springbacks. Perhaps the most pleasing of the older type of binder was the one made in the local bindery, often with the name

[3]D. E. Davinson, *The Periodicals Collection; Its Purpose and Uses in Libraries* (London: Deutsch, 1969), p.145.

of the periodical stamped in gold on the front cover. But all the earlier forms have quite generally been superseded by commercially made plastic covers, which, being transparent, allow the front cover of the periodical to display itself.[4] Plastic covers afford much needed protection to current issues which circulate or which stand vertically on display; in some libraries where the recent numbers are no longer in plastic covers, the covers are added before an item circulates.

Periodical racks are fairly widely used because they permit the latest issues to be lined up for effective display; but the display should be arranged artistically or much of the effectiveness is lost, particularly when taller and thinner journals are allowed to droop or when the magazines in front conceal the covers of those behind. Racks are found mostly in smaller public, school, and special libraries in which the total collection of current periodicals is small enough to fit into a few units. Miss Heintze says:

> No piece of furniture in a library can be made more pleasing than a periodical rack, where the brightly coloured covers of the journals are displayed conspicuously and clearly. The cover designs of periodicals have often an attractive appearance, and the most attractive way of displaying them is to show the whole front cover. But since the type of equipment needed in this case is rather space demanding, it must often suffice to use a rack where only the top of each periodical is seen. A third method is to lay the journals flat on the shelves, showing only the spine or the bottom edge of the number, and this may be a "must" for very large collections; but this method may advantageously be supplemented by some kind of display rack.[5]

In studying the display equipment, racks, and shelving which are illustrated in Miss Heintze's book, special attention should be paid to the use of glass, and still more to that of plastics, since the latter possibly has the most potential for the truly effective display of current numbers of periodicals.

Miss Heintze is right, too, when she argues against any formal arrangement in the reading area for current periodicals. She says:

> One of the first things to emphasize in any discussion of library furniture is the importance of the reader's convenience. Informal

[4]See Ruari McLean, "Cover Design," in his *Magazine Design* (London: Oxford Univ. Pr., 1969), p.5–88, for a discussion and illustrations of the qualities of the covers of periodicals.

[5]Ingeborg Heintze, *Shelving for Periodicals* (Lund: Bibliotekstjänst, 1966), p.10.

and comfortable chairs and tables should be located conveniently near to the periodicals in the reading area. In fact, this could be the most attractive part of the library, suitable for relaxation as well as for research work.

The necessity of saving space often prevents the librarian from considering the reader's comfort sufficiently, and so a traditional piece of furniture may be acquired, which is not adapted to the reader's physical comfort. The reader should, for instance, not have to bend to reach the bottom shelf or to stretch to reach the top shelf. A desirable height for shelving, easy to use, is about 145 cm from floor to the lower edge of the top shelf; and the bottom shelf should be at a minimum of 30 cm from the floor. The arrangement of the shelves should also make it possible to survey easily all the periodicals displayed.[6]

Several other studies, which do not aim at comprehensiveness, are of slighter value as aids in the planning and arrangement of periodical reading areas. Wheeler and Githens describe a typical older display rack and provide other details about periodical and newspaper rooms and their equipment.[7] Metcalf illustrates four types of display shelving, in addition to giving some details on periodical rooms.[8] And Davinson has three plates which illustrate display shelving in British libraries.[9]

Obviously provision must be made not just for the latest issue, but for the balance of the current volume, and sometimes of two or three volumes. Back numbers are often shelved flat on regular shelves, in pigeonholes, behind or under sloping shelves, or in closets. They may be put in containers with the rest of the set, but no open container, whether of cardboard or metal, is satisfactory when issues stand up in it unsupported, because the pieces gather dust and tend to be torn. The special library practice of housing some serials in vertical-file cabinets is satisfactory because there is adequate support and items are not exposed to dust.

Sloping and regular shelves can be alternated so that earlier issues lie flat immediately below the most recent number, which is on display on a sloping shelf. In the Columbia University Library selected

[6]*Ibid.*, p.12.

[7]Joseph L. Wheeler and Alfred M. Githens, *The American Public Library Building, Its Planning and Design with Special Reference to Its Administration and Service* (New York: Scribner, 1941), p.462–63.

[8]Keyes D. Metcalf, *Planning Academic and Research Library Buildings* (New York: McGraw-Hill, 1965), p.106–107, 170–72.

[9]Davinson, *Periodicals Collection*, between p.112 and 113.

titles are on display on counters with sloping tops, the earlier numbers being on shelves below the counter. The nonpreferred latest issues, together with their earlier numbers, are on flat shelves because in a large library space cannot be afforded to display all current titles.

A number of libraries have followed the Detroit Public Library plan or a modification of it. The latest number is on display; to secure an earlier one, the reader raises the sloping shelf and selects the item which is lying flat on a concealed shelf. The arrangement brings about a maximum of neatness for both current and earlier numbers. A less expensive form of bin storage was devised for the periodical room in the General Library at the University of Michigan, where the display factor was completely disregarded. Periodicals are stored in pigeonholes, each of which has its own little door with a label bearing the name of the periodical.

When issues other than the latest are directly available to readers, the staff must spend considerable time daily rearranging the files, returning misshelved items to their proper place, and watching for numbers that have been mutilated or need minor repairs. A larger measure of control can be gained by storing all but the latest issues on closed shelves. Readers must then fill out a call slip for every publication they want from the closed resource. The load on the periodical room staff is substantially increased when requests must be filled in this way, however. The Periodicals Division in the New York Public Library once said:

> The work of bringing to the reader and reshelving promptly larger numbers of magazines which are briefly consulted has been a strain on the staff. On one day, 3,085 periodicals were used in the rooms. Under such pressure, with the rooms crowded to capacity, it has been difficult to maintain the usual standard of service.[10]

Items are undoubtedly better preserved on closed shelves, but the call-slip system is not a guarantee against mutilation or theft.

Such factors must be taken into account in planning a new building or in converting older quarters. They were reviewed, for instance, when Harvard's Lamont Library was being planned. There a self-service scheme was wanted: a simple alphabetical arrangement on standard shelves spaced a few inches apart and with a neat label for each title. Even with constant attention to the files, the appearance of the current periodicals in Lamont leaves something to be desired, especially when issues are worn with use. Thus the matter of shelving

[10]*Report of the New York Public Library* 1931 (New York, 1932), p.41.

the file of current numbers boils down to a question of whether some degree of neatness should be sacrificed, fairly expensive equipment installed, or a closed-shelf system adopted.

Mutilation is a matter of constant concern to periodical room staffs, all the more so when files must be preserved for binding. The ever-present threat of it is a major reason for collation before binding, with its heavy consumption of time.[11] As a precautionary measure libraries sometimes withhold certain titles from current use; they become available to readers only after they have been bound. In other cases a duplicate set is acquired currently and set aside for binding purposes.

All too many periodical rooms have been and are designed without thought of the capacity that will be required in the future. In 1915 the periodical room in the Widener Library at Harvard was built to accommodate a thousand current periodicals; to provide more space, first the adjacent bookstacks and then the end of the reading room had to be pressed into service. Columbia University's Butler Library, opened in 1935, allowed for only 1,300 titles in the periodical room, a number that has subsequently been increased to 2,300; there it is planned to add wooden shelving to house the present titles in better fashion. The New York Public Library's great periodical collection has for many years overflowed from the Periodicals Division into the bookstacks some distance away. Examples like these can be multiplied over and over again.

Also, the periodical room in large libraries is an extremely busy place. In 1926 in the New York Public Library it had become so busy that the Periodicals Division had to limit its scope by removing from circulation all magazines of a distinctly popular nature. This was done to provide seats for those who came for current information as well as research.[12] In 1945 the situation in the Library of Congress was as follows:

> The Serials Division, broadly considered, is one of the busiest in our institution. Its custodial and service functions are exceedingly com-

[11]At the Library of Congress it is estimated that a collator averages twenty completed volumes a day, or about 4,260 a year; for newspapers the rate is twelve volumes a day, or about 2,763 a year. "These assistants select the files of serials, periodicals and newspapers for binding, examine each issue to see that all pages, plates, maps, supplements, etc., are in place and are not mutilated, arrange the issues in order, with title-page at the front of each volume and index at the back; initiate want cards for missing issues; and remove duplicates which are not needed." *Annual Report of the Librarian of Congress* 1946 (Washington, 1947), p.331.

[12]See the *Report of the New York Public Library* 1926 (New York, 1927), p.37.

plex by nature of the material in its charge, and it is confronted by more than its share of problems. Into the Division's hands come all of the newspapers and almost all of the current periodicals, the main receipts of government publications, domestic and foreign, and all uncataloged pamphlets. For service it must bring order into this heterogeneous and refractory mass of printed products (many of which are of the highest importance) and make them available to the most variegated section of the public that visits the Library of Congress.

The Division's three reading rooms last year served 390,768 items to about 75,000 readers. Only an approximation of the latter figure is given because of the impracticability of counting every visitant content with the daily papers on the reading room racks. It is known, however, that 93,791 of the items issued were government documents and were delivered to about 10,000 readers in a room where browsing can scarcely be indulged. No less than 46,284 volumes were loaned for use outside of the Library buildings, 26,183 telephone requests and orders were filled, and 614 letters were answered.

Serving the Congress, the Government and the public, the Division prepared reports on subjects as diverse as the following abbreviated list will indicate:

Admiral Farragut's capture of New Orleans.
Buddhist activities in southern California.
Business and finance.
Drugs and pharmaceuticals.
Farm machinery and tractors.
Horticulture.
Interior decorating.
Jewish newspapers and periodicals.
Lumber and woodworking.
Negro newspapers and periodicals.
Public speaking and lecturing.
Television.
Treaties with Switzerland.

Research scholars and students in the Library drew heavily upon the Division's resources as they explored subjects of equal diversity. Another brief sampling of their projects will bear this out.

Chinese newspaper editorials on the "Open Door" treaty.
Home conditions and the returning veteran—Civil War, World Wars I and II.
Early navigation on Maryland's Eastern Shore.
Life and death of John Dillinger.
Federal aid in education.
Editorial reaction to terms of the Versailles treaty.

Japan's plan of battle against the United States.
Evangelism of Billy Sunday.
Student youth movement in Southern colleges.
Vice in New York City, 1843.[13]

A somewhat similar story can be told in other libraries, particularly in big city institutions, which reflect major concern with business affairs. So, for example, the New York Public Library could report:

> The work in the Periodicals Division has continued to reflect the current thought and interest throughout the city. The tall office buildings which have closed in about the Library have increased largely the demands of the business world for a quick response to a pertinent question.
>
> Such opening phrases as "The latest statistics of ——," "The new markets for ——," "The newest fashions in ——," "The effect of the recent tariff revision on ——," serve to illustrate the type of questions which range from bottle designs and metal tubing for modern furniture to the output of gasoline in Russia.
>
> Illustrations of all phases of manufacturing have been much in demand. The predominance of such inquiries has made the trade papers of prime importance, and they have extended their interests far beyond the limits implied by their name.
>
> During the year the "digest" magazines with their abbreviated presentation of material have been in constant use. The faster tempo of American life as it expresses itself in the economic and business world demands the magazine of concrete ideas and facts, and these magazines have become each year of greater value in giving concisely the information desired.
>
> The searching for advertisements of employment has meant a continuous use of the latest issues of a great number of various types of magazines.[14]

If to the recorded interests of readers in these libraries were added the untold story of high-pressured as well as patient investigations in libraries of all kinds, the contribution of current periodicals to the advance of knowledge would be recognized as truly imposing.

Shelf Arrangement

On closed shelves the arrangement of current periodicals is as a rule alphabetical. Thereby the staff is helped in fetching and reshelv-

---

[13]*Annual Report of the Librarian of Congress* 1945 (Washington, 1946), p.75–76.
[14]*Report of the New York Public Library* 1931 (New York, 1932), p.40–41.

ing material, and readers do not have to supply class marks or call numbers for items they request.

On open shelves the usual arrangement is also alphabetical, but sometimes it is by subject, generally in broad subject groupings. In shelving and reshelving periodicals the staff is helped by the alphabetical arrangement; so, too, are readers who work from periodical indexes or whose interests are not narrowly defined. Readers who want to browse in a designated field are helped by the subject arrangement, which is therefore favored in college and university libraries. But all things considered, the balance may be slightly in favor of alphabetical arrangement.

The class should be recorded on the cover when periodicals are grouped by subject. What is recorded can be the first three digits of the Dewey number or the letters of the Library of Congress scheme, or it can be a completely arbitrary designation. The notation should be specified on the checking records; it can then be added to the pieces as they are posted as an aid in shelving and reshelving.

The Staff Collection

Dana says: "Of all of a librarian's reading perhaps the most profitable to him in his work is that which he gives to periodicals."[15] In addition to the reading of periodicals done in connection with the day's work, it is customary for librarians to keep abreast of their professional journals. Many libraries maintain a collection of library periodicals, often in a staff or work room. Multiple copies may be acquired when the journals circulate among staff members in large libraries.

Some librarians debate whether it is proper for the staff to read professional literature while on duty. Professionally informed librarians are, however, an asset to any library, so money spent on periodicals for them should be reckoned as a wise investment.

The Public Library Inquiry disclosed something of the periodical reading habits of librarians:

> Among the professional librarians, *Life* and *The Saturday Review of Literature* have the highest percentage of readers, 64 percent and 63 percent, respectively. *The New Yorker* and *Time* are next in popularity. Considerably lower in percentage of readers is the *Atlantic*; *Harpers*, *Newsweek*, and the *Saturday Evening Post* follow closely, about one fourth of the librarians being readers of each.

[15]John Cotton Dana, *A Library Primer* (Boston: Library Bureau, [1920]), p.69.

One or more of the digest magazines are read by 46 percent of the professional librarians.

The subprofessional librarians prefer to read much the same type of magazines as the professionals. The largest number, 70 percent, had read *Life*. Next in popularity were *Time* and *The New Yorker*, then *The Saturday Review of Literature* (read by 40 percent). About half of the subprofessionals read one or more of the digest magazines.[16]

The Newspaper Room

Periodical rooms have custody of bound volumes only by way of exception, but bound volumes have been the stock in trade of newspaper rooms. Format is the decisive factor in both instances. Bound periodicals can be shelved and serviced like books; they fit naturally into the classified stacks, even though they may form a group or groups by themselves, with or without call numbers. Newspaper volumes, on the contrary, are poor stack material; they are rarely classified. They require special shelving by virtue of their bulk; they are wasteful of space if they do not have special shelving. In the past they were often located in specially designed quarters adjacent to the newspaper reading area, but this picture is changing rapidly as bound volumes give way to microfilm copies or are transferred to storage libraries. The Library of Congress reached the peak of its holdings in 1961, when it had 169,993 bound volumes of newspapers. Since then the count has dropped steadily; in 1969 it was 130,227. In the same period the number of reels of newspapers on microfilm rose from 69,600 in 1961 to 197,256 in 1969; and the program of substituting microfilms for bound volumes, as well as that of microfilming in lieu of binding, is continuing.

Like many college and university libraries, the Library of Congress locates its current newspapers in the Periodical Reading Room. So the functions of the Newspaper Reference Room (formerly the Newspapers Section) are to make available to readers

> the Library's large collection of newspapers from all over the world; to provide a reader and reference service of the bound newspaper collections, and to prepare and keep current checklists of the Library's holdings. During the fiscal year 1949 the Section received 2,395,774 issues, prepared and submitted 3,685 volumes for binding,

16Alice I. Bryan, *The Public Librarian* (New York: Columbia Univ. Pr., 1952), p.48.

and assisted 17,334 readers in the use of 59,477 bound volumes. Readers using unbound issues are counted in the Periodicals Reading Room, and are not separately distinguished. However, statistics show that they used 189,411 unbound issues during the year. . . .

Historians and research students are becoming increasingly aware of the importance of newspapers as a basic source of information. It is only natural therefore that the Library's newspaper collections, unequalled by any other like collection, should be used as no other single collection in the Library is used. Last year reader demands resulted in a turn-over in the 128,878 volumes of the bound newspaper collection of 46 percent.[17]

Some periodical rooms take on a number of processing functions; newspaper rooms quite generally do, one reason being that newspapers lend themselves to checklisting rather than cataloging. The Library of Congress has published several of its checklists: *A Check List of American Eighteenth Century Newspapers in the Library of Congress* (new ed.; Washington, 1936); *A Check List of American Newspapers in the Library of Congress* (Washington, 1901); and *A Check List of Foreign Newspapers in the Library of Congress* (Washington, 1929). Supplements to these publications are maintained in the Newspaper Reference Room. The checklist for nineteenth- and twentieth-century American newspapers is in the form of a shelflist.[18]

Checklists in American libraries are arranged by state if domestic or by country if foreign, then by city and title. This is also the natural way in which to arrange the papers on the shelves, for which reason call numbers or class marks are unnecessary. The Library of Congress has a class AN for newspapers, but has not developed or applied it. Because the checking entry does not take on cataloging form, there are usually no cards for individual newspapers in library catalogs. This can be puzzling to readers who find other works issued by the *New York Times*, for instance, as well as works about it, but not the paper itself. The situation is changing as microfilms replace bound volumes and are consulted in the microfilm reading room; when this occurs, there should be newspaper entries in the card catalog.

In 1867 wood-pulp paper was first manufactured in the United States. The first American newspaper to employ wood-pulp paper was the *New Yorker Staats-Zeitung*, on 7 January 1868; it adopted wood pulp regularly in 1870.[19] Since that time the decay of wood-pulp

[17] Library of Congress, *Serials Division*, p.21.

[18] In the Harvard College Library the checklists are typewritten in loose-leaf volumes.

[19] See "When Did Newspapers Begin to Use Wood Pulp Stock?" *Bulletin of the New York Public Library* 33:743 (1929).

paper has been the biggest problem newspaper librarians have had to face. Air-conditioned quarters can help. For many years the New York Public Library attacked the problem by mounting both sides of each sheet of newspaper with Japanese tissue:

> Earlier reports have mentioned the progress of the Library's experiments toward the best method of preserving the paper stock of newspapers in bound files. The decision was that the covering of each sheet of the original with a thin sheet of Japanese tissue paper insured preservation for an indefinite period. Since June, 1916, the files of the New York "World" have been so treated, and the experience of five years has confirmed faith in the process. Little more need be said than that this year one of the volumes so treated came back to the bindery for rebinding. Under ordinary circumstances rebinding of a newspaper is impossible, the paper stock being so poor that though it is possible to sew it once when the paper is fresh and new, it is impossible to get the thread to hold when it is a year or two old. With this volume of the "World" it was possible to resew it like a book printed on good book stock paper; the buckram back had worn because of the constant use, but the sheets were as strong as the day they were finished.[20]

Microfilm proved to be the answer to the problem of preserving newspapers. It also reduces the great bulk of the stock. One bound volume of a newspaper may have upwards of a hundred times the cubic capacity of the corresponding microfilm.

Since the essence of a newspaper is its timeliness, airmail subscriptions are justified when they bring papers to research workers a day or two, rather then weeks, after publication. Many American libraries acquire the London *Times* and the Russian *Pravda* and *Izvestia* by air. Savings in money, but not so much in time, are possible when bulk shipments of the *Times* are sent by air to New York and from there are forwarded by surface mail. Libraries often subscribe to the regular edition of the *Times* as well, since the index relates to it and not to the airmail edition.

Newspaper bibliography is especially complicated because of the

---

[20]*Report of the New York Public Library* 1921 (New York, 1922), p.53–54. For further details see "How Newspapers Are Preserved," *Report of the New York Public Library* 1925 (New York, 1926), p.48–49. Figure 53 in Robert C. Binkley, *Manual on Methods of Reproducing Research Materials* (Ann Arbor, Mich., 1936), shows a portion of a newspaper page covered with Japanese tissue. For an account of the newspaper collections in the New York Public Library see Karl Brown, *A Guide to the Reference Collections of the New York Public Library* (New York, 1941), p.196–98.

number of editions that a paper may produce daily.[21] For some years *Notes and Queries* sought an answer to the question, "What is a newspaper edition?" It cited a London newspaper which had three editions, the first called the Fifth Edition, the second the Early Special, and the third the Special Edition. In another case five editions were issued, starting with the Third Edition and proceeding to the Fifth Edition, the Early Special, the Five O'Clock, and the Special.[22] Matter may appear in one edition and not in another, yet it is manifestly impossible for libraries to preserve files of all editions. Another problem is that lack of knowledge of what constitutes a complete set makes it difficult to determine the completeness of a file. Extra issues, omitted issues, and gaps in publishing due to holidays, strikes, and Sundays, as well as frequent errors in the numbering of issues, all conspire to make newspaper bibliography uncertain.

Historical societies, libraries, and other local institutions have undertaken much of the responsibility for preserving files and indexing them to make them more serviceable.[23] To some extent indexes to national newspapers serve as a key to local papers. But since national newspapers cannot cover local news, it is almost as important to index the distinctive parts of local newspapers as it is to preserve them. The outstanding example of newspaper indexing of this kind is to be found in the California State Library (see figures 25–26), which has a card index of two million entries to California newspapers from 1846 to date.[24]

Research needs are far from being the only justification for newspapers in libraries. As a community intelligence center a library should have newspapers on hand. News is listed by Learned as the first of the three types of knowledge which he distinguishes:

> The first type is essentially "news"—the flood of ephemeral print out of which is selected the limited group of facts that orients for each his daily life. The newspapers and periodicals possess this field, and furnish as excellent models of diffusion in their well-nigh

[21]On this problem see Folke Dahl, "On Quoting Newspapers: A Problem and a Solution," *Journalism Quarterly* 25:331 (1948).

[22]*Notes and Queries*, 10th series, 3:287 (1905) and 8:117 (1907).

[23]For a list of American newspapers which have been indexed in part or in full, see H. O. Brayer, "Preliminary Guide to Indexed Newspapers in the United States, 1850–1900," *Mississippi Valley Historical Review* 33:237 (1946).
of Increasing Reference Resources of the State Library," *ALA Bulletin* 25:644 (1931).

[24]See Mabel R. Gillis, "The Union Catalog and the Newspaper Index as Means

Richardson Bay
    Meeting to discuss plans by construction com-
pany to fill in part of Richardson Bay
                              Ch.9-9-1956   5/2
    Meeting of Belvedere
City Council; pros and cons   10-1   7/1
    Disapproval by council   10-2   22/1

Belvedere

Figure 25. Entry from the San Francisco newspaper index in the California State Library. This is a citation to the San Francisco *Chronicle* of 9 September 1956, page 5, column 2, plus later citations. A similar card is filed under Belvedere.

Vigilance Committee: 1851-
        Foreign convicts
                ALTA. Sept 29 1851   2-3

Figure 26. Index entry from the information in the California State Library. The citation is to the San Francisco *Alta California*; "2-3" refers to page 2, column 3.

universal contacts, as of qualitative bedlam in their ideas. Everything that possesses conceivable "news value" is pitched into the furnace of publicity. There public opinion treats and reduces it, drawing off at last for permanent use a product dependent upon the quality and acuteness of its own insight. . . .

The bulk of the town's new ideas are derived from newspapers and periodical literature that originates outside, that are subscribed for by a few interested minds, and that have no evident bearing upon the concerns of the locality.[25]

As if in support of Learned, the Newspaper Division of the New York Public Library reported in 1926 that "the seeker after news still constitutes about 75 per cent of the readers. Fully one-half of this number read out-of-town and foreign newspapers, difficult to obtain elsewhere."[26]

The Document Room

The two American libraries that have outstanding document collections also have fine document rooms. The Government Publication Reading Room in the Library of Congress and the Economics Division in the Research Libraries of the New York Public Library are centers of intense document activity.

Deficiencies in document collecting and servicing represent one of the most serious shortcomings in American libraries. Some of the trouble stems from uncertainty over a wise collecting policy. Libraries could be flooded with documents if they were acquired wholesale; rather than be overwhelmed, they have shown a tendency to temporize. In the Harvard University Library over a period of a dozen years there were no fewer than five surveys or special reports that proposed plans for developing and strengthening the document collections, none of which led to any course of action. In 1961 an Association of Research Libraries study pointed out the deficiencies in foreign government documents in American libraries.[27]

The Library of Congress is, in a very real sense, a national document center, largely because of the work of James B. Childs, for

25William S. Learned, *The American Public Library and the Diffusion of Knowledge* (New York: Harcourt, [1924]), p.5, 13.

26*Report of the New York Public Library* 1926, p.39.

27D. F. Wisdom, *Foreign Government Publications in American Research Libraries: A Survey Prepared for the Farmington Plan Committee of the Association of Research Libraries* (Washington, 1961).

many years chief of the former Documents Division. His thinking in part is:

> Government publications are of such importance for the Library of Congress that it is not a matter of selection but of ascertaining what has been and is being issued, of taking any necessary steps to secure copies, and of assisting in making them available. . . .
>
> Owing to the intricacies of governments and their publication activities, the difficulty of adequately representing all such material in the public catalog is rapidly increasing. More and more reliance for the use of these materials has thus to be placed on such printed catalogs as exist as well as increasingly upon the assistants and records in the Division. . . . While the Library of Congress has without doubt the most extensive collection of official documents in the United States and is regarded as a national document center, increasing demands seem to make it imperative for the Library to take all possible steps to establish and to maintain a much more nearly complete coverage for all current material, to survey and perfect the older materials, and to facilitate the use of these important publications.[28]

One of the most effective means that Childs devised for the expansion of the Library of Congress document collection was a series of bilateral agreements, now numbering fifty, between the United States and other countries whereby federal documents would be exchanged on an inclusive basis for the publications of other countries. The numerous agreements have brought a wealth of documentary material to that library.

The functions of the Government Publication Reading Room at the Library of Congress are:

> to have custody of the Library's collections of unbound serial documents of the United States and foreign countries, to provide a reader and reference service in government publications generally and the bound classified collections in J 1-999 in particular, to prepare the unbound serials for binding when complete, and to recommend the acquisition of materials needed to complete or augment the Library's collections. During fiscal year 1949 this section received an estimated 728,000 pieces of material to be shelved and serviced, prepared and submitted 8,377 volumes for binding, and assisted 16,501 readers in the use of 111,413 items in its custody.[29]

---

[28]*Annual Report of the Librarian of Congress* 1940 (Washington, 1941), p.48–49.
[29]Library of Congress, *Serials Division*, p.17.

McCamy's findings, based on a survey of sixty collections, show that public libraries have generally lagged behind research libraries in their document programs. He develops four theses:

1. Governments are a reliable and impartial source of authoritative information which should be accessible to citizens through numerous outlets.
2. The government's position should be known whether there is public discussion of foreign policy, public health, social security, etc.
3. Public libraries are charged with the responsibility for "making available to all citizens the more serious, more reliable and more permanent materials of all kinds."[30]
4. Because they are tax supported, public libraries have a natural interest in acquiring and disseminating those government documents which can help in bringing the citizen and his government closer to each other.

He brings out seven reasons why library programs for government documents are not as effective as they could be.[31] In general they relate to accumulated practices, tradition, laws which should be revised, and inadequacies in government bibliographies. Faults in bibliographies are that they tend to list documents by issuing agency instead of by subject, they do not differentiate between routine publications and those which contain important information on broad public problems, and they do not provide a sure way for the librarian to know which items will be of general interest. There is confusion in the distribution of documents, while some information is lost because it appears only in processed form and is neither cataloged nor distributed. Lastly, public libraries have not acquired as many government best sellers as might be expected.

In addition, McCamy expresses himself strongly about the cataloging of government publications, or rather the failure to catalog them:

> It is far from easy for an untrained person to find government documents and pamphlets in a typical library catalogue, where librarians tend to duplicate for their clientele the difficulties they themselves encounter in ordering from the government catalogues.

---

[30]James L. McCamy, *Government Publications for the Citizen* (New York: Columbia Univ. Pr., 1949), p.x.

[31]*Ibid.*, p.74–77.

Relatively few libraries, and those chiefly in the largest cities, list all their government publications in their general catalogues so that any reader searching for all the publications available on any particular subject would find the government publications included. Only seven out of forty-two libraries list all government publications in their general catalogues. Of the seven, five are in cities of more than 500,000 population; one is in a city of between 250,000 and 500,000, and one is in a city of 25,000–50,000.

Of the libraries in our sample half list in the general catalogue only titles which they think will be of general interest. This is roughly true of all the libraries in cities of 25,000 up to 500,000.... The other half do not list even the titles that might have general interest. In half the libraries, of various sizes above 25,000 and below the very largest libraries, government publications are apparently considered as "documents," to be classified for reference use, but not as publications that might be of interest to ordinary readers.

For example, a reader browsing in the catalogue for material on civil rights would not find *To Secure These Rights,* the report of the President's Committee on Civil Rights and a readable, popular book, because it would be classified as a "document." In half the libraries such a pamphlet would be in the same file with routine statistical reports from government agencies. The rule in these libraries seems to be: "If it's a government publication, bury it except for reference purposes!" In most libraries popular government publications have suffered because of their family connections. They belong to a category that is principally reference material and not expected to be interesting to anyone save specialized readers.[32]

[32]*Ibid.,* p.64–65.

15

Circulation

Even though photocopying machines may not have affected the lending of books to any marked extent, they have radically altered the patterns for the circulation of bound volumes of periodicals. The borrower commonly wants access to an entire book, but with a periodical it is an article of ten or so pages that he is interested in, not the whole volume as a rule, and the photocopying of a short article is a rapid and inexpensive process. For most other serials the patterns of use have remained fairly constant. Reference tools such as *Chemical Abstracts* and the *New York Times Index* have always been noncirculating. Other serials may generally be borrowed, e.g., annual reports and the individual volumes of monograph series.

Circulation of Bound Volumes of Periodicals

Ever since the photostat took hold in the 1920s, the trend has been steadily away from out-of-the-building use of bound periodicals. For public libraries Jennie Flexner says: "The fact that magazines are usually treated as reference books and held for use in most libraries adds to the reader's opportunity of finding what he wants when he wants it."[1] In an earlier work she says:

> Maps, pamphlets, bound magazines and other volumes belonging to the reference collection may be allowed to circulate, usually for a limited period, on special request to registered borrowers. A *temporary book card*, incorporating sufficient information to identify

[1]Jennie M. Flexner, *Making Books Work; A Guide to the Use of Libraries* (New York: Simon & Schuster, 1943), p.125.

302

the material lent, must be made to record the charge until the transaction is closed. In some libraries, material of this type circulates with enough regularity to warrant a permanent file of temporary book cards to be used over and over. Much used sets of bound periodicals may be circulated in this way, by inserting the year and volume number on the temporary book card when each volume is charged.[2]

Nowadays smaller public libraries do not bind the back files of the periodicals which they keep; as a result, an issue may be borrowed from the runs that are on hand.

In colleges and universities the traditional plan has been to lend bound periodicals to faculty members, certainly those of professorial rank, on a fairly liberal scale; to graduate students to a smaller extent; and rather infrequently to undergraduates. When faculty members and graduate students have studies or carrels in the library building, they are generally permitted to hold periodical volumes in those locations indefinitely because it is understood that items held in studies or carrels are available to others at short notice. Library committees have frequently been divided on lending policies for periodicals, some members wanting the volumes to be always on hand for consultation, others valuing highly the opportunity to borrow them. Chemistry libraries have been traditionally opposed to lending bound volumes because of the tie-in between abstracting services and runs of journals. There are two standard consultation procedures, in addition to working from abstracting and indexing services, which make it desirable to keep bound volumes in the university library. They are: (1) checking references for a new book or article, and (2) browsing through a set systematically to catch the type of information that cannot be found from abstracting and indexing services, that cannot even be found from the annual or cumulative index to the publication itself. With the coming of convenient and inexpensive photocopying machines, the tendency in college and university libraries nowadays is to restrict or end the lending of bound volumes of periodicals.

In most special libraries staff members can obtain photocopies of desired articles at no cost, so that here too the trend is away from out-of-the-library consultation; but bound volumes may still be borrowed in many instances, because they are as a rule not taken far from the library and so can be easily recovered when needed. In general a special library will do its best to accommodate a reader on the score

2Jennie M. Flexner, *Circulation Work in Public Libraries* (Chicago: American Library Assn., 1927), p.118–19.

that "books have only potential value as they stand on the shelves; it is the use made of them that is the ultimate measure of their worth. Good books are those that are read."[3] The thinking behind this philosophy is:

> In a small, closely knit organization it may be entirely satisfactory to circulate bound volumes without special restrictions. However, complications arise where the group is large and much literature searching is done in the library. The absence of one volume, borrowed to use one paper, puts perhaps fifty other papers out of immediate reach. Also the character of the particular literature involved is a determining factor as to whether bound volumes should leave the library. If a reference work such as the Beilstein *Handbuch der organischen Chemie* is used extensively, it would be a serious inconvenience not to have all of the volumes of the *Berichte* or the *Annalen* on the nearby shelves for immediate consultation. The question of the removal of bound volumes should therefore be weighed carefully, particularly if there are opposing points of view among patrons. Inasmuch as the majority of scientific libraries are oriented toward research activities, their most important resource, the periodical literature, ought to be available.[4]

Clearly a judgment factor is involved, in general as in special libraries. Heavily used sets or parts of sets may have restrictions placed on them, whereas less used items, especially the early volumes in a set and items in storage collections, may be available for lending. It is very annoying to a reader to be told that he may not borrow a volume not likely to be wanted by another person, which has not been consulted by anyone for many years.

Circulation of Current Issues

In many public libraries, and as a rule in branches, readers may borrow the latest issue of a periodical as soon as it is put on display; in others, though, it may be the next-to-the-latest number which circulates first. Sometimes a periodical must have been in the collection for three months before it can be borrowed, or it must have left the periodical room on completion of a volume. Some libraries permit

---

[3]Lucille J. Strauss, Irene M. Shreve, and Alberta L. Brown, *Scientific and Technical Libraries; Their Organization and Administration* (2d ed.; New York: Becker & Hayes, 1972), p.216.
[4]*Ibid.*, p.225.

reserves to be placed on current issues, some do not. As a rule a reserve may not be placed in anticipation of the receipt of an issue. If issues are displayed before they may circulate, reserves are generally accepted once an item has been put on display. The reason for restricting the circulation of the latest numbers is that thereby readers have an equal opportunity to browse among new arrivals and to place reserves for them. The theory is somewhat akin to that for a new-book shelf. However, the argument is less valid when periodicals do not circulate for three months, the time when requests for them begin to come by way of the periodical indexes.

In college and university libraries there is comparatively little circulation of current issues except among the library staff for official purposes and in departmental libraries. The reasons for noncirculation are, first, the tie-in with abstracting and indexing services and, second, conservation of the stock for binding. So most items circulate only by way of exception. The life expectancy of current numbers would be curtailed if they circulated freely for out-of-the-building use, though this statement is not as convincing as it was before the days of plastic covers. Some periodical rooms keep a supply of covers on hand to be attached to periodicals which circulate by special permission. Again, photocopying facilities have reduced the need for items in the periodical room to circulate. When they are lent, the loan period is usually shorter than for books. Three-day loans have been common, but more often readers may borrow an issue for a week. The arguments for limiting the loan period are: (1) it takes relatively less time to read a journal article, or even the whole journal, than it does to read a book; (2) since timeliness is the essence of current periodicals, they should be available to readers without delays and interruptions; and (3) the supply of periodicals in demand is not great, since service copies are seldom acquired.

In special libraries Walford says that "the majority . . . circulate at least some of the periodicals that they currently receive, on the generally accepted principle that the benefits of circulating periodicals outweigh the drawbacks."[5] The arguments in favor of circulation are considered to be: (1) if books are lent, periodicals should be, too; (2) issues are better in the hands of readers than lying idle in a central repository where they are usually not well displayed; (3) borrowers may be at some distance from the library, in other buildings or locations; (4) there are better ways of drawing readers to the library than by forcing them to visit it to consult current periodicals; and

---

[5]A. J. Walford, "Service Routine," in Wilfred Ashworth, ed., *Handbook of Special Librarianship and Information Work* (3d ed.; London: Aslib, 1967), p.365.

(5) staff members may not be able to come to the library regularly to consult items that may or may not be on hand when they are able to get there. The arguments against circulation are: (1) on-the-spot consultation of library materials is desirable because stock and facilities can be appreciated and exploited only when people work in the library regularly; (2) browsing should by all means be encouraged, and browsing is a library procedure, not one for the laboratory or office; (3) staff and librarians should be in contact with each other as much as possible, and the library is the best place for this; (4) when many people wish to see the latest issue of a periodical as soon as possible on receipt, they have a better and fairer chance if it is held in the library; and (5) some readers keep an issue far too long when it is circulated, and that is why some libraries set a time limit of one to three days. The arguments in both directions seem to agree on: (1) the cost of either controlled or uncontrolled circulation; (2) the need for service copies, in part to reduce the circulation load; and (3) the loss, marking, or mutilation of issues because they may not be circulated or because their readers cannot be supervised when they are out of the library.

Routing the Latest Issue

Despite all the problems, special libraries do very extensively circulate the latest issues of journals to members of the firm, laboratory, research organization, etc. The visible index serves as the control point; routing slips, which have been mimeographed or otherwise duplicated, are attached to the issues as they start on their way. Similar practices are employed in general libraries, but as a rule to a much smaller extent; the Library of Congress is an exception, as can be seen from the fact that in 1969 it had from two to fifty-three copies of 58,778 titles.

Contributors to *Special Libraries* have for long been exercised over the problems of routing the latest issue. The reason is, as Gertrude Bloomer says: "Of all the routine practices carried out in the administration of special libraries, probably none is more controversial, more varied in method, and at the same time more important in its aim and purpose than that of the circulation of current journals."[6] None will dispute the need for research personnel and others to be kept abreast of developments in their field. Much of the problem stems

[6]Gertrude Bloomer, "The Circulation of Current Journals in Special Libraries," *Special Libraries* 39:46 (1948).

from what has been called "magazine hoarding,"[7] which Miss Bloomer analyzes as follows:

> Failure of persons receiving journals to pass the journals along within the specified time, or within a reasonable period of time if no limit is set, is mentioned most frequently as the cause of delay and inefficiency in circulation. It appears that no library has been able to set up a system in which journals may be circulated freely, while at the same time, each receiver of journals is motivated to read and send them on promptly. The next most frequently mentioned cause of dissatisfaction is the tendency on the parts of many individuals to loan journals in circulation to persons not on the circulation list. This is actually temporary loss of a journal, and may even result in costly delay if the journal is needed, or in permanent loss.[8]

In an attempt to remedy the situation and to keep the staff informed of the whereabouts of any issue, some libraries have gone to the trouble and expense of controlled circulation, i.e., of routing an item to one person at a time instead of indulging in wholesale routing. After each individual circulation the item is charged to the next person on the list. The amount of work entailed in this operation is considerable, and the total procedure is protracted, as Cole and Rowley found. They report: "One girl spent 50 percent of her time checking in and out the periodicals and frantically sending overdue notices. Some of the journals with the longest routing lists were seen by the requester a year after the date of issue."[9] Experience at the Detroit Edison Company is somewhat similar:

> The first change made in our magazine circulation procedure was to discontinue having copies of the magazines returned to the library after circulation to a single individual. They are now returned to the library only after the circulation of ten names has been completed. At present, it takes on the average approximately twenty working days to circulate one copy of a magazine to ten names. This compares with over forty-three days under the old system of back-to-the-library between each circulation to an individual. Thus, this change, besides reducing the amount of labor required, has speeded up considerably the service to employes.[10]

[7]"Wanted: A Table-of-Contents Reprint Service," *Special Libraries* 41:257 (1950).
[8]Bloomer, "Circulation of Current Journals," p.49.
[9]Barbara R. Cole and Helen Rowley, "Current Journal Routing," *Special Libraries* 35:326 (1944).
[10]Harvey E. Bumgardner, "Labor-saving Methods Applied to Magazine Circulation," *Special Libraries* 43:92 (1952).

It is customary for periodicals to circulate directly from the checkers to the first person whose name is on the routing slip. The circulation desk, however, may come into play for later circulations, and some librarians prefer to have the circulation staff handle even the initial routing, at times utilizing a visible index for the purpose.[11] At the Detroit Edison Company introduction of a punched-card system was considered to be the biggest single labor-saving device in its program for reforming the routing system. As a consequence of this and other changes, Bumgardner reports that the time required for circulation of magazines dropped from a hundred man-hours per week to thirty.

A few special libraries have solved the problem in a radical way by giving up routing altogether; but in the Technical Division Library of the Rayon Department of E. I. du Pont de Nemours and Company the system was abandoned only after a number of substitute measures were undertaken. One was to acquire additional copies of the basic journals; the most significant was to route a weekly bulletin of abstracts of current journal articles, on the basis of which chemists could request any item which they especially wanted to see.[12]

The preparation of lists of current periodical articles, whether with abstracts or not, is a development of importance, since notable bibliographies, often of much more than local value, have resulted. The *Weekly Selected Reading List* at Brookhaven National Laboratory was one such publication, but it ceased to appear in 1970 since its value was felt to have decreased because of several commercial services which now cover the field. Herner describes the origins of a similar list in the Applied Physics Laboratory at Johns Hopkins University,[13] a list which is still being issued monthly as part of its *Library Bulletin*. Two professional librarians scan selected periodical titles weekly and choose articles which they believe will be of interest in the laboratory. Occasionally references are collected on a particularly timely subject. The library also circulates tables of contents in three areas which were selected by the scientists themselves: computer science, management science, and transportation science. With these aids at their service, scientists do not borrow bound or unbound periodicals; instead, request for articles which were noted in the

[11]For details on visible indexes for circulation work see David Grenfell, *Periodicals and Serials; Their Treatment in Special Libraries* (2d ed.; London: Aslib, 1965), p.91–97.

[12]Cole and Rowley, "Current Journal Routing," p.326–27.

[13]Saul Herner, "The Selected Reading List: A Means of Improving the Use of Periodical Literature," *Special Libraries* 41:324 (1950).

Library Bulletin or seen in the tables of contents are filled by means of photocopies. The library purchases extra subscriptions for routing or indefinite loan only in special cases for staff members who are in remote locations or who have a special need.

Interlibrary Loan

Although photocopying has bitten deeply into the interlibrary loan of serials, there is still a substantial volume of direct lending. In chapter 19 figures are given which show that in 1958 some 370,000 serials were borrowed on interlibrary loan in the United States, as against 380,000 photocopies which were made in lieu of loan. Among others, the National Library of Medicine reserves the right to determine whether material will be lent in the original form or as a photoduplicate. An application to it is made as a regular interlibrary-loan request according to the American Library Association interlibrary-loan code. With sufficient justification the library may lend complete issues or volumes of serials when such loans do not impair service; on the other hand, it will not photocopy a substantial part or all of an issue or volume as a substitute for a direct loan.

Commonly a serial is wanted on interlibrary loan because a reference to it has been found in an abstracting or indexing service, a footnote, or other source. As a rule, what is wanted is an article that is no more than ten or fifteen pages long, yet on interlibrary loan a volume of several hundred pages may be requested to satisfy the need. The service costs for locating, charging, wrapping, and shipping the volume can easily run into three or four dollars or more, whereas, a photocopy of the article can be supplied for a fraction of that sum. Further, while photoduplication undoubtedly leads to a certain amount of wear and tear, it is not as hard on a volume as shipping and returning it by mail or express, and the volume is out of commission for minutes instead of days.

In certain cases photocopies leave much to be desired, so access to the original is preferable. Most of the copying equipment found in libraries will not reproduce plates even reasonably well. Black-and-white reproductions are not satisfactory in art, botany, and other fields when color is desired. But in general photocopies serve adequately and are excellent for the re-creation of complicated formulas in scientific and technical publications and of drawings in patent specifications.

Photoduplication and interlibrary loan are valid alternatives in most situations (see figure 27). The interconnection between the two services was highlighted in 1943 when the National Library of Medicine began to provide microfilm copies free, except for postage, in place of interlibrary loan, not only to government establishments but also to any individual connected with an accredited institution. The idea behind the development was expressed in a statement issued on 1 September 1943:

> The Library recognizes that microfilm copying is a service which publicly supported reference libraries may well perform on an equal basis with that provided for readers and by interlibrary loans. In the pursuance of such a policy, microfilms will be sent without charge in lieu of the loan of books to those who prefer them or where books or journals cannot be loaned.[14]

At that time the library tended to avoid photostats and to concentrate on microfilm for long and short runs alike. Now it provides photocopies, which are made by means of continuous xerography.

Photoduplication

A library's photoduplication service tends to make heavy use of serials, just as the self-service equipment operated by readers does. As early as 1931 the New York Public Library said that "patents and papers from scientific and technical journals are the two predominant classes" handled by what was then its Photostat Section.[15] Orders for photocopies frequently require verification, especially when they are received by mail, and at times reference librarians have to exercise all their ingenuity to determine precisely what is wanted. Photoduplication is now a large business in national outlets.

Copyright is the question that vexes photoduplication services most. By a gentleman's agreement between librarians and publishers, tacit approval has been given to the making of a single copy. Some libraries post a notice of the agreement near their copying machines; others include a statement in the photocopies which they make. The National Library of Medicine, for example, prints on each photocopy the statement: "This is a single photocopy made by the National Library of Medicine for purposes of study or research in lieu of lend-

---

[14]Keyes D. Metcalf and others, *The National Medical Library; Report of a Survey* (Chicago: American Library Assn., 1944), p.38.

[15]*Report of the New York Public Library* 1931 (New York, 1932), p.27.

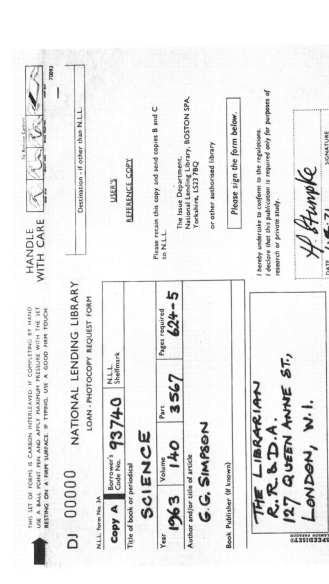

Figure 27. Three-part interlibrary loan or photocopy request, from the National Lending Library for Science and Technology. Copy B is on gummed paper to reduce clerical work. Copy C has a space to which the coupons for photocopies can be attached.

ing the original." Further, it will not process orders for material which is protected by copyright unless they are accompanied by written permission from the copyright owner. Formal arrangements have been made in a number of cases by the Library of Congress, which,

> being the home of the nation's Copyright Office, gives close attention to the presence of copyright restrictions in all of its photocopying activities. To make it possible to reproduce material from newspapers and periodicals without a specific request for permission from the copyright owner in each instance, a program has been instituted for securing permission from various newspaper and magazine publishers to copy within certain time limits.[16]

Because of its concern over copyright the Library of Congress refuses to process many orders for photocopies every year.

Most American libraries other than national libraries operate on the principle that "all the members of the ARL, SLA, ALA, and all the other library organizations . . . have what we think is sound advice of counsel to the effect that we can make one copy of any copyrighted work for anybody."[17] The copyright of books protects a publisher's market and hence his profits; not so with periodicals issued commercially, because nowadays publishers rarely carry any stock of them. Periodicals put out by McGraw-Hill, for example, consist of the number of copies required to fill subscriptions issue by issue, plus six. A publisher's interest in files of his periodicals really extends back only two years, the period during which benefits are considered to accrue from commercial advertising.

It has been said that no more than 60 percent of American periodicals are copyright. That figure is undoubtedly high. In 1969 the Copyright Office registered 80,706 issues of periodicals. If twelve issues per volume can be taken as the average, then some 6,725 American serial titles came under copyright protection. In addition, in that year 1,676 contributions to newspapers and periodicals were copyright. Almost no newspapers are copyright; there are few renewals of copyright for periodicals.

The question of copyright in relation to the photocopying of journal articles came into the open at a conference, where Stafford Warren proposed a National Library of Science System whose aim would be a complete storehouse of periodical literature in the field of science and technology. Regional centers throughout North America

---

[16]*Annual Report of the Librarian of Congress* 1948 (Washington, 1949), p.46.

[17]Allen Kent, ed., *Library Planning for Automation* (Washington: Spartan Books, 1965), p.188.

would then be able to provide bibliographies as well as photocopies of journal articles on a large scale. Naturally authors and publishers would welcome royalties derived from the making of photocopies in the various centers. Publishers' representatives at the conference said that there were then an estimated forty thousand Xerox 914 copiers in use in the United States, plus thousands of other makes. They went on to say that any system devised to prevent the photocopying of copyright material without payment of a royalty must operate on less than half the money brought in by royalties.[18]

The British Copyright Act of 1956 made provision for the fair copying of articles from copyright periodicals. A Board of Trade regulation requires that a person seeking a photocopy from a library sign a form which says that the copy is needed for research or private study and will be used for no other purpose, also that a copy has not been previously supplied by a librarian. The form must be signed in advance by a person in another country who wants Aslib or another outlet to make a copy for him.

The University of Chicago Library issues a North American *Directory of Library Photoduplication Services*. The Council for Microphotography and Document Reproduction produces *A Directory of British Photoreproduction Services*. Finally, the International Federation for Documentation publishes a worldwide *Directory of Photocopying and Microcopying Services*.

The National Lending Library for Science and Technology

The biggest single development in the circulation of periodicals came with the establishment of the National Lending Library for Science and Technology in Boston Spa, Yorkshire, which began gathering material in 1957. The subjects covered are all fields of science and technology, including agriculture and medicine, and (since October 1967) social science periodicals. The library acquires all publicly available technical reports, and it has over 200,000 translations of journal articles. By 1970 it was able to supply over 80 percent of the items requested from serials published before 1920 and 95 percent from serials published after 1966. Over 87 percent of all loan requests are filled from stock, about 8 percent being on loan when requested. Some 22,000 applications for loans are received

---

[18]For the proposal and the copyright discussion see Stafford L. Warren, "A Proposed National Science Library System," in Kent, ed., *Library Planning for Automation*, p.3–33, and "Copyright," *ibid.*, p.167–90.

weekly, as well as another 5,500 for photocopies, 14 percent of these being from overseas sources.

The library has a series of publications. Two of them are procurable from the Stationery Office. They are *Current Serials Received by the National Lending Library* and the monthly *N.L.L. Translations Bulletin.* Other publications include the monthly *British Research and Development Reports,* the monthly *Index of Conference Proceedings Received by the National Lending Library,* a *KWIC Index to the English Language Abstracting and Indexing Publications Currently Being Received by the National Lending Library,* and a *List of Current Serials Received from Asia.*

Serials and books are arranged on the library's shelves in alphabetical order, which enables the staff to find most items without having to consult records (see figure 28). Likewise, new publications go on the shelves without the delays normally associated with cataloging. On the other hand, Russian publications and translations are cataloged.

Figure 28. Alphabetical arrangement of the serial bookstock and the chain conveyor, which speeds up lending and photocopying services, at the National Lending Library in Boston Spa

Television Facsimile Reproduction

The standard method for carrying out interlibrary loan transactions is through the mail. In a number of university library systems and some metropolitan areas a station wagon makes daily runs between the libraries that are borrowing or lending books and periodicals; in Canada this type of service now operates between most of the university libraries in the province of Ontario. A third device, still in the experimental stages, consists of television facsimile reproduction equipment either for reading at a distance or the creation of a photocopy at the receiving end. At the University of Virginia the chemistry and main libraries were linked up for reading at a distance; a special cradle and page-turning equipment were developed to facilitate the transaction. At the University of California long-distance xerography was employed to link the main library with the Davis campus, some sixty-five miles away; the major portion of the transmission consisted of copies of journal articles from volumes in the Berkeley library which were requested by faculty members at Davis.

The findings in California were that surface mail, while it takes four to five days, is still the cheapest in terms of service cost (namely $5) except for deliveries in the immediate vicinity, which are best carried out by automobile. For distances of fifty miles or more television facsimile transmission costs less than the automobile. The general finding was:

> Because of continuing expansion in educational facilities, the increasing demand upon libraries may eventually create a significant need for telefacsimile. In any event, the results of this study imply that the manual procedures used in delivery of interlibrary loan materials need to be reorganized. Such reorganization must take place before telefacsimile systems can effectively be used.[19]

Still another form of transmission is by means of the regular telephone. At the moment the process is too slow, but when it is speeded up, it may well be what is required for metropolitan areas as well as for short to medium distances.

Bibliography

Bloomer, Gertrude. "The Circulation of Current Journals in Special Libraries," *Special Libraries* 39:46–50 (1948).

[19]William D. Schieber and Ralph M. Shoffner, *Telefacsimile in Libraries; A Report of an Experiment in Facsimile Transmission and an Analysis of Implications for Interlibrary Loan Systems* ([Berkeley]: Institute of Library Research, Univ. of California, 1968), p.84.

Bumgardner, Harvey E. "Labor-saving Methods Applied to Magazine Circulation," *Special Libraries* 43:92–93, 102 (1952).

Cole, Barbara R., and Rowley, Helen. "Current Journal Routing," *Special Libraries* 35:324–27 (1944).

Grenfell, David. "Circulation," and "Lending and Borrowing," in his *Periodicals and Serials; Their Treatment in Special Libraries,* p.83–115. 2d ed. London: Aslib, 1965.

Price, Robert F. "A Man-hour Analysis of Periodical Circulation," *Library Quarterly* 16:239–44 (1946).

Randall, G. E. "Journal Routing: Greater Efficiency at Lower Cost," *Special Libraries* 45:371–73 (1954).

Richardson, W. H. "Circulation Control," *Special Libraries* 51:493–96 (1960).

Simon, William H. "This Works for Us: Periodical Handling with Photocopy System," *Special Libraries* 50:206–207 (1959).

Strauss, Lucille J.; Shreve, Irene M.; and Brown, Alberta L. "Administration of Readers' Services," and "Dissemination of Currently Published Information: Library Bulletins—Other Methods," in their *Scientific and Technical Libraries; Their Organization and Administration,* p.215–60. 2d ed. New York: Becker & Hayes, 1972.

Thornton, H. "Is the Circulation of Periodicals Desirable?" *Aslib Proceedings* 11:106–107 (1959).

Walford, A. J. "Service Routine," in Wilfred Ashworth, ed., *Handbook of Special Librarianship and Information Work,* p.365–414. 3d ed. London: Aslib, 1967.

Warren, Stafford L. "A Proposed National Science Library System," in Allen Kent, ed., *Library Planning for Automation,* p.3–33. Washington: Spartan Books, 1965.

Copyright

Clapp, Verner W. "Library Photocopying and Copyright, Recent Developments," *Law Library Journal* 55:10–15 (1962).

"Copyright," in Allen Kent, ed., *Library Planning for Automation,* p.167–90. Washington: Spartan Books, 1965.

Freehafer, E. G. "Summary Statement of Policy of the Joint Libraries Committee on Fair Use in Photocopying," *Special Libraries* 55:104–106 (1964).

Price, Miles O. "Photocopying by Libraries and Copyright," *Library Trends* 8:432–47 (1960).

Television facsimile reproduction

Schatz, Sharon. "Facsimile Transmission in Libraries, a State of the Art Survey," *Library Resources & Technical Services* 12:5–15 (1968).

Schieber, William D., and Shoffner, Ralph M. *Telefacsimile in Libraries; A Report of an Experiment in Facsimile Transmission and an Analysis of Implications for Interlibrary Loan Systems.* [Berkeley:] Institute of Library Research, Univ. of California, 1968.

16

Binding

The library routines connected with the binding of serial publications are more complex than those for the binding of monographs, as can be seen from the following details. Serial librarians or binding-records assistants have traditionally maintained a card file of instructions for the treatment of each current title. The file is intended to make it possible for a set to be bound with reasonable uniformity, even though the component parts are as a rule sent to the bindery disjunctively over a period of years and decades. The collation of serials is often quite intricate, as was noted in chapter 11. The supply of serials for binding has peak periods, since most volumes tend to be completed at midyear or in December. Binders like to have a steady flow of material twelve months in the year, but that is not easy to achieve in the face of the peak periods. In order to satisfy readers, the staff may have to make frequent searches for titles which are on their way to or from the bindery; in urgent cases they may even have to recall a volume from the bindery.

In recent years much desirable standardization has been achieved through the work of the Joint Committee of the American Library Association and the Library Binding Institute. Their recommendations have been embodied in Feipel and Browning's *Library Binding Manual,* the relevant passages of which should be well known to serial librarians. (The principal references are on p.3, 7–8, 25–29, 36, and 48–50.) The biggest single achievement of the Joint Committee has been the approval and establishment of the practice of standardized lettering.[1]

---

[1]For an account of standardized lettering see Louis N. Feipel and Earl W. Browning, *Library Binding Manual,* prepared under the direction of the Joint Committee

Library Binding Practices

It is customary for service units to prepare volumes in their custody for transmission to the bindery. They may write out the instructions that accompany a serial, or that function may be performed by a binding-records assistant who is in a separate unit. The catalog department may do the preparatory work for items that have been acquired and cataloged in an unbound form.

The assistant who prepares a volume for binding cannot be content with seeing that all issues are present because a closer check may disclose that one or more of the issues has been mutilated, whereupon replacement copies must be obtained. Some types of publication are more susceptible to mutilation than others; for example, an art or a photography journal should be examined much more carefully than a library journal. In some libraries there may even be a double check. At the Library of Congress, for instance, the Binding Division reviews serials for completeness after they have been prepared in a service division.[2] Most binderies also collate volumes faithfully, even though they know that the library has already performed a similar task. At times they discover gaps and mutilations which had not been detected before, and then the volumes must be returned to the library to await the procurement of replacement issues. Yet bindery collation is expensive. One binder has expressed the opinion that "probably the most costly operation of any is the collating and arranging of the material that is to be bound."[3] In at least one library, the University of Oregon, procedures were reorganized so that collation at the bindery was no longer required. The various divisions in the library remove completed volumes from the shelves, collate them issue by issue, and send them to the Binding Unit, tied securely and with a notation of title, volume, and dates. The Binding Unit has found it necessary to collate once more issue by issue, but not page by page. The bindery does not collate.[4] Unquestionably there has

---

of the ALA and LBI (Chicago: American Library Assn., 1951), p.26–27. Standardized lettering did away with the need for rubs. Instead the binder knows where to put the lettering on the spine, measuring from the bottom up. As a result there may be slight variations in the size of the lettering and in the height of the volumes, but these differences are relatively immaterial.

[2] See Library of Congress, *Binding Division* (Departmental & Divisional Manuals, no. 5 [Washington, 1950]), p.17.

[3] Ernst Hertzberg, "The Binding Industry," *Serial Slants* 1:15 (July 1950).

[4] Cf. Emma G. Wright and E. B. Barnes, "Binding at the University of Oregon," *Serial Slants* 2:2 (Jan. 1952). Collation by the Binding Unit has been added since they wrote.

been duplication of effort in collating volumes in the library as well as in the bindery, so that economy is possible with delimitation of functions.

One of the recurrent questions of collation is whether the paper covers of issues should be discarded or whether they should be included in the bound volume. Some libraries preserve every front and back cover; some preserve only the front cover unless there is significant text on the back one; while others dispense with both as a general rule. When they are included, covers are usually bound in place, though an older practice was to bind them as a group at the end of the volume. Frances Warner has made a good case for preserving covers and binding them in place, especially in research libraries. She says:

> Some of our economies have been very irritating to scholars and scientists. Many of us have discarded the covers of scientific periodicals in order to reduce the size of the volumes. But on most of these covers, there is much information that is not found in the issue itself. Furthermore, covers serve to separate issues. When they are removed, a chemist, for example, who is running through the volumes of *Chemical Abstracts* to ascertain what is published in each number on the fundamentals of chemistry will have great difficulty in locating this section in the twenty-four issues published during the year. In one institution, during one month, over one dozen complaints were filed as a result of this rather common practice of librarians.[5]

Another moot point is the extent to which advertising matter, "the pages of advertisements which provide the financial life-blood of the periodical press," as Davinson says,[6] should be included in the bound volume. Shires says that "anything up to 80 percent of a technical journal to-day consists of advertisements."[7] Thus, if all the advertising

[5]Frances Warner, "Current Binding Policies at Iowa State College," *Serial Slants* 3:40 (1952).

[6]D. E. Davinson, *The Periodicals Collection; Its Purpose and Uses in Libraries* (London: Deutsch, 1969), p.173.

[7]G. A. Shires, "Information from the Advertisement Pages," *Aslib Proceedings* 2:23 (1950). A contributor to *Notes and Queries* (7th series; 3:336, 1887) said: "I cannot agree . . . that in binding up magazines *any* advertisement sheets should be removed; I would rather say let the loose ones be carefully secured by the binder as insets. The most interesting available material for a yet-to-be-written history of English lotteries is the multitude of amusing handbills distributed in now almost forgotten magazines by Bish and other giants of the trade in lottery tickets."

matter is retained, the issues of one bibliographical volume may have to be bound in two or three physical volumes. Some libraries feel that they must bind the whole work for the benefit of artists, the historian of a subject, or indeed anyone who wishes to study the advertisements of former times. Yet others are content with preserving merely the text, those advertisements that are on numbered pages along with the text, or at most the advertising matter from just one or two issues a year. Davinson says: "Anybody who has seen the skilful use which economic historians, for example, have made of the advertising sections of old technical periodicals is bound to feel some disquiet at the exclusion of material with a potential historical value."[8]

In 1935, as an attack on the problem of including the advertising matter in bound volumes or excluding it from them, an informal committee of the Conference of Eastern College Librarians checked thirty-four libraries and published *A List of Periodicals Bound Complete with Advertising Pages in New England and New York City Libraries.* The list still serves to some small extent as a guide to libraries that wish to economize by informing them that at least one recorded set has preserved the advertisements. At the University of Oregon an overall decision was given in favor of retaining the advertising pages:

> All advertisements...are bound in, unless they might result in serious structural weakness in the finished volume. The practice of binding in all advertisements...has been adopted for a number of reasons. From the standpoint of binding economics, we may pay more for binding, but we do not pay for the labor spent in cutting them out. These two factors probably balance each other. In addition to these considerations, our practice avoids the danger of mutilated volumes (text accidentally removed when cutting out advertisements). Certain bibliographical information which is frequently unobtainable elsewhere is retained as well as items that are often of most practical immediate interest (e.g. prices of instruments) and may very well be of considerable sociological interest in the future.[9]

Binders are inclined to agree with the decision reached at the University of Oregon, judging by the following statement:

> Is it necessary in all cases to remove ALL advertising material? A librarian not so long ago asked me—"Why do that in every case, are

[8]Davinson, *Periodicals Collection,* p.173.
[9]Wright and Barnes, "Binding at the University of Oregon," p.4.

not the ads a history of the times also?" If this were possible in some cases, the binder could leave the book fairly intact without going thru it page for page and eliminating all ads. A large part of the hand operation would be eliminated, and the saving passed on to the library. Probably those ads in the center could be left in each magazine and those on either end taken out, which would save the paging thru the text in the center to find the ads.[10]

Feipel and Browning urge librarians not "to remove pages of advertising" themselves "but to instruct the binder whether to remove or retain them."[11]

Steadily throughout the century the cost of binding has forced many economies on libraries. First to go were morocco bindings, their place being taken by buckram, which since the early 1900s has been the standard binding material in America. But leather bindings are still favored in Great Britain, at least for heavily used sets. Grenfell, writing for special libraries in Great Britain, says: "Good leathers are expensive, but if not handled or treated with a preservative, they will deteriorate in time. Its use should therefore be confined to such expensive reference tools as *Chemical Abstracts*."[12] When buckram was generally adopted in the United States, there was a tendency to retain colored panels and gold lines to represent bands, but those practices were abandoned. On the other hand, the use of quarter-flush binding for minor serials, which came in with the adoption of buckram, has continued. More recently machine sewing has been replaced in some libraries by the so-called perfect binding, in which the sheets are attached to the binding by means of a plastic glue. When perfect binding has been really well done, it has been reasonably satisfactory for smaller, lighter serial binding, but it should not be applied to large and heavy volumes.

The general trend toward economy in the face of steadily rising binding costs is reflected in the program developed at the University of Oregon Library:

> The work at the Bindery has been greatly simplified. First . . . there is no rub file. The size of type used in lettering depends on the thickness of the volume. Vertical placement for the lettering is determined by the heights and measured from the bottom. Color and wording are stated on the Bindery Slip. Trimming is the one

[10]Hertzberg, "The Binding Industry," p.15–16.
[11]*Library Binding Manual*, p.26.
[12]David Grenfell, *Periodicals and Serials; Their Treatment in Special Libraries* (2d ed.; London, Aslib, 1965), p.137.

operation that is not controlled. Different volumes of a set may vary from one-quarter to one-eighth of an inch, but since the lettering is all measured from the bottom, the titles of the volumes standing on a shelf are even.

In addition to instructions for individual volumes, there are a number of standing specifications. The materials used in all our binding are the same. The cloth binding is all standard quality Library Buckram. The board used is a #1 book binding board. .ʻ. .

In addition to standard cloth binding, the Press binds many items in what we call Board Binding. This consists of paper covered boards, of the same high quality used for cloth, with a vellum spine that is not lettered. Board Binding is specified in all cases where it appears the use will not be too heavy, where the paper is comparatively light and where other considerations make a cheaper binding advisable. Board bindings cost . . . [about] 50 per cent of cloth bindings.[13]

The University of Oregon Library realized that it must compromise between perfection and economic conditions. It was motivated by the philosophy that volumes are bound in order to make them serviceable and to preserve them for the future. With such a philosophy esthetics can still be regarded, but in a secondary way. This is a counsel of wisdom for the workaday serial publication.

Feipel and Browning take the attitude that "cheap binding, at best, is never cheap." Instead of resorting to it, they say, "it will usually be wiser for the librarian to determine what files must be preserved, bind them substantially according to Class 'A' Specifications and tie up the rest (or such parts as may not safely be discarded) into volumes."[14] But research libraries conserve many marginal serials which do not warrant standard binding and which should not be tied up except at the risk of exposing the pieces to physical deterioration or loss, and this is where devices such as quarter-flush bindings and plastic glues can make a significant contribution.

In recent years binding budgets have had to be reckoned with quite seriously. The situation in the University of Illinois Library may be cited as an example of the way in which the budget for binding has risen. In that library the annual appropriation for binding increased from $26,000 in 1946 to $50,000 in 1950. Even then—despite rigid selection of titles to be bound, reduction of duplicates, and

[13]Wright and Barnes, "Binding at the University of Oregon," p.3–4. A rub file has been established in the Binding Unit to record cloth or boards, color of cloth, wording, etc.

[14]*Library Binding Manual*, p.27–28.

other economies—the new figure was inadequate, so a supplementary appropriation had to be obtained to cover arrearages. The bindery was instructed: "(1) to collate volumes only if specially requested by our Binding Department, (2) to leave pages containing advertising in all issues unless directed otherwise, and (3) to omit lettering on less important and little used serials as designated by the Binding Department."[15] By 1970 the binding appropriation of 1950 had exactly tripled, but two interesting points emerge from a comparison of the 1950s and the late 1960s. First, for the two fiscal years 1953/54–1954/55, the books-serials-binding expenditures totaled $790,939, of which $115,933, or 14.6 percent, went for binding. The 1969/70 books-serials-binding expenditures were $1,749,332, and the $151,977 for binding amounted to only 8.6 percent. The lowered percentage seems clearly the result of the rise in the cost indices for books and serials, which has greatly exceeded the increase in unit binding costs over the same span of time. Second, during 1953/54–1954/55 the library bound 51,748 volumes at an average of $2.24 per volume. In 1969/70 60,569 volumes were bound at an average of $2.51, a figure which represents an increase of 12 percent over the earlier cost, small in relation to the inflationary rise during the period. The figure has been made possible only by the library's looking for every reasonable economy subject to giving volumes the level of protection they should have and its having an efficient binder who is engaged in an unending struggle to keep costs down.

In 1951 the Library of Congress reported arrearages of 435,000 volumes awaiting initial binding plus 259,000 volumes in need of rebinding, a large proportion of both groups being serials. The accumulation could monopolize the library's entire binding quota for ten years to come. A Binding Committee was therefore constituted to debate the possibility of reducing large quantities of material to photocopy form and of employing inexpensive types of binding. The following were among the points brought out by the Committee:

1. Prompt binding of serials is necessary for preservation and protection against loss; therefore serials should be accorded precedence in binding.
2. The greatest demand is for American serials listed in the standard indexes.
3. Large periodical volumes do not stand up well under heavy use. The quarter binding of single issues would

15Arnold H. Trotier, "Some Persistent Problems of Serials in Technical Processes," *Serial Slants* 1:11 (Jan. 1951).

probably cut down the need for rebinding certain periodicals. In many cases quarter binding for all the issues of a periodical would be more expensive than full binding an annual volume, particularly if the more desirable over-sewn quarter-binding style were adopted. Only those periodicals which are listed in standard indexes should therefore be considered for this special type of treatment.

4. Some lettering is desirable on the quarter binds. It would lessen deck-attendant error, help the attendants to correct reader errors in call numbers, and make it easier to spot mislabeled volumes.

5. Each volume sent to the Bindery for quarter binding would be accompanied by a prelettered buckram strip which would become the back of the book. The strip would be hand-lettered with a Leroy lettering set, using black ink on precut, light-colored buckrams.

6. The names of corporate authors would be condensed or abbreviated when necessary.

7. Because of the standardization of lettering panels, pattern volumes and dummies would no longer be required.

8. There were already sets on public reference which were in mixed Library of Congress and publisher's binding on which even the substance of the lettering differs. Likewise it was noted that the contract binding being done for what is now the National Agricultural Library was being done in red buckram with black-ink lettering. Therefore, when existing stocks of buckram were exhausted, the standard color for full binding at the Library of Congress would be ruby, except that the Congressional Document series and all law material other than periodicals would be bound in law buckram, and United States bills would be bound in olive buckram.

9. The Library should have in ink-print form at least one major newspaper from each foreign country. No more than three, preferably two, newspapers from a foreign country should be bound; even they should be microfilmed when their physical condition warrants. All other foreign papers which are to be retained should be acquired in microfilm form or be microfilmed and the originals discarded.[16]

---

[16]Abstracted from the Minutes of the Library of Congress Binding Committee, 1952–53.

Clearly there is much hard thinking for librarians to do about the binding of serials and in some instances about their reduction to microcopy form. The problem becomes doubly serious when arrearages of binding and rebinding are involved. Frances Warner cautions against allowing arrearages to occur:

> We have found that the practice of leaving unbound publications on the shelf, of tying up publications in brown paper or cardboard, only results in heavier costs later. In our experience, we have found no permanent economy in postponing binding or in placing unbound publications on the shelves for any considerable length of time. Issues of volumes of serials which are left unbound disappear. The cost of replacement is heavy both in time and money. Often missing numbers cannot be replaced. Deterioration of paper from age and infiltration of dust add to the damage. Binding is one item in the library budget which cannot be curtailed without serious loss.[17]

The problem of deferred serial binding is not new. It became acute, for example, during and after both the first and second World Wars. In 1919 the New York Public Library reported:

> With our present funds for binding we can do nothing but adopt makeshifts which are expensive and unsatisfactory. They require the double handling of material, once when it is temporarily put into Manilla-rope paper, and once when it is to be bound in some permanent form. These makeshifts are expensive in time, since it takes longer to tie, untie, and retie a volume in Manilla-rope paper than to consult a bound volume. They are unsatisfactory, because the volumes so treated are difficult to handle on the shelves; because they suffer more from wear and tear; and because they lend themselves to slipshod, careless and inconsiderate treatment from readers and attendants. Work deferred is not avoided; it has to be done at a later day, and usually costs more than if done when the occasion arises.[18]

To a large extent the problem of serial binding costs is most acute in the historical-research type of library, the institution which undertakes the responsibility of preserving files for future consultation. Most small public and special libraries do not bind their periodicals because they do not feel the same sense of responsibility. Instead,

[17]Warner, "Binding at Iowa State College," p.39.
[18]*Report of the New York Public Library* 1919 (New York, 1920), p.22.

they depend on larger libraries for work with back files and know that they can obtain fairly readily a photocopy of any desired article.

Some Special Problems

There are technicalities of many kinds which must be faced in the binding of serials, and each special situation should be thought through carefully. Paged-in cumulative indexes are generally left in place, but given special mention on the spine, so that the person who is working at the shelves can readily lay his hands on the volumes which contain these indexes. On the other hand, paged-in monographs are commonly removed. If they are called for in the table of contents, they may be left in place, or else the table of contents should be annotated to show the new location. Loose maps, such as those inserted in the *National Geographic Magazine*, are generally transferred to the map collection. A typewritten slip is often inserted in the bound volume in the place where a relocated part or section would normally have been. The same device is followed in a monographic series when the parts of a single monograph are bound together under the volume numbering for the first part, this for the sake of the continuity of the text. It is also followed at times when an issue of a document serial is restricted and therefore unavailable, as is often the case with United Nations publications.

Change of format within a volume can create a binding problem. The set of the British *Command Papers* has proved to be troublesome to bind and shelve because of constant changes in format, and because of such difficulties a number of American libraries have their sets made up and bound in Great Britain, where there is greater familiarity with the problems. In many cases the best solution may well be to bind the two sizes independently, but particularly so when one of them is to go on the oversize shelves. In general, the use of two different sizes for a serial does not affect the shelving, because in the purely serial parts of the classification folios are as a rule neither distinguished nor segregated as monograph folios are. The reason for holding serial publications together regardless of size is that there is not the same waste of space as there would be with the occasional monograph which is oversize. Most volumes of serial sets, other than newspapers, tend to be of a convenient size for shelving in a single sequence, an arrangement that represents a convenience to readers and staff who consult the shelves directly. It is only the very large serials that should be segregated; in fact, some of them can properly be shelved with the bound volumes of newspapers.

Spearheaded by the National Agricultural Library and the Library of Congress, there is a growing tendency toward putting all serials in a single color of buckram. The one color can be acquired and stored more cheaply than a variety of colors, and the binding-records file can be abandoned when there is only one color in conjunction with standardized lettering. In any event, most libraries have many mismatched bindings in their serial sets: a mixture of publishers' and library bindings, for example, of morocco and buckram, or of colors which were poorly matched during emergency periods. Some variations are simple errors in binding; most are caused by the process of building up sets from a number of sources.

There is a danger that should be guarded against whereby volumes of serials, like pamphlet volumes, may be made too thick from motives of economy in the first instance. This is a shortsighted policy which should not be adopted unless it can safely be assumed that the material will receive slight use over the years and that the issues will not have to remain unbound for too long a period while the desired thickness is accumulating. As has been found with newspapers, too great bulk can reduce the life expectancy of a binding. Some newspapers are now bound two or three volumes to a month; that has become standard practice for the *New York Times,* for example, resulting in thirty-six bound volumes a year instead of twelve or fewer. The lesson learned with newspapers has not been carried over to other types of serials as much as it should have been. On the contrary, two or three bibliographical volumes are often combined in the one physical binding. If three volumes of *College and Research Libraries* are bound in one (as was originally done in the Harvard College Library), the bulk is just too great when the work is consulted frequently. Such multivolumes are off the shelves for longer periods than they would be if each bibliographical volume were bound up separately; it is an inconvenience to the reader to have to search for three title pages and indexes scattered through the volume, if indeed he does find them as he browses through a set; and greater distortion of the inner text ensues when photocopies are made from overthick works. But the most serious trouble can develop from keeping unbound files in the periodical room or elsewhere for two or three years, instead of binding the titles on schedule and sending them to the bookstacks after the normal period of a year. The reader or staff member can be excused his irritation when he goes directly to the stacks for the file of two or three years back, only to have to retrace his steps and go to the periodical room where the file is by way of exception. Feipel and Browning point out that delay in binding results in heavy wear, and frequently in loss of numbers and parts. Unbound files are hard to shelve. Much time will be saved by the staff if it does not have to struggle with the job of keeping unbound magazines in order; and the public will be greatly pleased if it may have access to magazines which have been promptly bound.[19]

Yale University Library has established a rough working guide which says that no serial volume should weigh more than can conveniently be handled in the left hand of a righthanded person. Its instructions to staff members who are preparing serials for binding are:

1. In general, whatever kind of binding is used, a volume should not be heavier than a person can lift easily in his left hand.
2. Volumes which receive full binding should not usually be more than 3 inches in thickness; those which are bound in half-cloth should not be over 2 inches thick.
3. The following are usually bound singly:
   a. Volumes of monograph series, especially if they are bibliographies.
   b. Volumes 1½ to 3 inches thick.
4. Two or more volumes may be bound together if they are not monographic and are not more than 3 inches thick.[20]

Binding Units of Less than a Bibliographical Volume

The *Library Journal* has expanded so much in recent years that one of its bibliographical volumes must now be bound in two or more physical ones, and the case of the *New York Times* has already been noted. With the *Library Journal*, do the title page and index go in the first or the last bound volume each year? If the first, then the issues must be held back until the last segment is bound; if the last, then the person who goes to the current periodical room, expecting to find a year's file there, will have to go to the stacks if he wants one of the issues which has already been bound.

Libraries in various countries are increasingly binding serials in smaller quantities than the bibliographical unit. The principle deserves careful attention. It is possible, for instance, that it can be

[19]*Library Binding Manual*, p.3.

[20]Yale University Library, *Cataloging of Serials in the Yale University Library* (3d ed.; New Haven, Conn., 1969), p.73.

applied also to many an incomplete volume which, because of its incompleteness, was formerly bundled in some fashion or other. When there are only one or two issues on hand, and there seems little prospect of obtaining more, an inexpensive pamphlet binder may well serve. In these ways items are protected and should be in relatively good physical condition when the time comes to bind them in a completed volume. Yale makes use of both of these devices in addition to its regular quarter and full binding:

> Stitching is a *temporary* method of collecting into one physical volume incomplete volumes and those which are to be bound later with other volumes. The issues of the volume are stitched together, and a brown paper cover is pasted around the volume.
>
> Gaylords are cardboard covers into which lightweight, thin material is sewed. These should not be more than one-half inch in thickness.[21]

In addition to these methods, libraries have long had the binder insert guards in a bound volume so that one or two thin issues, missing at the time of binding, can later be inserted without having to dismantle the volume.

The National Lending Library in Great Britain has carried the principle to its logical extreme, primarily because it sends thousands of issues of periodicals through the mail every week. When the library was founded in 1962, it was decided to put each issue of a periodical into a quarter-flush cloth binding, with a clear plastic front cover which would do away with the need for lettering. The issue would thereby be protected in the mails, and there would be the additional advantage of its opening up flat, like a music score, when a photocopy was to be made. It was also decided to shelve separately issued indexes to a periodical in a pamphlet box at the beginning of the set; they would be bound up in five- or ten-year runs. As aids in keeping the masses of single issues in order on the shelves, a five-year color cycle was devised for the cloth spines, and a diagonal line, rising at an angle of 45 degrees, is drawn across the spines of completed volumes.

Russian libraries have also given up the bibliographical volume as the binding unit in certain instances. Klenov says that the two factors to be taken into account in binding periodicals are the use each individual title will receive and the type of library in which it is located. In Russian library parlance the terms *tonkie* (thin) and

[21]*Ibid.*

tolstye (thick) journals are used. Thin journals, such as *Krokodil, Ogonek,* and *Rabotnitsa,* which are widely read when they first appear but are less in demand later on, are bound by the quarter, half year, or year. But thick journals, such as *Novyi Mir, Oktiabr',* and *Voprosy Istorii,* where interest in the individual articles will persist over a number of years, are bound by separate issue and not by the year or half year. A periodical such as *Pchelovodstvo,* which although not large in size will have value for scientists for years to come, can be treated in one of two ways. From the point of view of economy it would seem wise to bind two, three, or more numbers in one volume. But it can also be said that if each issue is bound separately, circulation will be faster and fewer duplicate copies will have to be bought. Likewise, in a rural library the complete year of *Bibliotekar'* could be bound in two volumes, but in a large library, where library-science students consult the file extensively, it is wise to bind each number individually to make it available to the fullest extent.[22]

In the 1940s Fremont Rider developed a comparable scheme at Wesleyan University Library.[23] He put each issue of a monthly or quarterly in an individual pamphlet binder, and the twelve or the four issues which comprised a volume were then placed in a box. According to Rider, the faculty welcomed the innovation and wanted it extended. When a faculty member had an article to read in a back file, he could now carry home an issue that weighed a pound as against a volume that weighed four pounds. Moreover, one professor did not inactivate all the issues in a volume when he borrowed only one of them; the remaining eleven or three issues were left in the box for other professors to consult or borrow. Thus the change in binding methods resulted in an increase in accessibility.

Rider goes on to say that binding costs were notably less. For a quarterly like the *Yale Review* the cost per bibliographical volume dropped from $2.80 to $1.00, and for a monthly that was hitherto bound two volumes to the year the new figure was $2.40 instead of $5.60. Indirectly the Library of Congress cast doubt on these figures when it said that in many cases it would cost more to put the separate issues in quarter binding, particularly when oversewn, than to bind an annual volume in the regular way.

[22]A. V. Klenov, *Bibliotechnaia Tekhnika; Uchebnoe Posobie dlia Bibliotechnykh Tekhnikumov* (Izd. 4; Moskva: Gos. Izd-vo Kul'turno-prosvetitel'noi Lit-ry, 1947), p.43, 48–49.

[23]For details of Rider's plan see his *Compact Book Storage; Some Suggestions toward a New Methodology for the Shelving of Less Used Research Materials* (New York: Hadham, 1949), p.86–90.

In practice there are three disadvantages to Rider's scheme: issues are more easily lost, call numbers are longer, and there is no satisfactory way of dealing with the title page and index. Other factors should also be noted: the cost of extra lettering and boxes, and the facts that care and consultation of the shelves are more exacting processes and that the plan does not provide for high-frequency serials. As a final caution, the end processes in a library may already be suffering from a surfeit of pamphlet binders. No preparation-for-shelves unit welcomes the sight of large quantities of pamphlet binders fresh from the bindery, so a large addition to the number should be made only after careful consideration. At any rate, Wesleyan University Library abandoned Rider's scheme after he retired; from that time on regular binding procedures have been followed for monthlies and quarterlies.

Title Pages and Indexes

Libraries go to considerable pains to procure title pages and indexes whenever they are printed so that they can be inserted in the bound volumes. To the reader and the librarian, browsing for information, the index is a valuable addition to any set, even though the work may be covered by an abstracting or indexing service. The annual indexes to *American Libraries* and the *Library Journal,* for instance, are most useful, despite the fact that both are covered much more generally in *Library Literature.* So there are two advantages to having the periodical's index to its own contents: it is much more exhaustive than are the entries in any abstracting or indexing service, and it is a distinct aid in direct consultation of the shelves. Librarians in research institutions therefore take strong exception to Feipel and Browning's statement that "if the publisher's index is not easily available, and if the magazine is included in the *Readers' Guide* or other reliable compilation, the individual index to a bound volume becomes of little value, and is scarcely worth the effort frequently necessary to obtain or retain it."[24]

Naturally the title page is bound in front of the issues to which it relates, provided, that is, that bibliographical units are not bound up in two or more volumes, as is increasingly the case. When the index constitutes a unit with the title page, as often happens, it

[24]*Library Binding Manual,* p.26. The very fact that Stechert-Hafner compiles and issues checklists of periodicals which produce printed title pages and indexes in itself attests the value which research libraries place on these items.

also is put in the front along with the title page, even though readers and staff members are accustomed to looking at the back of a volume for the index. Research libraries generally prefer to place the index at the back of the volume whenever possible, but Feipel and Browning seems to imply that the index should always be bound at the front of a work. Actually either convention can be justified as long as it is carried out systematically throughout a set, which, unfortunately, is often not done. When two or three bibliographical volumes are bound in a single physical volume, the indexes are generally found in several places throughout the item. In the act of browsing through a set, it is disconcerting to find that the indexes are sometimes in front, sometimes at the back, and sometimes dispersed.

Lettering

Care and restraint need to be exercised in selecting the information that the binder is to letter on the spines of serial volumes. There can be extra charges for too many lines of lettering. There has been a tendency to follow the wording in the catalog entry in making out the binding instructions. Up to a point that practice is good, but on the shelves a finding title can suffice for all practical purposes. So "Building Science Abstracts" should be preferred on the spine to "Gt. Brit. Dept. of Scientific and Industrial Research. Building Science Abstracts." In the same way "Airway Bulletin" will serve instead of "U.S. Dept. of Commerce. Aeronautics Branch. Airway Bulletin." It is, of course, not difficult to find longer corporate names than these which are lettered on serial volumes. Acronyms may also be substituted for full corporate names. Thus "LC Quarterly Journal" and not "U.S. Library of Congress. Quarterly Journal"; "NYPL Bulletin" rather than "New York Public Library. Bulletin." Savings of this kind are being made by libraries in order to hold down the cost of binding.

On the spine, as in all serial work, arabic numbers should take the place of roman. Terms such as "Band," "tome," and "volume" should be omitted from the lettering unless two related expressions cannot otherwise be distinguished. Thus "72" is all that is needed, not "v.72," "Vol. 72," or any other form. But when volume 72, part 1 must be brought out, then "72, pt.1" can suffice, although some libraries adopt devices such as "72¹" to differentiate volumes and parts (see figure 29).

The library's name or seal appears on the spine of bound volumes less often than it once did. There is more than a sufficiency of

Figure 29. Four styles of library binding. The 1909 volume is in morocco, the 1910 in buckram with leather panels. Six double lines were later employed to give the effect of panels; by 1947 the lines also had been given up.

library marks of ownership in most bound periodicals, since every issue is stamped as it is received. Some institutions—the Library of Congress, for example—are effectively utilizing endpapers with the library's name and seal interwoven; in such an instance there is no reason for adding the name or seal on the spine.

It is better to strike a happy medium on all serial volumes, if possible, than to have an excess of lettering on some sets and nothing except the call number on others, e.g., on quarter bindings. At times the savings on less expensive serial bindings are offset when the items are hand-lettered in the preparation-for-shelves section; and sometimes typewritten labels are prepared and pasted on the side, occasionally on the spine.

Durability and Openability

The Library Technology Program has developed provisional standards for the durability, openability, and workmanship exhibited in library bindings. They appear in its *Development of Performance Standards for Binding Used in Libraries, Phase II* (LTP Publications, no.10 [Chicago: Library Technology Project, American Library Assn., 1966]); in 1967 they were approved as standards by the American Library Association and the Special Libraries Association. Two pieces of equipment have been developed, a Universal Book Tester for durability and an Openability Test Plate. The Library Technology Program is ready to carry out tests for any library on these instruments; or it is possible for libraries to acquire or build their own.

Newspapers

American Library Association specifications for class A newspaper binding are given by Feipel and Browning.[25] The Library of Congress no longer uses class A binding for newspapers or for journals that have newspaper format; its specifications are: cover of heavyweight buckram, no. 16 gray binders boards, hollow back, visible silesia joints, and backbone lettered in foil.

Some of the history of newspaper binding is revealed by the following statement of New York Public Library practice:

> Newspaper volumes in the Library were bound with leather backs and cloth sides a generation ago. The leather decayed, and full canvas or heavy duck was then used. Newspapers make large, heavy volumes that are sometimes stored flat on the shelves. The rough canvas sides proved to be such excellent dust collectors that full buckram was next resorted to. Even buckram proved to have insufficient strength for the backs of such large volumes, and we are now using strong canvas backs with buckram sides.[26]

Also in some libraries one or more grips were attached to the spine as an aid in pulling the heavy volumes off the shelves. There was less occasion for grips when the volumes rested on roller shelves, when several volumes were not piled on top of one another as they lay flat on the shelves, or when volumes were not made unduly big.

[25]*Library Binding Manual,* p.49–51. See also p.28–30 for the authors' views on newspaper binding.

[26]*Report of the New York Public Library* 1925 (New York, 1926), p.48.

In the past the natural binding unit for a daily newspaper was taken to be a month or even longer, but now the unit may be ten days or two weeks to avoid the creation of volumes too large for convenient handling. Bibliographical units are generally being ignored in terms of both the binding unit and the lettering on the spine. But most libraries do not bind newspapers as they once did; they prefer to conserve and service newspapers in microfilm form. For the most part it is only those libraries which have a responsibility for the collection and preservation of national, state, or local papers that continue to bind them.

Substitutes for Binding

Apart from reduction to microcopy, libraries must devise various ways of dealing with serials that are to remain unbound either temporarily or permanently. Some serials cannot be bound because the paper is too poor to stand binding. They should not be on the open shelves; they should be in air-conditioned quarters and preferably in storage libraries. Some must wait their turn in the periodical room or on the classified shelves until gaps have been filled. Others, such as college and university catalogs, may be given so low a priority that in effect they are never bound. Annual reports tend to be accumulated in the stacks until there are enough on hand to make a volume of a satisfactory size. And items which are sent directly to a storage library are generally left in an unbound state.

For many of these types binding substitutes must be found. The most common substitutes are manila-rope bundles tied with string, tape, or lawyers' pink pulls; boxes, envelopes, and containers of various kinds; and, in special libraries in particular, vertical files. When manila rope is used, it is bought sometimes in precut sizes and sometimes in large rolls that must be cut to size on every occasion. Manila rope is usually lettered in india ink. For large bundles it may be necessary to add boards as supports. Boxes of all types should be avoided because the unbound issues of serials tend to undergo an undue amount of physical deterioration in them.

Bibliography

Bunn, R. M. "Binding of Periodicals in the National Lending Library," *Journal of Documentation* 18:20–24 (1962).

Davinson, D. E. "Binding," in his *The Periodicals Collection; Its Purpose and Uses in Libraries,* p.164–78. London: Deutsch, 1969.

Feipel, Louis N., and Browning, Earl W. *Library Binding Manual.* Chicago: American Library Assn., 1951.

Grenfell, David. "Binding," in his *Periodicals and Serials; Their Treatment in Special Libraries,* p.134–43, 146. 2d ed. London: Aslib, 1965.

Hertzberg, Ernst. "The Binding Industry," *Serial Slants* 1:10–19 (July 1950).

Hughes, Margaret H. "Periodical Binding Schedules for Improved Reader Service in University and College Libraries," *College and Research Libraries* 13:223–26, 231 (1952).

Library Binding Institute. *Library Binding Handbook.* [Boston,] 1963.

Library of Congress. *Binding Division.* (Departmental & Divisional Manuals, no.5) Washington, 1950.

Ort, J. George. "Standardization of Periodical Bindings," *Serial Slants* 4:12–14 (1953).

Stratton, John B. *Library Binding Practices in College and University Libraries* (New York, 1952). Thesis, Columbia Univ. Library School.

Trotier, Arnold H. "Some Persistent Problems of Serials in Technical Processes," *Serial Slants* 1:5–13 (Jan. 1951).

Warner, Frances. "Current Binding Policies at Iowa State College," *Serial Slants* 3:39–42 (1952).

Wright, Emma G., and Barnes, E. B. "Binding at the University of Oregon," *Serial Slants* 2:2–5 (Jan. 1952).

17

Microreproductions

The great contribution that microreproductions make to research is found in their ability to provide copies of works which otherwise might be inaccessible, or relatively so, through scarcity or cost. Micro-copies are admittedly substitute mediums. As such they have their limitations, though they serve many purposes adequately. Being black and white, they cannot reproduce color; hence an art journal with colored plates should definitely be sought in the original, not in a microcopy. From the reader's point of view microreproductions limit consultation to those places in which reading machines are available, a shortcoming that may eventually be reduced by the multiplication of portable reading machines.

In so far as they restrict freedom of operation, microcopies are in a class with certain other important mediums of research, notably rare books and reference works. It is the printed page, not the microreproduction, which is conducive to the patient and quiet investigations which are carried on at home or in carrels, laboratories, studies, and elsewhere. One does not see people who are reading microcopies sit back to reflect on what they have been reading, then jot down the ideas that have come to them, a custom when the printed page is involved. A different psychology prevails. They may sit back, but then it is to rest their eyes; and reflection, if it comes at all, rather generally ensues from a rereading of notes or photo-copies. Additional work is entailed with microcopies; one must make extensive notes and then organize them, or else procure photocopies and annotate them; whereas with originals the tendency is to make jottings and to insert markers in the volumes to facilitate recovery of information. In these respects the offset reprint is to be preferred over the microreproduction, e.g., the offset editions of European serials which were produced to complete sets at the end of World War II, editions which were so good that some libraries discarded the original parts they had received in favor of the reprints.

It is of some significance to note that government research workers, particularly in the field of science and technology, utilize and accept microreproductions far more extensively than do those who are engaged in private or individual enterprise. In the first place they have far less option in the matter, and in the second place they think nothing of the expense involved in having numerous photocopies made for them, whole vertical files of photocopies in many instances. In fact, so important is it to be able to make photocopies from microreproductions that in the 1960s in the United States the microcopying of technical reports was changed from microcards to microfiche, the reason being that it is difficult to make a photocopy from the former but routine to make one from the latter.

The heart of the matter is that microreproductions are an invaluable aid to scholarship. They are welcomed when they can be used with moderation. Therefore, the philosophy for the general library should be to have as many of the originals as it can possibly acquire so that when the microreproductions must be resorted to, the research worker will be content, will have the feeling that the scope of his investigations has been desirably broadened. It is only in the company and government research library that space becomes a factor; but in those cases the ease with which a photocopy can be provided, often without the research worker's ever looking at the microreproduction, is decidedly a compensating factor. Multimillion-volume libraries rather generally have the originals; so many a smaller library should not argue space limitations when it knows that one day it too will be a multimillion-volume resource.

Davinson argues in favor of microreproductions because they can reduce the storage problem in libraries: traditionally this is very much a European rather than an American idea. He also feels that there is a great deal of prejudice against the consultation of microreproductions and that much of the opposition is on esthetic grounds. He says:

> Bulk reduction is . . . the most pressing reason why a library might resort to micro-copy material. The amount of space occupied by a micro-copy edition of a newspaper volume is only one-twentieth that of the original, and for a periodical about one-fifteenth.
>
> Despite the undoubted benefits to be had from storage in microform there is a great deal of resistance—some reasonable, but most prejudiced—to the application of such techniques, even by some

librarians near their wits' end with worries about the shortage of storage space. Users of periodicals do prefer the original. To read micro-copies a special, and relatively expensive, reading device is needed, and this fact virtually precludes the loaning of volumes of periodicals for use outside of the library. Microfilm volumes are almost impossible to "browse" through. Commercially produced, low cost, micro-copies of periodicals and newspapers do not produce satisfactory renderings of tonal illustrations and this sometimes reduces the value of microform storage. Some librarians argue that on aesthetic grounds alone the replacement of originals by micro-forms is undesirable, some that micro-copying eliminates all possibility of carrying out analytical bibliographical investigations.

The plea that readers prefer the originals to micro-copies is fair and reasonable. If all things were equal and no problems were met with in storing originals there would, indeed, be little justification for resorting to micro-copies. Things are not equal, however: shortage of space, lack of durability of originals, and the sheer expense of keeping them are real problems. Aesthetically, it is much more satisfactory to handle originals than micro-copies. How much do aesthetics matter if they cost a lot?[1]

The argument in favor of the user should be the compelling one. The library is a service institution; it exists to facilitate the work of its readers. On the one hand, it does so by permitting them to study originals as far as possible, and this is the reason why researchers go in large numbers to the great libraries of the world where the originals are sure to be found. On the other hand, it does so by providing microreproductions for works which otherwise could not be consulted locally. The sound philosophy for the workaday librarian, then, is to develop a judicious mixture of originals and microreproductions, with the original always being preferred whenever it can be obtained. The exception to this philosophy is in the special library, where space is at a premium and where photocopies can be supplied liberally to research workers.

Newspapers on Microfilm

There is one area in which the microreproduction is accorded almost complete priority. From the 1930s on, microfilms of newspapers have come to be valued over the original publications for most li-

[1] D. E. Davinson, *The Periodicals Collection; Its Purpose and Uses in Libraries* (London: Deutsch, 1969), p.136–37.

brary research. Because of their bulk and weight, sometimes also because of their fragile condition, bound volumes of newspapers are even less convenient to consult than microreproductions, and are not always welcomed by readers. Such was the experience of the Newspaper Division of the New York Public Library, which withdrew its bound volumes from service once microfilms were on hand. It reported that

> many readers, who have used both, prefer the film to the volume. It is largely a matter of getting accustomed to reading from a screen instead of from a book. The average reader has no difficulty in operating the projector after the film has been inserted by a library attendant, although others who insist that they are not "mechanically-minded," or do not like machines, prefer to use bound volumes, heavy and cumbersome though they be.[2]

Five years later a gain in housekeeping was noted in addition to continued reader acceptance of the films and reading machines.

> Readers seem to have come to prefer films to actual volumes. The use of film contributes in many ways to their comfort, for tables are no longer heaped high with huge volumes rendering it difficult to find working space. Tables and floors are not littered with showers of wood pulp. The disheveled appearance common to newspaper rooms is disappearing.[3]

The chief of the Newspaper Division in the New York Public Library analyzed the situation in the following terms:

> The advantages to the reader of the newspaper film as contrasted with the bound file are first, that the print of the newspaper as it appears on the screen is enlarged approximately 50 per cent above the size of the print in the paper itself. Again, the definition of the letters and figures on the screen is much sharper and clearer. This is especially noticeable in the case of financial quotations on which so much research work in a newspaper division is done. Then, the reader does not have to crane his neck to read the top of the newspaper page on the screen as he must when the volume is laid flat on a table or, even, if it is placed on a sloping table or easel.[4]

[2]*Report of the New York Public Library* 1934 (New York, 1935), p.44–45.
[3]*Report of the New York Public Library* 1939 (New York, 1940), p.63.
[4]Louis H. Fox, "Films for Folios," *Library Journal* 62:364 (1937).

Fox also reported improved service to readers, especially when more than one volume must be consulted:

> It was certainly much easier and quicker to take the film spool 3 11/16 inches in diameter and 1 3/8 inches in thickness from its box and insert this spool in the projector than to give a reader a seventeen-pound bound volume of the *New York Times.* The saving in time, when several volumes were wanted, was considerable.[5]

So successful was the transition from the bound volume to the microfilm that in 1941 the New York Public Library transferred its newspaper collection to a storage library. The microfilm collection of newspapers is all that has remained in the main building and is what readers have used almost exclusively since that time.

Clearly the case has been made for the microreproduction of back files of newspapers, and exclusively on the score of convenience to readers. The list of benefits to readers includes: (1) the increased size of the type as it appears on the screen; (2) the sharper and clearer definition of the characters; (3) the speed-up in service; (4) the ability to scan a page without having to crane one's neck; (5) working quarters that are not disheveled by the chaff which constantly falls from decaying wood-pulp paper; and (6) no need to lift volumes that weigh from seventeen to twenty-five pounds. In this recital by the New York Public Library no mention whatsoever was made of the saving in storage space, presumably because libraries have always been ready to find the space to store the valued and extensive files of bound newspapers.

This experience supports the argument that, apart from newspapers and other items on poor paper, libraries must generally plan to acquire and preserve the actual publications themselves in so far as they can be obtained by the most diligent and enterprising of methods. It may be entertaining to speak of the twilight of the printed book, but collection and dissemination of the printed page must be the primary objective of libraries as long as writers and research people are individuals who prefer to gather their data with as little regimentation as possible. It is still true, as Goethe said, that talent develops in quietude, character in the stream of the world.

[5]*Ibid.*, p.363. Cf. also Fox's "Turn a Handle and Get Your Page," *Library Journal* 60:675 (1935). In this he says: "Handling the film is, of course, infinitely easier than carrying a bulky newspaper volume weighing from 17 to 25 pounds and this results in greatly accelerating service to the reader."

Microfilm and Microfiche

Easily the most satisfactory form of microreproduction for serial files is microfilm and, to a lesser extent, its offshoot, microfiche. Microfilm has been successful in many large-scale serial projects: archives, government publications, newspapers, and periodicals, in particular. It is the preferred form in North America, whereas microfiche tends to be more highly regarded in Europe. Photocopies can be made readily from either form.

Microfilming of newspapers, which got the whole microreproduction program under way in the 1930s, has been undertaken in a number of centers to preserve papers, especially those of an area. In some instances publishers have arranged for the microfilming of their newspapers; in others, associations and institutions have accepted the responsibility, among them the Boston Public Library, the Canadian Library Association, the Center for Research Libraries, the Library of Congress, the Research Libraries of the New York Public Library, and the University of California Library. The Center for Research Libraries took over the project started at Harvard in 1938 whereby the leading newspapers from various countries are microfilmed for the benefit of North American libraries. Reels may be borrowed from the Center when they are wanted for local consultation. The Union Catalog Division of the Library of Congress publishes a union list of *Newspapers on Microfilm*. Companion publications are the *Microfilming Clearing House Bulletin* and the *National Register of Microform Masters*.

Since 1941 University Microfilms has reproduced some six thousand serial titles. It has covered many of the sets in thirty-two indexing services, including the *Wellesley Index to Victorian Periodicals*. It has six important series: American periodicals, the Civil War and Reconstruction, early British periodicals—creative arts, general, and literary—and English literary periodicals. The value of these undertakings can be gauged by the following statement, which was made in connection with the American periodicals for the years 1800–25:

> Good portions of the existing Americana must be had in the form of facsimiles if they are to be had at all; this is especially true of periodicals. Older libraries, fortunate enough to have the originals, control the supply; yet few can boast. It was necessary to use the resources of seventy-six libraries to complete the series under consideration. Except the Library of Congress, no single institution holds complete files of more than 30 per cent of the titles.[6]

[6]Robert E. Booth, "American Periodicals, 1800–1825; University Microfilms Commences a New Series," *Library Journal* 71:156 (1946).

University Microfilms has also devised a scheme for libraries to acquire microfilm in lieu of binding and preserving certain titles to which they subscribe.

Other producers are the American Society for Information Science (up to 1967 the American Documentation Institute), Bell and Howell, and the National Archives. With its duopage system, Bell and Howell can provide replacement copies needed for binding when there are missing or mutilated issues.

Microcards and Microprint

There are two opaque forms of microprint, both of which have the disadvantage that blow-ups cannot be readily made from them. The microcard in its inception was the most highly publicized method of microcopying. Unfortunately, it is the least satisfactory form for serials. Wilcox makes special mention of "the constant filing and refiling of 3 by 5 cards, and the tantalizing problem of misfiling."[7] One consumer suggested that microcards might be tied together, and the reaction of the Microcard Foundation was:

> It is true that a single tiny card is more easily mislaid than a fat book. And, for that reason, we are inclined to advocate that one's "microcard library" be maintained on a "closed stack" basis, i.e. as a file from which cards may be removed, and into which cards may be filed, only by a trained staff member. . . .
>
> It must furthermore always be remembered that one of the great advantages of microcards is that they offer material for use in small units, just as it is one of the great disadvantages of conventional, thick, periodical volumes, and of long reels of periodical film, that they tie up with one user a lot of material which he is not using but which he is keeping other library patrons from using. In other words, the more "separable" we make our research materials, the more usable we make them. This means that the moment we "bind" microcards together in any way we tend to destroy this flexibility and so to cancel one of their advantages.[8]

For current serials microcards can be supplied more promptly than microfilm can, the reason being that a single issue of a periodical may be microcarded while microfilm is delayed until completion of a volume. Microcards for *Newsweek* have been made weekly, for the Patent Office *Gazette* monthly, and for the *Federal Register* quarterly.

7Jerome K. Wilcox, "The Point of View of the Librarian," *American Documentation* 2:163 (1951).

8"Keeping Microcards in 'Bound' 'Volumes,'" *Microcard Bulletin* 7:8 (1951).

Microcards did not work out for newspapers. The Louisville Free Public Library had the *Louisville Courier-Journal* microcarded from 15 February 1949 through 15 February 1953. Shoemaker, in comparing the microcard and microfilm editions of the paper, points out that there are ten pages on each microcard compared with eight hundred on a reel of microfilm. For anyone who wants to go through the file of a paper, this means eighty loadings and unloadings for the microcards as against one for the microfilm. A full page of newspaper can be seen on the microfilm reading machine and only a quarter page on the microcard screen, so that four moves per page are necessary instead of one. He concludes that microfilming is the best method known today for the preservation of newspapers.[9]

Readex microprint cards are larger than microcards, so that there are fewer of them proportionately. They are housed neatly in cardboard boxes. There are three important items of serial interest in microprint form: the British House of Commons *Sessional Papers*, United Nations documents and, beginning with 1953, the current nondepository United States documents.

There has been much rivalry among the manufacturers of microreproductions. Consequently the same title may be available in more than one form. When duplication occurs, in general it is wiser to favor microfilm because of the relative ease with which a blow-up can be made from it.

Cataloging Microreproductions

A serial file can be a number of original issues or volumes eked out by microcopies, or it can be a complete microreproduction. Because there are mixed situations, it is wiser to catalog microcopies as though they were originals and to indicate the parts that are microreproductions. When the complete file is a microcopy, then the call number with the prefix "Film," "Microcard," "Microfiche," or "Microprint" suffices to disclose the form of the publication. The Library of Congress likes to specify whether a film is positive or negative and to give the size in centimeters for opaques. In general these refinements are not necessary elsewhere.

There should be a catalog or book-catalog entry for all titles in collections such as the American periodical series issued by University

[9]Ralph J. Shoemaker, "Remarks on Microcards and Microfilm for Newspapers," *American Documentation* 1:207–208 (1950).

Microfilms. Analyticals are not necessary for comprehensive programs, e.g., the set of United Nations documents.

Microcards, microfiche, and microprint are arranged archivally or alphabetically. Microfilm should be in two series: closed entries, which can be intercalated with books, and open entries with room left for future additions, e.g., the additional reels of the *New York Times* that can be anticipated year by year.

A Cooperative Program

In the late 1960s a group of college libraries in Colorado, Illinois, Iowa, Minnesota, and Wisconsin established a cooperative microfilm program with headquarters in the Newberry Library in Chicago. The undertaking was financed through the sale of bound sets from the shelves of the twelve cooperating libraries, as well as through a foundation grant. In 1970 there were 1,778 titles in the system, as disclosed by the second edition of the *Periodical Bank Holdings List*, twenty-five copies of which were made available to each member library. The purpose is rapid supply of photocopies. The theory behind the development is expressed by Williams as follows:

> At the midrange of costs found in the four libraries studied, and for a serial title with an annual subscription price of $20 (the average price per title found in the study), unless the title is used more than about six times per year, it is less expensive for the library to acquire a photocopy of articles from it when needed than to maintain its own subscription and file. . . . The saving to the library borrowing rather than subscribing to a title used an average of only once a year amounts to about $50 per title per year.[10]

Bibliography

Clapp, Verner W., and Jordan, R. T. "Reevaluation of Microfilm as a Method of Book Storage," *College and Research Libraries* 24:5–15 (1963).
Davinson, D. E. "Micro-Recordings," in his *The Periodicals Collection; Its Purpose and Uses in Libraries*, p.136–42. London: Deutsch, 1969.
Grenfell, David. *Periodicals and Serials; Their Treatment in Special Libraries*, p.65–74. 2d ed. London: Aslib, 1965.

[10]Gordon Williams, *Library Cost Models: Owning Versus Borrowing Serial Publications* (Chicago: Center for Research Libraries, 1968), p.iv.

Hawken, W. R. *Enlarged Prints from Library Microforms.* Chicago: American Library Assn., 1965.

Jolley, Leonard. "The Use of Microfilm for Completing Sets," *Journal of Documentation* 4:41–44 (1948).

Sale, Robert C. "Is Binding the Answer?" *Special Libraries* 42:380, 394 (1951).

5

Reference Aspects of Serial Publications

18

Reference Work

Many reference questions are answered with the aid of serial publications; that is, readers and staff constantly find their information in reference books that are serials in their own right, serials that are listed as reference works in Winchell and similar tools. Still other reference work has to do with the problems and routines which are involved as readers seek serials, or photocopies from serials, as part of their research activities. Included in this category are matters such as the interpretation of citations which are given in abbreviated, obscure, or translated form; the locating and acquisition of translations of periodical articles; and union-list operations that are connected with interlibrary loan or the procurement of photocopies.

Reference Work with the Aid of Serials

The prevalence of serials for reference work in the narrow sense of the term can be seen from even a glance at Winchell's *Guide to Reference Books;* its British counterpart, which is Walford's *Guide to Reference Material;* the French Malclès, the German Totok, and so on. For quick reference work serials play their part through titles such as *Books in Print,* the *Information Please Almanac,* and *Who's Who in America.* The stock-in-trade for standard reference work consists in no small measure of abstracting and indexing services, annuals, directories, government publications, newspaper indexes, statistical works, trade and national bibliographies, who's whos, and a host of other serial publications.

Special mention should be made of the reference role performed by cumulated indexes to periodicals. So useful are they that in 1942 the New York Public Library issued *A Check List of Cumulative Indexes to Individual Periodicals in the New York Public Library.* In public libraries it is customary to keep the series of cumulated indexes to the *National Geographic Magazine* in the reference collection or among the quick-reference books to be able to refer readers to colored plates on a wide variety of subjects.

A valuable starting point for reference work with the aid of serials, unfortunately no longer up to date, is Roberts' *Introduction to Reference Books.*[1] Among general manuals on reference librarianship this book is unusual in that more than half of it relates to the ways in which serials contribute to effective reference work.

The beginner at the reference desk must apply himself diligently and systematically in order to acquire the insights and skills which are necessary if serials are to be exploited to the full. Beatrice Simon maintains that the best preparation is "a stiff apprenticeship in some scientific research or business library"[2] where serial activities are the order of the day. And Kaplan points out that it is of fundamental consequence for reference librarians, as part of their training, to obtain first-hand knowledge of the periodicals themselves, not merely of the abstracts and indexes and how to use them to advantage. He says: "The truth is that it is not even possible to use the indexes efficiently without intimate knowledge of the periodicals."[3] It is certainly true that all too many serials in most fields are not covered by abstracting and indexing services, in part or in full, so that contributions in them can be overlooked if recourse is not made to the serials themselves; also, a journal's own index, including its cumulative index, may well be more exhaustive than is the coverage of almost any service. The search for a poem, e.g., to run down copyright data, may be more successful through consultation of actual periodicals rather than through indexing services, although both approaches should be made.

---

[1]Arthur D. Roberts, *Introduction to Reference Books* (2d ed.; London: The Library Assn., 1951). Because Roberts has made so notable a contribution, this chapter is much briefer than it otherwise might have been. He was the talented reference librarian in the United Nations Library in the 1940s and 1950s to whom UN personnel continually turned for expert help. Chapter 9 in David Grenfell's *Periodicals and Serials; Their Treatment in Special Libraries* (2d ed.; London: Aslib, 1965), p.147–82, is another important though shorter contribution to reference work with serials.

[2]Beatrice V. Simon, "Let's Consider Serials Realistically," *Library Journal* 71:1301 (1946).

[3]Louis Kaplan, "Reference Work with Periodicals: Recent Progress and Future Needs," *College and Research Libraries* 1:244 (1940).

There are two fairly common ways in which the reference staff makes use of serials to supply nonserial information. One is the consultation of newspaper indexes to discover when an event took place. The indexes can answer many quick-reference questions, just as they can disclose the approximate starting time for a literature search in abstracting and indexing services. The other, largely a telephone function, consists of informing small bookstores of the names of publishers of given books. The running down of publishers' names can consume much time because a search may have to be made in the various volumes of tools such as *Book Publishing Record Cumulative, Books in Print, British Books in Print,* the *Cumulative Book Index, Forthcoming Books,* the *National Union Catalog, Paperbound Books in Print,* the *Publishers' Trade List Annual,* and *Textbooks in Print.* Because of the amount of work involved, big city libraries often say that they cannot provide this type of service over the telephone, but that the reference works are readily available to those who will come to the library to make the searches for themselves.

Prior to World War II the annual reports of the New York Public Library afforded a valuable record of the way in which reference interests varied markedly from year to year at the same time that there was a solid base of constantly recurring questions. Certain of the *Annual Reports of the Librarian of Congress* and of the Departmental & Divisional Manuals, as cited in chapter 14, give insight into reference activities in the Library of Congress. Comparative experience of this kind should be discovered by reference librarians through reading and personal contacts with colleagues.

Serials are also basic for reference work in the larger sense in which all the resources of an institution are exploited. Here the pendulum may, in research libraries, swing in favor of serials over books. "The larger the library," says McCombs, "the greater the proportion of periodicals and pamphlets—those foundation stones of a research collection—and the more numerous the government publications from the far corners of the earth."[4]

As soon as a library aspires to be something more than a mere circulation agency, it must acquire and exploit serial publications. The Montclair (New Jersey) Public Library learned this fact from a survey, one of whose recommendations was: "You should certainly largely increase the number and variety of the current periodicals in

[4]Charles F. McCombs, "The Reference Function in the Large Public Library," in Pierce Butler, ed., *The Reference Function of the Library; Papers Presented before the Library Institute at the University of Chicago, June 29 to July 10, 1942* (Chicago: Univ. of Chicago Pr., [1943]), p.18.

your several reading rooms, main library and branches."[5] It responded by nearly doubling the budget for magazine subscriptions, developing a collection of 229 periodicals around the six outstanding periodical indexes, and emphasizing the purchase of yearbooks and other continuations. In 1971, some thirty-five years later, the figure of 229 had risen to 800, and the library maintains back files for approximately 700. About seventy-five of the number are on microfilm; there are three microfilm readers and a reader-printer to service the resource.

Equally effective was the locating and recording of serial resources in neighboring libraries and in commercial institutions in the vicinity, as well as the acquisition of the next-to-the-latest issue of many serials when they were discarded in those institutions. These activities should be carried out in communities in general to enrich the services and holdings of the local public library. The original program at Montclair was as follows:

> Recently reference purchases have taken cognizance of the library's ability to locate material in the immediate vicinity with a reasonable degree of speed. In consequence the library has been working to produce various substitutes for regional shelf lists. So far the Montclair Library has:
>
> 1. Catalogue cards in the main public catalogue of all books in the Montclair Art Museum, a half mile distant
>
> 2. A union list of some 680 magazines in 32 public and semi-public institutions of Montclair, and the terms under which these magazines will be loaned
>
> 3. A union list of newspapers on file in all libraries within a ten-cent fare of Montclair
>
> 4. A record of the holdings of the subscriptions of local banks to financial services, such as Moody's
>
> 5. The Granger and Granger supplement holdings of seven public libraries in the vicinity
>
> A reader who is not adequately served at the Montclair Library, or who believes that all material at his local library has been studied, does not need to take the long trip to New York only to find that he may not borrow books in the city library to take home, or that the collection he really needs to examine is in another building perhaps several miles away. If given the opportunity, the information assistant will direct such an inquirer to the special library which best suits his need and equip him with time-saving bibliographic references.[6]

[5] Margery C. Quigley and William E. Marcus, *Portrait of a Library* (New York: Appleton, [1936]), p.172.

[6] *Ibid.*, p.41–42.

The Public Library of Fort Wayne and Allen County, Indiana, has for many years demonstrated the contribution which government serial publications can make to the general reference program of a public library. The following are some recent reader requests which were filled from serial sources:[7]

REQUEST	WHERE THE ANSWER WAS FOUND
Address of the Seafarers' International Union of North America	Bureau of Labor Statistics, *Bulletin* 1665: *Directory of National and International Labor Unions in the United States*
Altitude of Des Moines, Iowa	Interior Department, Geological Survey, *Bulletin* 274: *Directory of Altitudes in the United States*
Average salary of keypunch operators	Bureau of Labor Statistics, *Bulletin* 1693: *National Survey of Professional, Administrative, Technical, and Clerical Pay,* June 1970
Explanation of farm parity	Agriculture Department, *Miscellaneous Publication* 1063: *Factbook of United States Agriculture,* 1970
How to drill a well	Department of the Army, *Technical Manual 5–297: Wells*
How to raise earthworms	Agriculture Department, *Farmers' Bulletin* 1569: *Earthworms as Pests and Otherwise*
Information about waterwitching	Interior Department, Geological Survey, *Water-supply Paper* 416: *The Divining Rod*
Operation of a flower store	Small Business Administration, *Starting and Managing Series* 18: *Starting and Managing a Retail Flower Shop*
Selective Service medical standards	Department of the Army, *Army Regulation AR 40–501: Medical Services Standards of Fitness*

Development and exploitation of the serial bookstock in a manner such as has been undertaken in the Public Library of Fort Wayne and

[7]Cf. Mary Armstrong, "Documents Please Fort Wayne Patrons," *Wilson Library Bulletin* 23:319 (1948). The list of requests and answers included in that article was reproduced in the first edition of *Serial Publications*, p.218.

Allen County can lend a touch of distinction to smaller libraries, opening up to them some of the serial resources of larger ones. Even in school and small public libraries steps should be taken to obtain worthwhile free and inexpensive government publications and to turn them to good advantage for reference and circulation purposes. The price lists issued by the Superintendent of Documents should be checked regularly, as should lists of state and local publications. John L. Andriot's *Guide to Popular U. S. Government Publications* (Arlington, Va.: Documents Index, 1960), and his *Guide to U.S. Government Serials and Periodicals* (4v. and supplements; McLean, Va.: Documents Index, 1964–), should be put to good use. Also of value are Ellen Jackson's *Subject Guide to Major United States Government Publications* (Chicago: American Library Assn., 1968) and W. Philip Leidy's *A Popular Guide to Government Publications* (3d ed.; New York: Columbia Univ. Pr., 1965). American libraries are able to obtain many United States documents free simply by asking the congressman or senator for their area for them.

Programs of this kind bring a sense of satisfaction to librarians who make the most of every potentiality. Hence the importance of building up the bibliographical apparatus of a library, because hidden wealth can often be uncovered by means of specialized reference tools. On occasion a tool may be a local manuscript record, e.g., a bibliography on a current or emerging topic with references drawn to a considerable extent from serial publications; it can be an index to committee prints and congressional hearings that are on hand; or it can be a union list of serials in local or regional libraries. The enterprising reference librarian is incessantly on the lookout for printed or locally prepared tools to open up serial literature to readers and staff alike.

Reference Work Concerning Serials

The reference staff is constantly called upon to help readers who have serial problems of one kind or another. Some of the more common serial services to readers are the following: (1) Readers who consult recent abstracting and indexing services from time to time require aid in locating periodicals which have left the current shelves but have not yet been added to the bound sets in the stacks. The binding records may show that an item is in the bindery or on its way to or from the bindery; if not, a search may have to be made in the catalog department or in the end processes. (2) Particularly in special libraries, the staff is regularly asked to discover whether a translation of a journal article or another document exists. Some of the services it employs for the purpose are discussed later in the chapter. (3) Activities with union lists of serials can be quite extensive. Files must be located for interlibrary loan or, increasingly today, to have a photocopy made. On the receiving end, skill may be required to interpret interlibrary loan and photocopy requests. (4) Readers frequently must be aided in obtaining items in kept-together monograph series or periodicals which have been indexed in the catalog, the reason being that they may fail to note the serial title and volume numbering on their call slips. Sometimes the reader must be asked to find the catalog entry again, more especially when subject analyticals only have been made, a fairly common experience in the Research Libraries of the New York Public Library. (5) Reference librarians generally take responsibility for the self-cataloging collections which are discussed later in this chapter. (6) The staff compiles timely bibliographies, which are apt to include citations from unindexed as well as indexed periodicals. (7) Abstracting and indexing services may be annotated to show which journals are in the main and departmental collections or in another resource in the neighborhood.

In addition, reference librarians have much to do with finding or interpreting serial entries in the card catalog, a good and sufficient reason for giving up catalog cards and relying on book catalogs for serial holdings, because it is easier to locate desired titles in book catalogs than on cards. In the Harvard College Library the head of the reference service used to make a point of telling new members of his staff that the most important preparation for their job was to become fully conversant with the technicalities of serial cataloging. It should be noted that the corporate entry is considered to be the single most troublesome element in reader use of catalog cards for serials. Yale cautions its staff by saying that "a cataloger must keep in mind that serials cataloged under corporate entries are difficult for readers to find."[8] With this in mind, then, catalogers at Yale are expected to make added entries for serials cataloged under a corporate name whenever such entries will be helpful to readers, a policy which is not always followed in other institutions. For instance, catalogers are generally unwilling to make an entry under an acronym that is not on the pieces themselves.

The most technical aspect of work concerning serials which the reference librarian must face arises from requests for help in inter-

[8]Yale University Library, *Cataloging of Serials in the Yale University Library* (3d ed.; New Haven, Conn., 1969), p.28.

preting the names of serials which have been cited in abbreviated form, official or unofficial, or names which have been otherwise altered or translated from the original, the last named being a fairly common practice, e.g., in the citation of titles in Japanese, Slavic, and other languages thought to be difficult. Miss Kinney says:

> Brief, cryptic bibliographical forms of citation to serials, classic works, and research and development reports are used extensively in the documentation of papers, dissertations, and books. In many subject fields, the coded references become major puzzles in locating the citation, and the abbreviations are confusing to those not thoroughly familiar with the field covered. . . .
>
> Cryptic, abbreviated citations cause confusion when the references are too brief and when the same abbreviation is used for different words. Decoding shortened-form citations for periodicals and initialisms standing for standard works poses problems. Fortunately, reference librarians are trained to pursue clues. The title of the article may be the only clue to a possible subject field; the appearance of the abbreviated citation in a given work may be the key to a source to consult; a personal name may be significant to pursue; the prefatory remarks in a publication or a single footnote may reveal that a title is given in its full bibliographical form the first time mentioned and thereafter abbreviated. So far as periodicals are concerned, the *Union List of Serials* and *New Serial Titles* may prove helpful in decoding an abbreviated periodical title, if one is astute to the word order and to the normal method of abbreviating, which is to omit a continuous group of the final letters of the word. Such approaches are seldom considered by the uninitiated student or the general public. Bibliographical methodology and bibliographical sources may be unknown to them.[9]

A valuable feature of Miss Kinney's book is the annotated list of ninety-four tools that can serve as sources for identification of abbreviated citations, as well as the list of fifteen tools for work with citations encountered in dealing with technical reports.

It is not possible to detail all the ways in which reference librarians resolve the problems caused by abbreviated and obscure serial citations. Each case seems to pose fresh difficulties, and in many instances solutions can be reached in several different ways. Nevertheless, the reference techniques involved with citations can to some extent be elaborated or illustrated as follows.

[9]Mary R. Kinney, *The Abbreviated Citation—A Bibliographical Problem* (ACRL Monograph no.28 [Chicago: American Library Assn., 1967]), p.1, 5–6.

1. The first step always is to rationalize the data on hand to see what clues they offer or what clues may be hypothesized from them. For instance, at Harvard a reader had footnote references in the same article to ZDMG and BSOS. The riddle began to be solved when it was thought that *Z* very likely stood for *Zeitschrift*. If it did, ZDMG was German, and perhaps *D* stood for an inflected form of the adjective *deutsch*. Guessing still further, *G* could possibly stand for *Gesellschaft*. Looking in the *Union List of Serials* for a *Deutsche m . . . Gesellschaft*, it was seen that the *Deutsche morgenländische Gesellschaft* was the obvious candidate, all the more so because the article was in the field of Asian studies. Success in the first instance gave added confidence in solving the second. *Bulletin* seemed a good guess for *B*, and because of the confirmed subject field *O* would almost certainly stand for *Oriental*. Pretty surely, too, it would be an English adjective qualifying a following noun, since French word order would tend to place *Oriental* last. It was then possible to suppose that BSOS stood for the *Bulletin of the School of Oriental Studies,* which actually was the case, but this serial is cataloged under "London. University." Belatedly it was noted that ZDMG, but not BSOS, occurs in Werner Rust's *Verzeichnis von unklaren Titelkürzungen deutscher und ausländischer Zeitschriften* (Leipzig: Harrassowitz, 1927). Operating through Rust in the first instance would have proved to be an equally satisfactory method.

Another example of rationalization involved a zoology professor who knew only the author and title, in French, of an article on birds. He felt that the quest was hopeless, but wondered if by chance there was anything that the reference staff could do. Here the assumption was that a scholarly article was apt to appear in a French learned-society publication. Winchell was accordingly checked for the index to these publications, and there the item was found through the index entry under the author's name. The full bibliographical entry was provided in less than ten minutes.

Sometimes the technique is to inquire of colleagues at the reference desk, especially experienced hands, whether they have encountered the problem before and whether they may even have noted the solution. Such, for example, was the case at Harvard with the *Annales Academiae Scientiarum Fennicae.* By word of mouth sooner or later everyone at the Reference Desk learned by heart the spelling of the Finnish entry under which the work had to be sought, "Suomalainen Tiedeakatemia, Toimituksia." In this serial the Finnish title does appear on the title page and comes first, although non-Finns are virtually unanimous in preferring the Latin alternative. Even the rare person who copied the Finnish heading would have had trouble in the catalog because of a case difference from *Suomalaisen,* which files an inch away. Another example of the same kind from the same part of the world has the title page, or at least the added title page, purely in Latin, whereas the publication can be found in the catalog only by discovering a corporate heading in Swedish to which there are no cross-references from the Latin forms. This is the *Acta Instituti Hungarici Universitatis Holmiensis,* which is entered in the catalog under "Stockholm. Universitetet. Ungerska Institutet." There is no reference "Holmia, see Stockholm"; no "Universitas Holmiensis, see Stockholm. Universitetet"; and, perhaps worst from a practical point of view, no reference "Stockholm. Universitetet. Institutum Hungaricum, see Stockholm. Universitetet. Ungerska Institutet." Only the skill of the reference librarian, direct or imparted to a colleague, or similar skill exercised by an unusually ingenious reader will ever uncover the catalog entry for this publication.

2. When the citation is secondhand, it is often wise to ask the reader, in person or by correspondence, the source from which the information was taken. In some cases the problem can be solved by a double check on the original source. One practice which is in fairly wide use is for the author to cite a serial in full when the footnote occurs for the first time in an article, book, or chapter; then in later citations the reference is drastically curtailed. So a check back to the first appearance of the reference may provide the needed information. Another device followed by authors is to list, at the beginning or ending of the publication, the special abbreviations which they have contrived in order to save space. German reference books in particular are noteworthy for the abbreviations and symbols which they employ in the interests of compactness; in consulting Beilstein, a periodical index, or a who's who, it is almost essential to find the key to the system employed.

3. The tools listed by Mary Kinney in her *The Abbreviated Citation,* which was mentioned above, should be consulted, and the list should be constantly updated.

4. When other devices fail, the standard procedure is to seek another and better citation to the article, monograph, paper, or technical report. This technique operates through abstracting and indexing services as well as bibliographies of all kinds; it requires the reference librarian to utilize every conceivable aid and clue available. It may be that the librarian is confronted by an author who is represented by surname and initials only, a brief title which is probably truncated if not hopelessly garbled, and a wildly abbreviated citation to a German scientific periodical. If further work establishes that the author in question was a nineteenth-century

writer on hydraulics, a very likely and hopeful place to look under the author's name is the Royal Society's *Catalogue of Scientific Papers, 1800–1900*. If the paper appears to be, from an examination of the title, a mid-twentieth-century study in organic chemistry, then one possible avenue would be to consult the cumulated author indexes to *Chemical Abstracts*; if in engineering, then *Engineering Abstracts*; and if in physics, perhaps *Physics Abstracts*. The point is simply this: that often a successful effort to decode a garbled or an absurdly abbreviated serial citation involves a search for a good and reliable entry in any one of literally thousands of specialized abstracting and indexing services, bibliographies, and checklists.

Special mention should be made of the effectiveness of works such as the *World List of Scientific Periodicals* which arrange their entries by key word or title, rather than by corporate entry as the *Union List of Serials* does. The *British Union Catalogue of Periodicals* belongs in this category; and a major library like Harvard has found the *Catalogue of Union Periodicals,* "Union" in this case being the then Union of South Africa, quite useful because of its entry by key word. This is not to say that key-word entry is better than corporate author or title, but it is a decidedly useful alternative. Computer-produced KWIC indexes of periodical titles would in fact be quite helpful in solving obscure references, because very often there is at least one word, often not the first, which may be guessed at with some degree of confidence.

There is another work which is particularly valuable in seeking a good and reliable citation to an article whose author and title are known but whose location is excessively abbreviated. This is Arnim's *Internationale Personalbibliographie*. Of course this is a two-stage process, but reference librarians are accustomed to making multistage searches.

5. When a citation is being verified for an item in a monograph series, the serial approach is generally to be preferred to the author and title. Readers are apt to depend on the author and title, reference librarians on the serial data. This technique comes into play from time to time with interlibrary loan requests. One reason for its effectiveness is that the work in question may belong to an unanalyzed monograph series. When a French book was requested in the Research Libraries of the New York Public Library, recourse to the *Bibliographie de la France* disclosed what the reader did not know, namely, that the item belonged in the monograph series *Cahiers de la quinzaine*. This better and fuller entry allowed the volume to be produced from the stacks; also, a decision was made to analyze the set.

6. The chronological conspectus of periodicals is another aid in interpreting incomplete and inaccurate citations. When the year of publication is known, or known approximately, it is possible in some instances to decipher a citation with a minimum of effort by consulting a conspectus and going through the list of titles which were published at that time. Tables of this kind occur in Beilstein's *Handbuch der organischen Chemie*; H. C. Bolton's *Catalogue of Scientific and Technical Periodicals, 1665–1895*; and *Poole's Index to Periodical Literature*, which covers the period 1802 through 1906. Also, as an aid to reference work in the libraries at the Oak Ridge National Laboratory in Tennessee, Helen H. Mason in 1954 issued *Synchronistic Tables of Selected Journals in the Oak Ridge National Laboratory Libraries, 1880–1950*. Her conspectus is intended in a limited way to complement Bolton's chronological tables.

Examples of Problems with Citations

Phyllis Richmond, who uses the expression "Misery is a short footnote" to indicate the troubles reference librarians may have with citations, says:

> In scientific writing, one functions on the principle that footnotes should be as short as it is humanly possible to make them. The result is that scientific literature is full of the most fascinating secret code for footnotes, particularly when reference is made to journal or report literature.
>
> Scientists employ initialisms as much as possible. Everyone is familiar with good old JOSA, PR, NOHC, AIEE, CA, PNAS, GSA, AFIPS and AAPG. They omit not only months from their citations, but series, sections, parts, numbers, volumes—in fact, everything but pages in some instances. Where issues of a journal are not paged continuously in a volume (some are still issued this way), this secret code is almost unbreakable.
>
> Books by corporate authors or conferences, seminars and congresses are not permitted to discourage anyone, even if several pages have to be perused to find a personal name to use as author. Subdivisions of corporate authors are almost always omitted, ensuring that there shall be several separate publications which can be identified by a single footnote. This is pure genius in economy. . . . Abbreviations make for a field day. They are obvious. Of course, but to whom? Place and publisher vanish all right, especially with governmental report literature where nothing is given but some hieroglyphics and a number. What fun for the Inter-Library Loan librarian! . . . Everything is published on the assumption that there

can never be a typographical error in a footnote, so no bits of information that could be used as check points mar the beauty of the brevity. Are the footnotes usable? Ask a citation indexer.[10]

Mrs. Richmond gives the following list of abbreviations, all of them taken from the *Physical Review*:

Am Chem Phys
Ann Math Monthly
L'Astrophysik
J Phys Math
J Sci USSR
Phys Bull
Physica Deil
Proc Cop
Wiss Ber Univ Mosh

She also cites the following extremely ambiguous names:

Acad of Sci USSR: 89 possible journals at least
Acad. Polonaise Sci. et Lettres Bull: 9 possible journals
Amsterdam Roy Acad Sci: 9 possible journals
Izvest Bulgar Acad Nauk: 23 possible journals
Preuss Akad der Wissensch: 28 possible journals
Sitzenber Akad Wiss Wien Math-Naturw Kl: 13 possible
    journals

She also gives the citation "Fachgruppen II," which proved to be "Akademie der Wissenschaften, Göttingen. Mathematisch-physikalische Klasse. Nachrichten. 2: Physik, Astronomie, Geophysik, Technik. Neue Folge."

Crane, Patterson, and Marr say:

The farther back one goes in the chemical literature the more difficult it becomes to identify journals from the abbreviations used for their names. To add to the confusion that resulted from a lack of system and standards, it was once a rather common custom to refer to a journal by the name of its current editor. So the older literature references to what seem to be different journals turn out to be

---

[10]Phyllis A. Richmond, "Misery Is a Short Footnote," *Library Resources & Technical Services* 9:221 (1965).

a number of references to the same journal edited by different men through a period of time.[11]

Rogers and Charen[12] note the six ways in which *Albrecht von Graefes Archiv für Ophthalmologie* has been listed in four abstracting and indexing services and two union lists, with only the last of them being really helpful:

Chemical Abstracts: *Arch. Ophthalmol, Graefe's*
Index-Catalogue of the Surgeon-General's Library: *Arch. Ophth., Berl.*
Index Medicus: *Graefe Arch. Ophthal.*
Quarterly Cumulative Index Medicus: *von Graefes Arch. Ophth.*
World List of Scientific Periodicals: *v. Graefes Arch. Ophthal.*
World Medical Periodicals: *Albrecht v. Graefes Arch. Ophthal.*

The following are examples encountered by reference librarians in the University of Chicago Bio-Medical Libraries in response to reader requests. The list shows the abbreviated form of the title as presented by a reader, followed by the catalog entry which the staff uncovered.

CITATION	CATALOG ENTRY
Acta horti botanici	Riga. Latvijas Universitate. Botaniska darzs. *Raksti*
Acta soc. scien. fen.	Finska Vetenskaps-societeten, Helsingfors. *Acta*
Arb. a. d. Reichsgesundheitsamt	Germany. Reichsgesundheitsamt. *Arbeiten*
Arb. neur. Inst. Wien Univ.	Vienna. Universität. Neurologisches Institut. *Arbeiten*
Arch. arg. ped.	*Archivos argentinos de pediatria*
Bol. inst. clin. quir.	Buenos Aires. Universidad nacional. Instituto de clinica quirúrgica. *Boletin*
Bul. Commonwealth bur. meteor.	Australia. Bureau of Meteorology. *Bulletin*
Jour. cons. perm. int. exp. mer	International Council for the Study of the Sea. *Journal*

[11]E. J. Crane, A. M. Patterson, and Eleanor B. Marr, *A Guide to the Literature of Chemistry* (2d ed.; New York: Wiley, 1957), p.155.
[12]Frank B. Rogers and Thelma Charen, "Abbreviations for Medical Journal Titles," *Bulletin of the Medical Library Association* 50:331 (1962).

Jour. de phys. U.R.S.S.	*Fiziologicheskii Zhurnal SSSR*
Phys. jour. U.S.S.R.	*Fiziologicheskii Zhurnal SSSR*
Pubb. del R. Ist. di studi sup. Firenze	Florence. Universita. Sezione di scienze fisiche e naturali. *Pubblicazioni*
Rep. A. M. Gorky All-Union inst. exp. med.	Moscow. Vsesoiuznyi Institut Eksperimental'noi Meditsiny Imeni A. M. Gor'kogo. *Otchet*
Rep. pub. health and med. Stat. off.	Gt. Brit. Ministry of Health. *Reports*
Russian biochem. jour.	Vseukrains'ka Akademiia Nauk, Kiev. Institut Biokhimii. *Biokhimichnyi Zhurnal*
Russian jour. biochem.	*Biokhimiia*
Russian jour. physiol.	*Fiziologicheskii Zhurnal SSSR*
Zeit. Phys. Sov. Un.	*Fiziologicheskii Zhurnal SSSR*

Instruction in the Use of Serials

Students are fairly generally taught by the reference staff how to consult the more obvious periodical indexes and keys to serial publications; they are informed of outstanding serials in the reference collection. The most difficult task of all, however, is to make students, and above all graduate students, keenly aware of the abundance of information latent in serials.

Since the hope for the best utilization of library resources at advanced levels lies with the foundation instruction given at the secondary-school level, it is imperative that high school libraries be equipped with an adequate supply of serials, both document and nondocument, as well as some of the tools for use with these publications. In the words of Dr. Bishop:

> We ought to be able to assume that freshmen have learned in their preparatory school days how to consult a card catalog, how to make out an intelligent call [slip] for books, how to use Poole's "Index," and what encyclopaedias and bibliographies are for. This is but little in the way of equipment for serious study in a university or research library, but the want of just such an equipment on the part of students, and of readers in a public research library, confines much of the work of assistance to most elementary first aid to the injured.[13]

[13]William W. Bishop, *The Backs of Books, and Other Essays in Librarianship* (Baltimore: Williams & Wilkins, 1926), p.68–69.

Handbooks that explain to students how to use library facilities and resources have been developed and put to good use in school and college libraries. More should be prepared, and they should give full attention to serial publications. Somewhat similar handbooks for graduate students and faculty should be the next objective, handbooks such as the *Guides to the Harvard Libraries*.

There is, for example, a series published by the Pergamon Press with titles such as *How to Find Out; How to Find Out about the Arts; How to Find Out about Physics; How to Find Out: Educational Research; How to Find Out in Chemistry;* and *How to Find Out in History*.[14] Quite invaluable are exhaustive studies such as Karl Brown, *A Guide to the Reference Collections of the New York Public Library* (New York, 1941); the Special Libraries Association, *Special Library Resources* (New York, [1941]–47); and the writings of Robert B. Downs, particularly his *American Library Resources, a Bibliographical Guide* (Chicago: American Library Assn., 1951) and its supplements, 1950–61 (ALA, 1962) and 1961–70 (ALA, 1972), *Resources of New York City Libraries, a Survey of Facilities for Advanced Study and Research* (Chicago: American Library Assn., 1942), and *Resources of Southern Libraries, a Survey of Facilities for Research* (Chicago: American Library Assn., 1938).

Required Reading

The coming of undergraduate libraries has somewhat decreased the problem of the wear and tear on periodical sets as large numbers of students consult articles they are required to read. Irreplaceable volumes have been marked, mutilated, and otherwise damaged through the excessive use made of bound volumes of periodicals by whole classes of students. Photocopying is the solution to the problem: the provision of multiple copies which can be consulted until they are worn out and then can be replaced quite easily. Since conservation of the bookstock is the oldest function of the librarian, it is important to see that periodical files are used and not abused, so that they will be available to generations of research workers in the future.

---

[14] A list of these and similar publications in various fields of knowledge will be found in Wilfred Ashworth, ed., *Handbook of Special Librarianship and Information Work* (3d ed.; London: Aslib, 1967), p.445–49.

Self-Cataloging Serials

Certain types of publication in the general reference collection lend themselves to economical yet efficient handling through self-cataloging. The reference staff must assume a great deal of responsibility for the arrangement, maintenance, and servicing of these resources. Some self-cataloging material may be located in the book-stacks, the reference room, or vertical files. At times it is desirable to assign an overall class mark to the category, with running numbers for the individual items, to facilitate circulation, general access, shelving, and reshelving.

Types of self-cataloging material vary greatly, particularly in special libraries which make a feature of vertical-file systems. The more common types, not all of them serial in character, are art-exhibition catalogs, auction catalogs, booksellers' catalogs, city directories, college and university catalogs, corporation reports and financial statements, government publications, out-of-town telephone books, prospectuses of private schools, prospectuses of summer camps, and reprints of periodical articles.

City directories are best checklisted because their coverage is by no means systematic. A given place may be included in a certain directory one year, in another the next year, and the third year be omitted altogether. Apart from this factor, city directories, both current and old, can readily be found by anyone when they are grouped together and arranged by country, state, and principal locality, ignoring the vagaries of their titles and hence of their conventional catalog entries. The Research Libraries of the New York Public Library has developed its shelflist so that it can serve as a checklist. Form cards under the name of the city, followed by the subheading "Directories," can be a useful adjunct in the card catalog.

Translations

Well over fifteen thousand translations of journal articles are made each year, that figure representing the annual intake in the National Lending Library for Science and Technology. Indexing services for translations have grown in extent and importance, so that it is possible for the reference librarian to discover with reasonable accuracy whether a translation has already been made or not. The National Translations Center at the John Crerar Library, Chicago, is the principal repository in the United States, just as the National Lending Library is in Great Britain.

In 1969 the National Translations Center published a *Consolidated Index of Translations into English*; it covers most of the translations which were announced in earlier publications during the period 1953–66. From 1967 it has been complemented by the semimonthly *Translations Register-Index*, which lists new translations acquired by the Center. Beginning with 1968 it includes translations which are listed in the *U.S. Government Research and Development Reports* or reported directly by commercial translating agencies, of which there are some 470 in the United States and Canada, and translation pools, of which there are some 342. On receipt of a complete citation by mail, telephone, or teletype the Center will search its files to see whether and where an English-language translation is available. It will also make a literature search for all translated works of a given author or all translations from a particular journal, the cover-to-cover translations being naturally excluded. The Center provides either paper or microfilm copies of translations in its collection.

The Clearing House for Federal Scientific and Technical Information, which is in the Department of Commerce, publishes *Technical Translations* every two weeks. It lists all American and foreign items acquired by CFSTI, as well as items added by the European Translation Centre, whose headquarters are in Delft, Holland. The latter agency publishes a monthly list of *Translations Notified to ETC*, as well as a quarterly cumulative *World Index of Scientific Translations*.

The National Lending Library for Science and Technology supplies translations on loan or in the form of photocopies. It publishes a monthly *N.L.L. Translations Bulletin*, which records new acquisitions.

The social sciences are covered by the Joint Publications Research Service in Washington, D.C. Microcopies of JPRS material can be obtained through Research and Microfilm Publications, which has issued a *Guide to United States–JPRS Research Translations, 1957–1966.*

Bibliography

Grenfell, David. "Reference Work with Periodicals," in his *Periodicals and Serials; Their Treatment in Special Libraries*, p.147–82. 2d ed. London: Aslib, 1965.

Hanson, C. W. "Subject Inquiries and Literature Searching," in Wilfred Ashworth, ed., *Handbook of Special Librarianship and Information Work,* p.415–52. 3d ed. London: Aslib, 1967.

Roberts, Arthur D. *Introduction to Reference Books.* 2d ed. London: The Library Assn., 1951.

Strauss, Lucille J.; Shreve, Irene M.; and Brown, Alberta L. "Reference Procedures and Literature Searches" and "Interpreting Services to the Library's Public," in their *Scientific and Technical Libraries; Their Organization and Administration,* p.261–334. 2d ed. New York: Becker & Hayes, 1972.

Citations

Boylan, Nancy G. "Identifying Technical Reports through *U. S. Government Research Reports* and Its Published Indexes," *College and Research Libraries* 28:175–83 (1967).

Kinney, Mary R. *The Abbreviated Citation—A Bibliographical Problem.* (ACRL Monograph, no.28) Chicago: American Library Assn., 1967.

Richmond, Phyllis A. "Misery Is a Short Footnote," *Library Resources & Technical Services* 9:221–24 (1965).

Translations

Brock, C. "English Translations of Foreign Social Science Materials," *Library Journal* 91:1995–2000 (1966).

Davinson, D. E. "The Language Barrier," in his *The Periodicals Collection; Its Purpose and Uses in Libraries,* p.193–208. London: Deutsch, 1969.

Lucas, Rita, and Caldwell, George. "Joint Publications Research Translations," *College and Research Libraries* 25:103–10 (1964).

O'Keefe, W., and Jacoley, R. L. "Spend Your Translation Dollar Wisely," *Sci-Tech News* 21:6–7, 16 (1967).

Owens, Charlotte G. "Translations," in Isabel H. Jackson, ed., *Acquisition of Special Materials,* p.66–72. San Francisco: San Francisco Bay Region Chapter, Special Libraries Assn., 1966.

Pflueger, M. L., and Walkley, E. M. "SLA Translation Center, an International Resource," *Special Libraries* 57:35–38 (1966).

19

Union Lists

The tools which are essential to the full utilization of serial publications are: (1) union lists, whose primary function is to record the location of serial sets wherever they may be found in libraries, and (2) abstracting and indexing services to disclose the contents of the sets by author and subject. The location function makes it possible for people to carry on their research wherever the resources are known to exist, to borrow some volumes on interlibrary loan, and generally to obtain photocopies of the parts of the sets that they need for their investigations. It also is an aid in discovering sets to be reprinted or to be reproduced by microcopying.

The Joint Committee on the Union List of Serials describes the role of union lists when it says:

> For his training and information the researcher must build on the work of colleagues in present and former times. In comparatively few instances can he gather his data from handbooks and other simple sources; as a rule he must draw on scattered contributions which occur in a variety of general and specialized sources, most of which are periodicals of one kind or another. As he carries on his investigations he should therefore be able to tap the countless millions of contributions to knowledge which are found in a profusion of serials (i.e., periodicals, publications of scientific and learned societies, government documents, etc.) Many of these serials should be close at hand in a working research library; but no library, however large and affluent, has been able to assemble even as many as half the serial titles in existence and, of the titles that have been collected in the United States and Canada, only 35 per cent are represented by complete runs. Accordingly the typical researcher is continually in search of data from other collections

than his own; and thus arises the demand for control records, by means of which files in other collections can be located and utilized. The interdependence of libraries is nowhere seen to better advantage than in the co-operative exploitation of serial resources; and for co-operative exploitation, the essential tools are union lists of serials, lists that disclose the location of periodicals and other serial publications.[1]

The first union list was a twenty-page pamphlet compiled by Luciano dell' Acqua and published in Milan in the first of three editions in 1859; it was entitled *Elenco dei giornali e delle opere periodiche esistenti presso pubblici stabilimenti a Milano*. It listed 562 periodicals in fifteen libraries. The earliest American union list was a *Check List of Periodicals*, which was published by Johns Hopkins University in the first of two editions in 1876. The Haskell and Brown bibliography, which appeared in the second edition of the *Union List of Serials* in 1943, recorded 387 items; the Library of Congress bibliography, published twenty-one years later, increased the figure to 1,218, which represents a world production rate of some forty union lists a year in the postwar period.[2]

The introduction to the Library of Congress bibliography says:

> Serials remain the most important means of rapidly disseminating to the learned community new knowledge in all fields of study, particularly in the natural sciences and technology. The great profusion of serial publications makes it impossible for even the richest libraries to obtain and keep more than a part of what their readers may require. Where economic or political conditions interfere with the procurement of foreign publications, library cooperation in the acquisition and circulation of scarce or costly serials is vital.
>
> The published union list is the most convenient device by which libraries located in a certain area, or specializing in a particular subject, may inform users of the serials which each one can make available. Union lists facilitate interlibrary loans and the procurement of photocopies and can be used to support other forms of library cooperation, such as exchanges and transfers, cooperative acquisitions and storage, and the discarding of excess duplicates. Dealers in serials find union lists of assistance as a means of learning

[1]Joint Committee on the Union List of Serials, *A Permanent Program for the Union List of Serials* (Washington, 1957), p.ii.

[2]Library of Congress, General Reference and Bibliography Division, *Union Lists of Serials, a Bibliography* (Washington, 1964).

which libraries lack serial issues that can be supplied from the dealers' stocks. The more carefully prepared union lists are invaluable bibliographical aids.[3]

The first edition of the *Union List of Serials*, published in 1927, recorded 75,000 titles in 225 American and Canadian libraries. The second edition with its two supplements, published from 1943 to 1953, covered 144,557 titles in 712 libraries. The third edition, published in 1966 in five volumes, listed 156,499 titles in 956 libraries. In its final report on this edition, the Joint Committee on the Union List of Serials says:

> Serials represent the larger part of the bulk of materials handled by libraries. In research libraries, especially, the dominance of the serial form is apparent; probably three-fourths of the total budget of the research library is devoted to the acquisition, processing, housing, and servicing of serial publications.
>
> The interest in and need for serial publications on the part of researchers is in direct ratio to the predominance of the form. . . .
>
> No library, however large, has been able to assemble even as many as half of the serial titles in existence. In the typical large research library, no more than a third of the titles held are held in relatively complete runs. Since no library can own more than a fraction of the total, the cooperative exploitation of resources is absolutely essential.[4]

The Committee also provides figures for interlibrary loans and photocopying in 1958, when 61 percent of all interlibrary loans and 95 percent of photoduplication were for serials. The breakdown by type of library is:

Type of Library	Total Loans	Serials to 1941	Per Cent	Serials 1941–58	Per Cent	Total	Per Cent
Government	175,000	35,000	20	113,750	65	148,750	85
College and University	250,000	27,500	11	82,500	33	110,000	44
Special	125,000	25,000	20	81,250	65	106,250	85
Public	50,000	2,500	5	12,500	25	15,000	30
Photoduplication	400,000	80,000	20	300,000	75	380,000	955

[3]*Ibid.*, p.v.

[4]Joint Committee on the Union List of Serials, *Final Report on . . . the Publication of a Third Edition of the Union List of Serials in Libraries of the United States and Canada* (Washington, D.C.: Council on Library Resources, 1966), p.17. The report gives a brief history of union list activities and details the production of the third edition of the *Union List of Serials*.

[5]*Ibid.*, p.23.

Exclusions from the third edition were: (1) all titles which began publication on or after 1 January 1950, since they are the province of *New Serial Titles*, which in that sense becomes a cumulative supplement to the *Union List of Serials*; (2) some 340,000 pre-1950 titles which are in the National Union Catalog and are in the course of being printed in the retrospective union catalog; (3) additional locations for serials when ten were already shown in the second edition, an omission which will constitute something of a handicap for interlibrary loan and photocopying because the geographical distribution of locations was disregarded; and (4) some 13,000 titles in Asian languages, which were omitted because most of them would have had to be recataloged before they could be included.

An organizational gap exists for new holdings, locations, and titles for pre-1950 serials. The third edition is considered to be the final one, and *New Serial Titles* is not concerned with pre-1950 titles except for the record of bibliographical changes which occur in any serial regardless of its starting date. The service began in January 1955; the changes are listed at the end of each monthly issue or cumulation. The scope is indicated by the following note which precedes each list:

> Changes are noted here for all serials, regardless of their beginning date. These changes include title changes in the name or catalog entry of corporate authors, cessations, suspensions, resumptions and the like. They do not include changes in frequency, format, price, or commercial publisher. For title changes or changes in names of corporate authors, the change is listed under the old title or name and, when appropriate, under the new title or name. The exact point at which the change took place is indicated insofar as possible. Unless otherwise indicated, the source of information is the Library of Congress.

In its earlier phases the *Union List of Serials* was complemented by three other publications, none of which has been updated. The *List of the Serial Publications of Foreign Governments*, published in 1932, covered the period 1815–1931, which leaves a twenty-one-year gap between 1931 and the time when *New Serial Publications* began. *American Newspapers* appeared in 1937 and covered the years 1821–1936, the earlier years having been pre-empted by Clarence S. Brigham, *History and Bibliography of American Newspapers*, 1690–1820 (Worcester, Mass.: American Antiquarian Society, 1947. 2v.). *International Congresses and Conferences* came out in 1938 and listed publications which were issued from 1840 through 1937.

Adams raises the question: "Are we on the way to creating a national serials 'unsystem' rather than a national system, and when shall we pass the point of no return?"[6] He anticipates the coming of a national computer system to take over the union list function, but he says that there are still lacking: (1) "a simple, standardized format for the identification and location functions performed historically by the *Union List of Serials*," and (2) "an adequate conceptualization of a search service system to provide nationally for the location function historically performed by the *Union List of Serials*."[7]

Closely akin to the *Union List of Serials* but with important variations is the *British Union Catalogue of Periodicals* in four volumes, published in 1955–58. It lists 140,000 titles held by 450 libraries. A supplement was issued in 1962, bringing the work down to 1960. Allied to *BUCOP* is the fourth edition of the *World List of Scientific Periodicals*, which appeared in 1965 in three volumes. It covers 60,000 titles in 3,000 libraries, again up to 1960. The two publications have now been amalgamated and are jointly supplemented by the quarterly *Bucop Journal*, which began publication in March 1964.

In its connection with the *World List of Scientific Periodicals* the British union list has to that extent provided international locations for serial publications. In 1947 Besterman suggested a European union list.[8] And Kuhlman, in dealing with the problem of speeding up the listing of publications in *New Serial Titles*, suggested that foreign libraries should be invited, and would be willing, to contribute to *New Serial Titles* in the same way that American and Canadian libraries do.[9]

Most union lists relate to a subject or to the holdings of a region or locality.[10] This is the sense in which Olson says that "union lists are more often wanted than they are available. . . . Regional and local lists could potentially serve most communicative needs best. These are never available enough, nor up-to-date enough."[11] His thesis is "that a sizeable transfer of effort could be made from local reporting

---

[6]Scott Adams, "Progress toward a National Serials Data System," *Library Trends* 18:520 (1970).

[7]*Ibid.*, p.531.

[8]Theodore Besterman, "Esquisse des projets d'activité du Centre de bibliographie et des bibliothèques en fonction du prêt international des livres," *La documentation en France, bulletin mensuel de l'UFOD* 16:22–25 (1947).

[9]A. F. Kuhlman, *A Report on the Consumer Survey of New Serial Titles* ([Washington, D.C.: Library of Congress,] 1967), p.31 and footnote 4 on p.31 and 33.

[10]David Grenfell, *Periodicals and Serials; Their Treatment in Special Libraries* (2d ed.; London: Aslib, 1965), has a useful selection of union lists for Great Britain and twenty other countries on p.202–205 and 208–12, with emphasis on subject lists of value to special libraries.

[11]Kenneth D. Olson, "Union Lists and the Public Record of Serials," *Special Libraries* 61:15 (1970).

of serials (to the users of individual libraries) to cooperative reporting (to a regional union list which would incorporate this function)."[12] This suggestion, a sound one, is in keeping with the idea,
which the Linda Hall Library has successfully put into practice, of
giving up the card-catalog record of serials in favor of a book catalog.

Since 1922 *Chemical Abstracts* has published a quinquennial list
of the periodicals which it abstracts. In 1969 the list became *Access.*
In addition to the names of more than 16,000 serial publications in
the field of chemistry, *Access* gives their locations in 325 American
libraries and 74 libraries in other countries.

Another subject list of note is the *Union Catalog of Medical Periodicals,* which is produced by the Medical Library Center of New
York.[13] Fifteen thousand titles are listed. The system can be readily
adapted for use in other localities by substituting local holdings and
adding new titles. It has already been adapted in a number of medical centers in the United States.[14]

Bibliography

Bibliography of union lists

Library of Congress. General Reference and Bibliography Division. *Union
Lists of Serials, a Bibliography.* Washington, 1964.

General works

Adams, Scott. "Progress toward a National Serials Data System," *Library
Trends* 18:520–36 (1970).
Brummel, L. *Union Catalogues, Their Problems and Organization.* (Unesco
Bibliographical Handbooks, no.6) Paris: Unesco, 1956.
Downs, Robert B. *Union Catalogs in the United States.* Chicago: American
Library Assn., 1942.
Joint Committee on the Union List of Serials. *Final Report on . . . the
Publication of a Third Edition of the Union List of Serials in Libraries
of the United States and Canada.* Washington, D.C.: Council on Library
Resources, 1966.
——— *A Permanent Program for the Union List of Serials.* Washington, 1957.
Kuhlman, A. F. *A Report on the Consumer Survey of New Serial Titles.*
[Washington, D.C.:] Library of Congress, 1967.

12*Ibid.,* p.20.
13See Jacqueline W. Felter, "Initiating a Mechanized Union Catalog for Medical
Libraries in Metropolitan New York," *Special Libraries* 55:621–24 (1964).
14Michael D. Sprinkle, "Regional Utilization of the Union Catalog of Medical
Periodicals System," *Bulletin of the Medical Library Association* 57:244–49 (1969).

Olson, Kenneth D. "Union Lists and the Public Record of Serials," *Special Libraries* 61:15–20 (1970).

Willemin, Silvère. *Technique of Union Catalogues, a Practical Guide*. Paris: Unesco, 1966.

20

Abstracting and Indexing

Although published abstracts and indexes have existed in one form or another for over three hundred years, the problems in the field are essentially contemporary ones.[1] They have come to the fore in the period since World War II, and a voluminous literature has sprung into being in that time. Among the serious problems are: inadequate coverage of almost all fields of knowledge; the increasing amount of financial support which the services require; the rising costs to subscribers; and the time lag in issuing the listings.

Much attention has been given even to the question of determining how many abstracting and indexing services there are. Just as it is difficult to arrive at accurate figures for the number of periodicals which are being published, either in general or in an area such as science and technology, so, too, it has proved difficult to give an accurate figure for the much smaller number of abstracting and indexing services in existence. The estimate quoted by Bourne in 1962 is still reasonably reliable. He says:

> There are currently an estimated 3,500 abstracting and indexing services throughout the world, about 550 of them in the United States. There are also an estimated 450 special information centers in the United States that maintain collections of information on special technical topics (e.g., Snow, Ice and Permafrost; Defense Metals; Air Pollution) for literature searching and reference services.[2]

[1] A good historical account will be found in Verner W. Clapp, "Indexing and Abstracting Services for Serial Literature," *Library Trends* 2:509–21 (1954).

[2] Charles P. Bourne, "The World's Technical Journal Literature: An Estimate of Volume, Origin, Language, Field, Indexing, and Abstracting," *American Documentation* 13:162 (1962).

In the following year the Library of Congress issued a carefully screened directory which listed 1,855 services in the field of science and technology.[3] But in 1969, in a volume which covered agriculture, medicine, science, and technology, the International Federation for Documentation recorded only 70 percent of the services noted by the Library of Congress in 1963.[4]

One reason why it is not easy to make a count of published services is the multiplication of current-awareness programs, KWIC indexes, and table-of-contents publications, many of which are only for local consumption, though they may be exchanged with other institutions working in the same or a related field. These compilations increase despite the studies which show that items examined because of their occurrence in a list of titles are, in general, not as satisfactory as those discovered by means of abstracts.[5] Among unpublished services there are considerable numbers of unrecorded card catalogs, computer listings, and sections of periodicals which generally go uncounted. Even for established systems a wide variety of forms occurs. Woods says:

> Many a & i services are separately published in bulletins which are printed periodically, e.g., *Tobacco Abstracts, Abstracts of Photographic Science and Engineering Literature;* others are issued in card form only, such as *Polymers Digest* and the several services of Lowry-Cocroft; some appear as a regular feature in a journal, such as the coverage of plastics patents in each issue of the *SPE Journal* (Society of Plastics Engineers) ; some services are issued in a multiplicity of forms—printed bulletins, cards, magnetic tape, or microfilm, as are *Biological Abstracts* and *Engineering Index (EI)*. *EI* further cumulates monthly issues into annual bound volumes. As far as I can determine, no continuing service is offered on magnetic tape only, yet this is both an economic and technical possibility (*EI*'s CITE-Electrical/Electronics has been an exception in 1968—

---

[3]Library of Congress, Science and Technology Division, *A Guide to the World's Abstracting and Indexing Services in Science and Technology* (National Federation of Science Abstracting and Indexing Services, Report 102 [Washington, 1963]).

[4]International Federation for Documentation, *Abstracting Services in Science, Technology, Medicine, Agriculture, Social Sciences, Humanities* (rev. ed.; Paris, 1969).

[5]See, for example, Jesse Bernard and Charles Shilling, *Accuracy of Titles in Describing Content of Biological Science Articles* (Washington: American Institute of Biological Sciences, 1963). But for a contrary view, see A. Resnick, "Relative Effectiveness of Document Titles and Abstracts for Determining Relevance of Documents," *Science* 134:1004–1006 (1961).

1969) ; searching of merged data bases from several services is also a new phenomena.[6]

The background to the abstracting and indexing problems of the day is expressed by Bourne as follows:

> The world's scientific community is presently generating a flood of technical literature, and much of it is not getting into the hands of people who could use it. It is probably missing these people for two main reasons: only a fraction of the literature is covered by abstracting, indexing, or citation publications; and only a fraction of those people who could use the information are familiar with the literature or aware of the tools and facilities for locating the information. We can measure the amount of literature that is actually covered by the abstracting and indexing services, but this does not indicate what fraction of the important information is getting to the potential users. In many fields the abstracting and indexing services may be covering only a quarter or a third of the estimated total pertinent literature, but this fraction may include all the significant research advances or applications while the remaining fraction consists of rehashes, popularized writings, and trivial contributions.[7]

All would be well if it were only rehashes, popularized writings, and trivial contributions that were not covered; but key items have gone unnoticed in the past, and undoubtedly some of them will escape notice in the future. Pollard gives several examples of advances in science and technology which were relatively unknown for a generation.[8] The classic case is that of Mendel's laws governing the inheritance of characters in plants and animals, which were published in the *Verhandlungen* of the Naturforschender Verein in Brünn in 1865 and 1869. There they remained comparatively unknown until 1900, when they were rediscovered and confirmed. Pollard says there is no doubt that the belated discovery of Mendel's work delayed the progress of biology by many years. He gives a parallel case in engineering:

6Bill M. Woods, "Bibliographic Control of Serial Publications," in Walter C. Allen, ed., *Serial Publications in Large Libraries* (Allerton Park Institute, no.16 [Urbana, Ill.: Univ. of Illinois Graduate School of Library Science, 1970]), p.162.

7Bourne, "The World's Technical Journal Literature," p.159.

8A. F. C. Pollard, "The Disordered State of Bibliography and Indications of Its Effect upon Scientific and Technical Progress," *Proceedings* of the British Society for International Bibliography 4:41–52 (1942).

the pre-jet airplane was detailed in a French patent granted in 1876 which came to light forty years later. Kronick gives several eighteenth-century examples, among them some of Diderot's mathematical papers.[9] Nowadays the risk of oversight is considerable whenever the coverage in a field is low as it was in 1954, for instance, when *Biological Abstracts* was able to record only 17 percent of the literature of biology.

At any rate, there has been a dramatic increase in the number of items abstracted since attention was focused on the shortcomings. Klempner has a table which shows that for fourteen services the lowest percentage of increase from 1955 to 1965 was 77.06 for the *ASM Review of Metal Literature*, the largest, 667.17 for *Scientific and Technical Aerospace Reports*. Numerically the smallest growth was from 3,280 to 6,865 for *Analytical Abstracts*, the greatest from 209,967 to approximately 700,000 for *Referativnyi Zhurnal*.[10]

While there have been deficiencies in the total abstracting and indexing program, there has also been an appreciable amount of duplication of effort. Some overlap is costly and unnecessary, but Woods says that it would be wrong to consider all overlap as duplication of effort and approach. He cites the following example:

> Compared were *Plastics Monthly (PM)*, published by Engineering Index, and *POST-J (Polymer Science and Technology-Journals)*, published by Chemical Abstracts Service. . . .
>
> Invariably the indexing approach is different—CAS stresses the chemistry (the monomers and the polymers) of plastics, while EI emphasizes the processing, the equipment, the final product and its use. Indexing terminology assigned also reflects this poles-apart interest.
>
> Another example of diversity is evidenced in the depth of coverage. In one sampling of eighteen journal issues (excluding hard core chemistry) which contained 205 papers, EI indexed for *PM*, while CAS indexed only forty-four in *POST-J*. If hard core chemistry titles were sampled, the balance in numbers would likely be similar and the difference in coverage would be reemphasized (in other words, relatively little real overlap).[11]

[9]David A. Kronick, *A History of Scientific and Technical Periodicals; The Origins and Development of the Scientific and Technological Press, 1665–1790* (New York: Scarecrow, 1962), p.215–17.

[10]Irving M. Klempner, *Diffusion of Abstracting and Indexing Services for Government-Sponsored Research* (Metuchen, N.J.: Scarecrow, 1968), p.52.

[11]Woods, "Bibliographic Control of Serial Publication," p.166.

Production costs and subscription rates are twin matters of concern. Federal government financial support has been necessary to help publications like *Biological Abstracts*, but Woods thinks that those days are over. He says:

> During the past decade numerous a & i services have had substantial government funding to create new services or to maintain or upgrade existing services. . . . Generally the day of heavy federal government support—particularly by the National Science Foundation —is past, and many services operated by not-for-profit organizations are being required to become self-supporting, a requirement which the information companies have always faced, through the sale of publications and services.[12]

A Unesco study says that the preparation of abstracts accounts for half the cost of publishing an abstracting journal.[13] The only solution would be to require each author to prepare an accurate, honest, and informative abstract which would be published with his paper. Otherwise it is possible that some abstracting services will become indexes to save on costs. In 1969 the *Bibliography and Index of Geology* discontinued abstracts, the aim being greater coverage of titles indexed as well as operation within the budget.

In order to meet the increase in production rates, subscription prices have continued to climb. In 1970 the average price index for 1,124 services, excluding Wilson publications, was 214.7, compared with a 1957–59 base of 100.00. Some libraries have been forced to cancel their subscriptions to *Chemical Abstracts* because of the great increase in price since 1955.

Prompt listing is, of course, the hallmark of an efficient abstracting and indexing service. Some steps have been taken to reduce the time lag. They include the use of preprints and airmail subscriptions, as well as a streamlining of internal and publishing procedures.

A number of libraries have organized to give reader and photocopy service for items covered in a publication. Those indexed in *Applied Mechanics Review* are available through the Linda Hall Library; those in *Biological Abstracts*, through the Center for Research Libraries and the John Crerar Library; those in *Chemical Abstracts*, through the Center for Research Libraries; and those in the *Engi-*

12*Ibid.*, p.171.
13Unesco, *Questions Relating to Science and Technology* (Unesco Report E/3618 [New York, 1962]).

neering Index, through the Engineering Societies Library. These developments are important because, as Tate and Wood say:

> The comparatively small number of periodicals held by any one library is the cause of one of the most frequently heard complaints from the users of A&I services. Both scientists and librarians serving them complain that cited originals are either unobtainable from local resources or that the time required to obtain them is excessive.[14]

They refer back to a 1961 survey conducted by Chemical Abstracts Service:

> Data accumulated during this survey indicated that of 334 U.S. and foreign libraries serving chemistry, only eleven U.S. and two foreign libraries maintained subscriptions to over 30 percent of the over 9,000 serials that were then being abstracted by *Chemical Abstracts.* Of the eleven U.S. libraries, only three subscribed to over 50 percent of the serials, the largest subscribing to only 5,256. Of the institutions polled in the survey, 65.5 percent of the U.S. and 71.1 percent of the foreign libraries subscribed to fewer than 1,000 of the serials that contained substantive chemical articles.[15]

Indexing Services

Germany has produced the most comprehensive national indexes. The former *Bibliographie der deutschen Zeitschriftenliteratur*, which indexed periodicals in the German language in all fields of knowledge, and its complementary *Bibliographie der fremdsprachigen Zeitschriftenliteratur*, which covered the foreign-language field, in 1965 merged to form the *Internationale Bibliographie der Zeitschriftenliteratur aus allen Gebieten der Forschung*. This monumental work indexes the contents of some 8,300 periodicals from all parts of the world. However, like all German abstracting and indexing services, it is not easy to consult because of its compactness and conciseness. Abbreviations are prevalent; the titles of publications indexed are referred to by number, not name; and the mass of entries under numerous topics makes checking a matter of patient endeavor, just as it is extremely rewarding.

[14]Fred A. Tate and James L. Wood, "Libraries and Abstracting and Indexing Services; A Study in Interdependency," *Library Trends* 16:356 (1968).
[15]*Ibid.*

In the United States the comparable systematic indexes are in subject fields. They include the *Bibliography of Agriculture,* which is published by the National Agricultural Library; *Public Affairs Information Service,* whose headquarters are in the New York Public Library; and the monthly *Index Medicus,* issued by the National Library of Medicine, which becomes the *Cumulated Index Medicus.* The latter is by no means as comprehensive as the former *Index-Catalogue* of the Surgeon-General's Office, since it covers by author and subject some 2,300 periodicals. In January of each year the *Index Medicus* contains a subject list of the journals it indexes. There is now an *Abridged Index Medicus,* which covers a hundred journals that ought to be in all medical libraries. At the beginning of each issue of the *Index Medicus* there is a list of reviews; the lists are cumulated annually into the *Bibliography of Medical Reviews.* The Medical Library Association publishes three times a year *Vital Notes on Medical Periodicals,* which lists new journals, changes in title, cessations, etc.

Beginning in 1900 the H. W. Wilson Company has published a series of general and special indexes; each one covers only a small range of periodicals, almost all of which are in the English language. They include:

> *Applied Science and Technology Index,* 1958 to date. From 1928–57 it was part of the *Industrial Arts Index.* It covers about 225 periodicals.
>
> *Art Index,* 1929 to date; 150 periodicals and museum bulletins.
>
> *Bibliographic Index,* 1937 to date. This is a subject list of bibliographies, both English and foreign language. The items listed contain forty or more bibliographical citations. Books and pamphlets are included: about 1,700 periodicals are searched for material.
>
> *Biography Index,* 1946 to date. The biographical listings are taken from approximately 1,900 periodicals which are covered in the other Wilson indexes.
>
> *Biological and Agricultural Index,* 1964 to date. From 1919 to 1964 it was called the *Agricultural Index.* It covers about 150 periodicals.
>
> *Business Periodicals Index,* 1958 to date. From 1928 to 1957 it was part of the *Industrial Arts Index.* It covers about 170 periodicals.
>
> *Education Index,* 1929 to date. It covers about 230 periodicals.

Index to Legal Periodicals, 1908 to date. It covers some 325 publications, which include annual institutes, periodicals, and yearbooks.

Library Literature, 1933 to date. This complements H. G. T. Cannons, *Bibliography of Library Economy* (2d ed., Chicago: American Library Assn., 1927) which covered 65 periodicals, also the supplement to Cannons (Chicago: American Library Assn., 1934). The main work indexed library literature from 1876 to 1920, the supplement from 1921 to 1932. *Library Literature* covers no more than a fifth of the professional journals.

Readers' Guide to Periodical Literature, 1900 to date. This was the first of the Wilson indexes; it was intended for small libraries and originally covered only 15 popular magazines. It now indexes about 160 American periodicals. There is also the *Abridged Readers' Guide to Periodical Literature,* 1935 to date, which covers 44 journals.

Social Sciences and Humanities Index, 1965 to date. From 1916 to 1964 it was the *International Index to Periodicals.* It covers 205 periodicals.

Vertical File Index, 1932 to date. This is a listing of free and inexpensive items which libraries should consider for acquisition.

The corresponding British indexes have undergone somewhat similar transformations. The Library Association published the *Subject Index to Periodicals* from 1915 to 1961. In 1962 this was succeeded by two works, the quarterly *British Humanities Index* and the monthly *British Technology Index.* Like their American counterparts, these indexes do not attempt to be comprehensive; they cover only a selection of periodicals.

There are several indexes to pre-twentieth-century periodicals. New York University prepared a card index to American periodicals from the beginning to 1850, with some periodicals continuing after that cut-off date. In 1964 the index was issued in microprint by Readex. The general list, which is in three groups by author, anonymous title, and subject, is followed by four special features. They are: (1) fiction, in two groups by author and anonymous title; (2) poetry, in three groups by author, anonymous title, and first line of text; (3) book reviews, in two groups by the author of the book reviewed or by anonymous title; and (4) songs, in four groups by author of the song, composer, anonymous title, and first line.

Poole's Index to Periodical Literature is a subject index to 470 American and British periodicals from 1802 through 1906. There is also the *Nineteenth Century Readers' Guide to Periodical Literature, 1890–1899* (New York: Wilson, 1944. 2v.), which is an author, illustrator, and subject index to 51 periodicals, fourteen of them being indexed as far as 1922. The *Wellesley Index to Victorian Periodicals, 1824–1900* (Toronto: Univ. of Toronto Pr., 1966) covers British periodicals.

Citations

In the field of law the judicial history of a case has been given in the form of citations for over a century. In addition to federal law, there is now a Shepard's citator for all the units of the national reporter system and all the states. Brown employed citations in various fields of science as an aid in ranking periodicals for selection purposes in libraries. Beginning with 1961 a *Science Citation Index* has listed references to the contributions of scientists as noted in a relatively small selection of periodicals; in the first volumes 613 journals were indexed by the citation method.

Coordinate Indexing

Taube forged the link between the static subject cataloging found in libraries, the Library of Congress in particular, and the relational system that is essential for the systematic retrieval of information.[16] His thinking developed during his association with the Science and Technology Project at the Library of Congress in the 1940s; the elements can be found in the list of subject headings which was drawn up under his direction and which, e.g., rejected the inverted heading. He became convinced that a static system would no longer serve the relational requests for information which are standard in science and technology, so he developed a system of uniterms which could be manipulated manually and eventually by computer.

In numerous fields a thesaurus of terms has been developed as an aid in the recovery of information. The system in use at the National Library of Medicine, MeSH, is an example of the practice. The future

---

[16]See, in particular, Mortimer Taube, *Studies in Coordinate Indexing* (Bethesda, Md., 1953–56. 3v.).

lies with systems of these kinds, which permit the connection of two or more concepts either manually or by means of the computer. MARC will never be successful as an instrument for the recovery of information by subject until it abandons Library of Congress classification and subject headings in favor of a relational system.

The Cranfield Investigations

Because of the rivalry that exists among various methods for the recovery of information, a number of tests were made at Cranfield to determine relative effectiveness.[17] The general finding was that most systems operated at about four-fifths of efficiency, although the real matter of concern is qualitative, not quantitative—i.e., whether all key documents are recovered or not. Efforts to increase the recovery rate from, say, 81 percent to 82 percent or higher proved to be particularly arduous. Cranfield-type tests should continue to be made until eventually a scheme is devised that will be truly satisfactory in quality and in quantity.

Indexing in Depth

In recent years there has been much discussion of the number of entries which ought to be made for a journal article in abstracting and indexing services as well as in computer systems. Traditional subject-heading practice in libraries has been to limit the number of entries to one, two, three, or four, but in abstracting and indexing programs the number has been appreciably higher. On the average *Nuclear Science Abstracts* makes eight entries per item, *Chemical Abstracts* twelve, and MEDLARS fourteen. No definitive number is ever likely to be set, either for a journal article or for a full-scale monograph. A judgment factor is involved, but definitely indexing in depth is on sounder lines than established library usage is.

Methods of Indexing in General

More attention has been paid to the theory of indexing in Great Britain than in the United States. It has had a Society of Indexers

[17]See, for example, C. W. Cleverdon, *Report on the Testing and Analysis of an Investigation into the Comparative Efficiency of Indexing Systems* (Cranfield, England, 1962).

since 1957 and a periodical, *The Indexer.* Important works in the field are Robert L. Collison, *Indexes and Indexing; Guide to the Indexing of Books, and Collections of Books, Periodicals, Music, Recordings, Films, and Other Material; with a Reference Section and Suggestions for Further Reading* (3d ed.; London: Benn, 1969) ; and *Training in Indexing, a Course of the Society of Indexers,* edited by G. Norman Knight (Cambridge: M.I.T. Press, 1969). However, Collison says:

> The finest manual on indexing is too little known: it is Marion Thorne Wheeler's *New York State Library Indexing: Principles, Rules and Examples.* 5th edition. (Albany, New York, University of the State of New York Press, 1957.) In spite of its uncompromisingly formal style and its undistinguished printing, this 78-page pamphlet covers every phase of indexing, and is full of good sensible advice and excellent examples of actual entries and of various kinds of indexes. A noteworthy feature of this work is its own index which, in just over five pages indexes the sixty-one pages of text in a thorough and workmanlike fashion.[18]

Recently American attention has been focused more on aspects connected with abstracting and indexing programs. There is, e.g., Frederick Jonker, *Indexing Theory, Indexing Methods, and Search Devices* (New York, 1964) .

Standardization

The British Standards Institution, the International Standards Organization, and the United States of America Standards Institute have all issued standards of one kind or another. The *USA Standard for Periodicals: Format and Arrangement* was issued in 1967. Its first ruling is:

> The cover of a periodical should contain:
> (1) title
> (2) subtitle, if any
> (3) number of the volume and issue in Arabic numerals
> (4) date of the issue
> (5) complete identification of the issue of the periodical in coded form to allow for a rapid input of compact, unambiguous

---

[18]Robert L. Collison, *Indexes and Indexing* (3d ed.; London: Benn, 1969), p.171.

identification into electronic or mechanical data-processing systems. This coded identification should include:

(a) ASTM Coden for the periodical title
(b) volume number
(c) issue number
(d) inclusive pagination
(e) date of issue

Example: JACSA 87 (24) 5525-5880 (1965) *Journal of the American Chemical Society* Volume 87, Issue No. 24, pages 5525–5880 December 20, 1965.

(6) title abbreviation as per USA Standard for Periodical Title Abbreviations, Z39.5–1963.[19]

Bibliography

Abstracting

Ashworth, Wilfred. "Abstracting," in *Handbook of Special Librarianship and Information Work*, p.453–81. 3rd ed. London: Aslib, 1967.

Bourne, Charles P. "The World's Technical Journal Literature: An Estimate of Volume, Origin, Language, Field, Indexing, and Abstracting," *American Documentation* 13:159–68 (1962).

Chemical Abstracts Service. *CAS Today: Facts and Figures about Chemical Abstracts Service*. Washington, D.C.: American Chemical Society, 1967.

Clapp, Verner W. "Indexing and Abstracting: Recent Past and Lines of Future Development," *College and Research Libraries* 11:197–206 (1950).

――― "Indexing and Abstracting Services for Serial Literature," *Library Trends* 2:509–21 (1954).

Davinson, D. E. "Abstracts," in his *The Periodicals Collection; Its Purpose and Uses in Libraries*, p.60–75. London: Deutsch, 1969.

Klempner, Irving M. *Diffusion of Abstracting and Indexing Services for Government-Sponsored Research*. Metuchen, N.J.: Scarecrow, 1968.

Mohrhardt, Foster E., ed. "Science Abstracting Services—Commercial, Institutional, and Personal," *Library Trends* 16:303–418 (1968).

System Development Corporation. *A System Study of Abstracting and Indexing in the United States*. Falls Church, Va., 1966.

Woods, Bill M. "Bibliographic Control of Serial Publications," in Walter D. Allen, ed., *Serial Publications in Large Libraries* (Allerton Park Institute, no.16) Urbana, Ill.: Univ. of Illinois Graduate School of Library Science, 1970.

[19]*USA Standard for Periodicals: Format and Arrangement* (New York: United States of America Standards Institute, 1967), p.7.

Indexing

Lawler, John L. *The H. W. Wilson Company; Half a Century of Bibliographic Publishing.* Minneapolis: Univ. of Minnesota Pr., [1950].

Strain, P. M. "Indexing a Periodical Run," *Sci-Tech News* 20:114–16 (1966).

Tashjian, Nouvart. "New York University Index to Early American Periodical Literature, 1728–1870," *College and Research Libraries* 7:135–37 (1946).

Citations

Malin, Morton V. "The Science Citation Index: A New Concept in Indexing," *Library Trends* 16:374–87 (1968).

21

Publications of International Governmental Organizations

In 1968–69, according to the *Yearbook of International Organizations*, there were 229 international governmental organizations, plus another 67 which were dead or inactive. In addition there were 2,188 active and 674 inactive international nongovernmental organizations. These figures give an idea of the acquisition enterprise that is required for a research library to have full coverage of the documentation.

The publications of international governmental organizations are predominantly serial in character. Actually, among United Nations documents the principal nonserials are the items which are issued in all manner of languages by the Department of Public Information for publicity purposes. Some of the documents put out by international governmental organizations are serials in their own right; i.e., they are periodicals, yearbooks, etc. But most of them are simply held together by symbols which enable them to take on the character of serial publications. Throughout the League of Nations period and until the *United Nations Documents Index (UNDI)* began publication in 1950, the serial control element was generally derived from the sales number.

Most libraries are unable to build up complete sets of the publications of organizations such as the United Nations. Some documents, especially Security Council items, are classified as restricted and are not procurable until they have been declassified; others are reproduced in small quantities and are limited to internal official use. The master microfilm file, which is maintained in the United Nations Archives, includes all items, restricted, limited, or not.

Distribution programs have often lacked thoroughness, so that one library may have an item that another lacks. In the 1950s the Harvard College Library and the World Peace Foundation used to compare their United Nations holdings several times a year; frequently they found that one collection had a document which the other lacked. At times differences in sets come about because of a personal connection; e.g., a professor who has held an important post in an international governmental agency may turn his files over to the library of the institution with which he is connected, and in that way the library acquires material which it would not have procured otherwise. It was owing to the enterprise of Verner Clapp and the other members of the Library of Congress staff who were present that sets of documents for the 1945 San Francisco Conference, which created the United Nations, were assembled for libraries, even specially run off from stencils in order to make the full documentation available.

The frequent issuance of addenda, corrigenda, and revisions is a major problem in collecting, organizing, and consulting the publications of international governmental organizations. When they are received after the items to which they relate have been bound, it is necessary to bind them separately, commonly in pamphlet binders. Even when the binding of a volume is postponed for a year or more to allow for the arrival of these additional items, the possibility always exists that more of them will eventually appear. The extent of the problem of handling these items can be judged by studying the list of addenda, corrigenda, and revisions which regularly is found in the *United Nations Documents Index*.

Most documents come out in an English edition, either originally or in translation. Sometimes, however, the only edition may be in French or Spanish; e.g., over the years most of the publications of the Universal Postal Union have appeared only in French. When a library wants to maintain just an English set, it may occasionally have to insert a document in another language to round out its holdings. And when sets in two or more languages are maintained, an item may have to be sought in the French or Spanish collection on the occasions when no English one is present.

League of Nations

The League of Nations Library (now the United Nations Library at Geneva) did not accumulate a definitive set of League documents as they were issued. The official repository was the League of Nations Archives, where the items were distributed archivally along with great quantities of other documentation. The United Nations Library at Geneva set to work to repair the omission and to assemble as complete a file as possible. In the meantime the best set was in the Dag Hammarskjöld Library at the United Nations in New York, a collection presented by the Woodrow Wilson Foundation, which had gathered it with great assiduity. The Geneva and headquarters libraries are cooperating with Research Publications in New Haven, Connecticut, which plans to microfilm as complete a set as possible and to make it available commercially. The problem is that there is no official checklist of League publications as there is for the United Nations. The unofficial checklist is Marie J. Carroll, *Key to League of Nations Documents Placed on Public Sale, 1920–1929* (Boston: World Peace Foundation, 1930) and its four supplements (Boston, 1931–38). More exhaustive than Carroll is Hans Aufricht, *Guide to League of Nations Publications; A Bibliographical Survey of the Work of the League, 1920–1947* (New York: Columbia Univ. Pr., 1951). Of value too is the work of the former librarian of the League of Nations, A. C. von Breycha-Vauthier, *Sources of Information, a Handbook on the Publications of the League of Nations* (New York: Columbia Univ. Pr., 1939). In some ways the Library of Congress cards, which include thousands of entries supplied by the Woodrow Wilson Foundation Library for items which are now in the Dag Hammarskjöld Library, afford the best check when taken in conjunction with the guides prepared by Carroll and Aufricht.

The problems of cataloging and classifying League documents gave rise to controversy in the United States in the twenties and thirties.[1] But the points at issue are for the most part no longer a matter of active concern. The problems stemmed from the Library of Congress cards which libraries acquired to go with their League collections. The cards were commonly not filed in the public or official catalogs, but were located near the publications themselves. The catalog so created consisted of four parts: main cards, subject cards, title entries, and added entries for the symbols. Now that the League no longer exists, the files should be incorporated in the card catalog, the symbols being arranged as a supplementary file under the heading "League of Nations."

One reason why the cards were turned into a special catalog was that the headings were often greatly simplified because of the diffi-

---

[1]See, among others, Clarence E. Walton, "Classifying, Cataloging, and Binding League of Nations Publications," *Library Journal* 55:155–59 (1930); also his "The Classification of the Documents of the League of Nations," *Proceedings* of the Catalog Section, American Library Association (Chicago, 1929), p.70–86; and T. Franklin Currier, "The League of Nations Publications, a Simplified Treatment," *Catalogers' and Classifiers' Yearbook* 2:99–102 (1931).

culties which were frequently encountered in attempting to determine a normal corporate heading. Walton found in the simplifications

> a tacit admission that our usual cataloging principles have broken down, to which some would object. I suppose the most direct criticism of the Library of Congress cards for League material lies in their frequent ambiguity on the question of real authorship; yet on this point we must remember that the truth about authorship is often very hard to discover, even in Geneva.[2]

Actually it was not so much a question of a breakdown in cataloging principles as of a gross misuse of library cataloging. The vast majority of League documents should have been checklisted, not cataloged, a situation which was fortunately realized by the United Nations Library in time to see that adequate checklists of United Nations publications were forthcoming.

In the transition from the League to the United Nations decisions had to be made about the treatment of serials which carried over from one organization to the other.[3] This was a matter for items classed by the Library of Congress in JX, not for documents of specialized agencies such as the International Labour Organisation which were carried over intact and which were classified by subject. A few other publications required attention; e.g., in 1928 the League of Nations Library had begun a *Liste mensuelle d'ouvrages catalogués*, which had to be recataloged under "United Nations. Library, Geneva" with an added entry for "League of Nations. Library." It did not require reclassification because it was in Z, not JX.

United Nations

There are English, French, Spanish, and Russian editions of United Nations publications in descending order of completeness. Unofficially some items have been republished or have been translated into other languages. Sometimes the unofficial edition will carry the symbol for the original.

Beginning in 1951, symbols have been assigned to United Nations

[2]Walton, "Classifying, Cataloging, and Binding League of Nations Publications," p.158.

[3]See Marie J. Carroll, "League of Nations Documents Comparable with or Continued in United Nations Publications," *College and Research Libraries* 13:44–53 (1952).

documents generally. The symbols should constitute the checking entries on the visible index or its equivalent. They simplify the checking procedures, and they make it comparatively easy to go through the issues of the *United Nations Documents Index* to discover gaps among the regular documents as well as the revisions, corrigenda, and addenda. This is an essential procedure because, unlike other serials, the notation in the symbols does not provide a control element. Ordinary routines for claiming missing numbers should not be undertaken until *UNDI* has been checked because many of the missing items will prove to be unavailable. An *R* or an *L* should be inserted in the checking square to indicate that an item is restricted or limited, and so unprocurable. Documents which are not serials in their own right should generally be checked off like numbered series.

Prompt follow-up work based on *UNDI* is essential. The stock of some items is exhausted rapidly, and processed material is held no longer than two years. The index discloses the publications that are available to depository and subscribing libraries; it omits restricted, i.e., confidential, documents and internal papers. Thus for follow-up work everything may be requested that is not marked "limited."

The Library of Congress is selective in the United Nations documents which it catalogs. Its cards therefore represent the limit to which libraries should go. The bulk of the documents should be organized as a self-cataloging collection, the approach to which is through *UNDI* and the other checklists.

Nixon and Chamberlin have questioned the catalog entries made by the Library of Congress and most other libraries. They maintain that the author heading should follow the structure of the United Nations in as much detail as possible. For all entries other than "United Nations. Charter" they believe that one of the principal organs mentioned in Article 7 of the Charter should be included, as well as, in most cases, a suborgan. They admit that an extensive system of cross-references is required under their proposals.[4]

Examples of this type of heading are "United Nations. Economic and Social Council. Commission on Human Rights," and not "United Nations. Commission on Human Rights"; "United Nations. Secretariat. Library," not "United Nations. Library." Some headings are unconscionably long and unsuited to catalog entries, e.g., "United Nations. Security Council. Sub-Committee on the Palestinian Question, to Consider Amendments and Revisions to the Second Draft

[4]Emily O. Nixon and Waldo Chamberlin, *How to Catalogue United Nations Documents* (New York University Conference on United Nations Documents, May 19, 1952, Paper 3 [New York, 1952]).

Resolution Submitted by China and the United Kingdom and to Prepare a Revised Draft in Consultation with the Acting Mediator in Palestine."

A desirable cataloging policy can be briefly stated. There are comparatively few true serials, i.e., annuals, periodicals, etc., among United Nations documents. These should be cataloged in the regular way. Then the question is the extent to which the factitious serials should be analyzed, and because of the existence of *UNDI*, relatively few of them should be. The index must serve as the approach to the collection, and it is more effective in every respect than cataloging records could possibly be. It should always be shelved at the beginning of the United Nations collection for the sake of convenient consultation.

The classification of United Nations publications should be just as simple as the cataloging. It should be based on the symbols, if it does not actually incorporate them; thereby the collection becomes self-cataloging to a high degree. The base notation in Dewey or the Library of Congress scheme should be changed to the practice followed in the Dag Hammarskjöld Library, where *UN* stands for 341.13. That library adds an *x* for works about the United Nations; thus, UNx, FAOx, and ILOx.

Microreproductions of United Nations documents are on the market in two forms, microfilm and Readex microprint.

The Future of United Nations Documentation

In 1963 *UNDI* dropped the listing of publications of the specialized agencies, but on the other hand it is considerably more analytical than it was. An attempt to produce a French version of *UNDI* failed. In 1967 a pilot project was undertaken to test out computer possibilities at the same time that another project explored the possibilities of reducing the documents to microfiche form. In 1969 a program known as *UNDEX* was inaugurated.

> *UNDI*, however, will be continued in its present form until *UNDEX* proves to be a really workable improvement over *UNDI*. Then, but not until then, the 20-year-old *UNDI* will be replaced by the new *UNDEX*, which will be made publicly available on a subscription basis that is yet to be determined. . . .
>
> The inescapable conclusion is that the complex problem of achieving bibliographical control of a body of documentation, such as that of the United Nations, can be solved *only* by the assistance of computers, and that in the end computer-aided indexing is more

economical—in terms of effectiveness—than conventional indexing procedures ever could be. . . .

The physical problem of managing a mass of paper which grows inexorably day by day is another matter. Miniaturization of the documents seems the only solution. Already it is excitingly clear that microfiche reproduction is appropriate, and that the combination of computer-produced indexes and the dissemination of microfiche copies of the documents indexed can provide a manageable and accessible resource for even the smallest delegation (or any library) .[5]

Organization of American States

Since 1948 the Organization of American States has existed as an agency somewhat like a regional United Nations. Its secretariat is the Pan American Union, which retains its name in spite of its change in functions. A number of serial publications carried over into the new organization. Some reclassification was necessary, especially since the Inter-American conferences, beginning with the ninth, fall within the province of the Organization of American States as well as that of the Pan American Union.

Other Organizations

The Union of International Associations issues a *Directory of Periodicals Published by International Organizations* (FID Publication 449; UAI Publication 212 [3d ed.; Brussels, [1970]]) . It lists 259 titles put out by 125 international governmental organizations, as well as another 1,475 issued by 1,071 international nongovernmental organizations. The directory can serve as a guide in knowing which organizations should be represented in a library's bookstock.

Bibliography

Brimmer, B., and others. *Guide to the Use of United Nations Documents, Including Reference to the Specialized Agencies and Special U.N. Bodies.* Dobbs Ferry, N.Y.: Oceana, 1962.

[5]Joseph Groesbeck, "Introducing *UNDEX*," *Special Libraries* 61:270 (1970).

Childs, J. B. "Current Bibliographical Control of International Intergovernmental Documents," *Library Resources & Technical Services* 10:319–31 (1966).

Duhrsen, L. R. "Classification of United Nations Documents Using the JX Schedule and Document Numbers," *Library Resources & Technical Services* 14:84–91 (1970).

Groesbeck, Joseph. "Introducing *UNDEX*," *Special Libraries* 61:265–70 (1970).

——— "United Nations Documents and Their Accessibility," *Library Resources & Technical Services* 10:313–18 (1966).

"Inventory of Lists, Indexes, and Catalogues of Publications and Documents of Intergovernmental Organizations Other Than the United Nations," *Unesco Bulletin for Libraries* 21:263–70 (1967).

Speeckaert, Georges P. *Bibliographie sélective sur l'organisation international, 1885–1964*. Brussels: Union des Associations Internationales, 1965.

Winton, H. N. M. "United Nations Documents," *Drexel Library Quarterly* 1:32–41 (1965).

Yearbook of International Organizations. Brussels: Union of International Organizations, 1948– .

22

Rarities and Archival Material

Many serial sets possess the two conspicuous characteristics of rare books: scarcity and commercial value. Their scarcity can be determined to quite an extent by a study of the holdings in major union lists. Most titles published before 1900 should be treated as rare books when only one complete set is recorded or when there are only scattered holdings. Certainly a case can be made for housing all serial volumes published before 1800 in the rare book collection. The commercial value of serial sets can be determined by the prices found in secondhand catalogs, if indeed the titles ever appear in them.

While scarcity and commercial value are factors in deciding whether serials should be considered for the rare book room, other factors must generally be taken into account. The twelve classes which follow constitute the principal categories of serial publications that are and should be treated as rarities.

Almanacs

The Library of Congress has over five thousand almanacs in its Rare Book Division. They were chiefly printed in America from the seventeenth through the early nineteenth century. The American ones are arranged by state, the others by country. The New York Public Library has some 2,500 pieces, with 1820 as the terminal date for automatic inclusion of American almanacs in the rare book room. Among its treasures is the only known copy of the 1649 edition of Danforth's *Almanack*, which was printed in Cambridge, Massachusetts.

Association Copies

Files of periodicals which belonged to notable people, and particularly to notable authors, should be kept in the rare book collection as association copies. Sometimes the volumes have the individual's autograph or bookplate, and in many cases they are annotated or corrected in manuscript.

An example is the Harry Houdini collection of legerdemain and spiritualism in the Rare Book Division at the Library of Congress. Among its 4,350 titles are numerous periodicals such as *The Magic Circular* (London, 1906–24) ; *The Mahatma* (New York, 1895, 1898–1906) ; *The Sphinx* (Chicago and Kansas City, 1902–19) ; and *The Spiritualist Newspaper* (London, 1877–82) .

Dime Novels

In 1950 the Rare Book Division at the Library of Congress had 19,543 volumes of dime novels, arranged according to the series in which they were published. A catalog has been published of the *Beadle Collection of Dime Novels Given to the New York Public Library by Dr. Frank P. O'Brien* (New York, 1922) . There were about 1,400 novels in that gift. The history of the Beadle dime novel has been written by Albert Johannsen, *The House of Beadle and Adams and Its Dime and Nickel Novels; the Story of a Vanished Literature* (Norman: Univ. of Oklahoma Pr., 1950. 2v.) . All dime novels should be classed as rare books.

Directories

Only a few city directories were printed in America prior to 1801; all of them should be on the rare book shelves. There is much consultation of the first London directory, which, however, has been reprinted in facsimile. Not many copies of nineteenth-century telephone books have been preserved; all of them should be treated as rare books.

Early Imprints

Conventional dates were adopted by American libraries at the beginning of the twentieth century; any serial or other work published prior to them must go automatically into the rare book collection. The general date for the United States was set at 1801, but for places other than the big cities, the date was either 1821 or else a decade after the founding of a locality later in the century. The year was 1601 for continental Europe and 1701 for Great Britain.

As the twentieth century draws to a close, the time periods call for revision. For Europe as well as Asia the date should be either 1701 or 1801, and for Great Britain 1801. Termination of the colonial period should be established as the automatic date for all former colonies. The time may well be at hand when the end of the era of the hand-printed book is taken as the dividing line for all countries.

First Appearances

Serials that contain the first printing of works of collected authors should be gathered into the rare book collection, e.g., the *London Magazine*, which contains original contributions by Keats and Lamb. Often the issues of these serials are single numbers of ordinary magazines in their original wrappers. They are frequently classified, not as serials, but among the works of the collected author, as though they were books. A rare book library may well have parts of the same magazine scattered among the writings of a number of different authors, but no serial record should be made for them unless the serials are unusually significant or represent good runs.

Mention should be made of the Tauchnitz editions because they may contain the first published edition of an author's work. For example, the first edition, even the only edition, of some of the works of Anthony Trollope appeared in that series.

For novelists, John Carter and Michael Sadleir, *Victorian Fiction, an Exhibition of Original Editions* ([London]: Cambridge Univ. Pr., 1947), gives an account of fiction series and magazine serials, especially on p.1–2 and 10–14. The relevant passages in *New Paths in Book Collecting* (London: Constable, 1934) should also be consulted. Useful passages can be found in John Carter, *Collecting Detective Fiction* (London: Constable, [1934]); Graham Pollard, *Serial Fiction* (London: Constable, [1934]); and Michael Sadleir, *Collecting "Yellowbacks"* (London: Constable, [1934]).

Mary Spalding says:

> Magazines containing the first printing of well-known authors often sell at fancy prices. One finds the *New York Saturday Press* for 1865 and 1866 containing articles by Josh Billings, James Russell

Lowell, Artemus Ward, and "Jim Smiley and His Jumping Frog," by Mark Twain, selling for $22; and the third and fifth volumes of the *New England Magazine* with contributions by Longfellow, Holmes, and Whittier, with Whittier's contributions corrected by himself in pencil bringing $190 for the two volumes! The *Godey's Lady's Book* and *Peterson's Magazine*, because of engraved fashion plates are often collectors' items. The first issue of most magazines is valuable. Collectors are on the outlook for these first issues, and competition in the market shoots their prices skyward. Los Angeles Public Library contained a complete file of the British aviation magazine, *Flight*, except for that valuable Volume 1, Number 1, and was glad to pay $50 for this issue.[1]

Of passing interest from a serial point of view are the issues of books which were published in serial form, especially after the success of Dickens' *Pickwick Papers*. The serialization of novels goes back much earlier—for example, to some of the works of Defoe. *Robinson Crusoe* first appeared in *The Original London Post, or Heathcot's Intelligence* from 7 October 1719 to 19 October 1720. Only three copies are known today, and, like similar serial publications of literary classics, particularly in the eighteenth and nineteenth centuries, they are naturally valuable. Strictly speaking, however, part issues of books such as *Pickwick Papers* are not taken to be serials, at least in retrospect, despite their original serial form.

Gift Books

Literary annuals, often intended for ladies and children, were numerous in the first part of the nineteenth century. They were collections of poetry and prose, sometimes by major authors such as Poe, whose "The Pit and the Pendulum" first appeared in this form, but more often by minor literary figures. Many of the contributions were anonymous or signed only with initials. The history and bibliography of American gift books is found in Ralph Thompson, *American Literary Annuals and Gift Books, 1825–1865* (New York: Wilson, 1936). All these publications should be preserved in the rare book collection. There was a revival of this form of publication in Great Britain during World War I, with contributions by the leading artists, authors, and composers of the day.

[1]Mary L. Spalding, "Current Use Versus Permanent Preservation of Periodicals as Reflected in Organization," *ALA Bulletin* 34:P–201–202 (1940).

Government Publications

Many of the earliest printings in a country or a community were laws and ordinances, as well as other forms of government publications. All of these belong among the rare books. Included in this category are the documents of the first fourteen Congresses of the United States. The Library of Congress has over twenty thousand volumes which are arranged according to the order given in Adolphus W. Greely, *Public Documents of the First Fourteen Congresses, 1789–1817* (56th Congress, 1st Session, Senate Document 428 [Washington: Government Printing Office, 1900]) and its supplement. There is no complete set of these publications; all of them are scarce.

Newspapers

The Library of Congress keeps all newspapers, American and foreign, published through the year 1800 in its Rare Book Division. American newspapers are arranged in the order given in the *Check List of American Eighteenth Century Newspapers in the Library of Congress*, originally compiled by John V. Ingram (new ed.; rev. and enl. under the direction of Henry S. Parsons; Washington, 1936). Similar checklists have been issued by other American libraries and by societies. The comprehensive checklist is Clarence S. Brigham, *History and Bibliography of American Newspapers, 1690–1820* (Worcester: American Antiquarian Society, 1947. 2v.), which, with *American Newspapers 1821–1936; A Union List of Files Available in the United States and Canada* (New York: Wilson, 1937), provides union list control for American newspapers from 1690 to 1936. Among the checklists for British newspapers are the *Tercentenary Handlist of English and Welsh Newspapers, Magazines, and Reviews* (London: The Times, 1920) and R. S. Crane and F. B. Kaye, *A Census of British Newspapers and Periodicals, 1620–1800* (Chapel Hill: Univ. of North Carolina Pr., 1927), the latter being a union list of American holdings.

Brown says of the papers in the New York Public Library:

> Newspapers constitute one of the important collections in the Library. Early files and rare issues are numerous, among them, Bradford's *New-York Gazette*, Zenger's *Weekly Journal* (best file known), Parker's *Post-Boy*, and excellent files of Holt's *Journal*, Gaine's *Mercury*, and of Farley's *American Chronicle* (the only known run;

incomplete) . Outside New York, the representation of Philadelphia newspapers includes the second-best known sets of Franklin's *Gazette* and Bradford's *Journal.*[2]

Periodicals

All journals which were published during the first two periods in the history of periodicals, i.e., through 1825, should be located in the rare book room. As guides there are William Beer, *Checklist of American Periodicals, 1741–1800* (Worcester: American Antiquarian Society, 1923) ; and for British periodicals the two items listed under "Newspapers." In the New York Public Library it has been possible to keep only the very rare, irreplaceable material among the rare books; but because sets of early periodicals are extremely scarce, space should be found to preserve all of them under rare book conditions.

It is important to point out that many sets published after 1825 also are rarities. For example, at Harvard the following nineteenth-century journals are located in the Houghton Library: *Butterfly* (London, 1899–1900) ; *Carpet-Bag* (Boston, 1851–52) ; the transcendentalist *Dial*, edited by Margaret Fuller and then Ralph Waldo Emerson (Boston, 1841–44) ; *Gentleman's Magazine* (Philadelphia, 1837–40) ; *Godey's Lady's Book* (Philadelphia, 1830–83) ; and *Pioneer* (San Francisco, 1854–55) . Also in Houghton are the children's publications *Aunt Judy's Magazine* (London, 1867–68) and *Oliver Optic's Magazine* (Boston, 1867–75) . Among twentieth-century periodicals there are *Broom* (Rome, 1921–24) , *The Egoist* (London, 1914–18) , *The Golden Hind* (London, 1922–24) , and *The Quill* (New York, 1921–25) .

Almost all libraries failed to collect little magazines contemporaneously, but because of their elusiveness and, in many cases, near-print form, little magazines quite generally belong in the rare book room. Two of the largest collections are in the New York Public Library and the University of Wisconsin Library.

Allen defines a little magazine as a periodical "designed to print artistic work which for reasons of commercial expediency is not acceptable to the money-minded periodicals or presses."[3] He goes on

[2]Karl Brown, *A Guide to the Reference Collections of the New York Public Library* (New York, 1941), p.218.
[3]Charles Allen, "The Advance Guard," *Sewanee Review* 11:425 (1943).

to say that little magazines were the first to publish the writings of about 80 percent of American critics, novelists, and poets in the post-1912 period. Some of the little magazines have had long runs, e.g., *Poetry, a Magazine of Verse*, which began in 1912 as a medium to encourage young poets and which in its early issues contained poems by Bodenheim, H. D., Eliot, Fletcher, Pound, Reed, Robinson, Sandburg, Tagore, and Yeats.

The University of Indiana Library published a *Union List of Little Magazines Showing Holdings of 1,037 Little Magazines in the Libraries of Indiana University, Northwestern University, State University of Iowa, University of Chicago, University of Illinois* (Chicago: Mid-West Interlibrary Center, 1956). A full-length study of them is Frederick J. Hoffman, Charles Allen, and Carolyn F. Ulrich, *The Little Magazine, a History and a Bibliography* (2d ed.; Princeton: Princeton Univ. Pr., 1947). A short work, with a list of forty prominent little magazines founded before 1950, is Reed Whittemore, *Little Magazines* (University of Minnesota Pamphlets on American Writers, no.32 [Minneapolis: Univ. of Minnesota Pr., 1963]). Something of a supplement to Hoffman is Len Fulton, "Anima Rising; Little Magazines in the Sixties" (*American Libraries* 2:25–47 [1971]).

Private Presses

Most of the publications of private presses are books, so that their principal serial publications consist of catalogs and prospectuses. But closely related to the private presses are the publications of societies of bibliophiles such as the Club of Odd Volumes, the Grolier Club, the Rowfant Club, and the Sette of Odd Volumes. The aims of these presses and societies are so closely linked with those of rare book libraries that their publications naturally tend to be treated as rare books.

Reference Works

Similarly the serial publications of bibliographical, typographical, and other societies which are connected with paper making and printing are kept among the reference works in the rare book room. Included in this category are certain periodicals such as *Colophon, a Book Collectors Quarterly* (New York, 1930–38).

Cataloging Records for Rare Serials

No special cataloging rules are required for rare serials; the features, such as provenance, can be brought out in the form of notes. On the other hand, the rare book cataloger *qua* bibliographer may be interested in checklisting some or all of the serials in the treasure room, thereby giving attention to variant issues and to issues with the original wrappers. Checklists which supplement the cataloging may in turn lead to the publication of significant bibliographies. Sometimes the card catalogs in rare book collections have special sections of serial interest. In the Rare Book Division at the Library of Congress there is, for example, a supplementary catalog for American almanacs arranged by title, date, and place of publication.

Manuscripts and Archives

There are many serials, a few of them in printed form and more in processed form, in collections of archives and manuscripts. They may not be organized as serial publications in the ordinary patterns, but rather archivally or as groups of manuscripts. For instance, the printed annual reports which are distributed throughout the files of the American Board of Commissioners for Foreign Missions in the Houghton Library at Harvard are not held or bound together, as they would be in standard library practice; instead, anyone who is looking for them must go through the file year by year, discovering each issue amid a mass of other material, all bound together by the Board to reflect a year's overall activities. In League of Nations days the file copies in Geneva were distributed archivally, not held together as a set.

Serials in manuscript, printed, and processed form occur in the archives of governments and other institutions such as universities, as well as in the local history repositories of libraries and societies. These serials vary from the extremely important through the routine down to the trivial. They include: annual reports; club publications; commencement, concert, football, and other programs; commercial catalogs; court records; examination papers; minutes of meetings; notices of faculty meetings, town meetings, etc.; political pronouncements and records of all kinds, including voting lists; student magazines, yearbooks, etc.; trade-union items; and a vast amount of other serial material. Serials in the National Archives in Washington include:

> messages, proclamations, orders, rules, and regulations; . . . census schedules and scientific data; statistical tables and compilations; reports of departments, bureaus, commissions, and officials; treaties, conventions, and records of diplomatic negotiations; laws, legislative journals, and minutes and reports of committees; petitions and resolutions; and court records.[4]

Sometimes the ephemeral material is mounted in scrapbooks without regard to its serial or nonserial character. Sometimes the more substantial publications, such as municipal documents, are bound in yearly groupings to give a cross section of life and activities. But more commonly an archival scheme provides a place for each type of publication, in which case the classification may furnish the most important approach to the collection. In view of the slight nature of much archival and manuscript material and the small amount of use it will receive, the catalog records should be simple and brief, despite the fact that they generally represent the primary or only listing for many of the items. Self-cataloging will suffice for large segments, and the shelflisting should be held to a bare minimum except when normal procedures can be justified.

These shortcuts are similar to the ones adopted in special libraries; but vertical-file systems are seldom practiced, since the material in archives and manuscript collections does not have to be particularly readily accessible. The objective is conservation rather than ready use or frequent service.

[4]National Archives, *Manual of Information about the National Archives for Government Officials* (Washington, 1941), p.1.

6

Postscript

23

Future of Library Work
with Serial Publications

Since the end of World War II a number of trends of interest and concern to administrators and serial librarians have become well defined. The following are among the more important of them.

1. From evidence supplied by *New Serial Titles*, there are at least fifteen thousand new serials being published throughout the world each year. The number will increase steadily. About a fourth of them are periodicals. Libraries must from now on be alert as never before to learn of the existence of new titles so that they can acquire the items they need with sufficient promptitude to guarantee the completeness of their files.

2. Tools to facilitate the use of serials have gained steadily in number and must multiply still further. They include abstracting and indexing services as well as union lists of serials. Definitive bibliographies of serials have lagged in most countries, the Soviet Union being a notable exception. Attention should be paid in the years ahead to the production of numerous definitive bibliographies.

3. Annual price indexes for serials have at long last become an established institution. As yet they are not sufficiently broad in their coverage, but they do make it clear that a library must anticipate constant growth in the size of its serial budget, if for no other reason than to maintain the subscriptions that have already been placed. So it has become almost essential for serials to have their own budget; that is the only sure way of providing for the inevitable

percentage increase that can be forecast from year to year and of allowing for additions to the collection to be made.

4. *New Serial Titles—Classed Subject Arrangement* has developed into the world's number one serial-selection tool. It is slated to become still more useful as titles are reported to it reasonably promptly as a consequence of the wide-scale introduction of first-issue cataloging. The list of contributing libraries should be extended to include at least: (1) as many national libraries as will accept responsibility for the prompt reporting of new titles which originate in their countries, and (2) North American libraries which produce, or are associated with institutions which produce, new serials and will accept primary responsibility for reporting those titles as well as changes in the publishing pattern of the new or continuing serials in their purview.

5. Since the 1930s the number of periodical sets which have been reproduced in print or microprint form has climbed steadily. Microprint has outnumbered print by a wide margin; in the process special libraries have gained, but general libraries, particularly in universities, have lost. The new general research libraries should as a rule avoid having too great a proportion of their bookstock in the form of microreproductions; in the years ahead corrective action should be taken to swing the pendulum much more in the direction of reprinting rather than microprinting.

6. Computer-generated book catalogs of serials have established themselves in recent years. As indicated below, much should be done to standardize certain aspects of the catalogs for the sake of the common good.

7. Coding and automation, which have made major advances since 1962, can be expected to make stronger and stronger contributions to serial control methods. With careful and diligent planning the day will surely come in the comparatively near future when computer systems for checking in current issues will become more economical and efficient to operate than the visible index.

A Period of Experimentation

Large-scale experimentation and research should be a prime objective in the years ahead. So far the load has been carried by an impressive number of medical libraries, one or two public libraries, a small array of special libraries, and three or four university libraries. The Biomedical Library in the University of California at Los Angeles believes that the reason why medical libraries are so interested in automated serial control is that current serial publications are the major information resource in the medical sciences. The great medical libraries have strong journal collections, and there is a proliferation of new important titles being published each year. The demands made upon these collections by medical researchers require better handling and control methods to provide the needed service. All of this is perhaps another way of saying that the clearly defined sense of purpose, which generally is evident in special libraries, is a powerful driving force to achieve library objectives by devising the best possible methods for the performance of the daily work, and particularly of the mass activities.

The spirit of the period of experimentation should be the greatest possible freedom of research. No one should have his hands tied by practice from the past. The cataloging entry, for example, should be the subject of considerable investigation because experimentation ceases the minute one says, as was the case in the Serial Record Division at the Library of Congress in 1952, that any detail such as catalog code headings must be followed. Well and good if after experimentation a detail is re-established; well and good, also, if adjustments, even major ones, must be made on the score of experimental evidence.

The library school is the one agency that is missing from the list of institutions which are carrying out profitable experimental work. Yet it should be capable of undertaking basic research and producing significant results. A concerted effort is essential if the best and fullest advances are to be made in the major area of mass activity which serials represent.

Book Catalogs for Serials

It is very important for administrators in libraries in general, and in the Library of Congress in particular, to give official recognition to the role of the book catalog. The major thesis that must be sustained is that the information which suffices for the visible index, a book catalog, or a union list of serials will also suffice for cataloging purposes. In the years ahead the essential data for serial listings of all kinds may well be: (1) *Coden* symbols; (2) dependable yet simple statements of holdings; (3) natural rather than technical headings; (4) notation for those libraries which wish to classify their serials or to provide the foundation for lists of serials arranged by subject; and

(5) a skeleton shelflist entry to be complemented by lists of holdings that will serve for any inventory that may be taken. That is, there can be an end to most of the descriptive detail that has gone on catalog cards in the past, as well as to subject headings for serials.

Insofar as there may be any loss from the elimination of cataloging detail, attention can be focused on the provision of two other types of listing. First, the national library in each country can develop a more detailed listing than is needed elsewhere, e.g., by country and language; then, libraries which desire greater detail can acquire tapes of the national lists so that they can produce their own country, language, or other arrangements. So it may be desirable for the Library of Congress to include in its program the eighty data elements which MARC has proposed; and if that is done, there is little need for other libraries to cover anything other than the minimum essential details. Second, with few exceptions, there has been serious neglect of the bibliographical side of serial publication. Systematic work should be undertaken in this area to complement the contributions which union lists make as well as the contributions of histories of newspapers and magazines.

There is little if any gain in having both a book catalog and the traditional type of catalog entry for serials. Whenever both exist in a library, they constitute an unwarranted expense. Since readers obviously benefit most from the book catalog, it should be developed and card cataloging should be terminated. The changeover to a book catalog is one of the clear gains that comes from the new program for serials. There can be no doubt about it: the book catalog is a major advance in library technology and every effort should be expended on perfecting it.

Libraries and *Coden*

Cooperation between libraries and the American Society for Testing and Materials (ASTM) has been slow in developing. It should come about as soon as possible. For one thing, it is not always possible to assign symbols without having an item in hand; not all institutions will supply the essential evidence. Errors are bound to occur when verbal or written communications from a wide variety of sources are accepted uncritically; all experience with union catalogs points in this direction.

At least two advances in the assignment of symbols should be considered. One is that libraries which inquire about titles for which symbols have not as yet been assigned might be encouraged to propose symbols which then would be reviewed. The other is that national libraries should be authorized to assign symbols for serials which originate in their countries, so that the system will develop internationally in a satisfactory way and with a bare minimum of delay in the determination of appropriate symbols. Complete centralization will not be adequate for worldwide needs, and *Coden* will not grow as it should without the cooperation of libraries, just as libraries will be handicapped if ASTM does not cooperate with them. Both sides have a vast amount to gain through insightful cooperation.

Union Lists of Serials

Not only does *Coden* lie at the foundation of the checking systems of libraries in the future, but it also for the first time makes it practicable to develop a network of union lists at the community, national, and international level. Once a book catalog is produced with *Coden* symbols and a standardized way of listing holdings, its data can be fed in a relatively simple way into a union list at any of the three levels. The method would be something of a variation on the technique developed by the Medical Library Center of New York for the interchange of tapes between medical libraries.

For the successful development of a network of union lists, the basic entry would cease to be alphabetical. Instead it would be the *Coden* symbol, to which professional staffs would have to become accustomed. At the local and regional level, and for subject listings on a national or international level, union lists in book form would appear periodically, preferably once a year. At the national and international level in general, however, there would be a tendency to rely on tapes that were held in strategically located centers. But all of this depends on the acceptance of a coding as the basic entry and of a standardized scheme for reporting holdings.

Abstracting and Indexing

As problems of coverage and financial support continue to mount, it will become necessary to develop international schemes somewhat akin to those proposed for union lists of serials. Again, coding, cooperation, and standardization lie at the heart of the matter. It is shortsighted to permit abstracting and indexing to continue with partial coverage of all too many subjects, no coverage of some, and duplication in the coverage of others. It is equally shortsighted for countries like Germany, Russia, and the United States to cover very much the same field independently of one another.

Printed abstracting and indexing services as they have existed in book form may in the future be limited to selected lists which cover the basic contributions to any subject, not to selected journals which may or may not perform such a service. Beyond that limit it can well be that computer tapes will be made at approved centers and distributed to major outlets so that cooperatively the serial literature of the world will be analyzed and made available with as full coverage and as little duplication as can be contrived.

Exchange and Reprinting of Serials

Quite apart from the needs of old-established institutions, every year throughout the world an appreciable number of new research libraries come into existence. They can employ microreproductions up to a point, but beyond that they should be able to acquire basic journals in print editions so that their service programs will not suffer through too great a reliance on microcopies. It will be necessary, therefore, for libraries and library associations to do all in their power to ensure a reasonably adequate supply of basic serials in regular book format. This means that unwanted sets of serials should be offered first to other libraries or to the United States Book Exchange or its equivalent in countries throughout the world. It also means that reprint houses should be aided as they seek to know which serials are in demand both by older and newly established libraries. The new library in particular is harmed if it simply gives in and acquires microreproductions. A concerted effort is necessary if readers are not to be handicapped through overreliance on microreproductions, which are an invaluable contribution to research provided that they do not exceed, in most libraries, a small proportion of the bookstock—a proportion which still remains to be determined with any precision.

A Period of Intense Cooperation

Each of the points which has been made in anticipating the future of library work with serial publications has as its essence the concept of cooperation. The development of successful methods and programs requires the cooperative efforts of librarians at the local, regional, national, and international levels. Only in this way will the mass activities which are intrinsically connected with a great and growing body of literature continue to be efficiently manageable. No one individual, no one institution can solve the problems or shoulder the responsibility. It will take a grassroots movement, enthusiastically and intelligently directed, to cope with the immense outpouring of the serial press, which will soon tally a million or more titles, if that figure has not already been realized.

Bibliography

Allen, Walter C., ed. *Serial Publications in Large Libraries.* (Allerton Park Institute, no.16) Urbana, Ill.: Univ. of Illinois Graduate School of Library Science, 1970.

Ashworth, Wilfred, ed. *Handbook of Special Librarianship and Information Work.* 3d ed. London: Aslib, 1967.

Davinson, D. E. *The Periodicals Collection; Its Purpose and Uses in Libraries.* London: Deutsch, 1969.

Grenfell, David. *Periodicals and Serials; Their Treatment in Special Libraries.* 2d ed. London: Aslib, 1965.

Strauss, Lucille J.; Shreve, Irene M.; and Brown, Alberta L. *Scientific and Technical Libraries; Their Organization and Administration.* 2d ed. New York: Becker & Hayes, 1972.

Index

417

DATE DUE

GAYLORD   PRINTED IN U.S.A.